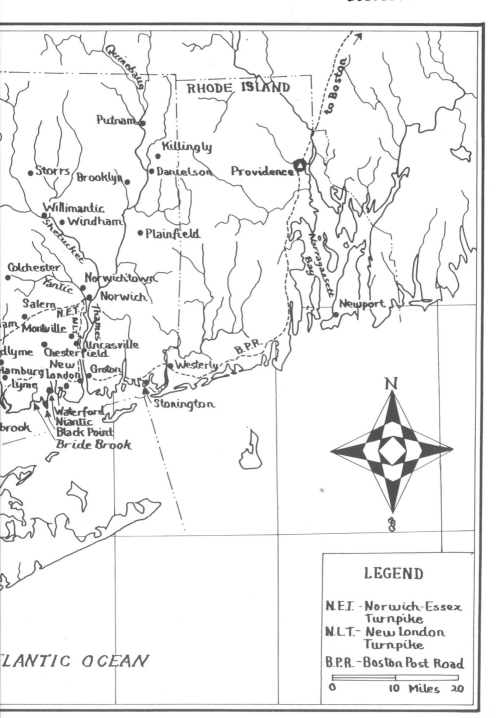

RHODE ISLAND

to Boston

Quinebaug

Putnam

Killingly

Danielson

Providence

Storrs Brooklyn

Willimantic

Windham

Plainfield

Shetucket

Colchester

Fantic

Norwichtown

Norwich

Salem

N.E.T.

N.L.T.

Thames

am Montville

Uncasville

dlyme Chesterfield

New

Hamburg London

Groton

Westerly

B.P.R.

Newport

Narragansett Bay

Lyme

Waterford

brook

Niantic

Black Point

Bride Brook

Stonington

N

ATLANTIC OCEAN

LEGEND

N.E.T. - Norwich-Essex
Turnpike
N.L.T. - New London
Turnpike
B.P.R. - Boston Post Road

0   10 Miles 20

The Tiffany Fortune

Also by Alfred M. Bingham

Insurgent America: Revolt of the Middle Classes, 1935

Man's Estate: Adventures in Economic Discovery, 1937

The United States of Europe, 1940

Techniques of Democracy, 1942

The Practice of Idealism, 1944

Violence and Democracy (with Jonathan Bingham), 1970

Portrait of an Explorer: Hiram Bingham, Discoverer of Machu Picchu, 1989

The Tiffany Fortune

AND OTHER CHRONICLES OF A CONNECTICUT FAMILY

Alfred M. Bingham

Abeel & Leet Publishers
Chestnut Hill, Massachusetts

Chronicle I, "Sybil's Bones," first appeared as "Sybil's Bones, A Chronicle of the Three Hiram Binghams" in Volume 9 of the *Hawaiian Journal of History* © 1975. Reprinted with permission of the Hawaiian Historical Society.

Sections of Chronicle VII, "The Explorer," are reprinted from Parts II and III of *Portrait of an Explorer: Hiram Bingham, Discoverer of Machu Picchu* © 1989 by Iowa State University Press, Iowa. Portions reprinted by permission.

Abeel & Leet Publishers
16 Gate House Road
Chestnut Hill, MA 02167
(617) 277-3857
1(800) 478-7090

Library of Congress Cataloging-in-Publication Data

Bingham, Alfred M. (Alfred Mitchell), 1905–
    The Tiffany fortune, and other chronicles of a Connecticut family / Alfred M. Bingham. – 1st ed.
       p. cm.
    Includes index.
    ISBN 0-9650357-1-9
    1. Bingham family. 2. Tiffany family. 3. Mitchell family. 4. Bingham, Alfred M. (Alfred Mitchell), 1905– —Family. 5. Connecticut—Biography. 6. Upper class families—Connecticut—Conduct of life. 7. Millionaires—Connecticut—Biography. I. Title.
CT274.B52B56   1996
974.604'092'2—dc20
[B]   96-1360
                                         CIP

Interior and jacket design: Kathe Harvey

Printed in the United States of America

10 9 8 7 6 5 4 3 2 1

CONTENTS

FOREWORD

The terrifying question "Who am I?" looms out of the darkness as a child develops a consciousness of self. The awful contingency of existence—each of us a tiny accident in an infinite universe—is often thrust back into the unconscious as too threatening to face.

A primary defense against that fear when it first arises in children is identification with the parents. But then a little later, with a shock, we discover the tenuousness of the incidents which, by bringing our parents together, brought us into being.

A second line of defense against anonymity comes into play if we are able to relate to ancestors—grandparents, great-grandparents, back through generations to more and more persons with names and individualities and so to communes and nations, and then, by a stretch of the imagination, to all humanity, perhaps even all nature. Only then can we gain a sense of really belonging.

This desire to feel a part of the universe, not an outsider, seems to increase with advancing years. The need grows as we approach final extinction. Older people often turn, when they can, to genealogy.

In my case ancestors were ready and available. Not only did they write voluminously and save much of what they had written, but their writings were considered of sufficient significance to be enshrined. The Yale University Library has thousands of letters, diaries, and other memorabilia of the Bingham, Mitchell, and Tiffany families.

One thing all these families of mine had in common was the concern with the relative importance of God and Mammon.

Children were brought up on the Bible and were familiar with the words: "No man can serve two masters: for either he will hate the one, and love the other; or else he will hold to the one, and despise the other. Ye cannot serve God and Mammon."

I have come to question this. In going over the lives of my forbears, I have found that they have all in some degree served the demands of both conscience and self-interest, the spiritual and the material. Even my missionary ancestors, my father's father and grandfather, were much concerned with money matters, being more than a little dependent on moneyed men to carry out their missions. My father, brought up to be a missionary himself, married

vii

the wealthy granddaughter of Charles Tiffany. His whole life thereafter was spent in trying to reconcile, with more or less success, the service of both God and Mammon.

To some degree this may be said of all humankind, perhaps even of all social animals, which must first survive and then nurture to reproduce. Human beings, the most dependent of all animals on their fellows, could not survive as a species without a development of the social virtues, that is, without an active concern for their families' and their neighbors' welfare as well as their own.

Alfred M. Bingham
Clinton, New York

DEDICATION
AND ACKNOWLEDGMENTS

This book is dedicated first of all to my wife, Kitty (Katharine Stryker Dunn Bingham), and to the members of the Stryker and Dunn families who have given me their wholehearted affection and moral support during the dozen years of my second marriage and the writing of this book.

I would also include in this dedication and acknowledgment the invaluable help of my editor, Judith Leet, without whose encouragement and editorial help the book would never have been published.

For patience and help in the research, I wish to express my gratitude and thanks to the following institutions: the Yale University Library Division of Archives and Manuscripts, the Hawaiian Mission Children's Society Library in Honolulu, the *Hawaiian Journal of History* for permission to reprint material, the New London County Historical Society for aid in research and in permitting reproduction of a portrait in their collections, and the National Geographic Society for access to their files on the Yale Peruvian Expeditions and for use of photographs in their collection; I wish to thank also the many friends and relatives who have helped in various ways to make possible publication of these *Chronicles*.

Hiram Bingham Genealogy

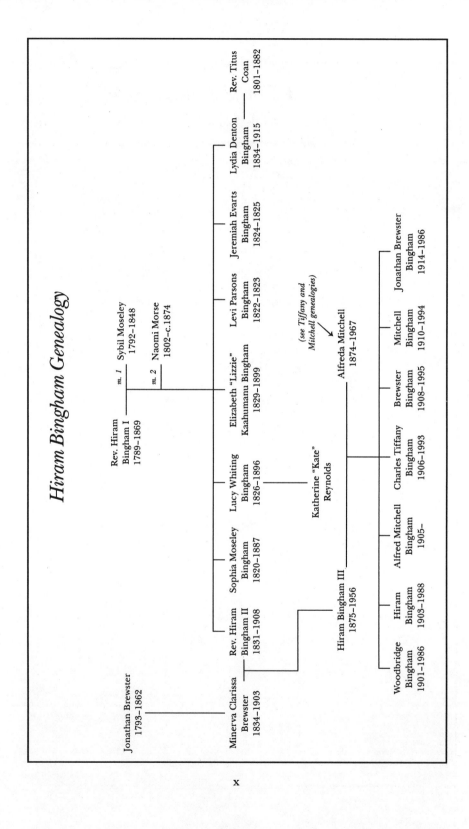

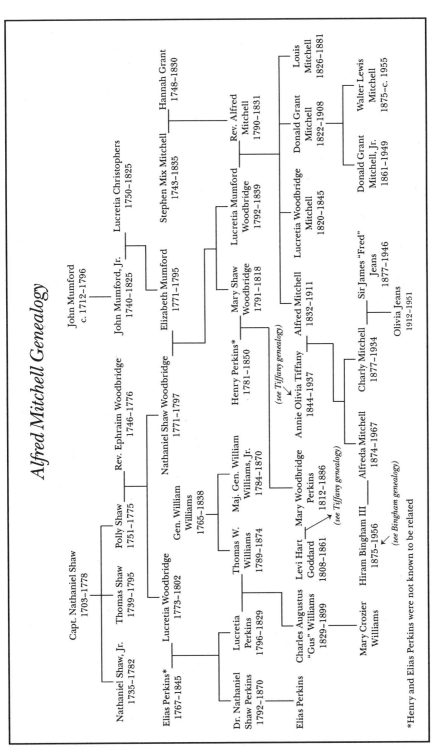

Alfred Mitchell Genealogy

John Mumford
c. 1712–1796

Capt. Nathaniel Shaw
1703–1778

John Mumford, Jr.
1740–1825

Lucretia Christophers
1750–1825

Rev. Ephraim Woodbridge
1746–1776

Polly Shaw
1751–1775

Thomas Shaw
1739–1795

Stephen Mix Mitchell
1743–1835

Hannah Grant
1748–1830

Elizabeth Mumford
1771–1795

Nathaniel Shaw Woodbridge
1771–1797

Gen. William Williams
1765–1838

Lucretia Woodbridge
1773–1802

Nathaniel Shaw, Jr.
1735–1782

Rev. Alfred Mitchell
1790–1831

Lucretia Mumford Woodbridge
1792–1839

Mary Shaw Woodbridge
1791–1818

Henry Perkins*
1781–1850

Maj. Gen. William Williams, Jr.
1784–1870

Thomas W. Williams
1789–1874

Elias Perkins*
1767–1845

Donald Grant Mitchell
1822–1908

Louis Mitchell
1826–1881

Lucretia Woodbridge Mitchell
1820–1845

Alfred Mitchell
1832–1911

Annie Olivia Tiffany
1844–1937

(see Tiffany genealogy)

Mary Woodbridge Perkins
1812–1886

(see Tiffany genealogy)

Lucretia Perkins
1796–1829

Dr. Nathaniel Shaw Perkins
1792–1870

Walter Lewis Mitchell
1875–c. 1955

Donald Grant Mitchell, Jr.
1861–1949

Sir James "Fred" Jeans
1877–1946

Olivia Jeans
1912–1951

Charly Mitchell
1877–1934

Alfreda Mitchell
1874–1967

Hiram Bingham III
1875–1956

(see Bingham genealogy)

Levi Hart Goddard
1808–1861

Charles Augustus "Gus" Williams
1829–1899

Elias Perkins

Mary Crozier Williams

*Henry and Elias Perkins were not known to be related

xi

Charles Tiffany Genealogy

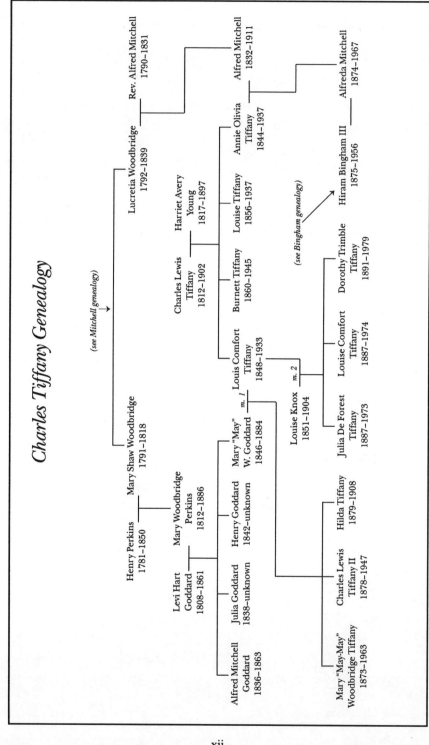

CHRONICLE I

Sybil's Bones

CHAPTER 1

The Missing Tombstone

I first heard about Sybil when my father took me to see her grave in the old New Haven City Burial Ground. The Grove Street Cemetery, as it was commonly called, was not far from the Yale College Chapel, where our family went on Sundays, so I suppose that it was after a service that my father walked us over to see where his grandfather and grandmother were buried. I was perhaps ten years old, and the year was 1915 or thereabouts.

My father was not a religious man, but as a college professor, at a time when attendance at chapel services was compulsory for all students, he may well have felt it incumbent on him, a supporter of the establishment, to attend Sunday services, when he was not off exploring in Peru, and he would have had an uneasy conscience if he had not given me and my brothers at least a grounding in the religion of his missionary ancestors. Moreover, the college invited the country's most prominent preachers, without much regard for doctrinal or denominational purity, to its pulpit, so his own skeptical theism was not offended. And he must have enjoyed the prominence of the family pew at the front of the faculty section, where his six-foot-four-inch frame, flanked by my mother and several small boys, was visible to the whole student body.

It would have been a five-minute walk from the Battell Chapel steps on College Street, with its slowly melting group of departing worshippers, to the cemetery. The setting today is unchanged from what it was then. On one side of Grove Street is the vast bulk of the university dining hall or Commons, the rattle of dishes in its kitchens next to the sidewalk alone disturbing the quiet of the Sunday street. At one end of the Commons, where College Street diverges gently to become Prospect, the street on which we lived, was the rotunda entrance to both the Commons and the university auditorium, Woolsey Hall. At the other end of the Commons was the blankly beautiful marble "tomb," in purest Ionic, of a college secret society, and, across from that, the great Egyptian gateway to the cemetery, over which was inscribed in letters visible a block away: THE DEAD SHALL BE RAISED.

Whether, on that first visit, I considered the incongruity of all this variegated architectural splendor to the simple elm-shaded graves of New Haven's colonial patriarchs inside the cemetery, or pondered the meaning of the resurrection, is doubtful, but I know I found my great-grandfather's gravestone less impressive than I expected. His name, in capital letters, HIRAM BINGHAM, was clear enough, and since it was also my father's name, I took it for granted. The rest of the inscription, to the effect that he "and his associate Asa Thurston were the first preachers of the Gospel to the heathen of the Hawaiian Islands," was not of the stuff to interest a small boy, even if the letters were more legible than they are today; still I recall a sense of slight annoyance, which I may have caught from my father, at the intrusion of Thurston's name to share the honors. What did impress me was the fact that Hiram Bingham had two wives. That seemed of sufficient oddity to be worth recounting if occasion arose.

Two wives, two similar slabs of marble, each naturally enough some inches shorter than their husband's—and one of them was Sybil's.

My father seemed to take a certain melancholy but possessive pride in the stones, as he explained that his grandfather had married again after Sybil's death, but all I remembered was what a queer name Sybil was and how the name of wife number two, Naomi, was even queerer. It was not till I was a grandfather myself that I learned why my father had such a proprietary interest in Sybil's bones. He had, in fact, brought them with him in his personal luggage when he had come to Yale as a freshman some twenty years before.

My own interest in them dates from the movie version of James Michener's *Hawaii*. Michener had made full use of the first Hiram Bingham's missionary record, *A Residence of Twenty-one Years in the Sandwich Islands*. The novel had obviously patterned its principal missionary character, Abner Hale, on an amalgam of Hiram Bingham and Asa Thurston, but Bingham was so much the dominant if not domineering character as to leave the major impress on the imaginary Hale. Sprightly Lucy Thurston, on the other hand, was more likely the model for Michener's beautiful heroine Jerusha than plain, conscience-ridden Sybil, if only because she too had written a book, while Sybil's story was locked in her diaries and in many scattered letters sent around Cape Horn between 1820 and 1840. At any rate, in my middle-aged reaction to the movie, I found Julie Andrew's depiction of Jerusha Hale so entrancing that I transferred all her charm to my side of the missionary family. If Sybil had not been my great-grandmother, and I had not been middle-aged, I would have fallen in love with her—or at least with Julie Andrews.

So on a romantic impulse, I took the next occasion to visit her grave in the Grove Street Cemetery. I was astonished to find only two stones where I had looked for three. There was HIRAM BINGHAM, as firm and straight as ever, and beside him the small stone of his "relict," the upstart Naomi, but nothing more—only a smooth area of turf between Naomi and the asphalt drive, and beyond that, outside the fence, the rushing traffic on Grove Street.

Had I then dreamed about being shown Sybil's grave by my father some sixty years earlier? Was it only something he had said about his grandfather's two wives that led me to conjure up a mental image of two similar slabs of marble? I checked the records in the cemetery office. The records did indeed show Sybil M. Bingham buried beside Naomi Morse Bingham, but unlike the listing of Hiram and Naomi, there was only one date opposite her

4

name, 1792, her birth date according to the family genealogies, with no year given for her death; and Mr. Monsoon, the Superintendent of the Cemetery, acknowledged that he was "at a loss to even guess what could have become of the stone."

His records showed the graves were in a plot that belonged to the United Church, one of the three landmark churches on the New Haven Green. I consulted the church records. I learned that only Naomi of the three Binghams had been a member of that church and thereby earned the right of burial in its plot, not only for herself but for her husband. Hiram had died in 1869, five years before Naomi, his "relict." But Sybil had died twenty years earlier, according to the family records. Hiram was, however, a "Reverend," and denominational loyalty to a retired Congregational missionary might have admitted his bones to this hallowed ground, even without Naomi's membership. But Sybil had no claim at all. And would Naomi have welcomed her sainted predecessor?

It occurred to me that Hiram might have extracted a promise from Naomi that after his death his first wife's remains would be brought from wherever they might be and re-interred beside him, and that, after his death, Naomi quite naturally balked, though the place for Sybil had been reserved. But neither the church nor the cemetery superintendent could tell me whether Sybil was really buried there, and if she was, what had happened to the grave marker.

By now my curiosity was thoroughly aroused. Curiosity may be a family trait. My father, after all, had been an explorer—in fact he listed his principal occupation as "explorer" in *Who's Who* even after he became a United States Senator—and if my urge to find "something lost behind the Ranges" took the form of searching old cemeteries, it might still be an inherited impulse.

The Bingham Family in the United States told me that "HIRAM BINGHAM" (the name again showed up in capitals), the "7th child of Calvin," had first married "October 11, 1819, Sybil Moseley, dau. of Pliny Moseley and sister to Judge Daniel Moseley of Westfield, Mass.," and went on to say simply: "She d. Feb. 27, 1848, at East Hampton, Mass., aged 56." Well, I thought, if she died in East Hampton, would she not have been buried there, or perhaps in nearby Westfield, where she was born, in some Moseley plot?

It would, I felt, have been ridiculous for me to make a special pilgrimage to Massachusetts just to search cemeteries for my great-grandmother's grave, but when other business found me in Springfield it took no further excuse to explore the graveyards of nearby Westfield and Easthampton (as it was spelled on my road map). I still had the image of lovely Julie Andrews in my mind's eye.

It was no use. I found no trace of Sybil's last resting place. Even in the weed-grown old burial ground off Mechanic Street in Westfield's factory district, where I made out the names of her father Pliny Moseley, who died in 1810 "at 62 years of age," and of his first wife Abigail, who died in 1788 at thirty, and of his second wife Sophia Moseley, Sybil's mother, who died in 1811—leaving nineteen-year-old Sybil an orphan to support herself as a school teacher, while other relatives took care of her younger sisters—even in the old family plot, there was nothing to indicate Sybil had ever been laid beside her parents.

Ten miles away, Easthampton, unaccountably west as well as south of Northampton, seemingly half asleep in the vacation period of its famous old Williston Academy, yielded little further information. At the Town Hall there was indeed a listing of the death of Sybil "wife of Rev. Hiram Bingham" on the page marked February 27, 1848, but the cemetery yielded no clues.

I knew from some correspondence of my father's that Hiram and Sybil had found a "refuge" in Easthampton with "kind friends," and that there Sybil had died, though it was not till later that I learned why it seemed a "refuge." I also knew that my father's father (whose name was also Hiram) had attended Williston Academy. I looked up the school's archives. Long a boys' preparatory school, it has now merged with a girls' school and is known as Williston Northampton School, but in its earlier days the Academy had admitted girls as students, and I was surprised to learn that two of Sybil's daughters were enrolled at the school with Hiram, the only son, at the time of Sybil's death. Also in the school's archives I found correspondence between its founder, Samuel Williston, and the Reverend Hiram Bingham.

Samuel Williston, it seemed, had played an important part in the lives of my missionary forebears, and, both consciously and unconsciously, in the disposition of Sybil's bones. As my curiosity led me on, the school's archives revealed further details of the Bingham family's benefactor.

Williston's father, a clergyman, was an early supporter of the American Board of Commissioners for Foreign Missions. This was the Protestant body, primarily Congregational and Presbyterian, that all through the nineteenth century had sent out missionaries, including Hiram and Sybil Bingham and later their son and daughter-in-law, to the ends of the earth to evangelize the heathen. Samuel Williston was brought up to believe a missionary's was the highest of callings, but his eyesight and perhaps his nerve failed him, and he made a fortune manufacturing cloth-covered buttons instead. He salved his conscience by giving lavishly to the ABCFM and less lavishly to individual missionaries, as well as founding the academy that bore his name, and donating substantial sums to Amherst and Mount Holyoke Colleges. In addition to helping the Binghams after their return from Hawaii, he had adopted two of the eight children of another mission family, the William Richards, who had been brought back and left with relatives or friends, as were so many mission children, including two of the Binghams, to be given a New England education.

It was a bombardment of the Richards' mission home at Lahaina on the island of Maui in 1827, by a whaling ship's crew, furious at the missionaries' attempt to deny them their accustomed visitations by island girls, that furnished the historical basis for a particularly lurid episode in the movie version of *Hawaii.* Hiram and Sybil had been visiting the Richards at the time, and, as Hiram later described the episode in his book: "We took our wives and tender babes to the cellar, and looked up for protection to Him whose shield was still over us."

A number of Hiram's letters to Williston were dug up for me by the school's archivist. They usually included, along with gratitude for past generosity, suggestions for helping other, sometimes rather grandiose, missionary endeavors. It does not appear, from some of Williston's surviving account books, that these appeals met with much success, and it is indicative of the humiliations this unemployed missionary, once the virtual ruler of Hawaii, had to undergo, that among the "benevolences" Williston listed for 1846 and 1847, along with $10,000 given to Amherst, appear the following entries:

Cloak to Mr. Bingham, value	$15.00
cash to Mr. B.	5.00
one bbl flour to Rev H. Bingham	7.75
Sundry other things	3.25

More valuable to the Binghams than these items, no doubt, was the opportunity offered to three of their younger children (of their seven children, two had died in infancy in Honolulu, and two had been sent back around Cape Horn some years before), who had been living with various relatives and at different schools when the family was homeless, to attend Williston Academy together, and to have them at last under one roof. Yet that was a bitter time for the family for their mother was dying, and their father had had to give up hope of returning to the one job he knew.

What Sybil's last years had been like I gathered from diaries and letters of hers and Hiram's that I found among the vast collections of papers they and their fellow missionaries had left behind them. (The voluminous files of the ABCFM are now at the Houghton Library at Harvard; the Bingham family papers are at Yale; other collections are in the Mission archives in Honolulu. My sporadic explorations have gradually taken me to all these rich lodes.)

Life in the Paradise of the Pacific was anything but healthy in the years when Honolulu was a village of grass huts on a dusty plain. Sybil was frail to begin with, if one can judge from her likeness in the portrait of the Binghams painted by Samuel F. B. Morse (of the Morse code and telegraph) before their departure for the Pacific: where an idealized Hiram gazes confidently from the little oval frame, Sybil's long thin nose and watery blue eyes make her look as if she had a head cold.

Actually it was Hiram who had a cold when their arranged meeting took place at his ordination in Goshen, Connecticut, early in the fall of 1819. But she had made up her mind to be a missionary, and if the only acceptable means for a girl was to go as the wife of a missionary, she was ready, whoever the missionary might be.

Two weeks earlier, on her twenty-seventh birthday, she had confided to her diary, as she had many times before, her concern for her "guilty soul," but she pledged anew her devotion to the "service of that blessed savior through whom all flows" and went on to express her deepest hope:

> Should I dare to pen a request for the year, if life be continued, it is that, wholly unfit, unworthy as I am, God would be pleased of his wisdom to fit me—I vow my desire strongly forth—and of his goodness to open a door for me among the heathen.

The door was already open. Hiram had just been refused by the only girl he knew who might consider sacrificing her life for the benighted heathen— apparently at the insistence of her father, the Reverend Samuel Shepard, a Berkshire village clergyman who did not think the pursuit of happiness was necessarily to be condemned. But Hiram had faith that the Lord, if not the ABCFM, would provide. Whichever the hand, it did provide, in the form of Sybil. Within a month Hiram and Sybil were married. Another two weeks and they were seasick together on the high seas, beginning the 18,000-mile journey to Hawaii.

The private diary was laid aside during that crowded autumn, and the next entry, after penning her prayer that the door be opened, begins as follows:

> *Jan. 15th, 1820.*   Conversation of a nature tender and interesting with my beloved friend in the silent hours of last night did deeply affect my heart. I desire to renew my resolution concerning my deportment towards this tender husband.
>
> *1st.*   I resolve that if moments occur when I cannot feel exactly with him in what may concern us, I will call to mind his attainments in the path of holiness beyond me, and set a guard upon my lips that no unkind word wound his feelings.
>
> *2nd.*   When I see that which (since in the flesh one is subject to infirmities) may want amendment, I will be faithful in my endeavor to exert a salutary influence to correct it, studying for the kindest manner in giving such reproof and exhortation as my sober judgment shall deem important.

Sybil had not been a schoolteacher for nine years for nothing. But she had been a wife for scarcely nine weeks.

She had much to learn about the domineering but "tender" Vermont farmer's son who was now her "beloved friend." She had moments of despair and terror, as I learned in going through the cramped pages of the diary where she wrote her secret thoughts—for her own eyes alone and those of her jealous God. (She kept another diary to send back to her sisters.) She prayed that she might be saved "from idolatrous affection, enabling me at all times to say, whom have I in heaven or earth that is once to be compared with *Thee.*"

8

Yet for all her worship of the "friend" with whom she found herself able to "reciprocate conjugal tenderness" (Sybil and three of her newly married "sisters" became pregnant on the five months' voyage), his continual prayers for the heathen must occasionally have irked her. For, tucked between the pages of her diary, at the point where the brig *Thaddeus* had "doubled" Cape Horn, is the nearest thing to a love letter from him to her that has been preserved: on the inside of a discarded envelope he had written what he had not the courage to say aloud, something between an apology and a confession:

> Think not for a moment, dear S., that I wish to reproach or grieve you in the least, but allow me to think my faithless and unworthy prayers can be of little avail to anyone; though if I pray at all, I hope that I do not always forget the friend who is dearer than myself. H.

On an adjoining page of her diary she wrote:

> I did not intend the reproof for him alone, myself was also included, but he received it so, and his heart is melted. Yet I trust it is wounded but to be healed. The command to us is to be holy. May we never cease aspiring to help each other to the work, however much it may cost nature. Compassionate Savior, thou wilt assist each joint endeavor.

The next entry was a month later, two days before they sighted snow-capped Mauna Kea. The terrible five months' voyage had taken its toll and she felt "weak and faint." But she prayed to her Savior, who by this time must have much resembled Hiram in her mind's eye, as she wrote:

> Thou meltest my heart by the kindness of my beloved husband whose tenderness towards me thou causest to increase daily, filling the tender names my heart has loved, in one, that of *bosom friend*. But, O my Savior, be Thou pleased to take the throne in my heart, and while I reciprocate his faithful love, let there be no idol there!

For twenty years she worked with him and for him and bore his children, but the cost to nature was a wasted body that finally came to seem to Hiram more important than his mission.

By then it was too late. Hiram anticipated that a few months' rest in what they considered the more healthful climate of New England would put her on her feet, and they would return to carry on the great work with which the Mission Board had originally charged them. In their eyes they had gone far to achieve the goals set for them: "Nothing short of covering those islands with fruitful fields and pleasant dwellings, and schools and churches, raising up the whole people—a nation to be enlightened and renovated and added to the civilized world."

Hiram confidently set about telling the world of their accomplishments, not only the Prudential Committee of the Board, which had by that time sent seven more shiploads of missionaries, including twenty-six ordained clergymen and eighty-seven others, to support the pioneer mission, but also the churches, mostly in New England, that supported the Board, and men of piety and wealth who gave to the cause, and even President John Tyler and the Secretary of State, Daniel Webster, telling all and sundry about the importance of the Hawaiian mission, its achievements and its needs.

No doubt he felt it was *his* mission, and there was no little personal pride when he presented to Congress a copy of the Bible printed in the Hawaiian language: he had led in the reduction of that language to writing and in the translation itself. He set about writing the history of his *Residence of Twenty-one Years*, which he believed not only would be a popular success but would bring additional wealth to the missionary cause and give him and his family an independent means of support.

When at the end of his book he summarized "what the Lord had done for the nation in respect to government, education, morals and religion," he knew he had been the Lord's chief instrument:

> The constitution and laws, the production of a people so recently barbarous, whose first lessons in their own language had been printed but eighteen years, may be pointed to as a monumental record of advancement. The Bible entire, printed in two editions of 10,000 copies each, and welcomed by the nation, as another: six boarding schools, 12 station schools and 357 common schools, embracing 18,000 scholars, as another; and as another still, the establishment and enlargement of eighteen churches to the light and glory of the land.

And as a final summation, these words:

> The age of darkness, of wars, of infanticide, and of human sacrifices had passed away, and the age of schools, of wholesome laws, of Bibles, of spiritual sacrifices, and revivals, had come.

Whatever contrary evaluations might be made, both then and now, both in the islands and in the homeland, it was a noteworthy achievement. Nowhere else could missionaries point to the transformation of a whole nation, at least in so short a time. It was, of course, a small island nation, and the missionaries had moved into the vacuum of an old culture already far gone in decay. Still, the mission had been a phenomenal success. And Hiram's open letters urging the churches of America to go on to "evangelize the world in the shortest possible time" and "to extend the gospel to these 600,000,000" did not seem too far-fetched, at least to him.

As the brief furlough he had envisioned lengthened into months and years, his confidence in himself and his cause began to wane. The ABCFM had heard enough complaints about the domineering character of its pioneer missionary—not only from the China trade merchants and whaling ship masters on whose financial contributions they were heavily dependent, but even from the later missionaries, who had found Bingham's continuing assumption of leadership intolerably arrogant.

Sybil's health did not improve. It became increasingly evident that she would never be able to return. Hiram fought on for five years, writing his book, traveling about the East, preaching and exhorting where anyone would listen, accepting the hospitality of relatives and friends, placing his children in a succession of schools, and carrying on a voluminous correspondence, with his children, with friends and supporters, with publishers, with the mission itself, and with the secretaries of the Board on whom his fate depended. Sybil, committed to their "joint endeavor," went along while her waning strength lasted, to Boston, to Brooklyn, to Philadelphia, to upstate New York, to New Haven, to Norwich, to Boston again, then to Hartford to be nursed by her sister. She had a chronic cough. Whether she or Hiram knew it, she was dying of the prevailing malady, "consumption." By the end of 1846, five years after their return, their world had collapsed.

The Prudential Committee of the Board, hardheaded businessmen, however pious, had discreetly sounded out Hiram's fellow missionaries as to whether they wanted Hiram back. The answer was no. "He assumes too much." He was "too much disposed to take precedence." Even his old friend, Levi Chamberlain, the Board's Honolulu agent, gave his opinion that Bingham's return is "on the whole undesirable" and "the majority of the mission" would be of this opinion.

At its September meeting, held in New Haven, the axe fell. The Board voted eight hundred dollars "for the use and comfort of Mrs. Bingham," but "dissevered" them both from its employ and "commended them to the churches." A couple of weeks later, Harper's, the publisher on whom Hiram had counted to bring out a big edition of his 300,000-word history, returned his manuscript. He had counted on the book not only to advance the cause but to contribute to the support of his family and himself.

Two despairing letters date from this time. One by Hiram, dated October 23, 1846, is addressed to "Rev. R. Anderson, D.D., Sec. ABCFM. My dear Brother." It thanks him, almost too fully, for the eight-hundred-dollar grant, and acknowledges that upon hearing the "kind terms in which our dismission was entered, my whole frame was convulsed with emotion." He went on:

A minister near me, as soon as I could attend, whispered, "The churches love you, and, ten years hence, will love you more." It *may* be so. May a merciful God grant that their love and confidence may not be forfeited.

With his hopes of a commercial publisher dashed, he had to accept the only alternative available, an offer from a Hartford printer to put out an edition of four thousand copies "by subscription," which meant that Hiram would have to sell that number of copies in advance.

11

For some ten days before and after accepting the terms I suffered as keenly as for any ten days of my missionary life. I could not rest. My health was affected. A paroxysm of my old bilious affection recurred. Fears that the cause of missions might fail of the benefits I had contemplated oppressed me.

He could not have known how many of his fellow missionaries disliked him. No doubt he attributed his dismission to Sybil's failing health. Perhaps he had her death in mind when he clung to the hope of going back to "the church and people once under my care, should it be possible for me to go again." He must have known she was dying:

This day is the twenty-seventh anniversary of that memorable day when we together stepped on board the *Thaddeus* for our long voyage and mission-ary campaign. She has been a true missionary, a firm friend of the Board and of the heathen, and a faithful counselor, and in my dangers, toils and trials, she, with what she calls a *feeble spirit*, has stood by me with un-daunted courage, and pursued her work with unfaltering patience, and is the same in spirit as on every former anniversary of our embarkation, having a heart large and buoyant, a mind clear and cheerful yet sober, a soul trusting in God and habitually looking upward. Her eye looks with calmness today on the blood-streaked expectoration from the lining of her lungs, which admonishes us of the frailty of her frame, though she is up from morning till night, and ready to labor or to suffer, or to be dismissed.

The other despairing letter is from Sybil herself, to her married daugh-ter Sophia, and is dated "North Haven, Ct., Dec. 20/46." She tries to sound cheerful and thanks God as always for his manifold blessings, but the picture of life in boarding houses, while Hiram is off in New Haven, seeking "winter quarters," or in Hartford making final arrangements for the printing of his book, is grim.

I thought we should have found winter quarters by this time, and I should have made full report of matters and things. But I must not sit here in this condition—fire all out in my stove—chamber cold—fingers numb. I have a foot stove with chestnut embers in it, or I could not stand it. So good night.—Will just say—I am all alone—your dear father in New Haven—went yesterday—returned the evening before from Hartford, to which place he went up in the cars Tuesday morning—no calculation in my mind but for his return in the afternoon train; but instead of that it was Friday after-noon, while not a syllable could I have, tho' the cars passed regularly, each way, twice in 24 hours. They were days of disquietude.

The next day she continued the letter.

Another day finds me comfortable. In great mercy the nights are generally made comfortable to me. As the day dawns I begin my work of hard coughing, but then strength is given me to get along with it, and find my place with others at breakfast table, then more or less coughing, till noon.

12

Not a day escapes—hardly any variation—occasionally someone will say, "It seems to me you cough harder than common today." But I can't tell—perhaps they chance to hear me more. I am looking for your dear father by the next train. One train has passed along from New Haven. I am expecting that he will find some place for us to board, and if so that we leave here today.

She goes on to say that they had come to North Haven seven weeks earlier hoping to board with a farmer who might allow them milk, but no farmer wanted to take in boarders, and the family where she has been staying, "with four hungry children, the fifth in arms, around a small kitchen table," can only afford to buy half a pint of milk a day and "one pound of cheese in the month."

The letter is continued two days later after they have moved to a New Haven boarding house, at the corner of York and Elm Streets. She ends with the expected prayer that "You all may have evidence of the Divine Spirit's regenerating work in your hearts, uniting in Jesus as blessed friend and Savior."

This was the time of Mr. Williston's "benevolences." He may have admired Mr. Bingham, but he had more personal feeling for Sybil, with whom he was connected on her mother's side of the family. He must have realized what it meant for her to have her children forever scattered, living with relatives, off at distant boarding schools as pensioners. With his button factory a success, and his fortune growing, he had recently founded, in Easthampton, his home town, the "Seminary" that bore his name, and built himself a handsome mansion next door. He arranged for the admission of the three younger Bingham children, and helped the family find a house nearby to rent.

And so for the last year of her life Sybil had a home—and three of her children with her.

Chapter 2

Man of God

It was Sybil's only son, Hiram, Jr., then fifteen years old, who made the final arrangements with Mr. Williston for renting the house in which his mother died a year later. Actually Hiram was her third son, but the two born in the early years of the mission had died in infancy. This third son—and sixth of seven children—may not have given thought to why he, and not one of his two brothers, was given the name of his redoubtable father. But there was enough in the choice of name to throw some light on his mother's early life and character. And now that he and his infant brothers all lie under the same turf behind their father's great stone church in Honolulu, a later descendant may speculate about those babies' names.

The first was Levi Parsons Bingham, born December 31, 1822, died January 16, 1823. "Nine days we folded it with sweet and tender affection to our bosoms," Sybil wrote her sister,

> rejoicing in its health, its growth, and fair promise. We gave him the name of our much beloved, deeply lamented brother, Levi Parsons, and, suffering our thoughts to run a few years down the vale of time, we said, "Perhaps, treading in the steps of him whose loved name he bears, he, too, shall be among those who, on the mountains of Jerusalem, shall lift up the standard for Israel's return." Our hearts rejoiced in this our pleasant child, while we desired to acknowledge God's superior claim. Sixteen days after He gave, He asked for the surrender of the precious gift.

They had named the baby after a fellow student of Hiram's at Andover Theological Seminary, a young man fired by the same zeal to save the souls of the heathen as brought Hiram and Sybil together. From the records it appears that he had been picked by the Mission Board to preach the gospel at the very fountainhead of his religion, in the Holy Land itself. Sybil, whose ambition, for years before she married Hiram, had been to give her life to save heathen souls, was first engaged to Levi Parsons, and it seems more than likely that, when she made that entry in her diary on her twenty-seventh birthday about hoping "the new year would open a door for me among the heathen," she was thinking of Jews and Arabs and Turks as the heathen whose souls were to be saved. For Levi Parsons was then about to sail for the Orient.

But the Prudential Committee of the Board had decided that, while missionaries to the Sandwich Islands would have to be married, missionaries to lands under Turkish rule must be single. I doubt if Hiram ever knew about Sybil's earlier engagement, any more than Sybil knew about Hiram being rejected by Sarah Shepard a month before he met Sybil. But their youngest daughter, Lydia, writing up her mother's life years later, reported that a fellow student of her father's,

> designated to the mission in Palestine, to which it was not thought wise by the ABCFM to send married men, had told him that if he were allowed to take a wife, Miss Sybil Moseley would be his choice.

In Michener's *Hawaii* the beautiful Jerusha had been engaged to a dashing whaling captain before she married Abner Hale. The real Sybil seems more likely to have waved her sad farewell to another missionary, as she was rowed out from the Boston wharf to the *Thaddeus*. Levi sailed a month later. After a year of language study in Asia Minor, he established himself in Jerusalem—"near the Holy Sepulcher" according to the missionary record; but about

14

the time that Sybil, on the other side of the world, was becoming pregnant for the second time, Levi, on a side trip to Egypt, fell ill and died. News of his death must have reached the Binghams shortly before the birth of their first son. So he was named Levi and not Hiram, Jr.

Another year went by, and another pregnancy, and with the birth of another son, still another name intruded: Jeremiah. Jeremiah Evarts was the Treasurer of the ABCFM when the mission was sent to Hawaii, and now as Corresponding Secretary he was the one on whom the missionaries depended at the end of the long life line around Cape Horn, so it may have been prudence as much as affection that led the Binghams to name their second son after him. But "my little Evarts" as she called him, "my cherished babe," lived only sixteen months.

The next two children were girls, and it was not till 1831, twelve years after her marriage, that the second Hiram was born. By that time the Binghams had a home of their own, an adobe cottage up Manoa Valley given them by Queen Kaahumanu, and Hiram's early memories were lush greenery and a mother at last able to give some attention to her children. Even the stern missionary father working on his translations was not altogether forbidding, if one can judge from the following mini-sermon preserved in the "Occasional Journal for the Children" in which he entered moralistic jottings for their edification:

> *31 Oct. 1839.* A little boy sat down to a nice breakfast with his parents and sisters on a beautiful morning in the charming sweet valley of Manoa where the cheerful birds sing and the green vegetation smiles around very pleasantly, and yet this little boy put on a very sour face amidst it all, and grieved his parents, and his little sister cried for the fly brush and the elder sister withheld it from her so the silly children disturbed the beautiful morning that God had given the family in that very delightful place.

Sybil was even then a semi-invalid, and the next year they left for the United States. That six-month sea voyage was the last time the boy saw much of his parents till he entered Williston Seminary. The 293-ton barque *Flora* with twenty passengers, eight of them missionary children, and with a cargo of sugar, molasses, hides, arrowroot, and raw silk, was a good place for intimacy if not privacy, and the "Occasional Journal" reports the following after almost five months at sea:

> Barque *Flora*
> Lat. 18. south

> *Dec. 26, 1840* Lydia said, "I want to be a good girl, and love Jesus Christ, and obey you, and love my mother, and make one another happy." [Lydia was six the day before.]
> Hiram went to the maintop of the *Flora* with his father. He recited also a page of Emerson's arithmetic, second part.

27. Hiram began to read the Book of Deuteronomy. He says he thought in the morning, when he was half asleep, that he was a naughty boy to disrespect his mother so much as he had done, that he felt discouraged, and did not wish to live in this world any longer, but to go to heaven.

28. Hiram said he thought the same thing again, and he was serious through the day yesterday. In the evening he went with his father to the maintop and they had some good conversation together.

Arriving in Brooklyn, nine-year-old Hiram was shipped off to relatives and then to a succession of schools willing to take a penniless missionary's son, and from then on his contact with his parents was mostly by letter.

He kept many of his father's letters, particularly after he was more permanently installed in the home of Mr. Amos Smith, a New Haven schoolmaster, who no doubt retained a share of the few dollars (eventually sixty dollars a year) allowed by the Mission Board for young Hiram's education. These letters, still to be read in the Yale Library, within a few blocks from where they were first read and treasured, are gentle and affectionate, in surprising contrast to the abrasive quality of some of the letters he wrote his fellow missionaries in those same first years after his return.

There is moral preachment enough, to be sure, in the first letter of the collection, when he wrote

I want to know that you love Jesus and are trying to serve him, trying to praise him, trying to please others and do the good, and preparing as well as you can to be useful in the world.

But even in that letter the emphasis is on "trying," and in the following letters there is far more evidence of concern that his children are homeless because of his own failures and frustrations than of concern for their morals. It was Sybil, if one can judge from the occasional postscripts she added to her husband's letters, who worried more over the state of her boy's soul. Perhaps that was why such letters as she was well enough to write were not preserved.

In one area young Hiram showed signs of independence. Significantly, his father seemed to have been more tolerant than his mother, when he wrote:

Your good mother has more than once spoken of your filial resignation and compliance with your father's wishes in consenting so willingly to have your hair cut so short as it was, while some even of the young gentlemen in college wished to wear theirs five or six times as long....A student or speaker should not have hair so long it distracts him.

The issue of length of hair was not settled for good. A couple of years later young Hiram, now fourteen, brought up the subject again. His father had always been clean-shaven and worn his hair short, but he said that he

16

considered length of hair and beard to be a matter "indifferent to God," only the boy should try to please others rather than himself. He had no small ambition for his son: "The world is to be reformed!" he wrote.

Many thousand active minds, such as yours is capable of becoming, need to be employed to remove the moral, mental and bodily maladies which now prevail so extensively throughout the world.

Now in his fifties, he saw the years slipping by, his wife an invalid, his mission interrupted, perhaps never to be resumed, yet the goal to evangelize the whole world was very real, and immediately attainable. With Hawaii "won for Christ," he saw China as the next field for conquest, and there he could imagine his son "the teacher of the Emperor of the Celestial Empire as your father was of the kings and queens of the Sandwich Islands."

Still, the need to have a family home, if not to live in, then for Sybil to die in, finally took precedence over dreams of saving the world. To young Hiram, not yet sixteen, was delegated the responsibility of finding a home to rent in Easthampton, with Mr. Williston's help.

His father wrote him from Brooklyn, in a letter dated April 19, 1847, that he had heard from Mr. Williston.

The principal question seems to be about getting our scattered family together in such a way as to benefit the children and comfort dear mother and promote the health, happiness and usefulness of the whole.

Mr. Williston says there are several chances of hiring a house, or several rooms in a house, at Easthampton if I apply *soon*, but I cannot very well leave my work here just now. [The deadline for finishing the proofreading of his book was three weeks off.]

You once proposed to have us run you as an "*express*," and here is a chance to begin. I should like to have you see Mr. Williston and his seminary, and have you look at the house and the apartments which Mr. Williston has mentioned. You may hire your board at about $1.25 per week [he first wrote $1.50, but crossed it out] and begin upon the garden to raise our summer vegetables, and thus wait for the rest of us.

As to your puppy—perhaps you had better sell him to somebody, or give him to the Sanford boys, or perhaps to Mr. Smith, if any of them want him. You may perhaps have promised yourself some pleasure in the company of your little dog, though I fear he would be a source of care, mortification and expense. It may cost a little self-denial for an hour to part with him— but I am confident that one manly effort to break away and rise above it, and please your parents and guard your reputation would be followed by more pleasure than any dog can give you. You can try it at any rate.

The boy must have parted with his puppy, for in his father's next letter, after praising him as a "pioneer" for the way he had carried out his assignment and, with Mr. Williston's help, found a house "in the precincts of the

Seminary," and indicating that it will be some weeks before the family can move in, his father goes on to say:

> It is natural that you should *feel lonely*, if neither hand nor mind find full employment. You have had a vacation of about three weeks. Now if you think yourself able to study two or three weeks more, you can take hold of Greek and composition or any other study at the Williston Seminary till the vacation there. You can practice your music some [Hiram had been given an old flute by a New Haven friend, which his father had gone to considerable trouble to have put in playing condition], and write to your sisters and aunts or cousins, for recreation.

In June, at last, his parents and his sisters Lizzie and Lydia arrived, and for a few months the dream of a family under one roof was realized. But Sybil was failing fast. Even her religious faith could no longer sustain her courage.

In December, in a letter to her sister, the last she ever wrote, she confessed that she was "trembling and afraid." Her "beloved friend," with his book finished, was without what he called "regular professional employment," preaching occasionally in vacant churches for a few dollars, or for nothing, still hoping, despite his resignation and the Board's "dismission," that he might again be sent to the field where he had preached to kings and queens.

This was how Hiram described Sybil's death in a letter to the secretary of the Board:

East Hampton,
Feb. 28, 1848

Dear Brother:

> The wife of my bosom, the youthful companion of my missionary life, is gone. And how shall I tell you the depth of my grief or convince you of the extent to which I feel my bereavement. I have had some trials, labors and cares before, when she stood by me to share them, or to soothe or dispel my sorrows, but now I painfully know she will never repeat those kind offices for me, or extend to her children or to the heathen those kind, maternal, or missionary counsels so valuable to them.
>
> But I would not murmur. It is the Lord's hand that touches me. He has taken away but what he gave, and I am bound to praise him, and think I do, that he allowed me to enjoy the rich gift so long.

He goes on to describe the course of her "multiplying maladies" and "excruciating troubles" over the last several months. She seemed most comfortable sitting in her rocking chair, the chair he had lovingly fashioned for her on their arrival in Honolulu twenty-eight years before—as a Vermont farm boy he had been handy with tools—and then brought back around Cape Horn. Now, as it became clear the end was near,

> in accordance with her former request to be in her chair when God should send the summons, we placed her there, and sustained her head and

hands and feet. I asked, how do you feel now, "I feel a little rested" (or "exhausted") not quite distinctly. I said again, "do you feel exhausted?" "Not as much as I should expect," she said, and soon repeated "Let His name be praised." "Be bold to speak the truth"—"The Lord cares for me"— then, in a low tone "Stop, Stop—I live." She took a spoonful of rice gruel. In a few minutes, toward nine o'clock—she said "Almost overcome" (sense ambiguous), then a few minutes later "Break the bonds." Then passed into a comatose state and spoke no more, but appeared to sleep.

The hours dragged along as the father and son and the two daughters watched and waited, wanting the labored breathing to stop, yet shunning the thought. Lydia, thirteen years old, in her later account, shortened the time to "a few more throbbings of her loving heart" while "father prayed, commending her to God," and sang two verses of a hymn beginning:

Go, pilgrim, to thy Saviour;
On joyful wings ascend.

But in her father's letter to the Board, he limited himself to this footnote:

*In this interval prayer was offered, hymns sung—O where shall rest be found? Rest for the weary soul? "The Dying Pilgrim" (*Sandwich Islands,* page 501.)

and briefly concluded that she "entered into her rest." The prayers and hymns were no doubt for the sake of the children. The footnote was perhaps to remind the Board that his book was finally in print, and that in losing a missionary they had also lost a poet. "The Dying Pilgrim" was a hymn he had composed for the funeral of another missionary's wife some years before, and it was quoted in full—six verses of eight lines each—on the indicated page of his great work.

For Hiram Jr., finally helping his father lift his mother out of the rocking chair, her death must have been deeply affecting. But he was young and strong. He finished his schooling at Williston, peddled the *Twenty-one Years in the Sandwich Islands* in his vacations (making as much as fifteen dollars on a two-week circuit), and went on to Yale. With the passage of time the image of his mother was naturally idealized. A generation later, when he was urging his own son to carry on the work of spreading the gospel, he wrote:

If ever there was in this world a woman who was noble, honest, generous, loving, tender-hearted and sympathetic, that woman was your grandmother, my own dear sainted mother; and how sincere was her belief in those doctrines which I hold to be essential to salvation, and to earnest whole-hearted service for our Lord Jesus.

Sybil was buried in the Williston family plot in the old cemetery not far from the Academy. The impoverished family was glad to accept continuing largesse from the button manufacturer, the friend of missions and mission families and of education. There was no money for a plot of their own, still less for a monument to her memory. Eventually Mr. Williston paid for a monument too, as I found out in my continuing search to find out why my father had been so concerned with where his grandmother was buried. The clue came in a letter the elder Hiram had written to Mr. Williston three years after Sybil's death, thanking him for taking care of the cost of an "extra nice and costly monumental article—a suitable and durable monument" to "that most precious wife and mother whose dear remains repose so securely under your kind protection and that of her unfailing Savior in your own peaceful family cemetery." But in the same letter he announced the prospect of a second Mrs. Bingham.

Naomi Emma Morse, the "Very worthy lady, of suitable age, say 47," to whom he said he was engaged (actually she was nearer fifty), came from the same part of Massachusetts as had Sybil. Like Sybil before her marriage, and like many another unmarried gentlewoman in her day, she was a schoolteacher. In 1843, the same year young Hiram became a boarding student at Mr. Smith's academy for boys in New Haven, Miss Morse and her elder widowed sister, Mrs. Mary Merrick, moved their Seminary for Young Ladies into a rented house on the north side of York Square (where the Yale Gymnasium now stands) in another part of the town. In the course of the five years Hiram spent at the "New Haven High School," before the family moved to Easthampton, his parents learned about the girls' school and its proprietors: in one of his mother's letters she asked him if he had been seeing Miss Morse and Mrs. Merrick, and in his last year at the New Haven High School his youngest sister, Lydia, became a student of Miss Morse's.

In an age when housework was not yet a male occupation, few men willingly remained widowers. It was natural for Sybil's husband to remarry, and all the more if Sybil had known and approved of the new wife. Nothing in the record suggests that Hiram fell in love with Naomi. Aside from her worthiness, there were other reasons why she attracted him. In his letter to Mr. Williston, he described her as:

> well adapted to elevate and refine society on a well cultivated missionary field, and give the finishing touches to the education of the daughters of missionaries, of merchants and chiefs at Honolulu, if we were quietly located there. But that is not to be just now. She does not think she ought to leave her school for it.

He was still cherishing his dream of a return "home" to the islands of his glory and his sacrifice. Not that he any longer had hopes of resuming his old position as self-appointed leader of the mission. He had even relinquished all claim to "his" church, with its two-thousand-member congregation and the vast stone edifice for which he had provided the plans, raised the money, and cajoled the chiefs into providing a thousand laborers, only to have his successor take the credit for completing the "new Solomon's temple." That had been thrashed out in a bitter exchange before his resignation and dismission (each volley taking six months to reach its target), in which Hiram had thundered:

> Lust of power may shake thrones. Usurpations and oppressions may jostle and agitate the institutions of men, but the kingdom of Christ is stable, and the relations of his churches and their pastors are not violently to be deranged.

A committee of the more worldly missionaries had confirmed his "supplanter," the Reverend Richard Armstrong, as permanent pastor and suggested to the Prudential Committee of the ABCFM that if Mr. Bingham ever did return—preferably in a more "accommodating and humble spirit"—he be assigned other duties, such as revising the Hawaiian translation of the Bible.

This had, of course, not been acceptable. Nor was the subsequent humiliating suggestion of Dr. Rufus Anderson, D.D., the Secretary of the Board, that he return as a "gospel laborer," dependent on Hawaiian piety rather than New England philanthropy.

There the matter might have rested if he had not conceived the idea of starting a school in Hawaii with Miss Morse. He even sounded out Dr. Anderson, as he wrote Mr. Williston:

> I told Dr. Anderson, as he asked me of my plans, that I had now the prospect of going into a Boarding School enterprise in company with a lady. "With your daughter," said he, "No sir, but with the teacher of my daughter." I spent two nights and a day with him without his suspecting my intention of marriage.

With Dr. Anderson apparently no more enthusiastic than Naomi about the school project, he played his last card. He was willing, he wrote in a final appeal, to postpone his marriage for a year and a half, if the Board would send him on a short-term assignment. He would make a tour of all the islands, and

> revisit those missionary stations most of which I helped to establish, to come once more among the churches with the fulness of the blessings of the gospel, to proclaim salvation once more to the thousands thronging at the missionary stations.
>
> The missionaries, the king and chiefs, the churches and people, I should hope, might be benefited by my labors and counsels a few months. It would, I think, do the race of Hawaiian Christians good to welcome their old friend among them, and to greet me once more with the warm "*aloha*," and to receive this friendly right hand in return; and to hear from my lips not only the messages of the gospel, and the results of my experience, but the assurances of the love and fellowship of their fellow Christians in this country.

He did not want to be a "supernumerary," but neither was he aiming to be "an antagonist or rival among my brethren." The Board well knew his qualifications, which he modestly admitted had been "given him from above." It was perhaps fear of being thought too old—he was now sixty-two—that led him to boast a little about his courage.

> Courage, which implies little or no merit, I had and still have in good measure. I felt it when thirty-two years ago I proposed to take the leap in the dark, and offered myself to the Board as the *first preacher* to carry the gospel to the Sandwich Islands, when no other preacher in the land was known to be willing to go thither. [Had he forgotten his brother, Asa Thurston?] I felt it too when I seized an angry chief there and delivered a white man out of his hand whom he was beating and kicking unmercifully, as I did also when in my youth I pricked with a bayonet a huge wounded bear in the night, and received the strike of his paw on my gun.

It was no use. Dr. Anderson was not open to this final appeal, however emotional.

Naomi, unfortunately, was in no hurry to offer him her bed and board. Perhaps she wanted to see how he would do as a business partner first. Yet her Seminary for Young Ladies must have seemed increasingly like his home. Lydia was again one of Naomi's pupils. Her sister Lucy, through school and engaged, was her assistant. Hiram, Jr., was a student at Yale, a few blocks away.

When they finally did get married a year later, it was Naomi's brother-in-law, a minister in Richmond, Virginia, not one of Hiram's old missionary friends, who performed the ceremony. Though in his old role he had been dubbed, half jeeringly, half admiringly, "King Bingham," and he was now only a partner in an enterprise known as "Mr. and Mrs. Bingham's Boarding and Day School for Young Ladies," he had at last found some security.

And there he passed the sixteen years of life still left to him. The school continued for most of that time, until the Civil War eliminated the Southern clientele that provided northern seminaries with their margin of profit, and it had to close.

He went on attending meetings of the ABCFM though they now paid little attention to him. With the school in difficulties, the Board voted him a pension of five hundred dollars a year, and he wrote Mr. Williston a fulsome letter of thanks for the one hundred dollars he had contributed to the pension fund. He preached when he could "in vacant churches," which brought in a little extra money. For over a year he was acting pastor "for the Congregational colored people of this city," as he wrote his oldest daughter; but he did not know "how long I shall supply them, with what compensation they will feel able to give me." The Temple Street Church had a reputation as a "haven" for fugitive slaves. It is unclear whether he was aware of that, but with the coming of the Civil War he became a passionate supporter of the "cause of our Country and of Human Liberty."

There was some pride and satisfaction for the old man when, after the war, his daughter Lydia, having served as principal of Ohio Female College in Cincinnati, answered a call to start a girls' school in Honolulu, and there, across the street from the great stone church, she carried out the project he had once thought of for Naomi and himself.

The greatest event of his old age was his delivery of the "charge" at his son's ordination as a missionary. To have a son his successor in the mission field had long been his most cherished hope; if he were not to be permitted to return himself, he had long told the Board, he wanted his son to take his place.

CHAPTER 3

Like Father, Like Son

Young Hiram had shown some tendency to break loose as a college student. Despite his father's earlier expressions of disapproval, he let his hair grow long in the new fashion. (Later, in an even more marked assertion of independence, he grew a beard.) A daguerreotype taken in college, as well as his class-book picture, depicts a gentle, almost sensuous face, quite unlike his father's Vermont granite. He won renown for kicking a football over the old Courthouse on the Green, a feat not before recorded. On one college vacation he paddled a canoe down the Connecticut River from the Canadian border, three hundred miles to Long Island Sound. From his early years his parents had worried that "he does not often enough think of his Savior," and that he was growing up without being governed by "the principles and feelings of a renewed nature"—which presumably meant he did not at all times have a proper sense of guilt.

Yet his father continued to remind young Hiram that he was expected to carry on the missionary work, which for himself had been so sadly interrupted, whether in Hawaii or farther out across the Pacific. In any case he must have impressed others with his seriousness, for upon his graduation from Yale he was offered the post of principal of the high school in Northampton, Massachusetts.

By this time he had learned to call his stepmother "Ma." But on moving back to within half a dozen miles of where his "own dear sainted mother" lay, he was not likely to forget Sybil or her concern for his soul.

Even so, he might never have become a missionary if on the staff of the high school under his direction there had not been an even younger teacher named Minnie Brewster. She seemed as concerned with the state of her own and others' souls as Sybil had been. "In early youth she sought her Savior's love and united with the church at the same time with her father." So it was said when her life came to be written. But her father, Jonathan Brewster, known in Northampton as the "genial landlord" of the Mansion House hotel, had apparently not felt the need of his Savior's love until his daughter's persuasions.

She had graduated from Williston Academy a few years after young Hiram, and must have heard the affecting story of Sybil's death and perhaps even visited her grave in the Williston plot—if not before, then certainly after she and Hiram became interested in each other. It takes no great flight of fancy to imagine the tall handsome young school principal on a Sabbath outing to his mother's grave, telling Minnie about his mother's sudden decision to marry and set sail around Cape Horn with the husband she had just met, on a mission to save heathen souls. And if Minnie's piety was sufficient to bring her father into the fold, it must have helped persuade Hiram that he owed his fellow man more than a career as a schoolmaster.

He was not immediately persuaded. At the end of that school year, he had a chance to see something of the world and he took it. He went to Europe on a grand tour. The auspices were irreproachable and the opportunity would not come again. His father's oldest and most worldly friend, James Hunnewell, who had sailed on the *Thaddeus* with the pioneer missionaries in 1819, carrying not Bibles but five casks of rum and other merchandise, and ten years later had returned to Boston with the beginnings of a large fortune, now lived in Charlestown, and there the Binghams had frequently visited when church or missionary business took them to Boston. Mr. Hunnewell saw in young Bingham, with a year of teaching behind him, a safe companion for his own son James, Jr., whom he was sending on an educational trip to Europe. Hiram was engaged to go along as tutor, friend, and moral guide.

Hiram kept a journal, as was the custom. It began, piously enough, probably for his father's eyes, with a farewell to his "dear pupils...committing them to the hands of Providence, that God would guide their youthful steps and bring them to an eternal home"—but with few pieties thereafter. His berth on the *Canada* required him "to make a slight kink in some part of my body." (He was six feet four.) James was seasick; Hiram permitted himself to play checkers, but not cards. Landing at Liverpool and going on to London, he was awed by the splendors he saw: the Crown jewels, a nobleman's palace, Queen Victoria in her coach, the Crystal Palace ("grandest of all sights"), riders on Rotten Row. For his father's sake, he visited a hospital for the aged, made a pilgrimage to the "abode" of Minnie Brewster's *Mayflower* ancestor, Elder William Brewster ("a man of property, but who adopted the views of the dissenters"), and attended Sabbath services (commenting on one sermon that the "arguments in favor of the Trinity were good"). But for the rest he was open-mouthed: it was all "like a dream."

If young James Hunnewell caused him any trouble, it does not appear in his journal. As decorous sight-seers, the two young men went on from England to do the continent. After this three-month glimpse of the great world, Hiram was ready to do what his father wanted. He entered Andover Theological Seminary, as his father had, to prepare for a missionary career.

Rebellion there must have been. His eyes bothered him. He developed respiratory and digestive troubles. In the second year of his course of study in Greek, Hebrew, and homiletics, he left Andover and showed up in New Haven. He seemed to have "broken down," as his father wrote Mr. Williston, under an attack of "bronchitis and dyspepsia. He cannot sing and must speak with a low voice. He does not go out of the house—and cannot expect to earn anything, and we fear he must relinquish his favorite profession." His father, of course, had no doubt what that profession was: "He has ardently longed to be a missionary."

If it was rebellion, it was soon stamped out. The Brewster girl probably helped. So did a few months of outdoor work on a farm. And before the year was out, he had begun to match if not surpass his father's achievements: within a span of twenty-five days his father had been ordained, married, and sailed from Boston as a missionary to the heathen of the remote Pacific. Hiram Bingham II accomplished the same in twenty-three days.

The ordination took place in New Haven, with the President of Yale offering prayer, and his father accepting him for the ABCFM as a "fellow servant of Jesus Christ." He was married in Northampton, November 18, 1856, to Minerva Clarissa Brewster (henceforth no longer to be known as Minnie, which gave recognition to a heathen goddess as well as her father's first wife, but as Clara, after her mother). And together they sailed from Boston on December 2, 1856, bound via Cape Horn not for the Sandwich Islands, only 18,000 miles away, but for the Gilbert Islands in Micronesia, 2,500 miles farther.

They did spend a few months in Hawaii, while their ship, the *Morning Star*, the first of a series of mission ships of that name, went off first to take supplies to the Marquesas mission. Hiram was pressed to stay and take charge of his father's great stone church, but that would not have satisfied the urge to be as much of a pioneer as his father. Hawaii was no longer at the edge of the known world. Even mail to and from New England went by way of California and the pony express in a matter of weeks instead of months. His father, learning of the offer to take over his old church, left the decision to his son. But the news that Clara was pregnant disturbed him: remembering the terror of acting the part of midwife for Sybil, he pleaded with his son to wait, arguing that God did not require that Clara should have her baby on a savage island unattended.

The young couple, having given their lives to the Lord's service, were not deterred, and when the *Morning Star* was ready to sail, they were aboard.

25

Their first landfall in Micronesia served to remind Hiram of his father's encounters with heathen "degradation." As the hermaphrodite brig sailed slowly by the first inhabited island, a man in a canoe paddled out to greet the visitors: his "constant theme," as Hiram wrote in his first report back to Boston, "was that there were 'waininini' (women) on shore. This, our first interview with the heathen, made us long to tell them of the blessed Savior." Hiram was to spend the rest of his life trying to convey the Gospel message to those heathen, and his response to the man in the canoe was symbolic; he wrote a letter, in English, hoping someone on shore might translate it, in these words:

Morning Star,
Aug. 29, 1857

To the Inhabitants of Menchikoff Island:

Glad tidings! "Glory to God in the highest; peace on earth; good will toward men." "God so loved the world that He gave His only-begotten
Son, that whosoever believeth in Him might not perish, but have everlasting life."

We hope soon to bring you the Gospel of Jesus Christ, and some of his missionaries to teach you.

Very truly yours,
Hiram Bingham, Jr.
Missionary to Micronesia

As he entered on his missionary labors, he brought, as his father had before him, not only the Gospel message but Western civilization, and he had no doubt about the relevance of either. During the next forty years of his life, along with much preaching, he was to give the Gilbertese a written language, and books, and schools. He translated the entire Bible, from Genesis to Revelation, and in that, too, he would outdo his father, whose contribution to the Hawaiian Bible was only that of one among many. Yet he must have wondered sometimes, and particularly when he dropped the "Jr." from his name upon his father's death, just where one Hiram Bingham left off and another began.

Clara, too, may often have felt Sybil as a daily presence. Not that she would think in terms of emulating Sibyl's large brood of children. But as she and Hiram and the Bible and a book on midwifery were dropped off at Apaiang, it was comforting to think that Sybil had successfully borne her first child with only her husband in attendance. At any rate, as she watched the *Morning Star* sail out of the lagoon, she kept her fears to herself.

Two months later the baby they had decided to call after Clara's *Mayflower* ancestor, William Brewster, was born. He never breathed. Hiram took the tiny body by night to bury in a secret spot that they would keep to themselves. For the Tarawans were readying a sanguinary invasion of Apaiang. And cannibalistic rites were not unknown.

26

Clara did not give birth to another baby for almost eighteen years. That baby was my father Hiram Bingham III, and thanks to a near miracle, a doctor attended his birth. It was also almost a miracle that he was not born a posthumous child. For during that pregnancy, the lives of two Hiram Binghams hung in the balance.

Missionaries to tropical lands, at least in our family, suffered from a common health hazard, referred to as a "bilious affection," more often as "dyspepsia." Diagnosis at this date is difficult. Intestinal disorders such as dysentery are still common in the tropics. But the Bingham missionaries, father and son, seem to have had recurring bowel disorders even when in New England, and the emotional stress of a continual guilty conscience may well have been a factor. On at least two occasions my grandfather was wracked and prostrated and near death.

The first was six years after he and Clara had set up the frame house— they called it "Happy Home"—that had come with them to Apaiang on the *Morning Star*. The times were turbulent and perilous. The kings of Apaiang and Tarawa fought their bloody battles, up to the very doorstep of the Happy Home. Open hostility to the missionaries was less of a problem than total incomprehension. The "heathen jargon" of the "savages" was difficult enough to master. Even more baffling were their manners and morals.

A later resident of the Gilbert Islands, with some cultural anthropology behind him, could describe them as

peopled by a race who, despite the old savagery of their wars and grimness born of their endless battle with the sea, were princes in laughter and friendship, poetry and love.

Hiram could only see

their extremely immodest manners and customs, their great licentiousness, their unbounded lying, their covetousness, theft, warlike spirit and bloody warfare, their ignorance of a final judgment, of heaven and hell, of Jesus Christ.

It was no wonder if conversions were slow in coming, and the Binghams were often near despair. A notebook for recording "Christians" lists only four in those first years. Yet they would have persevered if they could. The long black coat and top hat he wore on the way to preach in his almost empty palm-thatched church on a Sunday only accentuated the gauntness of his towering frame. When, with increasingly frequent and severe bouts of intestinal pain, his weight finally reached 128 pounds, his strength was gone, and he looked, as he wrote his sister Lydia, like a skeleton, he felt death not far off.

The *Morning Star* appeared just in time, on that occasion, and took them back to Honolulu. After two years of slow recovery there and in New England—not idle, however, for they were working on reducing the Gilbertese language to writing and beginning translation of the Gospels—they were ready for another voyage. This time, when they sailed from Boston for the long journey around the Horn, Hiram was not merely a "Reverend" but a "Reverend Captain" (which struck his sister Lizzie as funny), for he was the master of the second *Morning Star.*

The ship was used to maintain contact between a dozen mission stations in the Marshall, Caroline, and Gilbert Islands, an area as large as the continental United States. Hiram continued as captain for a year after reaching the Pacific. But for the time being, his main job was translating the New Testament. Clara translated hymns and helped his sister Lydia in a school for Hawaiian girls. They made three trips through the islands of Micronesia on *Morning Star II* and its successor, *Morning Star III,* with only brief visits to their "Happy Home."

The Gilberts were still islands of violence and misery. Progress in civilization, whether from the standpoint of church or school, seemed infinitesimal. The Hawaiian evangelists, who had kept the mission alive, were given to backsliding. A mob once burned the mission buildings. The little church was said to be used for prostitution. The secret grave of the Binghams' first-born was dug up and desecrated.

Believing as they did in the power of the word, and particularly of the printed word, once they had the New Testament in print, as well as a hymn book and a few school texts—the first literature ever produced in the Gilbertese language—they were ready to try another stint as resident missionaries. They returned to Apaiang determined to achieve for these turbulent islands what the earlier Binghams had done for Hawaii.

For almost two years they labored, before nature once more took a hand. They preached, organized a school, a women's group, always under the fear of violence. Murders were frequent. But their gentleness and persistence began to bring results. The notebook showed twenty joining the church in 1874, and in the first few months of 1875 there were seven more.

But Hiram's old intestinal troubles began to recur. And Clara's diary began to reflect a new concern about her own condition. His illness and her incredible pregnancy came to her awareness almost simultaneously. Here are some entries from early 1875:

Feb. 21. Darling suffered from severe dyspepsia.

Feb. 22. Our largest air plant is crowned with many buds which are just beginning to open into very pretty flowers.

Feb. 23. The little kitties grow cunning and pretty every day. They are very playful.

Feb. 24. Afternoon meeting, darling was very good on "gentleness."

Feb. 25. Usual school and other duties. We went out for a walk through the woods up to Tabouteba—picked sweet flowers. Caterpillars are plenty at T., and have eaten all the green from the grass on dear baby's grave.

Feb. 26. My darling had a better night than usual. His old difficulties are hanging about him. May the good Father spare him.

Mar. 10. Darling is quite poorly this month.

Mar. Afternoon meeting for those who wish to unite with the church. Over twenty were there. About ten may be received. Came home very tired. Darling was nervously weary.

Mar. 24. I am not very well these days. Is past experience to be repeated, or is it something else? I cannot tell.

Mar. 28. My darling was taken with great pains which continued at intervals.

Mar. 29. Darling was pretty weak and miserable all day. Did not come down at noon or evening. Is it a return of eleven years ago?

By the beginning of April she knew it was "something new" (had there been miscarriages before?), and they began to wrestle with their consciences. Only his breakdown could justify their leaving.

Apr. 1. Darling not so well. If only I were real strong and vigorous how glad we would be, but I *must not* be much on my feet these days.

Apr. 2. Weakness and often pain and depression are my loved one's portion. How like 1864.

Apr. 5. Capt. Daly's "Lady Alicia" came to anchor near Teirio before dark.

Apr. 6. Very light wind and the vessel could not get up to her anchorage. No special change in my darling for the better. My prayers are for his restoration. *The work is great—the workers few.*

Apr. 11. Dearest suffered all the afternoon, sweating and then pain. I try to "cast my burdens on the Lord";—but where is the path of duty?

Apr. 12. A question presses upon us this morning. Shall we seek passage somewhither with Capt. Daly? Strong reasons say yes—almost as strong— no. At first Capt. said impossible, but he came in in the afternoon and the matter was fully talked over, but we could not then decide. Capt. D. was willing to "do the best he could" for us.

Unfortunately the little *Lady Alicia,* a tiny trading ship, was still to complete her cargo of copra, and then would head for Sydney, in the wrong direction. They decided to wait. Perhaps the *Morning Star,* though not due for months, would come in time to take them back to Honolulu. Meanwhile the big signal flag, made of four white sheets bearing the word WELCOME in black letters, was atop a pole on the tallest coconut tree, and might be seen by a trader bound north for Hawaii. "Devoted natives in relay shifts," as she later told the story, kept watch in the top of the tree for a sail.

Finally on a "Sabbath," May 16, when Hiram was "so poorly" they did not go to church, "a fine, large, three-masted vessel" was "announced," and seemed headed their way. Hiram had "much pain in the afternoon." The wind was very light, the reefs at the entrance to the lagoon were treacherous, and the ship did not make their anchorage till late the next day. She was a "nice vessel" with a "very pleasant" captain, bound, after stops at some other islands, for Samoa, "where are physicians and milk."

Hiram, she wrote, was "excessively nervous and in severe pain. It seems as if he must have a change, or fail utterly. His life is surely worth saving for the work he can do for the blessed Master." They decided to accept the passage offered, even if this, too, was in the wrong direction.

Two days later they "left the dear, dear Happy Home; when, oh when to enter it again" (never, as it turned out), amid "much sobbing" and expressions of "tender love we have not been accustomed to see among our Gilbert Island people."

Hiram felt better for a while, and they went ashore on Little Makin Island when the ship put in at Butaritari, and for a week, while the vessel was trading goods for copra, they stayed with Maka, a Hawaiian fellow missionary.

Maka and his admiration for Hiram were described a dozen years later when Robert Louis Stevenson came that way in search of health. "I have never known a more engaging creature than this parson of Butaritari," wrote Stevenson in *The South Seas.*

> He had the morning cheerfulness of birds and healthy children, and his humor was infectious. We were next neighbors and met daily, yet our salutations lasted minutes at a stretch—shaking hands, slapping shoulders, capering like a pair of Merry-Andrews, laughing to split our sides upon some pleasantry that would scarce raise a titter in an infant-school.

That was Maka on weekdays, but his Sabbath appearance must have been patterned after Hiram's:

> On that day we made a procession to the church: Maka, a blot on the hot landscape in tall hat, black frock-coat, black trousers; under his arm the hymn-book and the Bible; in his face a reverent gravity:—beside him Mary his wife, a quiet, wise, and handsome elderly lady, seriously attired:—myself following with singular and moving thoughts.... To see him weekly flogging a dead horse and blowing a cold fire was a lesson in fortitude and constancy.

Stevenson must have known who had produced Maka's hymn book and Bible, and his later impression of Apaiang suggests Hiram and Clara had had more of an effect than they knew:

> Apaiang, the most Christianized of all these islands, where excellent Mr. Bingham lived and labored and has left golden memories; whence all education in the northern Gilberts traces its descent, and where we were boarded by little native Sunday-school misses in clean frocks, with demure faces, and singing hymns as to the manner born.

Even a hundred years later, it might be added, Gilbertese children are listening to the reading of Mr. Bingham's Bible and singing Mrs. Bingham's hymns, and those who continue their education do so in the "Hiram Bingham High School" on Beru Island.

But in 1875, Clara was recording Hiram's shipboard agonies in her diary, and ignoring her own condition, during a long month of beating south between Makin and Samoa. Towards the end they both began to doubt whether Hiram could make it to Apia alive. If he died, he told the captain, he did not want to be buried at sea, but rather, he hoped, in Apia. They did make it. Hiram on a mattress and a board was hoisted by block and tackle overside to a mission doctor's boat, and they found a respite ashore in the doctor's home.

The diagnosis: "no evidence of organic disease but of great nervous prostration and want of tone in the whole system, especially in the bowels."

Two weeks later Clara, for the first time, dared to put in her diary a direct reference to her own condition. She felt "two distinct throbs which sent a bound of joy through my heart." But Hiram is still bedridden and she feels miserable. "Oh, my heavenly Father," she prays, "take me in thine arms and help me. I am very weak. How can I do all I need to do and be."

She mentions the arrival—and departure—of vessels, but none headed their way. The weeks go by. The doctor thinks Hiram is well enough to travel. They have a chance to go to Sydney where there are steamers for Hawaii. But that would mean nine thousand miles of ocean instead of three. "Can it be that we shall be in Honolulu before the close of the year?" She counts the months. The baby is due in November. It is now September.

They decide to take a ship to Fiji, from where it should be possible to make New Zealand, and from there, perhaps, Honolulu. By September 15, they are at Levuka, a Fiji Island port, where they learn that the barque *Prospector* will sail for Auckland in two weeks. They take passage. Clara agonized:

> It is not likely that we shall reach Honolulu for some time. May the Lord direct and care for us. I do not feel very well equal to the task that is before me—but what can I do? My love "requires a change of climate" to reinstate his health, and I must go—trusting in the kind Father to keep me and my treasure safe from all harm.

Going aboard the *Prospector* she wrote she had never felt "*more forlorn.*"

> Our room was far too short for dear H. but he was allowed to take a longer berth.... A gentleman, Mr. Burwitt, took the upper berth in my room.

By now only too obviously pregnant, she must have felt her morals safe, and "I could not have my poor darling cramped up in the short berth."

A fellow passenger died and was buried at sea. A "terrific gale" hit them and they were "under very short sail for many hours. Oh, it was fearful." By

31

October 14 they landed in Auckland. Missionary friends had heard they were coming and took them to a lodging house. Doctors were consulted. They found Hiram had "atrophy of the liver and enlargement of the spleen." What they may have found as to her condition, now eight months pregnant, she does not say, but they thought Honolulu was as good a climate for Hiram's recovery as New Zealand.

Two more weeks went by. On October 29, they boarded the *Mikado* for Honolulu. "H. walked from carriage to our room without help."

There is one more entry in the diary:

> *Nov. 8th.* We have entered upon our 12th day, and *if the Lord will,* we hope to be in Honolulu sometime next Friday,—The Lord will provide.

Friday morning Oahu was in view. Some hours later they saw Hiram's sister Lizzie on the dock. "Friends came on board, and best of all, our good old physician responded to my note by coming on board and helping us get ashore." Hiram had to be helped to walk. A room was provided in the mission school for girls, now under Lizzie's direction.

Six days later "about seven in the evening, pains began." It was their nineteenth wedding anniversary. Clara duly chronicled the event:

> About 9 1/2 we sent by Charlie C. for Mrs. Morgan and also a note to Dr. S. Both came before eleven. Dr. got a rest for awhile in E.'s room. At half past 2 Mrs. M. called the Dr., and at quarter past 3 my heart was filled with wonderful love and joy at hearing the cries of my precious darling child, a fine baby boy. Everything went on well—except I had too little milk for my darling—which almost broke my heart. I must not forget to mention the coming in of the dear papa to see the baby boy in the morning about 10 o'clock.

CHAPTER 4

Checked Baggage

Though the first Hiram had died six years before, his powerful figure, and that of the sainted Sybil, loomed over his tiny namesake, the third Hiram. Kawaiahao Female Seminary, where my father was born, was across the street from the original mission buildings and the church that was his grandfather's great monument. His boyhood was spent surrounded by reminders of the power and the piety of the pioneer missionaries.

From Kawaiahao the family moved into a home provided for them on the old Bingham Tract at Punahou, in the lower end of Manoa Valley. The original 224-acre tract had been given to the first Hiram at the behest of Queen Kaahumanu fifty years before. All gifts to missionaries then were considered common mission property, but the Queen had built a thatched cottage for the Binghams, which the first Hiram had improved, and Sybil always thought of it as "home." She supervised the building of a wall to keep out roaming cattle, and started a twenty-acre sugar-cane and banana plantation for the support of the church; and a half century later, the night-blooming cereus she planted along the wall was still there, a block away from the new Bingham home, to remind the third Hiram of Sybil's good works. The site of the original cottage had been absorbed into the grounds of the school for the children of the missionaries, and title to the rest of the land had been released to the Mission Board by the original grantees.

Gilbertinia, as the new Bingham home was named, stood on Alexander Street in the lower part of the Punahou tract. (Today a four-lane expressway passes a block away with a large sign: Exit to Bingham Street.) The ABCFM, which was paying Hiram's meager salary, made the lot available, and its local supporters raised money for the house.

The largest contribution came from Mrs. Juliette Montague Cooke. She had known Sybil when she and Amos, her husband, members of the Eighth Company of missionaries, had started a school for Hawaiian chiefs. A dozen years later Amos and a colleague, Samuel Castle, had resigned from the mission and had gone into business together, and it was the phenomenal success of their firm, Castle & Cooke, that now enabled Amos's widow to make a generous donation toward providing a home for the penniless Gilbertese missionaries.

As a boy, my father could never be allowed to forget that while other missionary families might be rich, his family had renounced riches for nobler and purer goals.

His father labored at his translation of the Old Testament, working from a Hebrew text. His mother worked on Bible readings for prayer meetings and school books for Gilbertese children—an arithmetic, a reader, geographies. His aunts Lizzie and Lydia came to live with them. Lizzie had been christened Elizabeth Kaahumanu Bingham at the time the Queen Regent was Sybil's friend and patron, and perhaps that heathen strain accounted for the fact that she was the only member of the household with a sense of humor, and she taught her nephew how to play checkers and backgammon. Cards were, of course, taboo. Lydia, late in life, had married a redoubtable old missionary, the Reverend Titus Coan, and at his death, which soon followed, she joined her family, and her rustling black dress and sweetly solemn mien became a permanent aspect of Gilbertinia.

She, of course, assumed, as did his parents, that Hiram III would follow in the footsteps of Hiram I and Hiram II. He never got over the titters that went up when he first attended school and announced that his name was "Hiram T'ird." It did not help that about the time he entered Punahou School the trustees were naming a new building "Bingham Hall."

Like many another unhappy teen-ager, he ran away from home: with dreams of rising from newsboy to wealthy philanthropist, he took passage on a steamer for San Francisco, but the steamer's departure was delayed, he was missed at school, a schoolmate gave him away, and his father found and brought him home. Family friends were aghast, but his parents, however shocked and horrified, treated him with new consideration. Even the rod, which up till then had not been spared, was not used again.

Money, or rather the want of it, was of chronic concern. One of his grievances was that the pennies he earned, doing chores at home or for neighbors, were not his to spend but, after suitable deductions for the Lord's work, were put aside for his education. That he should have withdrawn all his savings from the bank on his daring escapade was a particularly heinous aspect of his relapse from grace. Presumably his father got a refund of the passage money, and the education fund continued its slow growth.

Education, in the Calvinist tradition of missionary families, was almost as important as godliness. The Hawaiian mission had its origin on the steps of a Yale building when Obookiah, the Hawaiian waif, was given refuge, taught to read the Bible, and inspired the pious to a concern for the souls of his people. A number of missionaries had studied at Yale, and their sons and grandsons went there as a matter of course. So when Hiram Bingham II, of the Yale Class of 1853, took his family on a long-planned trip to the mainland to see about the publication of his completed Bible, he decided that young Hiram, then sixteen, should transfer from Punahou to a school in New England and there complete his preparation for Yale.

Since his parents had both attended Williston Academy, in Easthampton, that was their first choice. Easthampton was near Springfield, where Clara's mother, and her brother Henry and his family, lived, and there were other family connections of the Brewsters, Moseleys, and Binghams in the area. But Samuel Williston, the old missionary benefactor, had died when they were still at Apaiang, and when they made a pilgrimage to Sybil's grave in the Williston plot in the cemetery, even that seemed not the same: her modest marble slab was overshadowed by a huge new monument to the memory of the philanthropic button manufacturer.

They decided on Phillips Academy at Andover instead. The fact that both Hiram I and Hiram II had studied at the nearby Theological Seminary seemed to make it appropriate. So in the late spring of 1892, Hiram III was deposited at Andover to take exams for entry into the Academy in the fall, while his parents settled down in New York for the arduous task of seeing the Gilbertese Bible into print.

The last verse of the Bible had been translated two years before, in a little ceremony in April 1890, duly photographed, with young Hiram, in a chastened mood after his escapade, behind his father's shoulder, and mission officials and members of the family standing in the background. Thereafter, with meticulous care, the whole translation had had to be reviewed and corrected, which took another two years, before it was ready for formal presentation to the Rev. Dr. E. W. Gilman, Corresponding Secretary of the American Bible Society, which was to publish it, at the Bible House in New York. A month later, having left their son at Andover, Hiram and Clara began reading the proof sheets of the first chapter of Genesis as they came from the composing room.

Day after day and month after month, Hiram and Clara strained their eyes to make sure that any mistakes of the typesetters, who of course knew nothing of the language, were corrected. Hiram estimated there were 3,350,000 letters and 120,000 punctuation marks to check, and as a Biblical scholar, he could state exactly, rather than in round numbers, that there were 31,173 verses. A year later, and again with due ceremony, the work was finished. As the *New York Times* reported:

> The last verse of the last chapter of Revelation was put in type. A proof was taken and carefully examined by Mr. Bingham, who then read the verse aloud in the Gilbert Islands tongue, his voice trembling with emotion. After a prayer of thanksgiving had been offered by the gray-haired missionary, the doxology was sung and remarks were made by Mrs. Bingham and others.
>
> The event marked the end of thirty-four years' conflict with almost insurmountable difficulties on the part of Rev. Hiram Bingham, the famous missionary.

His work, of course, was not finished. He still had to prepare a Gilbertese-English dictionary, without which the people whose language he had reduced to writing would have only limited access to the world's store of knowledge. That would take another dozen years, for after the first manuscript was ready for the printer, it was lost by a careless messenger and had to be all done a second time.

But the dictionary could be done in Honolulu, and the Binghams had no intention of spending another winter in the cold north. Hiram's ever chronic health problems had recurred, and now with his Bible finished, he underwent major surgery, long postponed. Then, in June 1893, he went to New Haven, and at the Yale Commencement ceremony, with classmates at their fortieth reunion applauding, he was accorded a recognition his father had never attained, the honorary degree of Doctor of Divinity.

A block from the ceremonies in the College Chapel was his father's grave. If he visited the cemetery, he must have thought of that formidable parent, perhaps now for the first time, with more sympathy than awe.

Whether it was on that occasion or subsequently there is no record, but the feeling grew that his mother's remains should not lie so far from his father's.

At any rate he was now ready to turn toward home. Young Hiram, with his first year at Andover behind him, joined his parents and went with them as far as Chicago to visit relatives and take in the World's Fair. From then on the record of what was done about Sybil's bones is to be found only in the letters from her grandson that her son so carefully preserved.

The first reference is in his last letter from Andover, written three days before his graduation.

Andover, Mass.
June 18, 1894.

My dear father,

Many thanks for yours of the 23rd of May and the enclosed check. I thank you for trusting me with so large an amount at one time. I hope I shall not have occasion to use it until I get to Springfield and then I would like to deposit it in the bank. I have been able to earn about $35.00 this past term, made up as follows: tutoring geometry $27.00, tutoring algebra $.75, collecting grand-stand fees $7.50. I wish you could be here June 21st, to hear your son make his debut on the commencement stage. I think there are to be only ten speakers. I hope Uncle Henry will be able to be here. How proud I would be if you and mama were able to be in the audience.

Then, after mention of a girl he met at the "Wellesley Float" and apologies for writing "so short a letter, but I am very tired and have to get up early," he remembers his father's letter. So he takes another sheet for a postscript:

P.S. Before I go to bed I must reply to your letter. All you say about the removal of my grandmother's remains from Easthampton to New Haven is right. At present I am very busy, and will be during the early part of the summer vacation. Probably during the early part of September I will be able to have everything done as you would like. I am glad that you have trusted me with this.

As a vacation job which he hoped would net him one hundred dollars, he had signed up as a traveling book salesman canvassing a Pennsylvania territory to sell a volume entitled *What Can a Woman Do?* The enterprise was not a commercial success, and it ended with what he said a doctor called "a catarrhal condition of the bowels caused by the intense heat, too much change of drinking water and nervous prostration caused by and due to the nature of my business," and what another doctor, back at his uncle's in Springfield, after he had "got scared about myself and bolted for home" told him might be appendicitis.

[The doctor] looked rather grave but said little and put me on a rather queer diet. "Nothing for forty-eight hours." "No, nothing, except brandy and water." "*No! not a thing!*" By Sunday night I was fearfully and awfully hungry—and still the famine lasted. He, the M.D., came to the rescue Monday noon, but only placed milk, eggs and toast on the "free list."

36

By Tuesday he was well enough to remember what he had been asked to do, and he wrote the sexton of the Grove Street Cemetery in New Haven to prepare for the reburial of his grandmother's remains next to his grandfather's.

It was getting near the end of August, and he had promised his father to have the matter attended to no later than September. But there were difficulties. He received a letter from Nathan H. Sanford, the Secretary and Treasurer of the New Haven City Burial Ground.

New Haven, Ct.,
Aug. 28/1894

Mr. Hiram Bingham, Jr.

Your letter of 21st inst. to Mr. Hickman, our Sexton, has been handed to me. There is no space for a burial in the United Society (North Church) burial lot, on the North side of Rev. Hiram Bingham's grave, it being close on to the north boundary line of said lot. At the south side of his grave is an unmarked grave, that I assume contains his second wife; this body that you wish to bring here, would have to be buried south of and next to this grave of second wife.

He went on to explain that digging up a body in summer would not be allowed in Connecticut, though it might be in Massachusetts, and in any case a zinc-lined pine box three feet long and two feet wide would have to be procured at a cost of about nine dollars. He further stated that the approval of the church whose lot it was must be obtained.

So young Hiram, recovered in health and beginning to enjoy his vacation, took time out, during a visit to some cousins in Holyoke, to move the project along. He wrote the church and, combining business with the attractions of "driving, playing tennis, calling on Katherine's young lady friends, etc. etc.," he drove over to Easthampton, seven miles away, and "got permission for the removal, and made arrangements with an undertaker for other particulars."

He reported all these events to his father, and told of receiving a discouraging letter from a representative of the church in New Haven, which he enclosed, but ended on a more cheerful note with an account of a "very fashionable full dress dinner party" where he had had a "very pleasant time."

The letter from the church, written by an old friend of the family, a Mrs. Champion, seemed to Hiram as good an excuse as any "why nothing has been done this Summer." It read as follows:

My dear Mr. Bingham:

Your letter came this morning. I have been to see Mr. Sanford. He says that the sexton is in error as to space on the north side of your grandfather's grave, and I have just come from the cemetery where we looked at the lot. There is not over six inches of space.

She went on to say that any new grave would have to be on the "south side of the second Mrs. B's grave and permission of the church committee may not so easily be gained,"

> for while the other space would never have been granted to anyone except to be used by your grandmother, she was in no way connected with our church, and the lot is for the church people who have no other burial spot. If the church gives space for a third grave coming toward the center of the lot I am not sure but your Father and Aunts would have to be consulted. Mrs. B. No. 2 could be moved and put No. 1 between Mr. B. and No. 2.

Mrs. Champion, out of delicacy perhaps, refrained from mentioning that "Mr. B" himself had never been a member of that church, always retaining his membership in the church in Honolulu, and that it was because of the membership of Naomi, "Mrs. B. No. 2," that he had been buried in the lot in the first place. However, Hiram's Aunt Lydia had joined the church when she taught at Naomi's school, and Mrs. Champion, who knew her, was sure she "wanted her Mother to lie next to her Father." So she hoped for a favorable decision.

The next letter in the manuscript collection, written two days before my father had to be at Yale for the beginning of his freshman year, tells the final grim details.

Springfield,
Sept. 24, 1894

My dear Father:

Last Saturday I went to Easthampton and shall try to give you a full account of all I did. I went directly to the undertaker's, Mr. Henry F. Pomeroy [Sybil's mother had been a Pomeroy, so this was probably a cousin]. We drove to the house of Deacon Ansel Lyman to get his permit for the removal. He was in the meadows digging potatoes, but stopped long enough to write a permit which I supposed would be O.K. Mr. Pomeroy, however, said I would make myself liable to a fine of $50.00 unless I secured a permit from the Board of Health. By the time I had found this out it was time for dinner.

I dined at the Mansion House, a very good hotel just across the river from where you used to live.

After dinner I went to the Town Clerk's Office to get the record, which he kindly made out for me, of the facts of the first death and burial. Then Mr. Pomeroy drove me to the express office to see what the charges would be if remains were sent by express. They don't carry a body for less than $5.00. This seemed rather steep, for I could go to New Haven and take the body with me for twice the first class fare, or $3.30, in the baggage car.

The thought occurred to me that it might be sent by freight. But the Freight Companies refused to take it, because no valuation could be placed on the remains and in case they were lost or went astray I could sue the R.R. Co. for any amount.

Finally one of the ticket agents came to my relief. Since I had a ticket to Springfield he would send remains to New Haven in the baggage car for one regular fare, i.e. $1.65. He was also the Board of Health Agent, so I left with him a 1st class ticket to New Haven and the govt. permit.

All of this required a lot of driving about and talk. Mr. Pomeroy was very good, however, and knew just whom to see and what to do. After this had all been fixed we drove to the Main St. Cemetery. He had provided a suitable box 3 ft. x 16 in. x 18 in., and had his man ready to make the exhumation.

The next page of the letter was marked "*Private*," and it is clear that young Hiram was concerned about upsetting his invalid mother (then showing the first symptoms of the shaking palsy that ended her life nine years later) and his aging aunts.

What follows you may not care to read aloud or have anyone else read, but I will write fully as I would tell you about it with all due reverence to the honored dead.

After digging down about three feet through a sandy soil we came upon the remains. They lay together directly in front of the stone. There was no trace of any box or container of any sort except two old fashioned brass handles which were probably on the coffin. The bones were all together. The skull, leg bones and ribs were all within a few inches of each other. We looked very carefully for traces of a box but found none. The bones had very evidently been taken out and laid in this hole without much ceremony. There were more remains than I had expected to find. The gravedigger searched very thoroughly, and I believe that all of the remains that lay there were safely removed. From the condition of the soil the burial was probably made about 17 or 18 years ago. Mr. Samuel Williston died about 20 years ago, and it is the opinion of Mr. Pomeroy that the removal was made at the time that the lot was graded and Mr. Williston's monument erected. The probability is that whatever remained there was quietly removed to this lot which no one seems to own.

Mrs. Champion has doubtless written you what we decided to do. I spent last Thursday in New Haven and talked the matter over again with her. As the remains will not reach New Haven until the latter part of this week I will be there to attend to everything.

The letter closes with a report of what he has spent to furnish his college room. He has bought a "very nice iron bedstead, with woven wire springs" for $4.95 and a "hair mattress all new" for $3.70, and goes on to explain the low price:

It is a regular $7.00 mattress but of special size 6.4 x 3, and was a special bargain which I happened to get at an immense drygoods stores. It was made to order for them for a lady. She wanted something larger, and they wanted to get rid of the mattress.

The next letter was written after college had begun. Sybil's bones were not on his mind. Yale was "fine, great, grand," but he was "green as grass," and at the first chapel service he had, to his horror, violated an ancient tradition by bowing to "Prexy" upon his entrance: "Only Seniors do." But two weeks later there is this brief note:

> Mrs. Champion has settled all the bills in regard to the removal. The stone has been cleaned and well set up. Mrs. Champion showed me the epitaph which you made out for the unmarked grave [Naomi's]. It seemed to me that the word "relict" is obsolete. By the way, Mrs. C. has made us a present of a very pretty sofa pillow.

Obviously Mrs. Champion had not secured permission of her committee to move Naomi. But Sybil was only a few feet from her "beloved friend" instead of sixty miles. And I had solved the mystery of her last resting place.

What I have not yet solved is what happened to the "costly monumental article," the stone of finest Vermont marble, that her Hiram had ordered, Mr. Williston had paid for, and her grandson had moved to its new location. The present sexton denies any knowledge. Perhaps it was not as "well set up" as my father thought. But at least I know now that it was there when he first showed me the graves.

CHRONICLE II

The Wanderer

CHAPTER 5

Origins and Early Years

In his old age my maternal grandfather, Alfred Mitchell, looked back on his life and made a belated record of events. He bought a leather-bound book of blank pages marked only with faint blue rulings. He decided to allow two facing pages for every year of his life. A rubber stamp with adjustable digits was used to mark each year, beginning with some significant years before he was born, the first entry being the birth of his grandfather, Stephen Mix Mitchell, in 1743. On subsequent pages in the later 1700s and early 1800s, he recorded the birth dates of his parents and five of his surviving brothers and sisters. He noted his own birth on April 1, 1832, four months after the death of his father, and from then on the page numberings are consecutive on into the twentieth century.

Most of the entries deal with his travels. He became a homeless wanderer even in his first year of life, when his mother left the parsonage of the Second Congregational Church of Norwich, where he was born, and moved in with relatives in New London. A few pages farther on, dated 1839, appears the brief entry, "March 29, Mother died," followed a few lines down the page with this: "Sale at auction of stuff and closing of house." For a while he apparently boarded with the new minister in the old parsonage, but the security of a settled home was forever denied him.

Financial security was another matter. Even as a posthumous child he was born, as the saying went, with a silver spoon in his mouth. His father had come from a well-to-do family, and his mother had passed on to each of her children a share of the considerable fortune she had inherited from the seafaring Shaws of New London. His wants were taken care of in his youth not only out of his own inheritance, but by wealthy relatives, and on his twenty-first birthday, as he duly noted in his date book, his guardian turned over to him the still substantial sum of $19,804.27.

From his earliest years he seems to have felt that the world owed him a living. He had the means to travel, and no sense of where he belonged. The record of his life that he jotted down in his later years is of continual journeying, much of it seemingly aimless. What was he searching for—perhaps the home he never knew and never found?

There are gaps, of course, in the written records available to me about my family. Along with the desire to preserve runs the fear of preserving. Among the neat packets of letters tied with silk ribbons by my grandmother Annie Tiffany Mitchell are references to the destruction of letters she did not want preserved. In one packet of letters on which she had revealingly—if unnecessarily—written in her strong angular script, "Letters I did not destroy," I found a long letter to her from a young man, my grandfather-to-be, that told me much about them both. Piecing together other letters and diaries of hers, I began to see my mother's parents as vivid and complex personalities.

The envelope of his letter was addressed to Miss Annie O. Tiffany at her father's house at 255 Madison Avenue—near Thirty-eighth Street—New York. The month and day given were November 26, but the year was not indicated; nor was it revealed by the smudged postmark. From the context I determined it was 1868, midway in a long and stressful courtship. The young man, Alfred Mitchell, was then thirty-six. It was perhaps characteristic that, although he had been informally engaged to Annie for over a year, he did not remember that the day after the date on the letter, when she might be expected to read it, was her birthday. She would be twenty-four.

It was also significant that he did not write her name and address on the envelope himself. They were in another hand. Was he afraid her father would intercept it? However concerned at her still unmarried state at an age when young girls were supposed to be safely established, her father could hardly look with favor on a young man twelve years her senior who was penniless and unemployed—as the letter reveals he was.

Her father was Charles L. Tiffany, merchant prince, founder and president of Tiffany & Company. As a young man he had left his father's cotton mill and general store in Danielson, Connecticut, a few miles up river from Norwich, to become partners with John B. Young, son of a neighboring mill owner and friend of the family; together they had opened in 1837 a small specialty shop on lower Broadway in New York under the name of Tiffany & Young, with an initial capital of one thousand dollars, all provided by his father, Comfort Tiffany. By the time he was in his mid-thirties, he already had an agent of his firm in Paris, buying the crown jewels of fleeing Louis Philippe, and was dubbed by an admiring press "the king of diamonds." Twenty years later, having made his fortune but still hard at work, as he would be to the end of his days, he was not disposed to encourage Alfred Mitchell's interest in his daughter.

Yet there was no doubt that Alfred was respectable and of good family. In fact his eastern Connecticut background, with Plymouth Rock not far away, was much the same as Mr. Tiffany's. Mr. Tiffany had every reason to know about that background, for his wife, Harriet Young, who was also the sister of his first partner, had intimate connections with Norwich, from where Alfred's letter to Annie was posted. John Young had retired from the New York business in 1853 and moved to that eastern Connecticut trading center, where two of his sisters were already living, having married into prominent local families.

The Youngs were the friends and neighbors of the Goddards and Williamses, who had brought up Alfred Mitchell after his mother's death, and knew as much as was to be known about him. And Annie, growing up in New York, thought of Norwich, where she often visited her aunts and uncles, as her second home. John Young's wife, Lydia Almy Young, was her favorite aunt, and the many letters to Annie from Mrs. Young make up the largest collection she preserved. "Auntie" had things to say about Alfred when the courtship began that were not favorable, but she certainly did not criticize his family background.

By the mid-nineteenth century when Norwich was the third largest city in Connecticut, thanks to the textile mills along the Quinebaug, Shetucket, and Yantic Rivers, the families that owned those mills were the local aristocracy, and Alfred belonged to that aristocracy. He was, in addition, identified with the seaport aristocracy of nearby New London, twelve miles to the south. If he had not wasted his inheritance, he was certainly well-enough connected to be an eligible suitor for a Tiffany. In fact, from the point of view of a family whose wealth had been inherited from previous generations, he could look down on the Tiffanys as somewhat nouveaux riches.

The Heritage

Alfred's forebears became wealthy from ownership of land and from seaborne trade. Some of their wealth, though he may never have been told, was undoubtedly made in the slave trade, but money once made could be passed on untainted. Some of his inheritance, moreover, came from English and Scottish ancestors who had brought wealth with them when they crossed the ocean. Thus his distinguished paternal grandfather, Stephen Mix Mitchell, delegate to the Continental Congress, United States Senator, and chief justice of Connecticut, found in Hannah Grant, only one generation removed from Scotland, as he was himself, "a young lady of large fortune." As his biographer put it frankly, "Being by inheritance and by marriage in easy circumstances he was not obliged to practice [law] for a livelihood" (he had trained as a lawyer) "and felt at liberty to indulge his inclinations for public life."

Alfred's ancestors were not all rich but many of them were, and many of them were pious. Piety and wealth in Puritan New England were seldom in opposition. When the Reverend Alfred Mitchell, Alfred's father, pastor of the Second Congregational Church of Norwich, died, he left not only a library of over a thousand volumes (including a collection of his own hand-written sermons, still preserved, with the dates of their delivery in Norwich and the surrounding towns), but also a large house and garden in the most fashionable part of town as well as sizable investments in bank stocks, school bonds, and mortgage notes. His estate was appraised at $14,973.61, no small sum in 1831 for a minister to leave his heirs, especially a minister who had been the youngest of eleven children.

My grandfather, the youngest of nine, was the second Alfred of his father's children; the first try at a namesake had died at birth. Two other Mitchell children had died in their first year. Life expectancy was low in the early

1800s. The second Alfred, though born four months after his father's death, was duly adjudged an heir, and so began life as a property owner. His mother was awarded her widow's third of the estate, and was named guardian of her six living children's shares.

Her name was Lucretia Woodbridge Mitchell, and she was my great-grandmother. She only lived a few years after her husband before the family illness of consumption struck her down, so Alfred hardly knew her. But she dominated his life, not so much because of her personality, which seems to have been more generous and warmer than her husband's, but because of her property, which was considerably greater than his. She was a wealthy woman in her own right, and her property continued to shape the lives of her descendants to the third and fourth generation. Unlike his wife's Tiffany fortune, which ultimately gave Alfred the life of opulent leisure he had been led to expect, Lucretia's wealth was mostly in land, and land can leave an even more lasting impress on the lives that follow than mere bank accounts and intangibles.

Part of the land was in New London, and it was to New London that Lucretia Mitchell, as a young widow, first moved her family. She left the big parsonage on the Chelsea Parade in Norwich for an even bigger house, the Shaw Mansion, overlooking the shipping in New London harbor, and there my grandfather spent his early formative years.

The Shaw Mansion was a symbol of established wealth. Even today, as the headquarters of the New London County Historical Society, emerging from a slum area in process of urban renewal, its granite facade is imposing. It was built in 1756 by Lucretia's great-grandfather, Captain Nathaniel Shaw, who took advantage of the arrival of a shipload of French deportees from Nova Scotia and built himself the finest house in New London. He was the founder of the most prominent of New London's shipowning and merchant families, and had prospered in trade with the West Indies and across the Atlantic. Yet the sea lanes were dangerous as well as lucrative, and three of his six sons never returned from their voyages.

The oldest son, Nathaniel Shaw, Jr., became the leading spirit in New London's support of independence for the colonies, when the British began enforcing restrictions on colonial trade and the family faced ruin. He took charge of outfitting and supplying the infant American navy for the Continental Congress. Ten of his ships were armed as privateers, and one of them, the *General Putnam*, took fourteen prizes. In the burning of New London by the British under Benedict Arnold in 1781, he was said to have had losses amounting to 12,000 pounds. Still, regardless of losses, the family emerged from the war richer than before.

None of Captain Shaw's sons had children to inherit their accumulations; only their sister Polly produced heirs. She and her husband, the Reverend Ephraim Woodbridge, both died at an early age—neither piety nor property was proof against the prevailing scourge of tuberculosis—but they left two small children. It was these two, Nathaniel Shaw Woodbridge, and his sister Lucretia Woodbridge, who became the heirs and in turn the transmitters of the Shaw fortune.

Newly orphaned, they too had found shelter in the big Shaw Mansion. A miniature painted at the time, and still to be seen in its collections, depicts them as wide-eyed and frightened, but they were probably pampered and spoiled by their grandparents and their uncles. The boy was sent to Yale at the age of fourteen. He was promptly sent back when his "puerile profuseness and dissipation" led to "tumults" for which the uncles had to pay damages. He was married at eighteen to Elizabeth Mumford, whose father managed the great landed estate acquired by the Shaws during the war, located in Salem, a few miles northwest of New London.

These thousands of acres of rich farmland and wooded hills had belonged to a Massachusetts loyalist, Colonel William Browne, who fled to England in 1776 when mobs were threatening the great houses of the wealthy in Boston. The General Assembly of Connecticut declared the Salem land forfeited and ordered it divided into lots and sold. Nathaniel Shaw, Jr., was the first and greatest purchaser. After he was killed in a hunting accident, his brother Thomas Shaw bought more of the confiscated land, and built a big new house for his nephew and heir (overlooking the spacious acres Nathaniel was to inherit). The young Nathaniel's father-in-law managed the property, collected rent from tenants and superintended farming operations, while Nathaniel, in the short span of years allotted to him, hunted, fished and entertained—a convivial country squire.

His manorial estate formed a background for family portraits painted in the 1790s, when Thomas Shaw engaged Ralph Earle, one of the country's leading portrait painters, to come to New London and do the family. Of Earle's six portraits, two still hang in the high-ceilinged rooms of the Shaw Mansion. Young Nathaniel Shaw Woodbridge was painted twice, first full-length, as a country gentleman in tailcoat and figured waistcoat, hunting on his estate with dog and gun. The second time he is shown as a father with daughter Mary on his lap, companion to a portrait of his wife Elizabeth holding the other daughter, Lucretia, later to marry the Reverend Alfred Mitchell. The young couple are depicted as a lord and lady, with powdered wig, silk gown, satin knee breeches, in a baronial setting suggesting the great houses of England. An idealized countryside is glimpsed through great tasseled velvet hangings behind their chairs.

The Salem land was a significant part of the wealth Lucretia Mitchell inherited and passed on to my grandfather Alfred Mitchell and her other children. But it served, as in the portraits, primarily as a symbol, denoting a patrimony more bucolic than profitable, and bestowing on Lucretia's descendants, in my generation and beyond, an aura of superior gentility.

Yet there was nothing bucolic about the original "subjugation" of that land. What may have been the largest aggregation of black slaves in New

England had been employed in clearing the forest, digging out the stumps, dragging the glacial rocks from the fields to make miles of stone walls, building farmhouses and barns. The Browne family had acquired the land as a speculation early in the eighteenth century. In 1759 the grandson of the original owner decided to bring the land into cultivation. His father-in-law, Governor Wanton of Rhode Island, who had grown rich in the slave trade, provided him with the manpower. One report has it that there were as many as sixty families of slaves brought over from Rhode Island for this undertaking.

Slavery was as acceptable in New England in the mid-1700s as in Virginia. To be sure, few northern estates were large enough to make slave labor profitable, though the Narragansett shore was one area where large plantations had been established. Newport, across Narragansett Bay, was a center of the triangular trade in rum, slaves, and molasses that shuttled between New England, Africa, and the West Indies, laying the foundation of many New England fortunes. Most of the slaves were sold in the West Indies to man the sugar plantations of Jamaica, Barbados, and Haiti, but the masters of the ships that plied the Middle Passage kept enough of their slave cargoes to meet the needs of their own households and farms in New England. So slaves were readily available for Colonel Browne's land clearing.

Browne engaged John Mumford (Lucretia Mitchell's great-grandfather) to take charge of the project. Mumford was the youngest son of a wealthy Narragansett planter family. In supervising gangs of blacks he was not out of his element. His father's first wife had been murdered by a slave rebelling against a flogging. Cousins of his had served as officers on slave ships. Other relatives who had migrated into southeastern Connecticut had helped give New London County the largest concentration of slaves in New England.

Of the slaves employed on the Browne lands, only nine were still there at the time of the Revolutionary confiscation. They were inventoried at 1,770 pounds, along with the forfeited acreage valued at 169,000 pounds, of inflated Continental currency. John Mumford, Jr., son of the original manager, asked to be relieved of responsibility for the slaves still in his lease. Slavery, in addition to being unpopular as a mark of ostentatious wealth, was uneconomic. Probably most of the original slaves, brought in under private contract, had been taken back to Rhode Island. But the remains of primitive shelters and numbers of unmarked graves in the woods just off the Browne land suggest that many who had worked on those lands were given a grim kind of freedom when they were no longer needed.

In any case, when Lucretia Woodbridge Mitchell first came to live in Salem as a child, after her dissipated young father Nathaniel Shaw Woodbridge died and she was taken in by her Mumford grandparents, she was in the care of black servants, survivors of the Browne slaves. The Mumford House where she grew up was more like a Virginia manor than a New England farm.

Not that she ever made any great pretensions. A portrait that survives shows a lady of subdued refinement. The values she brought with her when she married the Reverend Alfred Mitchell were expressed in the lines she cut with a diamond ring on a window pane in the parlor of the Mumford House on her wedding day:

In a narrow sphere,
The circle of Domestic Life,
I would be seen and loved,
The world beyond is not for me.

Her married life lasted seventeen years and produced nine children (only four of whom survived to adulthood). After her husband's death, Lucretia Mitchell moved with her family to the Shaw Mansion to run the household of her uncle, Elias Perkins. Perkins had been twice widowed; after the death of his second wife, Elias Perkins was glad to have Lucretia Mitchell, along with her children, live with him. Earlier, he had acted as Lucretia's legal guardian after her father's premature death.

Elias Perkins, then in his sixties, was as imposing as the Shaw Mansion in which he lived. Even today, his full-length portrait dominates the great stairwell in the entrance hall. Mayor of New London, he had been a member of Congress and, for many years, a judge of the county court. Active in banking and real estate, he had close ties to New London's burgeoning whaling industry, in which his son-in-law, Thomas W. Williams, was the dominant figure. Whaling may then have been of no interest to Lucretia and her infant son Alfred Mitchell, but it shaped the course of Alfred's life, and determined who his descendants were to be.

The few years that the Mitchell family lived in the Shaw Mansion were perhaps not enough to give a little boy grandiose ideas. But with all his family background conspiring to impress him with the importance of his ancestors, he could never forget that he was connected with the first families of New England—Saltonstalls, Winthrops, Gardiners, including divines, colonial governors, merchants, gentry, men of property and standing. Elder William Brewster of the *Mayflower* was in the family tree, and his son Jonathan Brewster was the first proprietor of the land on which the Shaw Mansion stood.

However, ancestral names and ancestral property did not necessarily provide security for descendants. Elias Perkins' oldest son, Dr. Nathaniel Shaw Perkins, recently married, had a prior claim on the Shaw Mansion. After only a few years of the Mitchells' occupancy, Dr. Perkins moved his family in, and the Mitchells looked for another home. Alfred had his first experience of the uncertainties of being dependent on wealthy relatives.

To be sure, his mother was more than amply provided for. As a gently bred woman, she was not equipped to handle her properties herself, but she had plenty of male relatives to advise and dispose for her. The house and farms she had inherited (in Norwich, New London, Waterford, East Haddam, and Salem) were all rented to reliable tenants. Her investments in real estate developments in other states (Maine, upstate New York, and Ohio) had been liquidated, and the proceeds put in Norwich and New London bank stocks.

She still owned the big house in Norwich that had served as parsonage as well as home during her husband's lifetime, but her health was becoming too frail to run a big household.

She was dying of the same "consumption" that had struck down so many young parents in her family and produced so many orphans dependent on others. Of her own parents and her father's parents, none had lived beyond the age of thirty. Her only sister Mary had lived only twenty-six years, but her early death now proved a kind of blessing for Lucretia, for her sister's daughter, Mary Perkins, had become a member of Lucretia's family, and grew up as an older sister to the Mitchell children. She moved with Lucretia to New London after the Reverend Mitchell's death, and was married in the Shaw Mansion, while Lucretia was still living there, to a Norwich lawyer, Levi Hart Goddard. As Lucretia became less and less able to care for her brood, Mary Perkins Goddard took increasing responsibility for their care, no longer merely an older sister to the Mitchell children but a substitute mother.

Lucretia Mitchell went traveling to the Caribbean, hoping a tropical climate would relieve her cough, taking with her two of the older children who had also contracted the dread disease. In the meager scraps of letters and memorabilia that still remain—including a locket with some of her husband's hair—is a letter she wrote in 1837 from St. Croix in the Virgin Islands to her cousin and legal advisor, Thomas Shaw Perkins: she said her health was not improving, and she was worried that financial panic was destroying the value of her investments.

Another document from St. Croix dated at the same time throws light on how a woman of piety and gentleness responded to the great issue of slavery: it is a certificate of the emancipation of a slave boy for whom she was willing to become responsible. The boy was mentioned in a codicil to her will, dated shortly before she died in 1839, and now preserved in the dusty files of the Norwich Probate Court, in which she set up a small trust fund for the benefit of "William Armstrong, a colored boy committed to my care by his mother in the island of St. Croix who now lives with me...to enable him to learn some good trade or business."

Neither family nor court records provide further information on William Armstrong or whether the little savings account was ever put in his name. But on the rest of Lucretia's substantial properties, and how they affected her heirs, the evidence is voluminous.

Under her will, her bank stock was left to her son Louis, on account of his "feeble health." He had a humpback, and at her death he was thirteen years old. The rest of her estate was to be divided among her six surviving children, including Louis, but before a division could be made two of the six had succumbed to the same endemic disease. That left four children, all minors, to share in their mother's extensive holdings of real estate.

The oldest, named Lucretia after her mother, was awarded farms in Waterford and East Haddam with some adjoining Salem land. Louis, in addition to his special legacy, was given the New London properties, the Daniel Shaw house next to the great Shaw Mansion, and the seventy-five-acre "Fort Farm" next to Fort Trumbull on the harbor. He also received a piece of the Salem land.

His older brother, Donald, in his second year at Yale, was allotted the bulk of his mother's holdings, several tracts totaling over four hundred acres, with two farm houses.

Alfred, the youngest, was given the former parsonage in Norwich, as well as a sixty-acre tract in Salem. Before he was seven, therefore, he was a person of considerable property.

The Orphans

Lucretia's childhood home, the Mumford House, had belonged to her sister Mary Perkins, and at the time of Lucretia's death it was occupied by Mary's husband, Henry Perkins, and his second wife. But he decided to make it available to his married daughter, Mary Perkins Goddard, who was trying to be a mother to the Mitchell children, and he moved into the other ancestral home, the Woodbridge House. So the Mumford House became home for Mary and her husband Levi Hart Goddard, and thereby as much of a home as Alfred would enjoy during the most formative years of his boyhood. Though not altogether a member of the Goddard family, Alfred could not help but feel a sentimental, even proprietary, interest in the wide bottom lands overlooked by the big colonial mansion.

Levi Hart Goddard was in his early thirties when he assumed responsibility for the farms inherited by his wife and her young cousins. He too had been born to wealth and social position; his father Calvin Goddard was one of the leading citizens of Norwich—successively a lawyer, a member of Congress, a judge of the Supreme Court, and mayor of the city. Hart—he did not like the name of Levi—set out on his own, after graduating from Yale, to read law and settle in Ohio; however, his marriage to a wife with inherited wealth led him to postpone that career and devote himself to managing his wife's Salem properties.

The Goddards had two children when they moved to Salem. Two more were born in the Mumford House. Mary Perkins Goddard, out of gratitude to the Reverend Mitchell who had been her foster-father, had named her first child Alfred Mitchell Goddard. This made for some confusion when they took in the young Alfred Mitchell, so they called him "Alf."

The second Goddard child, Julia, born in 1838, shortly before the Mitchell children arrived, came to seem as much a sister to Alf as to Alfred. But the younger ones, Henry and May, born after the families merged, were so much younger than the Mitchell boys that they were taught to call them, with due respect, Uncle Don, Uncle Louis, and Uncle Alf. Many years later when May's school friend Annie Tiffany first became aware of Alfred Mitchell, the solemn young man she was eventually to marry, she too called him "Uncle Alf."

To be called "Uncle" was, of course, appropriate for Donald, who was in college when the Goddards moved to Salem. He did not join the household, aside from vacations, till after his graduation from Yale in 1841. In college he had devoted his energies to writing voluminously for the Yale *Literary Magazine*, to the dismay of his legal guardian who thought he should be applying himself to more "practical" studies. Being chosen valedictory orator of his class further magnified his literary ambitions. He wrote his guardian he was thinking of becoming a lawyer, yet wondered if his "health and strength" were adequate, and proposed "residence on a farm for a year or two" to give him a "stock of health." He was afraid he might soon follow his mother and his older brother Stephen as a victim of consumption. His fourteen-year-old sister, Eliza, was dying of the same disease. So he came to Salem and lived with the Goddards not "for a year or two" but for three. Mary Goddard, only ten years older than he, was always more of a sister than a foster mother. Looking after his own and his brothers' farmlands was a congenial excuse for the life of a country gentleman, and provided him with ideas and impressions for the literary career that was soon to follow.

The practical-minded guardian whose advice Donald sought but did not follow, Major General William Williams, Jr., had been appointed guardian of the Mitchell children by the Probate Court in Norwich. The Court in picking General Williams made a logical and sensible choice. He was a shrewd man of large affairs—a bank president, shipowner, and manufacturer with business interests in Norwich but also in New London where he and his brother, Thomas W. Williams, owned or controlled a large part of the whaling fleet.

The Williamses, the Goddards, and the Mitchells all lived on the high ground, known as The Plain, on three sides of the Chelsea Parade in Norwich. General Williams' wife was the daughter of another wealthy businessman, Bela Peck, whose mansion also faced the Parade beyond the Mitchells. As neighbors and members of the Reverend Alfred Mitchell's church, General and Mrs. Williams had seen the Mitchell children grow up.

As young Alfred's guardian, General Williams was an impressive model not only of wealth and special position but of philanthropy and piety. He and his wife gave the land on which Norwich's high school, the Norwich Free Academy, now stands, and an adjoining tract of theirs provided the setting for the imposing Park Congregational Church. The religious faith of the Williams brothers carried over into their business operations: their whaling ships flew the Temperance banner; profane language was ostensibly prohibited; and on their voyages to the Pacific they occasionally carried passengers and supplies to the Hawaiian missions. General Williams was a corporate member of the American Board of Commissioners for Foreign Missions (ABCFM), and a vice president of the American Bible Society, the Seamen's

Friend Society, and the Home Missions Society. Those interests of his were of crucial importance to the ultimate connection of Alfred Mitchell's Connecticut family with the Bingham family of Hawaiian missionaries.

General Williams was in his fifties when he took charge of the Mitchell children's patrimony. No one could have given Alfred a stronger early impression that material wealth and moral rectitude were two faces of the same coin.

At the same time General Williams did not want his wards to live in idleness of their inherited wealth. The Puritan work ethic was strong in him. When Donald, the oldest of his wards, came of age and into his inheritance, the General prodded him into leaving the life of a country gentleman.

New England farming no longer provided anything but a bare subsistence. Donald loved the sight of meadows and growing crops, but he was not a "dirt farmer" and only dirt farmers could now extract a living from these rock-strewn family lands. Many Connecticut farms were being abandoned. Salem lost a quarter of its population between the census of 1820 and 1840. The rich farmlands of the great West opening up at that time were luring the more adventurous to pull up stakes and move. Others looked for new occupations or, if they could, simply retired. So it was with Henry Perkins, Mary Goddard's father, who was weary of trying to maintain a manorial estate on exhausted soil: in 1844 he sold the Woodbridge Farm with the fine old house built for his wife's father. About the same time Mary and Levi Goddard put the Mumford House up for sale, and Donald decided to sell the nearby farm he had inherited. The Salem properties were no longer good investments.

With a different bent from the young men who were heading West, Donald turned toward Europe. General Williams was willing to believe that foreign travel would enlarge his horizons and arranged a job for him with the American consul in Liverpool.

Yet the General had perhaps underestimated the extent to which inherited wealth could undermine the work ethic. Donald had inherited enough to feel he did not need paid employment. With poor health an excuse, he left Liverpool and began the rather aimless travels on the continent that almost fortuitously established him in a literary career. He fell in love, as he wrote, with "venerable old Europe, with its companies of nations, its relics of ages, its treasures of art!" On the strength of the anecdotal stories for which he had found a market, he put together and found a publisher for his first book, *Fresh Gleanings*. Its lightly humorous sketches, laced with sentiment and gentle philosophizing, won it moderate recognition, and both the style and the pseudonym he employed, "Ik Marvel," became the hallmarks of his growing reputation as a man of letters.

Not that success came at once, and he was practical enough to appreciate the hazards of an author's life. After his return he studied law in New York for a while. He toyed with the idea of running for Congress, mindful of the number of his family connections who had been there before him (his grandfather, Stephen Mix Mitchell, in the Senate; Elias Perkins, Thomas W. Williams, Calvin Goddard in the House). He went to Washington and wrote pieces, more in the nature of commentary than reporting, for the New York *Courier and Enquirer.*

Great events were, of course, in the making, both in Washington and in Europe. In the same year, 1847, that *Fresh Gleanings* appeared, the United States took California from Mexico, and in Europe Karl Marx and Friedrich Engels wrote the *Communist Manifesto.* In the following year the overthrow of the French monarchy in the February Revolution fired Donald's imagination. He left his law studies, secured credentials as a correspondent for the *Courier and Enquirer,* and sailed for Europe. In extravagant language suggestive of Thomas Carlyle he described his enthusiasm:

> Are they not acting out over there in France, in the street, in the court, and in the Assembly, palpably and visibly, with their magnificent Labor Organizations, and Omnibus-built barricades, and oratoric strong-words, and bayonet bloody-thrusts, a set of ideas about constitutional liberty, and right to property, and offenses criminal, and offenses civil, wider and newer and richer than all preached about, in all the pages of all these fusty Latinists?

He arrived in Paris just before the "June Days," when the revolution was suppressed, and was appalled by what he saw. "The battle is over, Mary, and I am safe," he wrote Mary Goddard.

> There has been dreadful work; from 10 to 20,000 killed, and twice as many wounded. Day before yesterday I went over the scene of the slaughter in a throng of soldiers and curious lookers-on. Houses were pillaged and shattered with balls, the pavement red with blood, every window broken, and weeping faces in almost every door.

He stayed on as a foreign correspondent for a year, but it was an unhappy year. His romantic sympathy for the oppressed gave way to fear that "with the Communists uppermost, heaven only knows what new state of terrorism might dawn on France." Perhaps the French were not ready for "republicanism." In his letters home, he poured out his doubts and longings. "You don't know how often my thoughts wander to that old country home at Salem," he wrote Mary Goddard.

> I tramp over those hills, and smoke on that porch, and rub up my gun, and pat Carlo nearly every night of the week. Surely my feelings will never attach to Norwich in the same way, of that I am ten times sure. I sometimes dream of having a great fortune, and going back there, and reinstating everything in the old way, and so dream on again of a life of happy idleness.

That dream of Donald's was also Alfred's, and many years later Alfred made it come true by repurchasing the family farms in Salem.

At the time, however, Donald returned to New York, to pick up again a desultory study of law and to add to a growing output of literary work. His book about the revolution, *The Battle Summer,* was panned by the critics, but he found increasing success with his light essays and social commentary. Within a couple of years of his return, he had produced the two books, *Reveries of a Bachelor* and *Dream Life,* on which his reputation rested for the balance of a long life. They were fictionalized sketches of his own life and loves. He was a warm-hearted and sensitive young man, and his romantic effusions happened to strike a responsive chord with the contemporary reading public. His popularity lasted, with innumerable reprints, new editions, and foreign translations of the two little volumes, for half a century.

Many of the scenes reflected the Salem background that was Alfred's as well as Donald's. The Salem farms had lost their economic viability but not their appeal to the imagination of the Mitchell brothers. The pathos with which the fourth of the "reveries" opens may have been flowery but it was genuine enough:

> It is a spring day under the oaks, the loved oaks of a once cherished home, now, alas! mine no longer. I had sold the old farm house, and the groves, and the cool springs where I bathed my head in the heats of summer; and with the first warm days of May they were to pass from me forever. Seventy years they had been in the possession of my mother's family; for seventy years they had borne the same name of proprietorship; for seventy years the Lares of our country home had held their place in the pretty valley.

The *Reveries* was published in 1850, *Dream Life* in the following year. Donald had signed the deed conveying his three-hundred-acre farm on April 2, 1850. The Goddards' conveyance of the Mumford House was signed a few days earlier. That opening paragraph was authentic history. The broad estates that had meant wealth and prestige to the Shaws and Woodbridges, the Mumfords and Mitchells, had passed to subsistence farmers. The era of landed wealth was over for New England.

Alfred's childhood was more secure than that of many orphaned children. Though his inheritance was drawn upon by General Williams for his support, it was otherwise safely preserved until the day he would be twenty-one. In Mary Goddard he had an affectionate foster-mother. In her family circle he was almost like one of her children.

But only almost. For when the Goddards moved to Salem, shortly after Lucretia's death, they took only the girls of the Mitchell family with them: Alfred and his brother Louis were left in Norwich to go to school. Alfred was seven and Louis thirteen when General Williams arranged for them to board in a young minister's family, and to attend the school that had been established in the

Mitchell parsonage after the minister's death. What was more logical than for the Mitchell boys, after their mother's death, to attend the school being operated in their old family home? Their tuition could be charged against the rent owed by the schoolmaster.

As legal guardian for the Mitchell children and responsible to the Norwich Probate Court, General Williams kept meticulous accounts of the properties entrusted to him. As a bank president he had clerical and bookkeeping staff available. His account book, with double entries made in varying hands, provides clues to Alfred's boyhood.

Board at $2.75 a week was paid for him and his brother Louis, beginning a few months after his mother's death, to Thomas K. Fessenden, while at the same time rent received from Mr. Fessenden for the old family home "House on the Plain," at the rate of $250 a year, was credited to Alfred's account. In the last years of Alfred's schooling, the "House on the Plain" became known as "Mr. Charles Abbott's Family School for Boys," and the account book indicates the rent was paid by the "Rev. Charles A. Abbott." With ministers as his schoolmasters, Alfred, the son of a minister, was assured of instruction in the fundamentals of Puritan theology as well as the usual academic subjects.

For a couple of years Alfred lived with the Williamses in their big house at the south end of the Plain; then when the Goddards moved back to Norwich, it was possible for him to continue his schooling while living with them—he and his brothers had always spent their vacations with the Goddards in Salem until the Mumford Farm was sold. He was, to be sure, not a financial burden: Mr. Williams paid Mrs. Williams for Alfred's board while he lived with them, and the Goddards had always been paid—at the generous rate of $4.00 a week—for boarding the Mitchell children.

Alfred was fifteen when the Goddards left Salem and moved back to Norwich. The new home they established was on Sachem Street, almost in sight of the parsonage house where he had been born. It remained the home to which Alfred kept returning till he was married.

This last taste of family life was not for long. He went off to college at seventeen, first to Amherst for part of a year and then to Yale. His college career was short. It does not appear that he was guilty of the "puerile profuseness and dissipation" that were his grandfather's undoing at Yale, but the discipline must have irked him; poor health was always an excuse; and before the end of the academic year he had set forth on the foreign travel that was to be a lifetime preoccupation.

Alfred was introduced to travel by Donald at age fifteen when they had taken a trip together to Niagara Falls and down the St. Lawrence to Montreal. Donald, ten years his senior, undoubtedly had a major influence on Alfred's development. During the years of Donald's wanderings and the building of his literary reputation, he wrote frequently to Mary Goddard, and his letters were most likely passed around or read aloud in the family circle. The romantic appeal of foreign travel, and the image of the sensitive but aloof wanderer, observing his fellow humans with sympathy but as a mildly sardonic outsider, took a firm hold on Alfred.

In the summer of 1851, he sailed for Europe and joined his hunchbacked brother Louis, then twenty-four, in an effort to follow if not reproduce Donald's peregrinations. They spent that winter and the following spring in Rome, Florence, and Venice, reaching Paris by summer. In Rome Alfred sat for a portrait, still extant, a pencil drawing of a young man with mild eyes and wavy blond hair in a Turkish costume, done in the style of Ingres. It is a picture of a young gentleman of leisure, affecting a bit of frivolity.

The following year, after some months back in Norwich, Alfred sailed for the Caribbean and spent the winter in Havana.

On April 1, 1853, he reached the age of twenty-one. His guardian's account book ends with a listing of the assets "passed" to Alfred in May 1853. In addition to the real estate in Salem and Norwich, now his to dispose of, there were substantial investments, mostly stock in various banks. The total came to just under $20,000, in present terms equivalent to perhaps a quarter of a million dollars.

In "passing" his inheritance over to him, General Williams no doubt gave him appropriate fatherly advice on how to use his wealth in order to gain more. The whaling industry in which the General and his brother Thomas W. Williams were so deeply involved offered great opportunities for a young man with some capital to invest. As a matter of fact, some of it was already invested—in the form of loans to Thomas W. Williams. Moreover, Thomas's son, Charles Augustus Williams, who was a cousin of Alfred's and of the same age, and another cousin, Elias Perkins, were about to leave for the Pacific to look after the interests of their families' whaling ships. Alfred was invited to go along. He was now on his own.

CHAPTER 6

Fortune Hunting in Hawaii

On the 12th of September, 1853, the clipper ship *Shooting Star* rounded Diamond Head, and three excited young men leaned over the rail and watched the cloud-draped mountain backdrop of Waikiki and Honolulu unfold. They sniffed the tropical scents on the offshore wind with a mixture of ecstasy and trepidation.

They were at the end of an eight-thousand-mile journey from Connecticut by way of Panama and California. Unlike the first New England missionaries who had gazed on those same mountains thirty years before, after the even longer journey around Cape Horn, they had come not to save souls from damnation but to seek their fortunes. Though they had been stirred by the dream of a quick strike in the gold mines of California during their stopover in San Francisco, their stake was not to dig underground for gold but to search for oil in the far reaches of the Pacific—in the bodies of whales. And as part of the still thriving whaling industry, they were helping build an American empire.

At the very time the *Shooting Star* was working her way into Honolulu Harbor, Commodore Perry was in Japan, negotiating a treaty that directly concerned the industry. American whalers in the Pacific were ten times as numerous as European, and as the nearer ocean waters were fished out, the whalers had to search for their liquid gold farther and farther, off the coasts of Alaska and Kamchatka and Japan, and it was not the least of Commodore Perry's missions to assure protection for American whaling ships wrecked or stranded on the shores of Japan.

It was with a certain pride that the three young cousins, all from New London, Connecticut, looked on the forest of masts in the harbor as they were rowed to the landing pier from the clipper's anchorage. September marked the end of the summer season when whaling masters brought their ships back from northern seas to be readied either for the journey home or for the winter season in the Southern Ocean. Most of the fleet were American, with by far the largest number from New England, with New London second only to New Bedford as their home port.

It was not merely as New Londoners that the three travelers felt pride in recognizing vessels from that city, but also as proprietors. For these three all were members of related families that dominated the New London whaling industry. They were arriving in Honolulu on behalf of their families' fortunes as well as their own.

The oldest of the three cousins was Elias Perkins, thirty-four years old. As a young proprietor, he was already a partner in the New London firm of Perkins & Smith that now owned or had a dominant interest in ten whalers. He had been to Hawaii the year before to help with the refitting and manning of ships returning from the north. The oldest of the fourteen children of Dr. Nathaniel Shaw Perkins, he had been brought up in the great stone mansion in New London built by his ancestor Nathaniel Shaw a hundred years before. It was the fortune amassed by that ancestor in the West Indies trade, enhanced by the business enterprise of his grandfather, the first Elias Perkins, that had enabled him while still in his twenties to establish his own firm—with whaling captain Franklin Smith as partner.

The two cousins accompanying him also owed to their common ancestor, Nathaniel Shaw, the start of the family fortune that enabled them now to embark on their business careers from a secure capital base.

Charles Augustus Williams, known as Gus to his friends and cousins, was the second of the trio arriving in Honolulu. At twenty-four he had not yet made his mark in the business world, but he had the drive to venture into new money-making enterprises, and he would die a rich man. His father, Thomas W. Williams, dominated the New London whaling industry, through his own and associated family firms.

Looking around Honolulu Harbor that September day, Elias Perkins and Gus Williams might well have spotted two vessels that bore their family names. The *N. S. Perkins*, a ship of 309 tons, belonged to Elias's firm, and was named after his father. The *Gen. Williams*, 446 tons and one of the largest ships in the fleet, was owned by a whaling firm (Williams & Barns) in which Gus's uncle, Major General William Williams, Jr. (guardian to the orphaned Alfred Mitchell) was the senior partner.

Both these vessels were in the Pacific that summer, as were the *India*, *John & Eliza*, *Neptune*, *Black Warrior*, *North American*, *Alert*, and *Candace*, all owned by Gus's father's firm (Williams & Haven). These New London whalers often spent several years at a time in the Pacific, shipping their oil home on other vessels. It was in order to handle those transshipments, to keep their firms' ships supplied, manned, and repaired, that Gus was to make Honolulu his headquarters for almost twenty years.

The third of the young men arriving that day—and the youngest—was Alfred Mitchell. Just twenty-one, a shy young man with wavy blond hair, his interest in whaling had till now been remote. But he had just come into his inheritance, and in turning it over to him, his legal guardian, Major General William Williams, had offered him the opportunity to add to his fortune by going to the Pacific with his cousins as an agent of his whaling firm.

With such a favorable wind behind him, Alfred Mitchell was determined to become a man of wealth and standing in his own right. But he had also inherited a more romantic strain: the fragrance of the offshore breeze and the curl of the Pacific breakers at Waikiki meant more to him than the cash that flowed from the whalers' try-pots. And he had a sense of serious purpose perhaps inherited from the father he had never seen, the Congregational minister of Norwich, Connecticut, who died before he was born. Brought up, however, by his mother's relatives—the Perkinses and Williamses and Goddards—all active in the world of business and most recently whaling, his youthful conscience drove him more to the search for wealth than to works of Christian piety.

Alfred's first duty on going ashore, he knew, was to look up a missionary. Not far from the dock where the three cousins landed he could make out the word "Bethel" on a large white banner fluttering from a church tower, which, he knew, must be that of the Bethel Union Church and Seaman's Chapel; there he was to present himself to the Reverend Samuel C. Damon, the pastor of the church and the chaplain of the American Seaman's Friend Society.

It was to be an important contact, not so much for the shaping of Alfred Mitchell's own life as for the very existence of the writer of this fragment of historical research. For the convergence of the search for wealth from whale oil with the works of missionary evangelism in Hawaii eventually brought about the meeting of my father, a son of missionaries, with my mother, daughter of New England wealth, from which my own identity was conceived. But that was far in the future when the three young men presented themselves to the Reverend Damon. Elias Perkins was, no doubt, impatient to revive the business contacts he had made the year before with the local merchants, but he was practical enough to know the importance of this chapel for the health and morale of his ships' crews.

It was the Williams family which had first seen the spiritual need of the crews, and Gus Williams' father, Thomas W. Williams, had in fact been responsible for the chapel building itself. Some twenty years earlier he had shipped the frame out from New London on the *Mentor*, one of the largest vessels in the whaling fleet.

His brother Major General William Williams, Alfred Mitchell's guardian, had been an early supporter and corporate member of that prestigious religious body, known in all the Congregational and Presbyterian churches of New England as the ABCFM. No doubt genuine piety impelled those early-nineteenth-century American capitalists, who provided the funds to Christianize the farthest reaches of the known world. But charity was also good business. Nowhere was the convergence of the profit motive with the demands of Christian belief and Puritan morals more apparent than in the symbiotic relationship between the whaling interests and the missionaries in the Pacific.

Of the cousins, Alfred Mitchell with his more religious and literary background was the most likely to have known the history that lay behind the Seaman's Chapel. He was a voracious reader, and his literary bent was enhanced by the sudden fame recently accorded to his brother, Donald Grant Mitchell, with the publication of his sensationally successful *Reveries of a Bachelor*. Alfred might well have read another recent book of an entirely different cast, *A Residence of Twenty-one Years in the Sandwich Islands*, by the leader of the First Company of Sandwich Island missionaries, the Reverend Hiram Bingham. The Williams family undoubtedly had a copy of that book since its dedication read to the "numerous and generous supporters" of the ABCFM, and Thomas Williams, Gus's father, was given special mention in its pages for his "liberality" in sending the frame of the Bethel Chapel out from New London.

If Gus had not already known of his father's initiative, he must have been told of it by the Reverend Mr. Damon when they met, and must have learned also something of the dramatic incidents, related in the Bingham book, that had made the chapel a sound investment for the whaling interests.

In the early years of Hiram Bingham's missionary career, the whalers were helpful and friendly to the missionaries. The first of Thomas W. Williams' whaling ventures, the brig *Mary*, was in the South Atlantic at the very time in 1819 that the brig *Thaddeus* was carrying Hiram Bingham through the same waters on her way around Cape Horn to Hawaii, and two other Williams' ships, the *Stonington* and the *Connecticut*, were among the first whalers to venture into the Pacific a couple of years later. Whaling ships carried missionaries out to the islands, and brought back their letters and journals, and, before long, their children on their way to school in New England. Whaling captains were invited to tea in the missionaries' homes, and exchanged precious items of Connecticut manufacture for the produce of the missionaries' gardens.

However, the killing of whales demanded not only the venture capital of church-going Yankee investors but muscle power to man the ships and hurl the harpoons and slice and boil the blubber; and after an early period when youth and adventure and partnership played a major role, the crews that endured the hardships of life before the mast were more likely to be there under compulsion of necessity or fear.

In 1826 the *Globe*, a whaling ship out of Nantucket, stopped at Honolulu to take on provisions and replace deserters from the crew. Not long after her departure, members of the crew murdered the captain and first mate in their sleep, killed others who would not join the mutiny, and set sail for a remote Pacific island hideaway. Six homesick crew members, appalled by the bloodshed, stole the ship while the mutineers were fighting and carousing on one of the Mulgrave Islands, and sailed her to Chile, from where the news of the mutiny was sent back to home ports. A U.S. Navy craft, the *Dolphin*, was sent to find the mutineers and bring them to justice. It was a sensational story at the time and has been retold many times since.

The Reverend Mr. Bingham was caught up in the aftermath. As he recounted in his history of the Hawaiian mission, the *Dolphin*, with two surviving mutineers aboard as prisoners—one of them a New Londoner—put in at Honolulu on her return voyage. There her crew joined other crew members from whaling and merchant ships in the harbor rioting to demand an end to the taboo which Queen Kaahumanu, the missionaries' prize convert and regent for the boy king Kauikeaouli, had imposed on the girls of Honolulu. They were no longer to swim out to arriving ships, according to long-established custom, to provide officers and crews with the sexual delights that were as important a part of the assets of the Paradise of the Pacific as its fruits, meat, and ships' stores. When the rioters were informed by the boy king that the taboo was God's will, and that he understood God's will because Mr. Bingham had told him what it was, they went looking for Mr. Bingham. He was saved from a lynching only by the late imposition of discipline by the commanding officer of the *Dolphin*.

If this was not enough to convince the missionaries of the need for the restraints of religion and Christian morals on the crews of the whaling ships, there was an equally frightening episode a year later, when the Binghams and another missionary family cowered in the cellar of the mission house in

Lahaina to escape cannon balls fired by members of the crew of an English whaler, the *John Palmer*, enraged by the same taboo imposed there by the governor of Maui.

Full reports of these incidents went back to the ABCFM in Boston. A waterfront church might help keep riotous sailors in line. Five years later Thomas W. Williams arranged the shipment from New London of the frame of the chapel which Mr. Bingham had prayed for.

Thomas Williams was in a position to help Mr. Bingham again after his return from the Islands in 1841. Mr. Williams was then in Congress, and Mr. Bingham went to Washington to plead the case for providing American missionaries with the same protection American merchants expected in foreign countries. He had interviews with the new president of the United States, John Tyler, and the Secretary of State, Daniel Webster, and was gratified to have Mr. Webster support his argument, that "missionaries, even more than merchants, ought to receive protection while engaged in such a work."

Congressman Williams was impressed with the powerful missionary figure on that occasion, and again a year later when the ABCFM held its annual general meeting in Norwich in his congressional district, and Mr. Bingham, as a returned missionary, expounded his visionary plan for evangelizing the whole world. Two years later he heard him again at the general meeting in Worcester, and invited him to come to New London and preach in place of Williams' own minister, then at death's door with typhus. Mr. Bingham spent a couple of weeks in the Williams mansion at the head of State Street in New London. But he was making more enemies than friends in those days, with his demands that the churches raise more money for his grandiose world plan, and it may be that the members of the New London congregation found him too self-important for their church; at any rate he was not offered a permanent pulpit.

While he was a guest in the Williams house, his son, Hiram II, then thirteen, came for a visit and stayed till his boarding school in New Haven reopened. It is possible that twelve-year-old Alfred Mitchell, whose guardian was Thomas Williams' brother, was invited to meet the famous missionary and his son, and it is an engaging fantasy to think of my two grandfathers meeting as boys at that time.

When, nine years later, Alfred Mitchell presented himself to the chaplain of the Seaman's Chapel in Honolulu, the name Bingham and the history of the Sandwich Islands mission were certainly not unknown to him. The Reverend Samuel Damon was no less aware of who his young visitors were, and no doubt treated them with the deference due to representatives of wealthy families whose philanthropy helped sustain his chapel and the whole missionary enterprise.

What transpired at that first meeting is not recorded. But not long afterward Alfred Mitchell picked up a letter addressed to him in care of the Reverend Damon. It was from Major General William Williams, so recently his guardian.

Norwich, Con.
28th October 1853.

Mr. Alfred Mitchell
Honolulu, Sand. Isls.

Dear Sir,

I have heard of your progress over the Isthmus and on the Pacific and at San Francisco, and hope soon to be advised of your safe arrival at the Islands.

I began some time ago a letter to you, but leaving soon after for Cincinnati from whence I have recently returned, I commence anew. I rec'd a letter from Revd. Mr. Damon of 15th June who says in anticipation of Augustus' arrival that he would receive a cordial welcome,—this will extend to you.

I understand from Messrs. Williams and Barns they are satisfied with the business transactions at San Francisco, and I trust that they will be so on all future operations that you may perform for them. Permit me to say keep them advised of any interest they have in ships at the Islands.

I trust the climate will prove congenial to you and if so I would adjust myself to such pursuits as may be useful to you, not only observations of the business of the place, but your leisure will permit you to know their language, and to review your French. I would be exact in my accounts, and keep my account books on the system of double entry.

Allow me to urge that you do not omit the daily study of the Scriptures, that your mind may be imbued with the truth, the greatest safeguard to the temptations that may beset your path. You will excuse these suggestions, they spring from an unchangeable interest in your welfare.—Make my kind regards to Augustus, and tell him that his Uncle and Aunt are fearful he has lost all interest in them....

Our town is on the march of improvement.... I think your property will be worth more at the close of your lease than when you rented it....

I remain Truly Yours
Wm. Williams

The business transacted with Williams & Barns in San Francisco on the trip out seems, from the letter, to have been vague enough and perhaps even trivial, but a young man with money to invest would not be unwelcome.

The knowledge of French that he was encouraged by his former guardian to "review" upon his arrival in Hawaii was no doubt derived from his travels in Europe a couple of years earlier. He had, to be sure, studied for part of a year at Amherst and another year at Yale, of which his father, grandfather, and older brother Donald were all graduates. But he left Yale before the end of his year there and never returned. The ostensible reason was one of health, and this was apparently a major reason for the voyage to Hawaii.

63

Certainly he was justified in worrying about his health: after his mother's own death of tuberculosis, three more of Alfred's brothers and sisters were taken by the dread disease. There was another less apparent weakness in his inheritance that may also have contributed to his dropping out of college and becoming a restless traveler: too much money can be as debilitating as tuberculosis.

The record of what he did with his inheritance is scanty. It does not appear that he kept in touch with the Seaman's Chapel or the Reverend Mr. Damon, except perhaps for the receipt of mail; and the connections he established with missionary families were strictly with the younger members who were becoming the business leaders, if not the owners, of the lush Pacific Islands.

Actually the time of his arrival coincided with the end of the dominance of the native Hawaiian monarchy by the missionaries. Only a month before, Dr. Gerrit Judd had been forced to resign his post as Minister of Finance and so brought to an end eleven years as the monarchy's most powerful administrative officer—a period during which Judd once half-seriously wrote, referring to the missionary leader whose mantle he took over: "I am at present the King Bingham of the Sandwich Islands."

It is more than likely that Alfred Mitchell and his cousins called on Dr. Judd, who had recently retired to a private medical practice. Sooner or later, in any case, Alfred Mitchell got to know many of the Judd family. One of Dr. Judd's sons, Charles, was associated with him in at least one venture.

That was after several years of varied activities, of which slight glimpses can be obtained from shipping notes. Some of these references are to be found in *The Friend*, a newspaper edited by the Reverend Mr. Damon and devoted to "Temperance, Seamen, Marine and General Intelligence." Others are from the records of the Honolulu Harbor Master, on arriving and departing ships.

From such meager sources, we learn that Alfred Mitchell, variously described as "whaling agent" or "merchant" or simply "traveler," was in and out of Honolulu half a dozen times in the 1850s, as was Gus Williams. On occasion this was to meet the whaling fleet on its spring or fall rendezvous for refitting and provisioning. Mitchell later referred to his having been in the ship chandlery business, and this may have been on his own account or on behalf of the New London whaling firms with which he and his companions were connected. In addition Alfred made at least two trips to Puget Sound, where seals were the objective rather than whales, and sealing was often more lucrative than whaling. Seals were sought for their skins as well as their oil. Elias Perkins' firm, Perkins & Smith, made a killing both literally and figuratively by discovering the chief breeding ground of the sea elephant, largest of the seals and most valuable for its oil, on Heard Island in the Indian Ocean. Gus Williams was one of the organizers of a sealing company, the Alaskan Commercial Company, that first raised the American flag over the newly acquired territory of Alaska. The company obtained a lease for an exclusive seal-ing operation on two small islands in the Bering Sea.

Other uninhabited islands, not in the Arctic but in the tropics, were the scene of the commercial venture with which Charles Judd was connected. This venture almost ended in Alfred Mitchell's death and brought some dis-grace on him and his partners. The enterprise involved the exploitation of guano deposits on the desolate Phoenix Islands two thousand miles south-west of Hawaii.

Many coral atolls in the Pacific are too small to provide fresh water or to support life except for millions of nesting sea birds whose droppings, over thousands of years, have left rich deposits of guano. In the 1850s Ameri-can whalers, finding whales ever scarcer, began bringing home cargoes of this rich fertilizer. Congress was induced to enact a law in 1856 under which commercial interests could claim title to guano islands. New London whal-ing firms, particularly those of the Williams family, were involved early in that profitable business. They organized a new firm in New London, the Phoenix Guano Company, which eventually claimed title to forty-eight islands.

Gus Williams was a moving spirit in this new business. Within a few years of his arrival in Hawaii, he had established his own company, C. A. Williams & Company, with Alfred Mitchell and a New London sea captain, James M. Green, as partners. One of the company's vessels, the *Agate*, after a voyage from New London to the seal islands in the Bering Sea, was diverted to the guano business. The *Agate* had brought out another cousin, Alfred Mitchell Goddard, the oldest son of Levi and Mary Goddard, to join his relatives in their spreading business empire. He and Alfred Mitchell made a number of trips to the guano islands. It was one of these trips that nearly ended in disaster.

Alfred Mitchell later wrote an account of that adventure, at a time when he was trying to emulate his brother Donald's literary success. Donald was then editor, with Harriet Beecher Stowe, of a farm family magazine, *Hearth and Home*, in which Alfred Mitchell was able to get some articles published, but "Forty Days on a Guano Island" remains in the family archives as an unpublished manuscript.

In it Alfred tells of sailing out of Honolulu on a "small brig"—possibly the *Agate* or the *Zoe*, another whaler converted to the guano business. The vessel was to pick up a load of guano on one of the smallest of the guano islands, and then to proceed to Sydney, Australia, where the cargo would be sold. On arriving at the island, Alfred found a gang of forty "Kanakas," hired by Gus Williams in Honolulu—illiterate Hawaiian natives who had scrawled an X opposite their names on a work contract calling for ten dollars a month and their keep. The expedition was running short of water, and the vessel was sent on to Samoa, a thousand miles away, to refill the casks. Alfred re-mained on the island along with the company's agent and the forty Kanakas.

As he wrote with somewhat forced facetiousness: "I have a high idea of the dignity and glory of honest toil, and it has always afforded me great pleasure to see other people work."

For a couple of weeks Alfred enjoyed his leisure. But the vessel that had been sent for water did not return when expected. With the lives of both white masters and Kanakas imperiled, Alfred set the Hawaiians to work digging under the sandy beaches in a search for pockets of rainwater that might have collected in the coral.

The brig eventually did return, and Alfred went on to Sydney. But after the Hawaiians returned to Honolulu, they brought suit against C. A. Williams & Company, and Alfred as a partner was served with a summons to appear in court.

The partners were charged with breach of contract for having failed to provide adequate food and shelter, and damages were demanded for the hardships endured. Among the witnesses called were Alfred Mitchell Goddard and Charles Judd. Despite the absence of native Hawaiians in the legal profession or on the bench, the plaintiffs won their case, but they were awarded less than forty dollars apiece for wages withheld and provisions not supplied according to the contract, with no damages.

Another business enterprise for which Gus Williams provided the initiative and Alfred Mitchell some of the capital was the establishment of regular steamship communication between the Hawaiian islands. In the official Archives of Hawaii, the following letter is preserved:

To His Majesty
   Kamehameha IV—

We, C. A. Williams and Alfred Mitchell and Jas. M. Green, comprising the firm of "C. A. Williams & Co." of Honolulu would hereby petition Your Majesty in Council to grant unto us your petitioners as follows:

That we, C. A. Williams & Co. for ourselves during the term of _____ years may be incorporated as a Company under the name and style of the "Hawaiian Steam Navigation Company."

That we may possess for a term of _____ years the exclusive right or monopoly of the Inter Island Steam Navigation of your Kingdom,...we covenanting on our part on such arrangements being made to provide a suitable Steam Propeller to be used in said navigation within about twelve months from May 1st, 1859, or sooner if possible.

> Most respectfully
> Your Majesty's obdt. servants,
> C. A. Williams & Co.

Negotiations between Williams and the Hawaiian government were protracted, but on March 7, 1859, the King approved "An Act to Promote Inter-

Island Navigation," under which "C. A. Williams, A. Mitchell, James M. Green and their associates and successors are hereby constituted a Body Corporate under the name of the Hawaiian Steam Navigation Company," and were given monopoly rights for a term of six years, provided the incorporators put into service a "good and substantial steamer of not less than 350 to 400 tons burthen within fifteen months from the date of the passage of this act."

Within the allotted time, the steamer *Kilauea*, a brigantine converted into a steamer in East Boston, had made her way around Cape Horn and was put into the inter-island service. How much money she made for her original owners does not appear, but she survived the buffetings of the Pacific swells far better than the side-wheelers that had preceded her. She was later bought by the government and continued, despite discomfort and near disasters, to ferry passengers between the islands for seventeen years.

With its varied interests in whaling, sealing, guano, and shipping, C. A. Williams & Company continued as a feature of the commercial life of Hawaii for many years. Gus Williams shuttled back and forth between New London and Hawaii, sometimes taking his family with him. He was the last of the New London whaling shipowners or agents, and continued to send out his ships for another thirty years.

Mitchell, on the other hand, left Hawaii shortly after the outbreak of the Civil War. Unwilling to continue as a silent partner of his aggressive cousin, he responded to the call of patriotism and was commissioned a captain in the 13th Connecticut Volunteers, a regiment organized in Norwich. So far as can be determined, he never had further business interests in Hawaii. Though he may have remained for a while as a partner in the Williams firm, it was without any substantial stake, for he later stated that he found himself penniless after his Civil War service.

Alfred did return to the islands, where so much of his inheritance as well as his emotions had been committed, but this was after he had married the Tiffany heiress, and later still when he brought his two young daughters along to learn to savor the tropics. By that time he had become a resident of New London, and Gus Williams had returned and become the city's mayor.

As for the third of the three cousins who arrived in Honolulu in 1853 to seek their fortunes, Elias Perkins suffered the ups and downs of any entrepreneur. His firm, Perkins & Smith, prospered for a few years, but the financial crisis of 1857 affected its investments in Connecticut real estate and railroads, and put it into bankruptcy, and Alfred Mitchell had a hand in transferring some of its whaling assets to the related firm of Williams & Haven. Within a few years, Elias's diversified business interests both in Hawaii and on the mainland enabled him to recoup his losses, and he continued through the Civil War and afterwards to carry on business activities in both New London and Hawaii. For a while he served as United States consul in Honolulu, a position that was said to have lucrative perquisites in the handling of funds for the hospital care of sick and injured seamen.

The Civil War had a devastating effect on the whaling industry. It disrupted many lives, even in Hawaii. Elias Perkins did not return to join a volunteer regiment as did his cousin Alfred Mitchell, but he may have been more torn in his sympathies, for two of his brothers lost their lives in the Union Army while another brother, who had settled in South Carolina, served in the Confederate Army and died of typhoid. Yet Alfred Mitchell was not without some conflict of feelings, for his brother Donald had married a Southern girl, two of whose brothers were killed while fighting for the Confederacy.

Alfred saw action in the Gulf campaign in 1863 and once had a horse shot from under him. He resigned his commission at the conclusion of that campaign, and urged his cousin Alfred Mitchell Goddard, who had continued in the guano business, to keep out of uniform. But young Goddard did not follow his advice, and responding to the urge of patriotic duty, returned to his native Norwich where he was commissioned a lieutenant toward the close of the war.

After the Civil War the special link between New London and Hawaii was no longer in evidence. Some whalers still appeared in Hawaiian harbors for a few years. But whale oil as a staple of commerce that had brought prosperity to both New London and Honolulu was being supplanted. Lamps were burning kerosene.

CHAPTER 7

Civil War Letters

When news of the fall of Fort Sumter reached Honolulu in the spring of 1861, it was for most Americans, whether missionaries, merchants, or crews of whaling ships, not more than a distant rumble, a cause of concern for the war's possible disruption of the already ailing whaling industry, but not a clarion call to participate. Sympathies were more likely to be with the North, since missionaries and whalers alike were New Englanders, but the exploitation of the labor of brown-skinned Kanakas was too much like that of black Africans to encourage a strong stand on the slavery issue. Even the missionaries had felt the abolitionist cause diverted moral and financial resources from what was to them of vastly greater significance, Christianizing the heathen.

When the news came, Alfred Mitchell and his cousin Charles Augustus Williams, partners in C. A. Williams & Company, were putting most of their energies into the extraction of guano from the distant Phoenix Islands and into the operation of their inter-island steamship service with the new propeller-driven *Kilauea.* Williams was then thirty-two, energetic, a true entrepreneur, the moving spirit in all the partnership's undertakings. Alfred Mitchell, three years his junior, provided capital and assisted as needed, but he had little real enthusiasm for the details of the firm's activities, and was little more than a sleeping partner.

A fourth cousin, Alfred Mitchell Goddard, had joined them a few years before and had become the field manager of their guano business. He had spent months at a time on the guano islands supervising operations, had taken at least one cargo to Australia, and on one business trip had returned home via the Indian Ocean.

Alfred Mitchell Goddard and Alfred Mitchell were very close. The Goddard home was the only home Alfred Mitchell had known since his mother's death. Now the two Alfreds, both in their twenties, were hearing in letters from home of the growing war fever in Norwich. In 1861 the spirit of dedication and sacrifice was running strong, and both the young men had brothers who were responding to the patriotic enthusiasm of the hour.

After the fall of Fort Sumter, Lincoln called for 75,000 volunteers for what was then expected to be a short show of force, with the enlistment period only three months. But Lincoln also sensed the length of the struggle ahead and, on May 3, issued the first call for a major expansion of the army by forty volunteer regiments to be raised by the states. They were to serve for three years or for the duration. In the organization of volunteer regiments, much was left to local leadership.

Alfred Mitchell heard from his older brother Louis of the patriotic fervor with which recruiting had begun in Norwich. Louis, a cripple from birth, was unfit for military service, but several of his close friends, some of whom Alfred knew, were joining up and organizing companies. When this news reached Alfred out in the Pacific, he was prompted to return and volunteer himself. Anything but indispensable to the Williams business, with no independent responsibility, he had failed to make the fortune he had hoped for. True, he had a financial stake in the enterprises he had helped finance out of his modest inheritance, but there was no assurance he would ever get his money out, and he disliked being dependent on others. He took ship for San Francisco.

Alfred Mitchell Goddard would have liked to go too—his younger brother Henry, only nineteen, was enlisting—but he had an active role in the Williams business and felt he could not leave.

By summer, Mitchell, crossing the continent by stagecoach and rail, had reached Norwich. He found his native state already mustering in some of the new volunteer regiments. Governor Buckingham was exceptionally energetic in responding to Lincoln's call: seventeen of the forty volunteer regiments to be raised under the May 3 proclamation were raised in Connecticut.

Officers were commissioned by the state governors. Recognized community leaders and political friends were often given positions of command. It has been said that the Civil War was "the last gentlemen's war." Men from the upper classes were assumed to be natural leaders and filled the officer ranks in the first regiments to be formed.

Alfred Mitchell had had no military training or experience, but he had connections with some of the leading families in Norwich. His former guardian, William Williams, had been a major general in the militia. Governor Buckingham was a Norwich man, and fellow townsmen were commissioned early. One of Louis Mitchell's friends, Henry Birge, was commissioned a major in a regiment mustered as early as June 1861, and soon there was talk of his being made colonel of another regiment in which a number of Norwich men might find congenial posts.

Alfred waited through the fall. He sold his inherited Salem properties to his brother Louis for a thousand dollars. The old family home in Norwich, part of his inheritance, had been under lease to Charles Abbott's Family School for Boys at $250 a year, but he had had his brother sell that property for him while still in Hawaii. He was living off the last of his inherited capital.

Early in 1862, Colonel Birge was put in command of the 13th Connecticut Volunteers. Alfred was commissioned in February. Almost thirty and older than most of those now volunteering, he was commissioned a captain. Seven other officers besides Colonel Birge were from Norwich. A strong feeling of common local origin and class origin gave Alfred a greater sense of comradeship than he enjoyed at any other time of his life. In a matter of weeks, the 13th Connecticut Volunteers, with Alfred as a company commander, was ready for a combat role.

In the North's grand strategy of encirclement of the South, control of the Mississippi was a major objective. The 13th Connecticut Volunteers was assigned to the Army of the Gulf. On the transport that carried the regiment to its first base on an island near Mobile Bay, Alfred's hunchbacked brother Louis went along, thanks to his friendship with Colonel Birge, as unofficial civilian historian.

New Orleans fell on May 1, 1862, after naval action led by Admiral Farragut. Baton Rouge surrendered a week later. With astonishing ease, the mouth of the Mississippi came under the control of the Union forces. But the Confederacy retained strong positions upstream at Port Hudson and Vicksburg with two hundred miles of river between, and still had an army in southern Louisiana. It took fifteen months and much loss of life before the forts fell and the whole river was in Union hands.

The 13th Connecticut Volunteers served as part of the occupation force in New Orleans and then was sent into the field in operations against the remaining Confederate forces in the area and against Port Hudson. Alfred Mitchell served first as commander of Company K, but when his superior, Colonel Birge, was given command of a brigade and then a division, Mitchell went along as a staff officer.

Three letters to his brother Louis by then back in Norwich, describing battles he was in, have been preserved and are notable for both their revelations of his personality and their vivid account of engagements fought among the bayous of the Mississippi delta. In writing them, he was obviously conscious of Louis's self-appointed role as local historian.

The first letter describes a minor engagement that took place October 27, 1862, at Labadieville about fifty miles west of New Orleans, an episode in the year-long campaign aimed at destroying the Confederate force still challenging Union control of the lower river.

> In the field near Thibodaux
> Saturday, November 8, 1862

My dear Lou:

You will have already heard through the Fishers of our little affair of last week.

The Regiment conducted itself very well indeed under a fire which I am told would be generally called fairly hot, but which lasted but a short time, say half an hour. As we were held in reserve during the greater part of this time and were lying down, the grape and canister passed mostly over us, though the range was very exact, particularly on the left of our line. I expected any moment to see the Colonel and Adjutant who remained mounted picked off by a stray grape shot, many of which I saw pass very near the colonel who was nearly behind the Company next on my right.

When an advance was ordered I was so busy in keeping my Company dressed in the line of battle (as we were crowded on the left by the nature of the ground) that I saw very little more of what happened until we arrived up to the enemy's abandoned position and the fight was over.

I was tolerably well scared during the whole business but too much so to think of running away, though it would have pleased me beyond account to have been *ordered* to some other place.

The worst part of the business was our march directly away from the enemy's fire on the other side of the Bayou in order to reach the bridge where we crossed over. During this time, some twenty minutes probably, we were exposed to a constant fire of shells, but being behind a high levee and marching by a flank they did us little hurt. But as we were all ignorant where we were going, and most supposed we were retreating, the screaming and exploding of shells within a few feet of us had a demoralizing effect. The grape and canister, when we reached the other side and had got into a position to do something, though much more effective, did not produce nearly the same effect upon the men.

All things considered we all got off very well.

Last night an accident occurred upon the railroad which has much more serious consequences to us than the fight. A train came up from New Orleans bringing about 90 of our men who had been left in hospital. A car laden with ammunition exploded when within a quarter of a mile of this place. Feet and hands were picked up this morning at an eighth of a mile from the train.

I don't enjoy camp life particularly, as we have no tents and are obliged to sleep these frosty nights with very little or no shelter. We hope to be sent back to the city before many weeks or at least before the winter rains. The enemy have all fled to the other side of the Atchafalaya River where they are said to be strongly intrenched and well supplied with artillery. I do not think we shall follow them any farther, and do not anticipate any more fighting for some time to come.

If the gun boats sent around to the river to intercept the rebels had been in time we should have bagged quite a lot of them. As it is the expedition is infructuous except that it has given the men some experience and given the Government possession of a large tract of country, which contains a very large stock of sugar. The growing crop which is large will be entirely lost as all the Negroes have deserted the plantations and the whole country is abolitionized. Two Negro regiments are guarding the line of the railroad.

I hope soon to hear from you as I have received no letters for a long time. The Colonel says he has received your letter and will answer as soon as possible and hopes a continuance.

> Yours truly,
> AM.

Six months later he wrote again. He had just heard from his brother Louis, and from his cousin Alfred Mitchell Goddard, who was back from the Pacific and had been trying to get into the army as an officer. Mitchell was now on the staff of Colonel Birge, newly put in command of a brigade. They had just been through the most severe engagement of the desultory Louisiana campaign, the battle of Irish Bend, fought on a bayou between the Mississippi and the Gulf coast on April 14, 1863.

> Barres Landing on
> Bayou Courtableau
> 6 miles East of Opelousas, La.
> April 29, 1863.

My dear Lou:

I have today four letters from you and one from A.M.G. [Alfred Mitchell Goddard]. I have had hardly any chance of late to write as we have been constantly on the move since we left Baton Rouge a month ago. The accounts of our fight at Irish Bend on the Teche about 2 miles above Franklin you will probably get in the papers. To give you a better idea of it than you can get from them I will make a little diagram of the grounds.

Mitchell then drew a crude sketch map, and described the deploying of two regiments, with artillery support, in a cane field facing some woods from which the first fire had come. As another two Union regiments were moving into a battle line, they all came under sudden attack:

A galling fire opened from the thicket on our right flank (we had passed the line parallel with the wood and running through its outer edge). The 25th Conn. which was on the right endeavored to fall back but broke in some disorder and the 26th Maine followed suit, which being seen by the rebels in the thicket they made a charge in order to take prisoners, and firing as they advanced, the 159th got the whole benefit of it and lost about a hundred men in about five minutes.

We could not stand the pressure and fell back in disorder. My horse got a bullet in his back side (entering the ham and coming out some days after between his hind legs) which produced such an effect upon him that I concluded he was badly shot and might fall on me in the rough ground so I attempted to dismount and got a fall for my pains. My horse cantered off to the rear and as that seemed to be the direction in which all hands were bound I followed slowly after my horse. As my wind was never very good and was moreover somewhat damaged by the fall I had got, I had to walk very slowly, and, the bullets coming in great abundance from the front, my promenade on foot was the most disagreeable part of the fight. I got my horse again soon and found he was not so badly hurt as I had supposed, so mounted again and went to look for the brigade.

What was left of the three Regiments were already forming and I marched them down to the farther edge of the wood just now occupied by the rebels where they remained in observation for most of the day. The 13th meanwhile had steadily advanced on the left of the road and driven everything before them until they had actually got in the rear of the enemy's line, when Col. Birge, who had been dismounted at the same time with myself but had soon got another horse, ordered them to fall back and wait support. As soon as this arrived they advanced through the wood and I found them there when I came up with the other part of the brigade.

The fight was a very sharp one and if our Brigade had been promptly supported we should have driven the rebels out without so much loss of life. The new Regts. stood very well but a flanking fire so close as we had it is too much even for veterans.

The delay in our march caused by this fight, which in the opinion of many was so ill fought, caused the failure of the main object of the expedition, as the enemy thereby gained time to make his retreat by a cutoff road which we were striving to reach.

Our Brigade went into the fight with between 1400 and 1500 muskets and we lost in killed or wounded 312 men (including some valuable officers) and in prisoners about 30, about 20 percent of our force, which is a good butcher bill for volunteers, three regiments of whom had never before smelt gunpowder.

The loss in the 13th was not so large as in the other Regiments owing to the good order they preserved. But two men in my old company were hurt and they not seriously.

We shall probably have no more fighting for a long time except a few shots from guerrillas and I am in hopes that we shall have the good fortune to be ordered back to New Orleans as soon as we get through with our present duty—viz—clearing out this section of the country of its cotton, cattle, sugar and niggers.

Last news from the North, including the defeat at Charleston and no success anywhere, is not encouraging and I begin to think that my term of service will expire long before the war is ended.

I will write Alf Goddard later and meantime do not advise him to enter the Army except it may be as a Staff Officer. Coming so late he will find it hard work making a beginning.

Yours truly,
AM.

Love to all at home.

In his advice to "Alf" Goddard, Alfred Mitchell obviously felt himself the battle-hardened veteran for whom the war had long lost its glamour. But Goddard was eager for action. He already had secured a lieutenant's commission. For a while he served on the staff of General Harland, another Norwich friend of Louis Mitchell, but a year later, during the siege of Petersburg, he sought a transfer into the lines, and was killed in his first battle.

Meanwhile Mitchell was becoming increasingly disillusioned with what he considered a bungled campaign. After the battle of Irish Bend, his brigade, enlarged to become a division, took part in the siege of Port Hudson attempting two costly assaults that ended in failure. With 25,000 Union men concentrated there, much of the area taken in the Louisiana campaign, including the base at Brashear City, near the Gulf coast, from which Mitchell's brigade had been deployed, was retaken by Confederate forces. And even though the Army of the Mississippi under General Grant finally took Vicksburg in July 1863 and Port Hudson surrendered shortly thereafter, Mitchell, like most soldiers doing the fighting in any war, was less and less enthusiastic about risking his life for blundering commanders.

His third letter was written shortly after the fall of Port Hudson had put the entire Mississippi River under Union control.

Headquarters 4th Division
Donaldsonville
July 21, 1863

My dear Lou:

We are now a division as you will see by my date—the Colonel having temporary command of Grover's troops, he (Grover) commanding the forces here, seven brigades. Our Division is however hardly much larger than our Brigade was before the commencement of this campaign. We have lost out of the 1500 or 1600 men with which we moved to Brashear City about 500 by death (in action) or wounds and used up a great many more by hard marching, bad water, exposure etc., though the place of these have been in a measure supplied by convalescents joining their commands from the hospitals at Baton Rouge, Bayou Boeuf and New Orleans.

You will have known by the papers of the disgraceful loss of the whole LaFourche Country during the siege of Port Hudson. This Division are heavy sufferers, all their camp and garrison equipage, soldiers' knapsacks containing all their spare clothing, and nearly all the Officers' baggage having fallen into the hands of the enemy at Brashear City. The Colonel and staff have fared no better than the rest. We, Captain Norton, Lt. Siemann, and myself have lost everything, so that the dirty flannel suit which I have worn and slept in for the last three months with a spare shirt and pocket handkerchief comprises the whole of my personal property in this Department.

Our trunks were left in private hands at Brashear City, and, about a week before the place was taken, judging from the general mode of conducting business in this Department that they might be in some danger there, we sent down for them, but our messenger dilly-dallied about the place until it was too late and was finally taken prisoner himself. I have however one consolation, all my company papers, ordinance returns, clothing rolls, etc., were in my truck and in no condition to pass the inspection of the 2nd Auditor of the Treasury, and now I am made even with Uncle Sam. I regret more than anything else the loss of some private papers and little articles, silver spoons, guide colors, etc.

We have had a very tedious campaign, one of the most laborious of the whole war, though we have done no great things in the fighting line. Everything seems to have been badly managed and with the loss of life which we have suffered we ought to have accomplished much more. Both of our assaults upon Port Hudson were shocking bungles from beginning to end. Taking it all together the Army of the Gulf has very little to brag of, and a great deal to lament over.

Our brigade was never fairly engaged, and [in the second assault] on June 14th was under the command of Col. Morgan of the 90th New York whose cowardice so disgusted me on that day that I would not stay with him. He is now in arrest on a charge of misbehavior before the enemy.

The casualties in the 3rd Brigade only amount to about 170 (all killed and wounded) during the operations before Port Hudson. Warner of the 13th left the place shortly after the 27th on sick leave and although he was soon fit for duty did not return but preferred to report to General Emory at New Orleans who put him on duty there to organize a Regiment of Home Guards for 60 days. His stock is low in the Brigade.

Alfred went on to tell of the call for "a storming party of 1000 volunteers to take the post or perish in the attempt." Though Port Hudson surrendered before this final assault was made, the courage of those who volunteered was none the less, and Alfred took pride in the part he and his old regiment played, though he apparently was not among the volunteers:

It is probably lucky for us that the storming party was never called upon as, although I have no doubt we should have been successful, we should probably have lost many men and of the best we had left. Out of 1000 men and officers who volunteered for this party, 241 were from the 13th Conn.

and only 65 from all the 9-months regiments of which there were 15 or
twenty. The 12th Connecticut furnished 4 officers and 41 men. Col. Birge,
Col. Benedict (brother of the Norwich man), and Col. Chickering were the
only officers of that rank who volunteered, but Benedict was taken sick
and Chickering who is a pet of Banks was not allowed to join the party. Of
90 odd officers in the party only three besides these were field officers.
The Colonel with his field staff was to command the column. As the
assault did not come off, we had the honor of leading the column of
occupation into the place after its surrender.

The 4th Division moved down to this place a day or two after Port
Hudson was occupied and in condition to move upon the Rebels, and they
are now evacuating the country as fast as possible carrying off an immense
amount of government property into the Teche country whence they will
probably go into Texas.

All the Negroes who have been forced to labor upon the government
plantations and those owned by planters who had taken the oath of
allegiance, have been carried off. So ends General Banks' famous reorganization of the system of labor in Louisiana. If instead of putting these
same Negroes upon plantations he had continued Butler's plan of drilling
and arming them they would have defended the country in quite another
way from the 9-months men in whose hands it was left. But Banks began
by ill-treating the Black soldiers and when forced to change his tactics it
was too late to make them of any service in this campaign. Burton's three
regiments have done good service and I would rather be supported by one
of them than four regiments of 9-months men.

This is a long letter for me and it is the only way I can make up for a
long silence. I have however been constantly waiting for something of
importance to turn up, and after reaching Port Hudson did not wish to
write till the job was done. I have been quite well until the last few weeks
when the fatigue and exposure of the campaign began to tell on me. I am
not sick now—only worn and tired. As soon as I have written up my returns
for the Adjutant General's Office I shall go to New Orleans and try to get
leave of absence for as long a time as possible. I think I can get a furlough
for 30 days without much difficulty and hope to see you before October. I
do not know whether I have enough shirts at home and wish you would
have some linen bought and a dozen made with turn-over collars.

Remember me to all at home.

Yours truly,
AM.

No more of Alfred Mitchell's Civil War letters have been preserved. By
gaining control of the entire Mississippi River, the Army of the Gulf, of which
Mitchell had been a part, had fulfilled its major mission. Yet Texas remained
to be brought under Union control, and Louisiana was not wholly secure for
another year.

For another nine months, Mitchell continued on the staff of now General Birge, and saw further action in the unsuccessful effort to invade Texas

by way of Shreveport and the Red River. He had been offered a promotion to the rank of major, but, according to the record, he declined the promotion. When Birge and his old regiment moved to Virginia, where they saw some fierce fighting in the Shenandoah Valley in the fall of 1864, Alfred was no longer with them. He had resigned his commission in March of that year.

One may speculate as to the reasons. He no doubt felt he had done his part, though only two of the three years for which he had donned a uniform had expired. He was proud of his record, and after the war he had his canteen and sword mounted on a plaque and hung over a doorway. Perhaps his oldest brother, Donald, had something to do with it: Donald's wife, a South Carolinian, had five brothers in the Confederate army, two of whom were killed. One of Alfred's Perkins cousins who had moved to the South also died in a Confederate uniform. It was a war of brother against brother, and Alfred no longer had a stomach for it.

CHAPTER 8

Alf and Annie

Annie Olivia Tiffany kept a diary from 1865 to 1867. Her first mention of the man she would eventually marry was in January 1867, when she wrote simply that "Mr. Mitchell and Mr. Norton called." She was then twenty-three years old, the daughter of the millionaire merchant of luxury goods, Charles Tiffany, and eminently marriageable. She was out when the two gentlemen called at her Madison Avenue home, but they left their cards. She knew Mr. Mitchell only as an older relative of her dear friend May Goddard. She would not have realized how characteristic it was that he had only mustered the courage to call on her in the company of another man, also presumably interested in getting to know her better.

That first mention of Alfred Mitchell in her diary was brief and casual. The next entry, four months later, was evidence that she had to take him seriously. For he had brought her "a little bunch of trailing arbutus," all the way from Norwich, a hundred miles away in eastern Connecticut. Trailing arbutus is a small shy wild flower, anything but showy, and she was not overly impressed. She found it "flattering" that he was paying court to her, but "thirty years old cannot love like twenty-three." Actually he was thirty-five, twelve years older than she.

When she had first met him at May Goddard's home in Norwich, she could not remember. It might have been in 1861, the first year of the war, when he had just returned from Hawaii, in response to President Lincoln's call for a volunteer army, and had sought a commission in a Connecticut regiment in his hometown. Or it might have been a couple of years later when, as Captain Alfred Mitchell, he was back in Norwich on leave from the Louisiana front in a tattered uniform. All his spare clothes and personal effects had been lost when a counterattacking Confederate force had seized the base of operations of the Army of the Gulf, and he had written his older brother Louis, whom Annie knew, to have some shirts made for him in Norwich. His uniform must have meant something to Annie Tiffany, for a photograph of him in uniform was preserved by her till the day she died.

Yet his photograph was not the only one she kept. Harry Goddard, one of May's older brothers, had sent her his picture, also in a Union officer's uniform, in the middle of the war, four years before Mr. Mitchell's flowers. Harry was only a year or two older than Annie, and, as he once signed himself in one of the many letters of his she kept, he was "half your lover, all your friend." A gay and bantering correspondence went on between them for some years after the war, one of its features being a contract, not very well lived up to, under which she would give up chocolates if he would abstain from tobacco.

May's oldest brother, Alfred Mitchell Goddard, killed in the last year of the war, had been given a hero's burial in Norwich. Annie had not known him as well, as he was several years her senior, and he had been out in Hawaii engaged in the same business enterprise as his cousin Alfred Mitchell until 1863. The connection between the two Alfreds was one more link in the chain that brought Alfred Mitchell and Annie Tiffany together.

Yet until that first call at 255 Madison Avenue, she had never thought much about Alfred Mitchell, only that he was May's "Uncle Alf." May's parents, Mary and Levi Goddard, had given him the only home he ever had, but he was seldom there when Annie visited. He had, as she knew, resigned his commission in 1864, and gone to California to try his luck in the gold fields. She knew his older brother better, the kindly hunchback whom May called Uncle Lou, who had come to live with the Goddards after Levi Goddard died, and was always there when Annie visited May.

Of course, Uncle Lou and Uncle Alf were not May's real uncles but her mother's first cousins, who had been treated as members of the Goddard family as long as Annie could remember.

May Goddard was the closest of a group of friends and relatives Annie knew in Norwich. The Tiffanys, of course, lived in New York, but they had come from the Danielson area, a few miles up the Shetucket River from Norwich. And several members of the Young family—Mrs. Tiffany had been Harriet Young—lived in Norwich. Annie's favorite was her Aunt Lydia. She had been the wife of John B. Young, Charles Tiffany's original partner, when he opened his shop in New York in 1837. John Young had sold out to his more aggressive partner in 1853, and gone to live in Norwich next door to his wife's father, a wholesale grocer and a man of substance. The spacious house he built at 73 Washington Street, only a block or two from the Goddards, often seemed like home to Annie when she came to visit her beloved "Auntie," especially after Mr. Young died, and it was on the lawn behind that house that she first induced the shy Mr. Mitchell, a couple of months after his first gift of flowers, to join in a game of croquet. That, too, was in her diary.

There was a direct steamboat passenger service between Norwich and New York, and from Norwich, the Norwich & Worcester Railroad followed the Shetucket River to Danielson less than an hour away, so Norwich was connected with Annie's early memories of being taken from New York to visit her grandparents in Danielson.

One of her Norwich cousins, Hattie Backus, was a student at Wheaton Female Seminary in Norton, Massachusetts, as were the daughters of some friends of the Tiffanys in Danielson, and it was doubtless through them that the Tiffanys had decided to send Annie away to school when she was twelve years old.

Her first serious schooling, then, was at Wheaton Female Seminary, later a women's college. It seems likely that the reason for sending her to boarding school was to get her out of the city, at that time prone to deadly epidemics that decimated families, especially striking children. Even the wealthy Tiffanys lost two children in infancy, and Annie's sister Louise was a sickly newborn dependent on a wet nurse, at the time the decision was made to send Annie away to school.

After two years at Wheaton, however, her parents found a suitable school, Mlle. Rostand's Young Ladies Institute, within walking distance of their New York home. The study of French was a major emphasis in that school. Foreign languages and music were important accomplishments for young ladies then, and some of Annie's French notebooks are preserved; but there is also evidence of her study of history, mathematics, and English composition.

Her education did not stop there. At the age of eighteen she went on from Mlle. Rostand's to a two-year finishing school, Mrs. Hoffman's, almost equivalent to a junior college of today, where the curriculum provided an unusual amount of science, including both chemistry and geology, also a course in "intellectual philosophy," as well as the more usual courses in history, literature, and foreign languages.

Annie received a better education than might have been expected of the daughter of one of New York's newly rich first families. She was not brought up to be a social butterfly.

Charles Tiffany, her father, after all, had not come from the bottom, nor become wealthy by means of any bold gambles. He worked long hard hours all his life, and built up a business whose trademark was integrity. If he had genius, it was in his imaginative appreciation of what the carriage trade wanted in the way of luxury goods. And even if his own personal style was stodgy, he had the flair to cash in on passing events of note. Thus he obtained exclusive rights to a leftover piece of the first Atlantic cable, polished sections of which, mounted as paperweights or on snuffboxes, became popular gift items. The Civil War opened a market for officers' swords and military accoutrements, and Tiffany's became a principal supplier. When monarchies fell, crown jewels found their way to Tiffany's. But flashy episodes in the history of Tiffany & Co. were rare. More significant was the fact that the American standard for sterling silver was set by Tiffany's.

Annie's parentage on both sides was of established respectability. The Tiffanys were an old New England family. Annie's grandfather, Comfort Tiffany, used a modest inheritance to good effect to acquire textile mills powered by the waterfalls of the upper Shetucket Valley. Her other grandfather, Ebenezer Young, was a competing mill owner in the same area. He could boast of an even more distinguished ancestry, including several of the *Mayflower*'s select company. Not that either the Youngs or the Tiffanys made any great pretensions. Even in his later years, when Charles Tiffany was one of New York's civic leaders and a patron of the arts, he was essentially a small-town product, and his standards were those of the solid gentry of a small town.

So Annie was brought up to feel that her family's wealth and social position were part of the order of nature. And the school friends she made and kept, such as the Huntington and Perkins girls in Norwich and her special friend May Goddard, though not as obviously rich as the Tiffanys, were of the same comfortable class of small-town gentry.

In addition to her ties to Norwich, Annie had other social contacts at the Tiffany country estate up the Hudson, at Irvington, where she spent her summers. Morgans, Rockefellers, and Vanderbilts were neighbors there, but Tiffany Hall was an old remodeled farmhouse with wide porches, magnificent only in its view of the Hudson. Croquet, riding, driving, and rowing on the river were among the leisure-time activities open to a proper young lady. The Morgans were apparently the most congenial family, and her diary mentions sharing a prayerbook with Colonel Morgan in church, and seeing him at a dance. The first J. P. Morgan was seven years older than she and about to be married when she described him as "the jolliest chaperone I ever knew, but then, he says, he is not one yet." George Morgan was the one she went driving with alone, which was not quite proper.

Yet her diary is as often concerned with the state of her soul as with the young men who paid her attention. She began the diary in January 1865 at the age of twenty; she had graduated from Mrs. Hoffman's school the previous June. Her immediate concern was self-improvement:

> My principal reasons for writing this are to improve myself in writing, by constant practice and, although I cannot tell exactly how I shall be benefited, to make myself better and nobler.

After some doubts about the worthwhileness of the effort—her father had criticized her spelling, which was actually not bad at all—she went on to specify the qualities she sought in herself.

I want to be more amiable and better contented and good and useful. I don't know why it is that I am of so little use in the world, but certain it is that I am of so very little consequence.

She wished she would be more like her Aunt Lydia who seemed to be "always doing some kind of action." She wished she could be more attractive. She felt her parents were not very helpful.

Papa always thinks people will come without an invitation which they won't always do. It is not his natural "make" to be cordial, however; if he were, it would be much pleasanter. People I suppose, think him stiff, as they do me, whereas nothing is farther from my intentions. I suppose neither of us can help it. I try to be as sweet as possible to everyone but I am always considered cold except to people who know me well.

A few days later she wrote:

Why am I so utterly miserable when I have everything that a girl could possibly desire to make me happy, but one?

The one lack, clearly, was a husband. "That one I could also have if I were different." She felt she had an "unfortunate disposition." She wanted to be "amiable" but yet "it is hard for me to be anything but cross." Then, too, though she did not try to explain it, the young men who were most attentive were not the most congenial. Mr. Dyer, for instance, whom Auntie had thrown at her on her last summer's visit to Norwich, she could not abide. And Mr. Dalley, who took her driving in Irvington, was so boring.

She worried, too, about her spiritual condition. Her cousin Amy Tremblay was joining a church. Yet Amy allowed herself to read novels on Sunday, "which my conscience would never let me do." She was strict with herself, but she felt her faith was weak, and getting weaker. On June 9, 1865, this entry appeared:

Oh, if I could be a Christian. Yet I am always longing to be good and always praying for help. Is our religion one that can suit every kind of disposition? It must be so, and yet why am I not one? Oh, God, help me or I shall perish.

Then with a touch of humor, she wrote that all she was good for was "to teach Mama patience by so trying her."

Apparently her mother, still a country girl in the big city, was not much help, either with Annie's religious doubts or her social life. The young men she mentioned most often were those she had met on her visits to Auntie in

Norwich. Her mother did let her invite some of them, along with May Goddard and a couple of other girl friends, to a big house party in Irvington at the end of the summer of 1865. May and Lillie Perkins were the first to come, on Monday. The next day the ever faithful Henry Goddard arrived, with two other young men from Norwich, Newton Perkins and Fred Terry. Annie was more in love with May than with any of the men.

> May is the loveliest girl I ever knew. If only I could be like her in a small degree. Besides being the prettiest, she is the best girl I ever knew.

Annie's brother Louis Comfort Tiffany, though only seventeen, was in the party, with no idea then that he would eventually marry Annie's May (Louis in later life became the well-known artist and stained-glass maker). Another party guest was Louis's tutor, Emile Kingsland. Annie was not above a touch of snobbery in her references to him.

> Poor Emile! I think he is one of the kindest, most obliging fellows I ever knew, and yet I cannot help treating him as I do.

> The festivities lasted through the weekend: On Thursday afternoon quite a party of us went to Yonkers and had our pictures taken in a group. Fred Terry invited us to row on Friday morning, and in the afternoon we drove again: of course all the spaces of time were filled up by croquet, walks, and so forth, besides which Emile continued to read *Nicholas Nickleby*, which he had commenced to read to us before they came, whenever there was time.

There was a dance Saturday evening, to which the occupants of some of the big houses nearby, including the Morgans, were invited. House guests went to church Sunday morning with the family, before leaving on their separate ways.

The memory of that happy house party was still fresh in Annie's mind when she next wrote in her diary a few months later. She was then at the beginning of a European tour with her Aunt Lydia and her brother Louis, and trying to set down memories of her recent doings before they were crowded out by new impressions. Her "darling Papa" had decided to send her to Europe. Her Aunt Lydia, recently widowed, was an excellent chaperone. But her sentimental thoughts turned back to Irvington and "my last ride on Willie on Saturday before I sailed, when Mr. Morgan and I went to White Plains." There was also a Mr. Amster whom she had found "more interesting"; he took her driving, and "actually had on light kids [spats?]." Yet she knew she was not really in love with him. Nor in fact with anybody.

Once she wrote that she had almost fallen in love with the seventeen-year-old son of the local minister whom she got to talking with on the train going from New York to Irvington. "I never find men half so splendid as I have seen boys."

For the good part of a year, another young man, Harry Gray, was much in her thoughts—till Alfred Mitchell appeared on the scene. As a suitor Gray had the great advantage of being a member of the Tiffany household for the whole summer of 1866, as a kind of tutor-companion for Louis. Annie first wrote about him on July 13.

> I do not know how it came about exactly that he came to teach Louis. Seeing him at Columbia College one evening Louis proposed to Papa to ask him to be his teacher for the summer. Papa, much to my surprise, consented. The arrangements were made and the young man arrived the day after the fourth of July.

She confessed to fantasies about him before his arrival. She "planned delightful flirtations and even went so far as to say to myself 'Perhaps he is to be my destiny.'" Yet in spite of finding him "as near perfection as I could imagine a young man, in truth nearer," she sadly admitted she was not in love with him either.

Gray was somewhat older than she and sported a full beard, and, perhaps aware of his responsibilities in the family, he told her parents she should not go driving alone with Mr. Morgan. She did not like him for that.

There was another house party at the end of that summer with May and Henry Goddard and other friends again coming from Norwich. Again they went to Yonkers for a group photograph. But the diary entries were fewer than before. More exciting was an extended visit to Norwich where her Aunt Lydia gave a party for her. She began to wonder whether she was becoming a social butterfly.

> I am old enough to have had plenty of experience in life, if I am ever to have any. I think I must be in a sort of state of blasé, used up, burnt out— or not yet commenced to burn at all. "Better to have loved and lost than never to have loved at all." I believe I think so.

She was grateful that she had had so little pain in her life, yet at the same time she felt she was missing something.

> It is hard to make up my mind that this is all—that I am still to walk in a calm path, and never bask in the intense heat of the sun. I would rather be scorched than always moderate.

On reading over these words, she realized she was talking like a romantic schoolgirl.

> What fine sentiments, Miss Tiffany! Really you are wise, even for a young woman of your age.

She thought of Henry Goddard; he would call her a "consummate fool."

But Harry Gray was still center stage. He called on her and read her poetry. He took her riding. On one occasion when May was visiting her in

New York, he took them both to lunch at Delmonico's, and afterwards they went with him while he bought himself a high hat. She was impressed with his appearance.

> I did not know he could look so well in any hat, and really I have more respect for him. I think a high hat imparts quite an amount of dignity.

She enjoyed his company. She felt he was truly in love with her, and his love was "pure." What's more, her parents seemed to "favor" him. And his father and mother were already treating her almost as a daughter-in-law.

About the time Alfred Mitchell brought her the little bunch of flowers in the spring of 1867, she made up her mind about Harry Gray. Though she liked him as a "friend," she was not in love with him, and she found the courage to tell his mother. Shortly thereafter she received a letter, which she always treasured, from Harry's father. He was a well-known portrait painter, and she had admired his work at an exhibition at the National Academy of Design to which Harry had once escorted her. The letter read:

Studio, 14th May '67

My dear Miss Tiffany,

I feel under the deepest obligation to your kind father, for many favors to my dear son; I would be delighted to only pay the *interest* on the debt, as a slight expression of our gratitude, by painting for him a portrait of you.— Will you favor me with the necessary sittings?

If not *perfectly* agreeable to your fancy or convenience or feelings in any way—please take no notice of this and I will understand; but if you should be pleased to assist me, tell Mrs. Gray.

I would prefer that Mr. Tiffany should not know of it until accomplished, if you coincide with me.

Very truly and respectfully,
Henry Peters Gray

Whether Mr. Tiffany knew about it is not in the record. He was busy all day every day at the store, where he was getting ready for a move uptown to a new building on Union Square, and for the incorporation of Tiffany & Co., until then a partnership.

Annie went for sittings to Mr. Gray's studio. He was obviously fond of her, and the portrait was painted with love. He might have lost a daughter-in-law but he had a charming model for a picture, and even if given to Mr. Tiffany, and accepted as a gift, it would lead to other commissions. As a matter of fact, he did paint another picture for the Tiffanys that summer, a shimmering idealization of the view of the Hudson River from the porch of the Tiffanys' Irvington house, with specks of sailboats on the placid Tappan Zee in the distance. The portrait was described in a preview of the fall exhibition at the National Academy of Design, in a column by the art editor of the *Sun*, as "altogether beautiful in its subject and treatment."

By that time, however, the name Gray was no longer appearing in Annie's diary. She was wholly under the spell of May's "Uncle Alf."

Alfred Mitchell spent several days in New York that spring. He had come to the city with Henry Goddard, ostensibly on business, but bringing the flowers to Annie. Henry had not progressed further with Annie than the "contract" that she would give up chocolates if he gave up tobacco. But with Alfred Mitchell, life was more serious. He called several times, and went out with her when she went shopping. "I do like to dress prettily," she confided in her diary, "but I wish I need not spend so much time thinking about it." No doubt Mr. Mitchell was disapproving. She decided that what she wanted in a husband most of all was a man of "goodness and nobleness and honor." Presumably Mr. Mitchell, even if he was a "dignified, critical, over thirty-year-old gentleman," impressed her with the moral qualities she had said she was looking for. She wanted a husband she could look up to.

Her Aunt Lydia Young heard from Henry Goddard on his return to Norwich about Alfred Mitchell's attentions. She wrote Annie that she had been told of "your going out several times with Uncle Alf," and went on to bring up, none too subtly, the name of "our Mr. Dyer."

In June, Annie got her mother to invite Alfred Mitchell to Irvington. After the visit she had to tell her Aunt Lydia about him.

> I think he is the most interesting person I ever listened to. Don't you know, Auntie, there are some persons with whom you always feel at ease, and get so interested in their talk you forget they are actually doing it all. With Mr. Mitchell I feel as if I were being very brilliant while I am only enjoying his conversation.

But Auntie was not impressed, and wrote back:

> I do not doubt that Mr. Mitchell had a nice time at Irvington. I thought he looked particularly smiling and happy the last time I met him in the street, which was only a day or two ago. Take care, my love, don't become too much fascinated. I know he is just the kind of man to fascinate a young lady to whom he took a fancy, and I don't think he would take the trouble to make himself particularly agreeable where he did not take a fancy, and I don't believe he is the right kind of man for you to enjoy a happy married life with. He is too cynical, too whimsical, and I am not sure but too selfish. I don't know that there is any particular danger in your case, but there is my warning. I don't think there would be any harm come from a little flirtation, if a free and pleasant intercourse between a young man and a young lady can be called "flirting." But I think I will leave the management of the matter to yourself.

At the end of July, Annie spent a week in Norwich visiting. Under her aunt's watchful eye, there was little chance for intimacy between Alf and Annie, but as he was staying with the Goddards, only five minutes' walk from Aunt Lydia's, and May Goddard was, after all, Annie's favorite friend, he could hardly be kept away. Yet as an older man and a Civil War veteran, he was an awkward participant in any gathering of young people. Annie wrote noncommittally in her diary: "Mr. Mitchell condescended to play croquet with us quite often."

May began to take a hand. She worshiped her "Uncle Alf," and as she realized he was becoming seriously interested in her "darling Annie," the notion of a match between two people she loved dearly, however unlikely it had first appeared, took root in her mind. She was going to visit Annie in August and suggested Uncle Alf be invited at the same time. If it had occurred to her that Tiffany money might be a factor in her penniless Uncle Alf's interest in Annie, she would have put it out of her mind as unworthy of him.

Annie was finding the summer dull with only her brother Louis for adult company. As she wrote in her more and more sketchy diary:

> Most of the time we were all alone with the children. How I love them, all my brothers and sisters! my darlings! [Louis was then nineteen, Louise ten, Burnie seven.] I expect May this week and I shall be so glad to see her.
> And Mr. Mitchell, too, I hope will stay to have some croquet.

In May's company, she began calling him "Uncle Alf," which was not conducive to romance. But in October he was back for another visit at Irvington, this time without May, and he was again "Mr. Mitchell." On this occasion he was serious. He screwed up his courage and asked her to marry him.

He asked Mr. Tiffany's approval, but Mr. Tiffany was anything but cordial. True, Annie was at an age when she should be marrying. But a husband was expected to support his wife. Alfred Mitchell could only talk vaguely about how the war had ruined his business career, and how he was considering certain new prospects, perhaps in the Reconstruction South, perhaps back in California. Mr. Tiffany could not take his suit seriously. And as for Annie, she was too taken aback to know what to say, and told him she would think about it and write him.

She did write him. He later referred to that "first letter I ever got from you" as a "bitter disappointment." But it led to a stronger resolve than ever to make some money so that he could in good conscience seek her hand.

He consulted his former legal guardian, General William Williams. Now almost eighty, with a long and successful business career behind him, he could not have had much confidence in Alfred's ability to make money. Alfred had dissipated the inheritance so carefully preserved by Williams and handed over to him at age twenty-one. At that point, fourteen years earlier, General Williams had helped Alfred establish a partnership with his energetic nephew, Charles Augustus Williams, but Alfred now had nothing to show for the various business enterprises undertaken in the Pacific, though his former partner Gus Williams was still adding to his fortune.

The General had staked him after his return from the Civil War, and sent him to California to try his luck in the gold fields. But gold mining was no longer rewarding to the lone prospector, and there was nothing left of that investment. His former commanding officer, General Birge, had offered him a job in a manufacturing enterprise he was promoting in Georgia. But General Williams felt Reconstruction business in the South was too risky, and thought California still offered better prospects, particularly with transcontinental rail services on the near horizon. He offered to stake Alfred once more in another mining venture.

Mrs. Williams no doubt helped persuade him to that decision, for to her Alfred was always her "dear boy." The Williams' only son had died a few years before, and they had no living children; Alfred had often stayed in their big house fronting the Parade when he was in Norwich. Moreover, Mrs. Williams knew Annie from Annie's visits to her Aunt Lydia, the Williams' near neighbor, and Annie's family was distantly connected with hers so she would have liked to see Alfred make enough money to satisfy Mr. Tiffany and get married.

Alfred prepared to go back to California, more desperate than ever to prove himself. Annie, no doubt influenced by her father's disapproval and her Aunt Lydia's unfavorable opinion of him—and perhaps not understanding why he was going—concluded he was a "selfish, cold-hearted man," as she wrote her aunt. Aunt Lydia again told her that she thought him "too fastidious, and perhaps too exacting, to make any woman happy who wouldn't find her happiness in yielding everything to him, and believing him in everything the one above all others." She again recommended Mr. Dyer.

But Alfred had an advocate to plead for him. May Goddard had always considered him a big brother, even if she called him "Uncle Alf." Now she undertook to soften up Annie on his behalf. Ignoring grammar in her eagerness, she wrote Annie:

> You do not feel his love is deep enough to satisfy you. You doubt his capacity of loving you as you would be loved—but Annie, is it a little thing for a man who has reached all these years (as I truly believe he has—for if he has loved before it was many years ago) courted and admired as he has always been by ladies, delighting in their society as you well know, to offer to one whom he has closely watched, openly admired and met constantly for a whole year—the wealth of love which I know lies under all the cold skepticism of which you deem him proud, but which I believe he would give worlds to rid himself? He has passed through years of lonely living in the midst of varied continued temptations untainted by one breath on his moral character.

In May's eyes Alfred had a character of "spotless purity." She believed him "capable of any good, and totally incapable of insincerity, falsehood or any meanness." She tried to arrange another meeting between them before Alfred's departure. They missed connections: Alfred was in New York when Annie was next in Norwich. Then Annie went visiting relatives in New Bedford, and he offered to call on her there. Nothing worked out, and he left without seeing her again. It was November 1867. But Annie did write him that she hoped to see him on his return.

This was enough to raise his fallen spirits. He wrote May's older sister, Julia, who was becoming his closest confidante, as May was Annie's:

> Oh, Jule, think how our life hangs upon a thread—suppose I had gone away without receiving those letters. I should have left home with scarce a wish ever to return—with such a different idea of Annie from any I had ever had—and with my faith in human nature utterly shaken.

Julia was ready to back May's matchmaking efforts. She told May, and May passed it on to Annie, that she believed Annie

> could give the kind of love which Alf had never had, and which is the one thing wanted to make him wholly noble and self-sacrificing.

Julia wanted May to assure Annie that Annie was "really and truly Alf's first and only love." And May concluded her pleas to Annie:

> Will you not trust him and the opinion of those who know and love you both so dearly! Good night! God's blessing rest upon you. God's angels guard and keep you both.
>
> May

Back in California, Alfred had no better luck than before. The gold he was seeking was as elusive as ever. He ran through General Williams' second stake. On the way back from California in the summer of 1868, empty-handed, he met some promoters who fired him with a new money-making scheme, the promotion of coffee plantations in Guatemala. They sent him to Guatemala to make a thorough study of the prospects. Two months later he was back in Norwich. As he wrote in his report to the promoters, and in a November letter to Annie, a coffee plantation would take years before producing a profit. He still had other prospects, not so far in the future.

He went to New York and pressed her to agree to marry him as soon as he had a position that would win her father's consent. She said she would write him her decision. Back in Norwich waiting for her reply, he found the suspense unbearable. After four days of waiting, he wrote pleading for a letter:

> I haven't written you since I left you Saturday night, dear Annie, because I wanted to give you time to find out whether you wanted to see me again, for you know you said you were in great doubt about it. But I am afraid to wait longer lest the decision should be against me.

Her changes of mood were driving him to despair.

> I try to think it is only a little wilfulness on your part that so distresses me but I can't always make up my mind to trust you. There was no need of your dropping my arm half a block away and hurrying up the steps in such

haste. What you had just told me, that you were "never happy with me" was quite sufficient to prevent my soliciting any affectionate manner of leave taking.

The next day Annie's letter finally came. She did not want her parents to know she was writing him, so she enclosed it in a letter to May. For the first time she addressed him by his first name, though she had never dared to call him Alfred to his face. She told him she needed to know him better but did not discourage his suit. He went from despair to exuberance, and immediately sat down and wrote her a twenty-page reply, telling more about himself than he had ever revealed before or perhaps ever would again. "My own darling Annie:" he began.

> Your letter of today has been a balm to my soul and I can never thank you enough for it. I have been more dismal and desponding since I left you in New York than I can ever tell, and have been hoping so much and yet fearing to get a letter from you, going to every mail until this morning when I had given over to despair. But Henry came in this morning with two letters for May, and I knew one of them would be for me, and when it was given to me and I had opened the envelope I knew at once from the mode of address that you had repented of the wilfulness which had caused me so much anxiety and pain. And as I read I felt as if I were passing from dark night and peril into sunlight and safety again.

He accepts her invitation to tell more about himself, and goes into a long recital of his efforts to make a living. He obviously feels an inordinate compulsion to explain and justify his penniless state.

> Your letter makes me feel more than I have ever done before that I can trust to your affection, even though I had added more serious offenses to the sin of poverty. For it is a sin, and to a certain extent a shame that a man of my years and opportunities should be obliged to confess that but for the kindness of friends he would not know where to get his dinner. I set it down rather bitterly, more so perhaps than I should, but you will see in a little that I am rather the victim of ill luck than of my own lack of effort or industry.

He tells of the failure of his "mining adventures," of his turning down the offer of a job in "another industry in the South" in order to try again in California, and of the failure of that effort, of his investigation of starting a coffee plantation in Guatemala, and of his deciding he could not face "an absence so prolonged from all I hold dear in the world." He would at this point be willing to accept the job his "southern friend" had offered, but it is no longer available: "he has filled the place he desired me to occupy." He has "one campaign" left. His brother Donald, the successful novelist and essayist, has just been named editor, with Harriet Beecher Stowe, of the new magazine *Hearth and Home*, and "desires me to assist him in the work (making translations and other such literary work) but I hate New York, and the prospect of earning more than a bare subsistence is not promising."

He goes on to tell of his "uneasiness and discomfort" whenever he has been in the Tiffany home. "I was well aware that to a man of your father's industry and great success in life there could be no excuse for need or penury. Neither do I desire him to change his opinion until he shall be forced to by an apparent change in me."

He wants Annie to wait till he has some "steady persistent work."

> Had I not known that your father's position with respect to fortune was such as to place you always beyond the fear of want, whatever might happen to me, I never should have dared to have avowed my love for you. The constant pressure of poverty has been so long and bitterly felt by me that I would never have ventured to ask anyone to share it with me, least of all you who has never even dreamt what the word meant.

Is this all rationalization? He knows he will be thought, if he ever wins her hand, to be marrying her for her money. She is "so little versed in the hard and practical ways of the world" that she might not understand that.

> I have never done aught of which I would feel ashamed or which should make you ashamed of me, but I so stand in dread of the evil interpretations of those who have no reason to be charitable toward me that their presence is a terror to me.

With this long confession behind him, he feels better. "If you will only tell me that you are glad I have so written," he goes on to say, he could "really feel as if you belonged to me, however far off and distant the culmination and crowning of my hopes may be." He agrees that no engagement should be announced till her parents have given their consent.

That consent was not forthcoming for another year and a half, and their marriage would not take place for still another year after that.

It was a difficult period for both of them. He wrote her so many letters that he once suggested, if she kept them all, her father would have to build an addition on his house for space to store them. Many years later she found them so painful to read that she destroyed most of them. What survived may have been letters she did not find, but they are enough to show the shape of his doubts and fears.

A recurring theme is his concern that he will be thought to be attracted to her only by her father's wealth. He has to tell her over and over again how much he loves her:

> You are the one woman whom I have been hoping for and waiting for and seeking for all these long years, and I should have known you and claimed you in my heart under no matter what circumstances, whether I were rich or poor, in prosperity or adversity, hopeful or despondent.

And he wants constant reassurance that she believes in the purity of his love.

I want you to tell me over and over again that you believe that my love for you is true and honest and clear of any taint or suspicion. I need not only this belief of yours but its constant expression, for there are many of my friends who I know will never believe it, and their doubts I shall discern though unspoken to me. And the eager desire I sometimes feel for unlimited wealth is mainly prompted by the wish to be able to give the lie to malicious tongues.

For a while he made the most of his brother Donald's willingness to pay him for "literary work." The second issue of *Hearth and Home* contained an unsigned article on "Coffee Culture in Guatemala." A little later appeared a short piece about native Hawaiian customs—the making of tapa cloth, lomi lomi massage, the eating of dog meat—entitled "Pictures of Hawaii" by T. M. Coan, M.D. Dr. Coan was the son of a famous Hawaiian missionary, Titus Coan, from Killingworth, Connecticut. During Alfred's years in the islands before the Civil War, he had become acquainted with several missionary families, and he was probably responsible for procuring that article.

In July 1869, *Hearth and Home* began the serialization of a French novel, *L'Histoire de Sibylle*, by Octave Feuillet. Published in translation as *The Romance of a Rich Young Girl*, the translator's name does not appear, but this was Alfred's work. In several letters the previous winter, he had mentioned to Annie how hard he was working at it, and he told her proudly that his brother had told him it would be worth five hundred dollars: "So you see I am beginning to earn something." The serialization of his translation ran seventeen weeks. But that was the last of his published work. Perhaps he had hoped to follow this translation with another, of Feuillet's even better-known novel of that period, whose title described his own situation—*Le Roman d'un jeune homme pauvre*. Among the papers he left for his posterity is the manuscript of his completed translation.

The only other evidence of his effort to emulate his successful literary brother was his manuscript "Forty Days on a Guano Island," the account of his own near death from thirst ten years earlier; written for *Hearth and Home*, it was never published.

He was already convinced of the futility of trying to make a living by his pen when he received another offer of a job from his former commanding officer, General Birge, in Georgia. This time he accepted with alacrity. In December 1869, he took ship from New York for Savannah, leaving Annie with a farewell letter and a florist's bunch of violets.

His new decisiveness had apparently breached her last uncertainties, and she was now very much in love. The letters she sent after him during this separation are the only letters of hers of the courtship period that survived her later ruthless housecleaning. She needed to repeat so often how much she loved Alfred—variously described as her "little boy" and her "old man"— that her letters contain little else.

The first one was written within hours of his departure.

My own dear, dear Alfred,

Your letter came this evening just before dinner and I have not read it all yet for I cannot keep my tears from blinding me. But I want to commence my answer before I sleep. I want to say again, I love you, I love you. Already you are far away at sea. Are you thinking of your little girl who is so lonely without you? She wishes so much so much that she could rest her head on your shoulder and have a goodnight kiss.

I did not know how badly I felt to lose you, Alfred dear, until your letter came this afternoon. I am sure you would be glad you wrote it if you knew how precious it is to me now that you are gone. And yet it makes me miss you more, it makes me long so to put my arms around your neck and say I love you and have you kiss me again. Are you thinking of me now, my naughty boy, and would you smooth my head and call me "sweetheart" if you could?

Two days later was Christmas Day, and Alfred had ordered fresh violets delivered at the Madison Avenue house. She wrote of her "sweet surprise."

The faded ones have reminded me all this morning how long it is since you gave them to me, now these fresh ones seem to bring me a kiss directly from you.

She thought of him on shipboard "all alone among strangers." He had written that her love was all the more precious because he had spent so much of his life alone. She had been afraid that he would get tired of loving her "because you have been so much more accustomed to living without anybody to love you." But she was confident of him now. The love and kisses and terms of endearment went on by the page. She was impatient to hear from him again. In the meantime May would be coming for an extended visit "so that we may commence our lessons together the first week in January."

May was, of course, delighted with the fact that the engagement of her Annie and her "Uncle Alf" was now so definite. But it was still not official. The Tiffanys had not yet consented. Alfred must find steady employment before they would agree. Yet their resistance was weakening. May Goddard's presence in their house in January 1870 helped soften them up. She had been the chief promoter of the match between her Uncle Alf and Annie, and she was not going to give up now.

Just what "lessons" she and Annie undertook together, and with what tutors or governesses, is not recorded, but one product of the winter's educational activities that survived is the minute book of the "Thought Exchange Society," kept by May as "Secretary." Mr. and Mrs. Tiffany were induced to allow their names to appear as "President" and "Vice-President." Annie was designated "Motioner" and her brother Louis, who decorated the minute book, was elected official "Artist." Some of Annie's Norwich cousins came for visits that winter and spring and were enlisted in the society's literary exercises. Two of Annie's suitors, Harry Gray and the eligible Mr. Dyer, were brought into the meetings, perhaps in a last vain attempt of the family to find an alternative to Alfred Mitchell.

But it was no use. Annie was too deeply in love with her "little-boy-old-man." The ties between the Tiffanys' Norwich connections and Alfred's Goddard family were too close. Even Annie's Aunt Lydia Young had been won over to becoming a partisan of Alfred's. And Alfred had surmounted the last barrier by getting a permanent job.

It was not too clear just what his work consisted of. General Birge's business at the Satilla Mills in Camden, Georgia, had not been able to make use of Alfred's talents after all, but another prospect had opened up. Alfred's brother Donald was married to one of the Charleston Pringles, who were still, in spite of the Civil War, among South Carolina's most prominent families. Alfred visited Charleston and, thanks no doubt to the Pringle connection, landed a job in the railroad business.

This was the era of the most rapid expansion of the nation's railroad system. The first transcontinental rail line had been completed the year before. Charleston interests had been responsible for the first rail passenger service in the country; and in the Reconstruction of the South's railroads, and its industry generally, Charleston played an important part.

Alfred's contributions to the growth of the American rail network were not of historical significance. But in an autobiographical note some years later, he stated that "for ten or fifteen years subsequent to the war he was engaged in the railroad business in South Carolina first and later in Kansas."

His employment was enough to satisfy Charles Tiffany's scruples, and won his consent to the announcement of the couple's engagement, provided they would not get married for another year.

On April 27, 1871, Alfred and Annie were finally married at her parents' home. The two hundred guests were treated afterwards to a sumptuous wedding breakfast catered by Delmonico's. Among other gifts, Mr. Tiffany gave his daughter a diamond and pearl brooch with matching earrings.

A few months later May Goddard wrote her brother Henry, by this point a lawyer in Hartford, of her own engagement to Louis Tiffany, Annie's younger brother: "We are both very ridiculous," she wrote, "and I am afraid are just as silly as Alf and Annie have been."

CHRONICLE III
Child of Privilege

CHAPTER 9
Alfreda's Romance

The 1874 Christmas trade at Tiffany & Co.'s new location on Union Square had fully justified Mr. Tiffany's belief that society and business were continuing to move uptown. The homes of some of his customers were nearby, and within a few blocks developers were building luxury apartment houses. In one of those buildings, on East Seventeenth Street, Mr. Tiffany's daughter Annie and her husband Alfred Mitchell had recently rented an apartment, and there, with Christmas decorations still brightening the rooms, on December 29, their first child was born.

Annie was just thirty years old; Alfred twelve years older. They had wanted a boy, and Annie would have named him for the husband she adored, but the baby was a girl, and they named her Alfreda. They began calling her Freda for short, and Freda she was in the family for the rest of her life.

Like other upper-class mothers, Annie felt keeping her figure was more important than nursing her baby, and a "wet nurse" shortly became a member of the household.

Alfred had always been restless. In the railroad business that occupied him in his early married life, he never felt tied to a desk and was able to indulge his inclination to travel. Business trips often took him to the Midwest where the railroad tracks were spreading out over the plains. In addition he always felt free to take holiday trips farther afield. The birth of his children only temporarily interfered with overseas travel.

Two years after Alfreda's birth, another child was born. Again they wanted a boy and found themselves with a girl, and again they gave the child an adaptation of a man's name, this time of Annie's father Charles; but instead of Charlotte or Carola or any of the more usual feminizations of Charles, they called her Charly, a name she came to hate. She was also handicapped from birth by a congenital disease that remained hidden for thirty years.

For the first eight years of Alfreda's life, her father suppressed his penchant for travel and the family lived in New York apartments, first on East Seventeenth Street, then on East Twenty-sixth. But New York in the 1870s and 1880s, as European immigrants swarmed in and the slums grew, was a pestilential place, especially in summer, with yellow fever, diphtheria, and typhoid rampant. The Mitchells began spending summers in New London, where much of Alfred's childhood had been spent. It was now a summer resort almost as fashionable as Newport. After a couple of years in boarding houses, the Mitchells began buying property in the Pequot section fronting on the harbor, with a beach for the little girls to play on.

Adjoining tracts were acquired over the next few years. An old gambrel-roofed cottage fronting on Pequot Avenue was added to in successive expansions; and as the estate grew, a brick wall was built around the main tract, and more acres were acquired all the way to Ocean Avenue and beyond. Though it remained principally a summer home, it was the only home Alfreda and Charly knew during their childhood and youth. Their father's restless travels came to dominate their lives.

Their first extended trip began in November 1881, and for a full year the family lived in hotels, first in London, then wintering in Madeira, then through the spring and summer in Portugal, Spain, France, Switzerland, and Germany. A pattern was set with the family continually on the move. Being so often in transit, the girls had no regular schooling. They were taught by a series of governesses, taking lessons in foreign languages, French, German, and Italian, and in music—Alfreda on the violin, Charly the piano. Sometimes they settled for a few weeks or months in a rented villa. Summers were usually spent behind the high brick walls of the estate in New London. In spring and fall, when not traveling, the family would visit with the Tiffanys on Madison Avenue in New York or at the Tiffany mansion up the Hudson at Irvington.

In 1886 when Alfreda was eleven, and Charly was nine, the winter was spent in Hawaii. Their father was nostalgic for the "Paradise of the Pacific" where he had tried and failed to make his fortune in the 1850s. He had previously taken his bride there on a belated honeymoon and now he wanted to have his daughters know the islands and some of the old families, descendants of the early missionaries, whom he had known thirty years before— Judds on Oahu, Rices on Kauai. For six months, they made their home in a cottage on Waikiki Beach, later occupied by Robert Louis Stevenson.

Hawaii was still at that time an independent kingdom, with kings and queens and royal princesses providing an elite society, along with rich merchants and descendants of the missionaries. A sister of King Kalakaua, married to a wealthy Scottish business man, Archibald Cleghorn, lived nearby with a little daughter, Princess Kaiulani, who had prospects of becoming queen, and a high point of the Mitchell girls' social life was an invitation to a formal children's party for the princess on her tenth birthday. The party was out-of-doors under the palm trees where high-rise hotels now crowd the beach.

After a winter and spring in Hawaii, the Mitchells returned to their New London home for a few months before setting forth on another long trip to Europe. This time the winter was spent in Italy in a villa in Fiesole overlooking the towers and domes of Florence. The girls were in the care of a German governess, and the diary Alfreda kept was written in German, but she was also learning Italian, Latin, and ancient history. One of the few friends she was able to make on her constant travels was Susan Metcalf, whose American father and Italian mother were wintering in a nearby villa. She was the same age as Alfreda and equally devoted to music and art.

Some years later, Susan and Alfreda were fellow students at the Brussels Conservatoire, Susan preparing for a professional career as a concert singer, Alfreda with similar ambitions as a violinist. (A good many years later, when Susan was the wife of Pablo Casals, and Alfreda had a family of her own, Susan and the great cellist, then on concert tour together, were house guests in the Binghams' New Haven home.)

Alfreda's father had promised her a fine instrument, and in anticipation she had written a poem to it. Approaching twenty, she was a very green and unworldly girl.

Will I be with you soon,
Oh my dear violin?
Were you ever made mine
But in a dream?

Could I pour out my soul
Into that soul of yours,
Tell you all and having told
Burst into tears?

Ah! to my violin,
My own secret's friend,
My pleasure, grief, my dear,
My life to my life's end,
To you I will tell it all...

When the family was in London en route to Brussels, her father took her to Hill's, the great violin dealer, and she picked out a pedigreed instrument, made two hundred years before in Cremona by a member of the Guarnerius family. She fell in love with Mr. Hill as well as the violin, and later was inspired to write a poem about his "pale dear face" in which "all the world is to be seen."

At the Conservatoire she took singing lessons as well as violin lessons. She was thrilled to be told by her violin teacher that she was "gifted": "Je suis doué, on m'a dit," as she wrote in her diary. For a week she was "very happy," but then she came down with a persistent cough, which was finally diagnosed as whooping cough. She had to give up her singing and then her violin lessons, and, at least for the time being, her dream of a professional career.

As her parents resumed their travels, first to Holland, then to Paris and back to London, she comforted herself with more versifying.

All flowers are not made
To shine for all the world,
Or be admired ere they fade.
        . . .

Many a flower has passed unsought for,
While all the rainbow colors from above

Were poured into its cup, while with its odors
It told the silent sky its sweetest love.

With the coming of spring, however, her spirits rose. In a poem entitled "After the Winter in Brussels," the last verse strikes a more hopeful note:

Ah have I ever felt so loving sunshine,
Have I been e'er delighted at such bird songs,
So truly happy at this nature's wakening burst,
Ta'en such sweet flowers?

As if each tree was now first blossoming
Each flower with surprise was rising high,
Each bird was overjoyed with power of singing,
And each heart to its climax be nigh.

Alfreda's romantic yearnings were further stimulated the following winter by a houseboat journey up the Nile. On all her previous travels with her parents, she and Charly had been together, always dressed alike and treated almost as twins. But in 1894, Charly had broken loose, persuaded her parents to let her go to college, and after intensive tutoring had been admitted to Bryn Mawr. Alfreda now had her parents to herself.

She would be twenty-one that December, and no doubt it was with some feeling that she should not be less well educated than her younger sister that the trip to Egypt and Italy was planned. Foreign languages had been a mainstay of the tutoring that she had received before, and the ancient Mediterranean cultures offered, in addition to languages, a wealth of history. So for the three-month cruise on the Nile, Alfreda was to be given a rigorous course of college-level work in Greek, ancient history, and music by an English governess-companion, Blanche Anderson. Alfreda's educational program included the writing of long letters to Charly, to be preserved in lieu of a diary.

In one of the first of these, she describes the great sailing yacht or "dahabeha," the *Ida*, which the Mitchells had chartered in Cairo. In addition to Alfreda, her parents, and the young Englishwoman, the passengers included Mr. Mitchell's thirty-one-year-old niece, Hesse Mitchell. There was also a "dragoman," or tour guide, who took care of all arrangements.

Dec. 10th, 1895

My dear Charly,

This is our first evening at home. We started from the hotel this morning at about eleven and drove over to Gizeh which is about a mile from the town. We were all excited, especially Hesse and I, as Blanche is more sedate, when we saw from the carriage road, looming over the bank of the river, the high masts and American stars and stripes of our dahabeha.

This is to try and show how it looked when we drove up, looking from the Gizeh side over to Cairo. The view was beautiful especially as the sun went down and the opposite shore with its sand hills and the minarets of the mosques were for a minute flushed with a bright pink. Well, to look inside, our crew were all dressed in bran[d] [here as elsewhere the original spelling has been retained] new linen gowns tied at the waist with red scarves, and the bands of white muslin tied round the red fez looked as fresh as could be. They are noiseless people with soft shoes, and as they do not speak English we only looked at each other with interest. We will probably soon see enough of them to know them apart. They all seem to have nice faces, and there is but one white man among them, the cook I think.

We did not sail today as the wind was against us...At lunch time some friends we had made on shipboard came to bid us good-bye and brought a maiden-hair fern for our dining table. The lunch was most sumptuous and quite strange.

The dragoman presided over the table standing by Papa with a fly brush while an Arabian in sedate silence served one dish after another. I shall tell what came from their small kitchen at the bow as I hope our lunches will not all be so remarkable. There were "or d'oeuvres," cold fish with a grand decoration, steak with numerous vegetables, birds, cheese and Turkish coffee, while the table was covered with nine kinds of fruit. What a meal for a boat on the Nile, it was fit for Cleopatra.

In the evening the crew began to make the most wonderful noises. There was a drumming and a kind of singing with nasal voices. Good lights were not put in when the ship was built a long time ago, so we have to use candles. Papa and Mama are playing dominoes while the rest of us are writing.

There is a great silence about us, the river is as calm as a lake although there is a strong current which we do not see in the darkness. Hesse, Blanche and I have been sitting on a large divan on deck. One could hear hardly a ripple and the lights of Cairo looked pretty reflected into the water. We shall probably start tomorrow...I hope you will write to me soon and tell me all about what you are doing. I must say good night now. With a kiss and much love from

Your Id [Charly's nickname for Freda] on the Ida.

Alfreda's next letter remarks that in four days they have gone only four miles. The wind filled the sails only occasionally, and manpower was needed to move the houseboat upstream.

This is the way they go. Some seven or ten men walk slowly along the bank with the rope which is tied to our mast upon their shoulders. They usually sing while doing this. Sometimes we come to shoals and then there is a great scrambling and pushing with poles to get off again. Another way to go on is to take the anchor in a rowboat far ahead and pull up on it with lots of noise. I think the crew earned a good supper today but they only had a gift of a fish from the dragoman, besides their black bread. They sit in a circle on the lower deck.

We pass our time reading a great deal. Hesse, Blanche and I read aloud. We do not get any exercise except for a walk which we took after we anchored for the night.

The next day with a strong favorable wind they made good progress.

> Our boat must have looked like an immense swan with her two great
> white sails spread and puffed out. I wish I could have a picture of her. She
> is all white on the outside with green blinds for the windows and we have
> many green palms and plants on deck. The crew add to the effect in their
> red and blue dresses and white turbans.

Alfreda admired the "muscular" men with their "rich brown skin," and
was amused by the captain's little son, dressed like the rest as a working
member of the crew.

> We never have seen him smile. Once when we were looking at him
> whilst he was opening the front of his little gown to search after fleas, he
> looked up at us seriously and went on.

Alfreda's subsequent letters are full of vivid descriptions of what she saw
on the banks of the river as the *Ida* sailed by or when they went ashore for
exercise.

> A camel walking on the horizon or standing in his stateliness near the
> water's edge. A woman robed in black bringing a great earthen jug to the
> river on her head. Children bearing burdens as great as themselves. It is
> strange to see such intelligent but care-worn faces on boys so young.

The contrast between the luxury enjoyed by the passengers and the abject
poverty of the natives—even the boat's crew lived mostly on black bread—was
described without comment in a long Christmas letter. But it was the beauty
of the setting that most attracted her.

As the *Ida* neared Aswan, some two hundred miles from Cairo, Alfreda
began to long for people of her own kind. She knew there were other
dahabehas on cruises but had seen none. A steamboat carrying mail for the
family had stopped by, but they had seen no white faces in two weeks. Alfreda
hoped the tourist steamer would be at Aswan at the time they arrived there.
Her craving for romance was for more than scenery.

Arriving at Aswan they found company. Three other dahabehas were
there ahead of them. One had as passengers a member of the Austrian royal
family traveling incognito with his retainers. On another was an American
family named Dane, whom the Mitchells found congenial; the Danes' son was
a young doctor, thirty-one years old, on an extended vacation trip with his
parents. On the slow journey down river, the two families kept in touch with
each other, often mooring side by side at the nightly stops.

The name of Dr. Dane began appearing more and more frequently in
Alfreda's diary and in her letters. Hesse Mitchell, Alfreda's cousin, being
more nearly his age and more lively and outgoing than Alfreda, was probably
the chief attraction for Jack Dane on his visits to the *Ida*, and on the two

families' walking tours of the famous temples and tombs down river. By the time they reached Cairo, Alfreda was in love.

Fortunately for the ripening of her unrequited romance, the elder Mitchells and Danes arranged to follow parallel paths on the travels in Italy that both had projected as a sequel to their Nile journey. So at Rome, Florence, Venice, and Lake Como, the two families' routes often overlapped.

Alfreda's diary tells more of the story than her letters, though in the briefest of entries:

March 29.	Rome.
March 31.	Nice call from Mr. and Dr. Dane.
April 1.	Dr. Dane came after dinner.
April 5.	A perfect Easter. Met Danes.
April 6.	Nice call in evening from D. Dane.
April 9.	D. D. asked us to go with him and his father, to Vatican statuary. It was great pleasure and delight. What perfect beauty. Devine [*sic*] inspiration.
April 12.	D. Dane took Hesse and I in carriage to churches. It was rainy but we had a splendid time.
April 14.	Florence.
April 20.	We went with D. D. to see the frescoes of Giotto. We read Ruskin.
April 22.	D. D. came to take us out.
May 1.	To Venice. Expected call from D. D., but did not find us.
May 2.	D. D. came in afternoon to take us in his gondola about the canals. Hesse and I are very enthusiastic.
May 3.	Evening. Gondola again. Music and lovely night.

The families met again at Lake Como, and similar entries appear in the diary. Alfreda seems never to have achieved a first name basis with Dr. Dane; even in her diary she most often refers to him as "D. D.," and Hesse seems to be always present on their excursions. When the Danes left for home on May 23, the Mitchells saw them off at the station. Alfreda noted in her diary that she was "cheerful." Two days later she wrote: "How happy I am, how I love living!!!"

Her hopes were kept alive when she received two letters from Jack Dane in Paris. It is clear that she was very much in love, but there is no evidence that the young doctor looked on her as more than a shy ingénue and a travel companion who was acceptable for want of anyone more lively.

On the Mitchells' return to New London, contact with the Dane family continued. In November Dr. Dane came to New London for a weekend visit. Alfreda played golf and went driving with him, and again wrote in her diary how happy she was.

But still there was no proposal. Mr. and Mrs. Mitchell gave up counting on him as a possible son-in-law. Concerned that their two marriageable daughters should know more eligible young men, they invited a group of Yale students from Hawaii, sons of the missionary families Mr. Mitchell had known as a young man, to come to New London over Thanksgiving. As Alfreda briefly noted in her diary, the house party included "2 Baldwins, 2 Cookes, 2 Judds, 1 Bingham."

This was the first meeting of Alfreda and young Hiram Bingham, then a junior at Yale, but Alfreda was too wrapped up in her romantic attachment to the Boston doctor to take much notice of the "1 Bingham." A photograph taken at a luncheon picnic in a wooded area on the estate shows Hiram shyly seated in the outer edge of the group, nowhere near Alfreda. In her diary the next day, there is a simple mention of a ball at the Tylers' mansion down Pequot Avenue. If Hiram felt attracted to either of the Mitchell sisters, it was to the younger, Charly, the Bryn Mawr student who was also in her junior year.

After the Yale students had returned to New Haven, Alfreda's only comment was, "They are very nice boys."

A winter in Palm Beach came and went. Alfreda's mother tried to tell her she should stop thinking about Jack Dane, but agreed to invite him to another house party in the spring. It was set for the middle of June when New London's social life would be at its height. Tiffany cousins, Charles and May-May (Louis's children), came from New York, and Charly's Bryn Mawr college mate, Katrina Ely, whom Charles would later marry, and of course Dr. Dane from Boston; they were joined for tennis and golf and dances by New London friends of the Mitchell girls. Alfreda's diary again indicates her infatuation; she wrote that she was "supremely happy," and after his departure came this entry: "We have not spoken much but I love him."

He invited her—but alas also Charly—to attend a baseball game, probably the Yale-Harvard game, in Cambridge, putting them up at a Boston hotel. The "happiness" she wrote of then and on the other rare occasions when she saw him seems to have rested on the merest shreds of evidence that he cared for her. She was "dreadfully disappointed" when he failed to make contact with her on an occasion when the Mitchell family was in the Boston area.

In November the blow fell. She was again in Boston for a wedding. She had written him that she would be staying at the Victoria Hotel with some other wedding guests. All one evening she sat in her hotel room waiting for a call that never came. The next day at the wedding, she saw Jack Dane and his parents, and had a few empty words with him at the reception. His mother, who had shown some fondness for Alfreda since their first meeting on the Nile two years before, took her aside. She evidently felt it was time Alfreda knew the truth, that Jack was not interested in her. Alfreda's diary told the story, with only a misspelling to indicate her agitation: "I had a nice talk with Mrs. Dane. Sad knews!"

The following winter her parents decided she should learn to be more independent. She was twenty-three and had never yet lived away from home. As they were planning a trip to Mexico, they arranged for her to spend the

winter of 1897–1898 in a rented New York apartment under the chaperonage
of a somewhat older cousin, Cornelia ("Nina") Nevins. She was encouraged to
set up a rigorous schedule of violin and singing lessons, concerts, lectures,
and physical exercise in a gymnasium. But she was in poor health and spirits,
and the experiment in independence was unsuccessful. In May she was back
in New London with her parents, lonely, sad, and bored.

In June at the Yale-Harvard boat races, there was another house party.
This time Jack Dane was not invited, but another uninvited guest did appear.

In his senior year at Yale, Hiram Bingham had become an ardent small-
boat sailor. Lacking money for a boat of his own, he was in demand by classmates who needed an experienced man as crew in the regattas that took
place in New Haven harbor. One boat-owning classmate, who wanted to sail
up the coast to New London after graduation to watch the Yale-Harvard
races on the Thames, invited Bingham to come along as crew.

A good breeze brought them by mid-afternoon to New London harbor
where they anchored, as it happened, just off the Mitchells' beach. Hiram
had his friend row him ashore. He made his way over the dunes to Pequot
Avenue and rang the bell at the Mitchells' gate. He found Mrs. Mitchell all
alone with an elaborate tea spread, her daughters and their guests not yet
returned from a golf game. She was delighted to have the polite young man
fill in for them. Then when it turned out that one of her male house guests
would not be back for dinner because he had won a yacht race and had to
attend a dinner at the local yacht club, young Bingham was invited to take his
place. Apparently Mrs. Mitchell was charmed by him, and for the first time
Alfreda gave him favorable notice in her diary: "We enjoy Hiram immensely."

But it seems Hiram was again more attracted to Charly, and the day after
the races it was Charly whom he invited to New Haven for the Yale-Harvard
baseball game that followed the New London boat races.

Alfreda was still pining for Dr. Dane. She tried to comfort herself with
writing poetry. A poem entitled "Duty" began with these lines:

I have not the grace that I had once of yore,
  The facility to write down my thoughts.
The spring of my love floweth no more,
  And therefore my verses are nought.

My mind is as full, my soul is as clear
  But my heart was the source of their flow,
And my heart is deserted, lonely and drear;
  It contains but mind-images now.

She tried to reassure herself that Truth and Beauty were still at hand
even if she had to wait for Love. Thoughts of Jack Dane still obsessed her; his
image inspired verses in French and in German. Her parents, alarmed at her
obvious depression, decided to take her traveling again, this time on the
longest journey yet, across Canada and the Pacific to the Far East. As she was

leaving home, she confided to her diary that she was still "unchanged," adding mournfully: "I long for what I leave behind. Behut ihm Gott! Ich habe geliebt und belebet." (God protect him! I have loved and lived.)

Finally she decided to put an end to an obviously hopeless fantasy. Perhaps if she told her mother the whole story, it would help. Perhaps if she wrote "him" a final farewell, she could make a clean break.

In San Francisco on November 14, 1898, she wrote in her diary: "I tell Mamma, but not all. I should feel much better if I opened my heart to her." The next day: "I write my letter. Am very happy." Four days later she sailed for Hawaii on the *Archer*, a partially square-rigged barkentine her father had chartered for the first leg across the Pacific.

It was a sentimental journey for him, recalling his early trips by sailing ship. For Alfreda it filled her romantic soul with new hope.

> *Glide, glide, glide, ever onwards go*
> *Towards the setting sun, the sunset glow,*
> *On, on, on, from East towards the West*
> *To where the clime is soft and sweet winds blow,*
> *To where the kindred souls of summer rest,*
> *Where in eternal springtime flowers grow.*
> *Nearer, nearer, nearer, towards the sinking light*
> *Steer her to where the sun dips into the sea,*
> *For slowly o'erwhelms us the soft night*
> *Of balmy tropic breeze and sweet tranquillity.*
>
> *Sweet, sweet, sweet is this soft balmy air*
> *Coming from ocean deserts wondrous far,*
> *Breezes that bring us nearer to that hour,*
> *When we again may tread that island shore,*
> *When we may live in Paradise so fair.*
> *And should you there be welcomed by a kindred soul*
> *Meet it with all your heart for God hath sent it thee.*
> *God leads your ways, and love is wonderful,*
> *Which he sends to men's lives eternally,*
> *Granting a sight of heaven from our planet here.*

When she wrote of "kindred souls of summer," was she thinking of more than one? The Thanksgiving party when she had met Baldwins, Cookes, and Judds—Yale students from Hawaii—may have been in her mind, but that had been two years ago, and it was only the "1 Bingham" who had visited in New London the following summer. In her second verse, only one "kindred soul" comes to mind. And it was Hiram Bingham who came to call at the Mitchells' Waikiki beach cottage soon after they had moved in. He had read in the *Advertiser* of the arrival on the Honolulu waterfront of the brigantine *Archer*.

106

CHRONICLE IV
Child of Mission

CHAPTER 10
A High Calling

For the six years that young Hiram III worked his way through Andover and Yale, he wrote letters faithfully to his parents, who just as faithfully preserved them. His father also kept copies of many of his own letters to his son. Together they tell the story of the boy's ordeal. He not only had to struggle with a continual shortage of money, even for barest necessities, but he also had to cope with his demanding conscience in a never-ending effort to meet his father's expectations that he would devote his life to God and carry on the work of saving heathen souls.

The first year at Andover was Hiram's hardest. He had to repeat his junior year—a good academic record in the little school out in the Pacific was not enough to meet Andover's more rigorous standards. His education savings only paid for the year's tuition and a room, and he had to earn his board by working five hours a day as a kitchen helper in a student boarding house. On one occasion the boarding-house proprietor scolded him for not getting up at 5:30 in the morning to make the ice cream for Sunday dinner. His dormitory room was unheated, and after his father finally sent him money to buy a stove, coal smoke often filled the room. In his first January at Andover, even with the stove, he wrote that he could raise the temperature in his room only to 53 degrees. He wanted to play football and sing in the glee club, but the cost of football clothes and a dress suit were out of reach. He tried to raise money by selling candy, and for a while reported that he was making thirty cents a day. He answered advertisements for salesmen and was intrigued by an offer of a 50 percent commission for selling plaster casts of famous sculptures.

Eventually he found the best way to earn money was by private tutoring of wealthier but duller boys, and in time he earned enough by this method to pay most of his expenses through Andover and Yale. This tutoring suggested teaching as a potential means of livelihood, if not a path to riches.

In any case his conscience did not let him dwell on material wealth. The state of his soul in his parents' eyes and in his own was far more important. In the spring of his second year at Andover, he attended a national convention of the Student Volunteer Movement, a nondenominational religious organization that had grown out of the late-nineteenth-century religious revivalism of Dwight L. Moody. There young Hiram's sometimes flagging piety was given a new impetus. He was ready, even eager, to become a missionary.

"I have been led to consecrate myself anew to the service of my Master," he wrote his father. "It is my purpose to save souls for Christ." His father, back in Honolulu with his Bible coming off the press, was delighted, yet not without some misgivings. He feared young Hiram was being exposed to the new theological liberalism, and warned him against the "higher criticism." Hiram had visited the Andover Theological Seminary where both his father and grandfather had studied and had found its fundamentalism unattractive.

All through his four years at Yale, the battle continued between the allurements of this world and his parents' expectations of a life of piety. As well as tutoring "rich men's sons" at a dollar an hour, he worked at summer jobs such as peddling books door to door. His social ambitions were gratified when he was able to pledge the fraternity of his choice. His parents' strictures against dancing, which had prevented him from feeling "in it" during his Andover years, finally gave way; he wrote his mother begging her forgiveness but arguing that courtesy and consideration for his hostess at the parties he attended required him to join in the entertainment provided.

He had early become aware that social success at school and college depended heavily on athletic prowess. He failed to make any team and had to recognize that his tall thin frame—he was six feet two and a half inches when he entered Yale and six feet four when he left—was not adapted to football. "I am not built for athletics," he wrote. He took up tennis, arguing that it was "good for me."

Debating at that time was much admired; interscholastic and intercollegiate contests attracted almost as much attention as major sports events. When Hiram led a Yale debating team in defeating Harvard for the first time, he at last achieved the recognition he craved, and with it came a new self-confidence. All his life he felt at home on a public platform, and the ability to argue either side of a question at issue proved useful at a number of critical moments in his life.

Academic excellence was perhaps not at the top of his list of priorities, and to his later expressed regret, he did not win a Phi Beta Kappa key. Nor was he "tapped" for one of the Yale senior societies that would have symbolized success. Yet he always viewed his years at Yale with nostalgic affection. For him they were, in the words of the Yale hymn he sang in the Glee Club, "bright college years, the shortest gladdest years of life." His narrow Honolulu background was far away, and a new world was beckoning.

At the same time, with continual prodding from his parents, he remained faithful to his cultivation of things of the spirit. He sang in the college choir at the daily chapel services and was active in the student YMCA and in the campus religious activities centered in Dwight Hall. He joined the Yale Volunteer Band, a group interested in the foreign mission field. By the end of his college years, he was still fervent in his commitment to a life of religious dedication.

In Hiram's own words in one of his many letters to his father, he felt "a strong call to be a medical missionary in China." It was his "purpose to save souls for Christ.... My motto is, What would God have me to do?...O father, pray for me that I may be kept by the power of the Holy Spirit from all unrighteousness. I do so want to do His will." His plans began to take shape. "I long to get home and begin with you my work of theological Bible study."

He knew his father wanted him to attend a theological seminary, but except for one college vacation, he had not been home for six years. Moreover, he was acutely aware of his lack of money. He compromised by returning to Hawaii and taking a job in a "home mission" settlement house, as pastor of the Palama Chapel in the slums of downtown Honolulu, while starting theological studies with his father at home.

Six months later, all thoughts of giving his life to save the souls of the heathen were abandoned. Life had brighter adventures to offer than his parents' dreary piety and the noisome drudgery of work in the world's slums. The opportunity for escape suddenly opened up.

CHAPTER 11
New Horizons

The arrival of the barkentine *Archer* in Honolulu harbor on December 3, 1898, two weeks out of San Francisco, with the Alfred Mitchell family aboard, signaled a turning point in Hiram Bingham's life.

Two days after their arrival, when young Hiram Bingham called on them at their Waikiki beach cottage, Alfreda was poised for romance. As a Yale student, Hiram had twice been invited to house parties at the Mitchell home in New London, along with other sons of missionary families whom Alfred Mitchell had known from his early years in Hawaii. Himself a freethinking Darwinian, Mitchell was no admirer of missionaries. Undoubtedly, however, he had felt young men of such a background—particularly a Baldwin or a Judd, who were two generations removed from their missionary past—might be suitable for his marriageable daughters. But now it was young Bingham who had come to call.

Thereafter events moved swiftly. Alfreda's diary mentions long walks and horseback rides together. She played her violin in a Christmas concert he arranged at the settlement house. She even tried her hand at "drilling" a group of "native" girls in the Palama school. She prevailed on her father to provide a picnic on the beach for a group of Hiram's slum children. By New Year's Eve Hiram was "confiding" in her, telling her of his growing alienation from the fundamentalist beliefs of his parents, his growing doubt about being called to the life of a missionary. He talked with her about other possible careers.

By February she was writing her cousin and closest friend, Louis Tiffany's daughter May-May, about the wonderfully dedicated young man of God, who had ahead of him two more years of study in a seminary before being ordained as a clergyman and taking up the work of a missionary. Could she conscientiously "encourage this youth's love (which I am sure is there)"? Was she not too "worldly" for him? Her father was "cross" and wanted to take her off and continue on their planned visit to Japan.

By the middle of April, when the Mitchell family, covered with leis, moved away from the Honolulu pier on the deck of the steamer *Doric*, Hiram and Alfreda were deeply in love and pledged to each other. It was not a formal engagement. Neither the Mitchells nor Hiram's parents were ready to give their consent. Ironically, since he had been in a similar position, Alfreda's father saw Hiram as a young man of no prospects, probably more interested in his daughter's presumed wealth than in her. The Binghams feared for their son's soul. No doubt both families hoped that time and distance would end the romance. It was a fond hope.

For Hiram his whole life's pattern had suddenly changed. The fundamentalist religious beliefs of his parents, already seriously undermined by his college years, had lost all appeal. The strain of living under the Bingham roof, the uncongenial demands of the settlement house, and his mounting revulsion at the prospect of a life of poverty and sacrifice had made him desperate for an escape. It had come in the shape of a loving, ingenuous young woman from what appeared to the provincial young man as the glittering world of wealth and social position. And he was in love.

He resigned his job at the Palama Mission, giving poor health—a persistent throat infection had affected his voice—as the reason. Actually he felt he had to get out from under his parents' influence to think through how he could make good the escape that now seemed possible. He could not expect the Mitchells to let him marry their daughter even if he gave up the missionary career, so long as he was penniless, unemployed, and with no prospects.

A first requirement was to get another job. Some of the missionary families whose younger members he had known in school and college—the Baldwins and Cookes, for example—were building fortunes in sugar. With Hiram's contacts he had little difficulty in being hired by the American Sugar Company, then developing new cane plantations on the island of Molokai. Naturally enough, in these islands where natives did the manual work, his was a white-collar job: having a college degree, he was employed as a "chemist" to test the salinity of subsurface water in the cane fields.

This, he knew, was only a stopgap. He was not ready to seek his fortune in sugar or any other business. Yet years of penny-pinching, coupled with his brief glimpse of the glamorous world of wealth and high society, had given him a strong sense of the value of money, of what it would buy and the power it conferred. He could hardly know at this stage whether marriage to the Tiffany heiress would automatically provide the affluence he craved. It was part of the American tradition that sons even of wealthy parents should make their own way without help. And he was too proud to seek a life of ease at someone else's expense. In any case, Mr. Mitchell had not been encouraging. And Hiram, for all his rejection of a religious calling, had not given up the idea of serving humanity.

Teaching as a career appealed to him. Individual tutoring had been his chief source of income as he worked his way through school and college. College teaching not only offered a means of livelihood but also afforded opportunities for research in new fields of knowledge that might satisfy his inborn craving for exploration of the unknown.

He found it not too difficult to decide to return to the mainland and go on with his education. His father had wanted him to go to a theological seminary either in California or in the East. He knew by this time that theology was not for him, but he could not decide on an alternative field of study.

The Yale professor most responsible for his intellectual emancipation was William Graham Sumner, prophet of the new "science of society." In "sociology" Hiram saw a fascinating new field for exploration. Astronomy also attracted him. If the Bible story of creation was no longer to be taken literally, then how had the planet Earth come to occupy its place in the cosmos? And if the purpose of human life was not to glorify God in the hope of Heaven, then what was its function? Moreover, in talking over his future with Alfreda, he had found that astronomy appealed to her romantic interest in Nature.

In August 1899, just a year after his return home from college, he gave up his job on the sugar plantation, and with his four months' earnings there, and with what he had saved from his settlement house salary and from his college earnings, he bought passage on a ship for California. He let his parents believe that he had found the tropical climate debilitating and that he wanted to get on with the advanced studies for his life's work. He mentioned his new interest in sociology and astronomy, but he had too much heart to tell his father outright that he had given up all thought of studying for the ministry. His father gave him a letter of introduction to a professor of theology at the Pacific Theological Seminary in Berkeley.

Once in San Francisco, young Hiram had no intention of going to the seminary. But he was beset by indecision. He consulted a doctor and was advised that his eyes were not up to a life at the eyepiece of a telescope, but that his general health was good. The choice of a career was wide open. He was not even sure he wanted to be a student again. He considered journalism as a possible career that did not require graduate study. A job in a business would have the same advantage.

Too much freedom can be painful. He had not wholly cut the cord that bound him to his parents, and he wrote his father seeking advice:

Please answer these questions as soon as you can.
(1) Would you prefer a business career for me to a Prof. of Political Economy?
(2) My health being good, what would you say to (a) Forestry? (b) Agricultural Chemistry? (c) Business? (d) Sociology?

Before his father could reply, he had opted for sociology, and enrolled in the University of California graduate department of history, sociology, and political economy, as a candidate for a master's degree. The head of the department, Bernard Moses, persuaded him to switch to history. And there at length the decision lay.

His parents were desolate. What had happened to all his early pledges of consecrating his life to the service of the Lord? Hiram only made matters worse when he wrote that his love for Alfreda was now the "major premise" of his life. He asked his father to forgive him:

You and my precious mother have taught me faithfully and lovingly as you have believed. I thank God for you and ask him each day to bless and keep you. All that I am today I owe to you and my heart is full of love for you. And yet I feel that *She* has her first claim on me, for Her love is life to me and my life is love for Her.

Those capitalized pronouns must have seemed almost blasphemous to the old theologian. In anguish he wrote his son again.

The greatest force in a man's life should be supreme love to *Jesus*, supreme loyalty to the Saviour of the world. If such loyalty is controlling all your life, I have nothing to fear for you. If it is not, I have everything to fear for you.

He hinted at the "everlasting fire" that awaited any whose "first premise" was not to "love the Lord thy God."

If his father was distressed at the choice his son had made, his future father-in-law began to look on him more favorably. Alfreda's mother even let it be known that if Hiram earned his M.A., he might indeed be able to have his "A.M."

With this incentive Hiram buckled to the task of winning a master's degree in history in a year. In addition to his courses, he would have to produce a thesis. He took as his subject "The Growth of American Supremacy in Hawaii," a subject he knew a good deal about. The saga of the American missionaries' role was ever present in his childhood. His school days had been spent under the flag of the Hawaiian monarchy, but he could hardly have failed to observe that Americans dominated the political and economic life of the islands. A revolution led by a small group of foreigners, mostly of

American descent, had ended the monarchy while he was at Andover, and his return to Honolulu the year before had coincided with America's annexation of Hawaii as a consequence of its war with Spain.

His finished thesis was a respectable two hundred pages. It covered the history of the islands from their discovery to their annexation. He made good use of his sources, but there were hardly enough footnotes to satisfy the usual standards of scholarly writing. Such references as he had were often to entire chapters rather than pages. In fact he had copied a number of long passages without the use of quotation marks. Still it was a solid piece of work, his plagiarisms were not detected, and the thesis was approved by his professors.

By the time he had completed the requirements for the degree in May, Hiram had decided on his future course. He would become a professor of history, specializing in the history of South America. His study of American dominance in Hawaii made him aware of the convergence of religious and commercial interests that had extended American power into the Pacific. He had seen American soldiers on their way to the Philippines marching through Honolulu streets. The Spanish-American War, which had formed a backdrop to his last year in college (his roommate had enlisted even before graduation), had resulted in America's acquisition of Puerto Rico and the occupation of Cuba, and the Caribbean was now an American lake. But this was only an extension of the Monroe Doctrine, which had long asserted the primacy of the United States in the Western Hemisphere. With the annexation of Hawaii and the occupation of the Philippines, the United States was moving toward primacy in the Pacific.

Once the era of American imperialism had begun, it seemed inevitable that South America, whose settlement and economic development had been left to Europeans, would become of primary interest to Americans. Professor Moses believed that South American history would be an important new field in university classrooms and persuaded Hiram that he could hope for rapid academic advancement as an early specialist in that field.

The tall, handsome young man from Honolulu evidently made a favorable impression on Professor Moses. Halfway through the academic year, he brought Hiram to the attention of the president of the university, Benjamin Ide Wheeler. Hiram was invited to the president's house for dinner and later took charge of a class President Wheeler was teaching on "ancient Greek institutions" while Wheeler was away attending a conference. For a graduate student to substitute for the president of the university in this way was sufficiently unusual to be noted in the San Francisco *Call*. During that winter he gave a series of lectures at the university's extension program in San Francisco, using material from his master's thesis on Hawaiian history, and this also received publicity in the press.

Young Bingham early recognized the advantages of knowing important people, whether college professors or presidents, and of getting his name in the paper. He sent clippings about these events to his parents and to Alfreda.

He also sent clippings from the society pages, of which he no doubt was equally proud. But his father, already near despair over his religious backsliding, was further distressed by these reports of "worldly gaieties."

Young Hiram's personal life was indeed undergoing a sea change. The rigid pattern of self-denying piety, already undermined by secular influences at Yale, had been shattered by the Mitchell family's visit to Hawaii. At Berkeley he felt free for the first time to enjoy life. He was living in the home of a history professor where he had obtained lodging in return for doing household chores. Professor Bacon and his wife took pity on the awkward young man from Honolulu and encouraged him to take advantage of the cultural and social life of the Bay area; they were young enough and well enough connected to introduce him to at least the fringes of the glamorous world he longed for.

In college he had obeyed his parents' strictures against card playing and dancing as well as alcohol and tobacco, although he had begun breaking the rule against dancing at the Mitchell house parties. At Berkeley the lid was off. He joined dance clubs and was invited to parties. A society editor included his name among the "most popular men" at the first gathering of a club known as La Jeunesse Cotillion, and on one occasion he even led one of the dances. His Yale fraternity connection gave him acceptance in Berkeley campus organizations. He took part in student theatricals and wrote a farce about a football team of giant Vassar girls that was presented as a "curtain raiser" at a benefit show at the San Francisco Opera House. It was no wonder that his father feared for his soul.

Despite his ebullient social life, Hiram completed the requirements for a master's degree by the beginning of May. Professor Moses had recommended that he go on to work for a doctorate at Harvard and gave him the necessary credentials. Without waiting to receive his new diploma at commencement, he took the first train he could for the East Coast to present his credentials at Harvard and—what must have seemed at the time far more important—to claim his "A. M."

It had been over a year since Alfreda's parents had taken her with them to Japan. On their return trip across the Pacific, the Mitchells had sailed by the northern route, thus avoiding Honolulu, and had reached their Connecticut home by way of Canada. But separation had not lessened the young couple's romantic attachment. In February 1900, Alfreda noted in her diary the arrival of "a little ring." The "little" no doubt reflected the slimness of Hiram's purse. But she was joyful and reassured.

A stream of letters went back and forth, keeping their images bright in each other's mind's eyes. The images were, to be sure, in important respects unrealistic. Alfreda saw Hiram as the young man of God who had given up his calling to the ministry out of love for her but was no less dedicated to the service of humankind. For him, the four months of his Hawaiian courtship

The Reverend Hiram Bingham I and his wife Sybil Moseley Bingham, by Samuel F. B. Morse, 1819. (Courtesy of Yale University Art Gallery.)

The Reverend Hiram Bingham II and his wife Minerva Clarissa Brewster Bingham, Boston, 1866.

The completion of Hiram Bingham II's translation of the Bible into Gilbertese, April 1890. Seated left, the Reverend Hiram Bingham II; seated center, Moses Kaure, Gilbertese interpreter. Hiram Bingham III stands behind Kaure.

Nathaniel Shaw Woodbridge (1771-1797) with his daughter Mary, painted after his early death by Ralph Earle. Woodbridge was Alfred Mitchell's grandfather.

Charles Tiffany, seated center, with his wife Harriet Young Tiffany and family.
From left: son Louis Comfort Tiffany, daughter Annie Tiffany Mitchell, Louis's
second wife Louise Knox Tiffany, and Annie's husband Alfred Mitchell. In
Louis Tiffany's apartment on Seventy-second Street, New York.

Founder of Tiffany & Co., Charles
Tiffany with his granddaughter
Alfreda Mitchell, 1877.

From left: the retired missionary Hiram Bingham II, his wife Clara, his son Hiram Bingham III, and his sisters Elizabeth and Lydia on the steps of "Gilbertinia," Honolulu.

Above: Alfred Mitchell, about 1870.

Left: Mary "May" Woodbridge Goddard, cousin of Alfred Mitchell, close friend of Annie Olivia Tiffany, and first wife of Louis Comfort Tiffany.

Alfred Mitchell paddles an outrigger canoe with his daughters Alfreda and Charly, at Waikiki, 1886.

Annie Tiffany Mitchell, on the veranda of "Sans Souci," a cottage overlooking Waikiki beach, 1886.

Alfred Mitchell at home in New London, Connecticut, in the 1890s with, right, his wife Annie Tiffany Mitchell and daughters Alfreda and Charly.

Annie Tiffany Mitchell, in the music room of her recently enlarged New London home, about 1885.

Annie Olivia Tiffany Mitchell, center, and her daughters Alfreda and Charly, about 1890.

Above: Alfreda Mitchell studied the violin in Europe and played chamber music throughout her life, 1893.

Right: Hiram Bingham III on the Yale debating team, 1897.

had inevitably altered his first impression of her as the glamorous product of wealth and high society. She was shy and unsophisticated. But her sweetness and gentleness, so beautifully expressed in her violin playing, more than made up for her evident immaturity, and her social position was no less real.

After their reunion in New London in May a year later, a first step was for Hiram to win the Mitchells' consent to their marriage. He did not feel it necessary to have his own parents' consent. In any case, Alfreda's letters during the past year had gradually melted their resistance. Her cause had been supported by Hiram's Aunt Lydia, whose romantic soul had been sufficiently stirred to tell Alfreda of an early love of hers: "When I was just your age, I loved very ardently the man who sought my love, but there was a sad drawback to my happiness; he was not a Christian, and joy ended in sorrow." Her confession may have been meant as a warning, for Alfreda was not a member of a church. She had promised Hiram's mother early in the engagement, "When the time comes and I can speak for myself independently, I will with joy and great willingness become a member of the church; my faith is strong and large enough to make me think I can do such a thing." Her profession of faith, such as it was, gave Hiram's parents "exceeding joy," though the elder Hiram urged her to confront her father immediately.

The big stumbling block for the Mitchells was how the young man, still studying for a career, could possibly support a wife, much less give Alfreda the material amenities to which she was accustomed. According to the old New England ethic, a man should not marry until he is able to provide for a family. Mr. Mitchell, to be sure, could not in good conscience insist on that, for he had married the daughter of Charles Tiffany when his own financial assets and prospects were of the slightest, and the employment he had secured to please his father-in-law only lasted a few months before he settled into a life of cultivated leisure.

Annie Mitchell, on the other hand, had good cause to be concerned at the prospect of her daughter having to wait. She would soon be twenty-six years old. She had always lived with her parents, except for the experimental and carefully chaperoned winter in a New York apartment. Such an upbringing had inevitably enhanced her natural shyness and a tendency to withdraw into depression. The Mitchells could not help but wonder whether she would ever find a more suitable husband.

Just what understanding was reached between them and Hiram is not clear, but Alfreda was assured of an allowance that would amply take care of her needs. Hiram took the train to Cambridge and enrolled as a graduate student, confident that if he did not have to support a family, he could pay his own way from his savings and with what he could earn by part-time teaching. Three weeks after his reunion with Alfreda, their engagement was announced.

A round of visits and parties followed at which Hiram was introduced to Mitchell relatives and friends. He then returned briefly to Honolulu to visit his ailing and querulous parents. As his worldly course was clearly set, they began to feel that their only remaining hope for his religious salvation lay with Alfreda.

Back in New England, Hiram started his graduate studies at Harvard, and a date was set for a wedding. Alfreda and her mother traveled to Cambridge to find what Mrs. Mitchell felt would be a suitable home for her daughter, and they arranged for the rental of a house.

On November 20, 1900, the couple was married in a small and decorous ceremony at the Mitchells' New London home. Timothy Dwight, president of Yale, officiated. The day before had been Hiram's birthday, so on their wedding day he and Alfreda were both twenty-five.

CHRONICLE V

The Tiffany Fortune

CHAPTER 12

Inventory

When Charles Tiffany died on February 19, 1902, three days after his ninetieth birthday, he was referred to in the obituaries as a philanthropist. His philanthropies had always been modest and unpublicized, and the designation was only the conventionally polite way of saying that he was believed to be very rich. But how rich?

One biographer, Joseph Purtell in *The Tiffany Touch,* estimated his estate at thirty-five million dollars. Records of the New York Surrogate Court indicate that when his will was probated his executors filed an inventory amounting to only $6,542,096.55. But this was of personal property only, and did not include any of Mr. Tiffany's real estate holdings. Nor did it include the value of his 679 shares of Tiffany & Co. stock, which was treated as if it were tangible personal property not expected to appear in a cash account. A value was, however, given in a later report to the New York state tax authorities, where it was estimated at $4,000 a share.

If the Tiffany shares are added to the items of personal property, we get a tabulation like this:

679 shares of Tiffany & Co. stock	$2,716,000
50 issues of other stocks	1,102,000
88 issues of corporate bonds	2,573,444
9 issues of federal, state, and municipal bonds	1,433,700
cash, receivables, and bank deposits	1,121,000
personal property	9,000
	$8,955,144

While the tangible personal property was probably undervalued, Tiffany was never a collector of paintings, gems, or other valuables, and always remained a man of relatively simple tastes. Real estate, not listed in the inventory, would have added at least a million dollars to the value of his estate. The principal holding was the monumental "house" containing three apartments at Madison Avenue and Seventy-second Street, which he had allowed his son Louis and architect Stanford White to design and build for him and his married children in the 1880s, but which he never chose to live in. His will provided that it be sold by his executors, and it was bought by his son Louis, himself one of the executors, for $665,000. His younger brother Burnett protested that the price was too low, charging a conflict of interest. But when it was finally sold by Louis in 1929, to be demolished for a modern apartment building, it brought only $450,000.

121

The brownstone house at 255 Madison Avenue, near Thirty-ninth Street, which Mr. Tiffany had bought in 1860, and in which he died, was assessed for tax purposes at $60,000, but was probably worth twice as much. Numerous real estate holdings on upper Fifth Avenue and Amsterdam Avenue were valued in one accounting at $357,000.

Mr. Tiffany also owned a sixty-five-acre summer home at Irvington-on-Hudson, fifteen miles upriver. Adding these real estate holdings to his personal wealth, the Tiffany fortune might fairly be estimated at $11 million. This would not be a vast sum by today's standards, but considering that the dollar was then worth at least ten times as much as today, he died a very rich man.

His rise to millionaire status did not begin in poverty. When he was born in 1812, his father Comfort Tiffany was part owner of one of the largest cotton mills in New England, located on the Quinebaug River in Danielson, Connecticut. When Charles was in his mid-teens, his father was prosperous enough to build his own mill downstream in the neighboring town of Brooklyn; he took Charles out of school to run a company store established as an adjunct of the mill, and the Brooklyn Manufacturing Company was soon renamed Tiffany & Son.

Early in life, then, Charles had substantial if not great wealth behind him, and when in his mid-twenties he left his father's business to go into business for himself in New York, his father staked him. Five hundred dollars was not a large stake, to be sure, but when matched with another five hundred dollars brought in by his partner John B. Young, the son of another Danielson mill owner, it provided the initial capital to establish the new business in stationery and "fancy goods" that opened at 259 Broadway in September 1837 under the name of Tiffany & Young.

The first day's sales amounted to only $4.95, but the two young men held on and the business grew. They took in another partner in 1841, and the firm became Tiffany, Young & Ellis. After the French monarchy was overthrown in 1848, they bought some of the crown jewels, and gold, diamonds, and jewelry became major items in their inventory. In 1853 Tiffany bought out Young and Ellis, and the firm became Tiffany & Co.

In the 1860s the company expanded from retail merchandising into manufacturing. Its silverware factory in Newark employed as many as five hundred people. The company's stamp of "Sterling" was recognized as a standard. But it was jewelry, particularly diamonds, that gave most luster to the name Tiffany. Blatant and showy extravagance was a mark of high society in the post–Civil War period. It was said that Mrs. Belmont's knees might buckle under the weight of the diamonds she wore to a ball.

Charles Tiffany could be a flamboyant promoter, as when he sold polished bits of the new Atlantic cable as paperweight souvenirs, or when he teamed up with P. T. Barnum to celebrate the wedding of the midgets Tom Thumb and Lavinia Warren with a magnificent silver horse and carriage.

But he was thoroughly conservative in the way he ran the business, and the ethical standards he imposed on the quality of his wares made the name Tiffany a byword for honest value. And in his personal life, by all accounts, he was upright and hard-working.

Tiffany & Co. remained a partnership until 1868 when it was incorporated. Initial capital was $2,400,000, represented by 2,400 shares with a par value of a thousand dollars each. Of these Charles Tiffany received 1,124, just short of half; an equal number went to Gideon F. Reed, the other major partner, while E. T. Moore and C. T. Cook, who held top management positions, were given the balance, respectively 61 and 91 shares. No shares were offered to the public, and for almost a hundred years the company was closely held among a few families. Charles Tiffany at one time brought his own stock ownership up to over 2,000 of the 2,400 shares. Not traded on any market, the value of the company's shares was never easily determined, but it is clear that by his middle years he was already a multimillionaire.

Meanwhile, along with building a business and making a fortune, he was building a family. In 1841, four years after founding the firm, he married his partner John Young's sister, Harriet Young. She brought an aura of quiet respectability from the Connecticut countryside to their several New York homes. They had five children. The first, named for his father, died in childhood. Annie Olivia, the oldest of the surviving children, was born in 1844, Louis Comfort in 1848, Louise Harriet in 1856, and Burnett Young in 1860. No whiff of scandal ever touched the family until the erratic behavior of their two sons began to cause them anguish.

Louis showed signs of an artistic temperament at an early age, but his father wanted a son who could carry on the business. He once wrote Annie:

> I often think if you had had a twin brother just like you, and he had taken to the jewelry business, why I could have gone bass fishing all summer... You are the smartest girl I ever knew.

But in the nineteenth century, it would have been unthinkable for his daughter, no matter how smart, to go into business. He tried to teach Louis discipline and sent him to a military school, but Louis was very unhappy there, and his father finally let him go abroad to study art. Louis won early recognition as a painter. His father's wealth enabled him to stake out a career in the decorative arts, and he eventually set up his own business, the Tiffany Glass Co., which became the Tiffany Studios.

The name of Louis Comfort Tiffany is far better known today than that of his father, Charles Lewis Tiffany. The stained-glass windows, produced by the Tiffany Studios and a team of artists he assembled, decorate many American churches. Some of those he created for the mansions of the rich in the late 1890s and early 1900s, such as the Mark Twain House in Hartford, may still be seen in their original settings; others have been preserved in museums. The American Wing of the Metropolitan Museum in New York links his creativity with that of his contemporary John LaFarge. "Tiffany lamp" is almost a generic term for any lamp using colored glass to make a lamp shade that glows in daylight as well as by its nighttime iridescence. It was not as a favorite artist but rather as my mother's Uncle Louis that I first became aware of him.

CHAPTER 13
Uncle Louis and Uncle Burnie

When Louis Tiffany married May Goddard, he was marrying his sister Annie's best friend, but May was also a cousin of Alfred. So there was a double tie between the Mitchells and the Tiffanys.

The couple's first child, named Mary Woodbridge Tiffany after her mother, was always known as May-May to distinguish her from her mother May. So May-May was a cousin of Alfreda's on both her mother's and her father's side.

By the time the couple's first child was born, Louis's fame as a painter had already justified his pursuing an artistic career instead of going into his father's business. He took his family abroad to continue his painting in France and North Africa, and it was in France that their second child was born, about the same time as Alfred and Annie's first daughter Alfreda. But to the distress of both families May's infant son lived only a few days.

Louis Tiffany was always a dim and shadowy figure in my childhood. On the few times I may have seen him at my grandparents' house in New London or New Haven, he showed no interest in me. I only gathered in a vague way that he was to be considered an important man. When my mother spoke of him, she seemed to regard him with awe but without affection.

I was once taken by my mother to visit the Tiffany Studios on Madison Avenue, the large showroom and shop where his wares were displayed, the business being quite separate from his father's jewelry store.

I think it was on that occasion that my mother took me for a ride, my first and only ride in a horse-drawn hansom cab. I can still recall the musty stable smell of its cushioned interior, and the little trapdoor over our heads through which my mother could tell the driver up on his seat above and behind us where to go.

I don't know just how or when my mother acquired the various Tiffany lamps that graced the new house on Prospect Street, New Haven, where my first clear memories begin.

A lotus-leaf-patterned lamp in green glass hung like a parasol upside down over the dining room table, where its reflection appeared in the soup plate with which our family evening meal usually began.

Another lamp stood on the floor next to the golden-maple grand piano in the big high-ceilinged living room sometimes called the music room. This bronze standing lamp had a glass mosaic shade of glittering red and orange panels. On my mother's desk in an alcove off the little hallway that led to the library was a small table lamp of bronze and emerald-green glass. Most admired was a decorative but generally useless table lamp in the form of a bunch of lilies—each golden flower with its separate small electric bulb.

The Tiffany Studios were also the source, I believe, of an elaborate but uncomfortable sofa and two easy chairs, upholstered in green and gold silk velvet with a stenciled pattern, all so uncomfortable that they were almost never sat in except on special occasions like Christmas day for the opening of presents.

As the son of a rich man, Louis had always felt able to indulge his rather extravagant tastes. After his father died and he received his inheritance, he engaged in a lavish expenditure on the house of his dreams. This was a Moorish palace built in Cold Spring Harbor on the north shore of Long Island, distinguished by fountains and hanging gardens and a chimney disguised as a minaret. The views from this house appear in some of his stained glass windows. I don't remember ever seeing his house. It burned down shortly after Louis's death in 1933 (and is known only by descriptions, found in various biographies of his life).

I do recall a much more modest winter home he built during his last years in Miami, Florida, on a tract of land within walking distance of my grandmother's home on Brickell Avenue. Like my grandmother's, it was built on a little coral cliff on the shore of Biscayne Bay. Louis wanted a view of the water so his house gave the effect of a tower overlooking the coconut trees. It was roughly circular. A balcony ran around the entire second floor, supported on columns of coconut tree trunks.

Louis's first wife, May Goddard Tiffany—so instrumental in the courtship of Annie Tiffany and Alfred Mitchell—died in 1884 in her late thirties of tuberculosis, another victim of the family disease, leaving three young children—May-May, Hilda, and Charles Lewis II. Louis also outlived his second wife Louise Knox, whom he married in 1886 and who died in 1904. With Louise Knox, Louis Tiffany had three daughters, a set of twins, Louise Comfort and Julia, and Dorothy.

Louis Tiffany's fame was in eclipse in my school and college years, and it was fashionable to sneer slightly at his extravagant tastes. I gathered that my mother's cousin May-May and Louis's other children were angry at their father for squandering their inheritance after his second wife died. And there were other reasons for his family to disapprove of his way of life.

They could not accept his having a female companion in his later years. My mother described her only as his housekeeper. Known as Miss Hanley, she had reddish, golden hair, which seemed to be appropriately matched by her being dressed always in yellow, at Louis's request.

I did once accompany my mother and my grandmother to a luncheon party at Louis's Miami house. The mysterious Miss Hanley in her yellow dress was the gracious hostess. I later learned that she was a trained nurse who had cared for him in an illness after his second wife died. He had fallen in love with her and wanted to marry her, but she felt the hostility of his grown children and chose to remain his housekeeper and devoted companion during his last years.

Louis and his children over time inherited half of the Tiffany fortune, comparable to that of his sister Annie Tiffany Mitchell and her descendants. What happened to his half of the inheritance is not part of my story.

I never heard of his younger brother, my mother's Uncle Burnie, until I was grown up. Then when his name inadvertently came up and I asked about him, my mother quickly pigeonholed him as the family "black sheep," something any family might have but the less said about him the better. Only fourteen years older than my mother, Uncle Burnie was a figure of some ambivalence to her. On the one hand she spoke of him as a kindly man who lived, when she was a girl, on the top floor of the Tiffanys' Madison Avenue house with a collection of small pet animals. On the other hand she implied that he did have to be excluded from the family circle, without saying why.

One clue to this mystery came from a faded photograph in a family album that had belonged to my mother's father Alfred Mitchell, an early camera enthusiast. It was a picture taken in 1892 of a family picnic on the far side of the Pali, the great mountain pass above Honolulu. On one side of the family circle sat Alfreda, a shy seventeen-year-old, looking apprehensively across at her Uncle Burnie, then thirty-one, who, with a wide grin that might be called a leer, was at that moment uncorking a bottle.

Though her father had an amply stocked wine cellar in his New London home, with a particularly fine selection of Madeira wines, Alfreda grew up with an almost pathological fear of anything alcoholic, and I have wondered whether this might have developed from some frightening encounter with her alcoholic uncle.

Burnett Young Tiffany was the probably unwanted child of his father's middle age. To Charles Tiffany, himself a workaholic, managing the store and building his fortune were obviously of greater importance than parenting his dim-witted younger son. Burnie was sent away at a tender age to live in Norwich, under the care and schooling of a family connection, Julia Goddard Piatt, a retired schoolmistress.

In later years he seems to have tried his hand at various jobs, sometimes in his father's store, but never for long. At one time he wrote his father from California that he was considering a job as a stagecoach driver, a plan which

Charles Tiffany promptly vetoed, and he was ordered home to live with his parents.

He obeyed, but one day, in March 1887, he disappeared, and the next day his father received a letter:

My dear father,

You will be much surprised to learn that I was married last evening to Miss Emma Pierson. She is a real nice young lady, with a very charming mother. We will be at the Everett House for the present. I hope you will please call and see me and my wife. I know you will never regret it. She is so kind and good. I hope you will call this evening.

Your aff. son,
B. Y. Tiffany

Whether his father did call is not recorded, but a few days later he wrote an anguished letter to his daughter Annie, then traveling abroad, quoting Burnie's letter and describing his new daughter-in-law as "not bad of the kind, but of the worst kind. They went from a house of prostitution to the house where they were married, both under the influence."

Charles Tiffany was a man of power and wealth. He hired detectives to get the facts, but he could not prevent the yellow press from exploiting the story. He set about trying to undo the damage. He got his son home and shipped him off to Europe with a Tiffany & Co. employee who was about to leave for Russia on a jewel-buying trip. He wanted to get the marriage annulled on the ground that it had not been consummated. But his son and daughter-in-law had lived together for a week. At least he could change his will to make sure that none of his wealth went to the child of a prostitute.

The making of a will is a serious enough undertaking for anyone, and for a man of property like Charles Tiffany, a will affects generations yet to come. As a matter of fact, the will he had signed the previous year, June 30, 1886, was still affecting his descendants a hundred years later. Though he was to live another fifteen years, he never made another will, and the only change was in the form of a codicil dated March 6, 1887, a week after he got the bad news from Burnie.

The 1886 will had already indicated a lack of confidence in his younger son. But it discriminated against him no more than against his younger daughter Louise, unmarried and a semi-invalid. In their father's mind, they were equally incapable of managing a fortune.

Though it ran to ten pages of legal jargon, it was not a complicated will. To his wife Harriet and his two older children, Annie and Louis, he gave $200,000 each and 150 shares of Tiffany & Co. stock (par value $1,000 a share, but probably then worth twice that). His two younger children, Louise Harriet and Burnett, were each to receive comparable portions of his estate, $250,000 and 50 shares of Tiffany stock, but these were to be held by his executors in trust. Though their inheritance would not be fabulously large, still, considering that the dollar was then worth ten times what it is today, their portions were obviously more than enough to keep them in comfort for the rest of their lives. At their death the funds were to go to their "issue," a key if imprecise term, or if they left no issue, then to Annie and Louis or their issue.

Charles Tiffany left his home on Madison Avenue and his country estate at Irvington-on-Hudson to his wife (as it happened, she died in 1897, a few years before Tiffany, so the real estate was included in his general assets).

Most important was the "residuary" clause leaving all the rest of what he owned—and this was bound to be a lot more than all his specific bequests—to be divided between his children. But not equally. Annie and Louis, both of whom were married and had children, were each to get three-eighths, while the trusts for the other two children were to receive one-eighth each.

Charles Tiffany also had reservations about his older son Louis: although already famed as a painter and glass maker, he was inclined to extravagance and had never shown a proper respect for money. Annie, on the other hand, was thought by her father to have good judgment; even her choice of a husband, the impecunious if well-born Alfred Mitchell, had not shaken Mr. Tiffany's admiration for his older daughter.

The changes made by codicil after Burnie's disgrace did not alter the amount of the trust for Burnie's benefit, but it gave the trustees unlimited discretion to limit the amount of the income they were to "apply" for his support. It also provided that no "issue of his present marriage" was to share in the ultimate distribution of the fund. The codicil further stated, in a non-binding clause, that if "his habits do not change, in my opinion $3,000 a year is sufficient for the support of Burnett." Finally the codicil contained the very questionable provision that excess income not needed for Burnie's support was to be paid by the trustees to Louis and Annie. But Louis was one of the trustees and another was Annie's husband, Alfred Mitchell. That last provision would ultimately provide considerable business for lawyers.

During his father's lifetime, Burnie was kept under a tight rein. For four years he lived abroad, but having a propensity for gambling, he was sent only limited sums to live on, and was allowed to come home only after his divorce from Emma Pierson became final. She was undoubtedly paid handsomely for bringing the suit. On his return he was expected to live at home with his parents. Occasionally he was taken traveling with his older sister, Annie Mitchell, and her family, as was the case when he went to Hawaii with them and frightened his niece Alfreda. For a while he worked as a sales clerk in his father's firm, at an annual salary of $750. He seems to have been a kindly man of weak will and little ambition, who made trouble only when he got drunk.

After Charles Tiffany's death in 1902, and after his eccentric will went into effect, Burnie married again. His wife, Lucille Kaufman, was not a prostitute but a recent divorcée, whom he first met at a Madison Square Garden Exposition. The Tiffany family tended to believe that she and her former husband, who was in bankruptcy at the time, had plotted the divorce and the seduction of the presumably rich son of the jewelry tycoon as a means of recovering their solvency. When Lucille Kaufman discovered that Mr. Tiffany's codicil had tied up Burnie's inheritance, she prodded him to try to break the will. In the long litigation that followed, he repeatedly tried to eliminate the trustees' discretion over how much he should get of the income.

Whatever may have been Lucille's original motives, she apparently became fond and protective of her slow-witted second husband. There is no evidence that she diverted any of the Tiffany money to her first husband.

The trustees never did follow Tiffany's suggestion that they limit payments of income for Burnie's support to $3,000 a year. The trust fund after all amounted to over $1,500,000, with an anticipated income of at least $50,000 a year. Alfred Mitchell felt so embarrassed by the discretion that allowed him to enrich his wife and brother-in-law Louis at Burnie's expense that he was at first unwilling to accept his role as a trustee. But he and Louis finally agreed on a compromise, allowing Burnie $21,000 a year, and $16,000 each to Louis and Annie. How much they were influenced in this decision by Burnie's challenge to the will and objections to subsequent trust accountings—legal maneuvers the rest of the family tended to attribute to Lucille—and how much was due to Alfred Mitchell's and Louis Tiffany's conscience is unknowable.

Burnie and Lucille moved to Santa Barbara, California, to the relief of the rest of the family. To live like a Tiffany, however, seemed to impel Burnie and Lucille to extravagance, and Burnie went into bankruptcy. Some of his creditors joined him in his legal assaults on the custodians of the Tiffany fortune.

Later, after Alfred Mitchell's death in 1911, with evidence that Burnie had gotten his drinking under control and was now a "total abstainer," the trustees raised Burnie's allowance to a generous $40,000 a year. And so it remained even through the Great Depression, as Tiffany & Co. continued to pay dividends out of hoarded reserves.

Lucille died in 1927. Burnie went to live in Beverly Hills with her married sister as a well-heeled boarder. There, for the first time since his fall from grace, he was visited by his older sister Annie, then in her eighties. The family rift seems to have been healed—after a fashion.

Burnie lived on until 1945. The Tiffany fortune had sustained him in a lifetime of idleness, but thanks to his father's caution, his share of it was still intact to go to the children and grandchildren of Louis and Annie.

What little property he possessed at his death went to the sister-in-law who had cared for him in his old age.

CHAPTER 14
Spending Father's Money

When Alfred Mitchell, the impecunious and unemployed young man from Connecticut, asked Mr. Tiffany for Annie's hand, the response was anything but enthusiastic. Mitchell had to wait three years and demonstrate that he could get and hold a job before he won the parental consent so essential to becoming a beneficiary of the Tiffany fortune.

Even though the job did not last long, and his son-in-law eventually lapsed into a life of idle traveling, Mr. Tiffany still seems to have been impressed with his sobriety and reliability. Only four years after the Mitchells' marriage, he took a first step toward distributing his wealth by giving Annie fifty shares of his company's stock. And when a few years later, he named Alfred Mitchell an executor and trustee under his will, he demonstrated his growing confidence in his son-in-law. Within a few months of Tiffany's death in 1902, Alfred bought a qualifying share for $4,500 and was elected to the board of directors of Tiffany & Co.

But it is one thing to be trusted with other people's money, and quite another to have a fortune in one's hands without obligation. Annie was too much in love with Alfred to put the brakes on the grandiose ways he soon found for her inheritance to be spent.

It was indeed a lordly inheritance. In addition to the specific legacies of $200,000 and 150 shares of Tiffany stock (then worth at least $675,000 at $4,500 a share), Annie's three-eighths of the residuary estate turned over to her by the executors within the year was, as they reported to the court, $2,796,700. This made a total of $3,671,700, on top of her previous holding of fifty shares, which she now put in Alfred's name.

Even before his father-in-law's death, Alfred had become involved in developing real estate in Salem. He had a strong sentimental attachment to the properties that had once belonged to his Woodbridge and Mumford ancestors. The orphaned Alfred's only childhood home was the Mumford house, where he was taken in by his first cousin, Mary Perkins Goddard, almost twenty years his senior, as a member of her family. Until the Goddards moved to Norwich eight years later, the old colonial mansion was the home to which he came back from boarding schools for vacations. A mile away across the valley he could see the house built for his grandparents, Nat Shaw Woodbridge and Elizabeth Mumford, and in the field below the house the grave markers where they were buried after their brief lives.

Neither the Mumfords nor the Woodbridges had produced any male heirs, and the marginally profitable farms were sold when Alfred was a young man. But after his marriage and his establishment of a home in New London, his interest in the Salem lands, only a two hours' drive from New London, revived. Just before his daughter Alfreda's marriage in November 1900, he bought the old Woodbridge farm, two hundred acres of exhausted crop and pasture land and scrub woodland, including the family cemetery where his grandparents were buried, as well as his grandfather's house, which was in a ruinous condition. What he had in mind to do with the abandoned farm is not clear, but the following summer, when he learned that his daughter was pregnant and that his family had a future, he set about restoring the old house. He undertook to modernize it, putting in running water, bathrooms, and a central heating system. When his daughter, at his urging, named her first-born son Woodbridge instead of the expected Hiram Bingham IV, he put the property in his grandson's name, reserving only a life use for himself.

At this point he had not overreached himself. The farm had cost him only five thousand dollars, and he probably spent a comparable amount for the renovations, which were well within his family's resources at that time. But when his Tiffany father-in-law died and his wife became heir to millions, he let his fancy roam.

Within months of the distribution of the Tiffany estate, he bought the Bailey farm and the Rix farm on the valley floor below the Woodbridge house. The Bailey place had belonged to his literary brother Donald, whose romantic stories about the farm being sold out of the family, published under the name of Ik Marvel, had made *Reveries of a Bachelor* and *Dream Life* popular best-sellers, and led to the house being marked on maps as the "House of the Reveries." The Rix farm was an even more important acquisition since it included the old Mumford house, which had once been home to both Alfred and Donald. Its 312 acres included some of the richest farmland in the area.

Following the precedent established with the Woodbridge farm, Alfred Mitchell deeded the Mumford farm with its 1769 mansion to his second grandchild (reserving a life use not only for himself and his wife but also for his daughter Charly). The Bailey farm and the hundred-acre pasture above it that had been part of the Rix property he gave outright to Alfreda. A couple of years later, in 1905, when she had produced a third grandson and named him Alfred, he rounded out the holdings that had belonged to his grandfather, Nat Shaw Woodbridge, by acquiring the Beebe farm, including most of the rest of the valley floor, and assured the perpetuation of his extended family holdings by putting that farm in his third grandson's name (subject again to his own and his wife's life use).

He was now proprietor of four farms, an almost feudal domain of over two thousand acres. What was he to do with them? He felt he had unlimited funds at his disposal.

Among the family portraits he had been exposed to as a child were portraits of his grandparents, Nat Shaw Woodbridge and Elizabeth Mumford Woodbridge, painted a hundred years earlier by the fashionable portraitist Ralph Earle. It seems likely that he had been impressed by these portraits, done in the style of the English aristocracy, with powdered hair, silks and satins, vast draperies, and background views of an English deer park.

His dream of a great landed estate had no doubt been further prompted by his brother Donald's writing on the beauties of English and French estates, as compared with the slovenliness of American farms. His ideal was further expressed in an English print he hung in the Woodbridge House, entitled *Home from the Honeymoon*; it depicted a handsome young English lord and his beautiful bride arriving in a coach at the gate of his castle park, to the welcome of his household and village tenants.

Farming in Salem, and most of New England, had been in decline through much of the nineteenth century. Unable to compete with the rich soils of the West, many of the remaining farmers at the beginning of the twentieth century were selling their impoverished farms to recent immigrants from Europe. In Salem the newcomers were mostly from Poland; the Zeleznickys, Wlodarczyks, and Swiders had worked in the Pennsylvania steel mills or coal mines till they had enough money to buy a run-down Salem farm. Alfred Mitchell was able to hire gangs of Polish immigrants who needed the cash income to help them develop their own farms.

Within a few years, Alfred Mitchell had transformed his ancestral properties. In addition to restoring the old houses, he added new wings to the Woodbridge and Mumford houses to provide quarters for tenant caretakers. He enlarged the hay barns and cattle sheds. As if to impress his own personal overlordship on the far-flung estate he was creating, he had all the dwelling houses and farm outbuildings painted the same dark red with orange trim that he had adopted for his New London properties.

At the same time, he was improving his acreage. Gangs of laborers cleared the fields and pastures of encroaching brush, repaired fences and old stone walls, restored neglected drainage ditches, and rebuilt depleted soils. The hundreds of acres of second-growth forest land on the hills surrounding his valley he envisioned as park lands. He opened up miles of wood roads, installing stone culverts to cross streams and swampy areas, so he could drive around his estate and through his woods with horse and buggy.

A major undertaking was the clearing of a maple swamp in the center of his best arable land, building a dam a hundred feet long and eight feet high across the brook that drained it, and creating a scenic lake as the centerpiece of an idyllic landscape.

Then to have a better view of the landscape he was reshaping, Alfred Mitchell indulged himself in the most extravagant whim yet. He had taken his family to Japan in 1899 after traditional Japanese architecture won his admiration. He conceived the idea of erecting a Japanese tea house at the end of the Woodbridge House garden where the whole of his estate could be viewed to advantage, and where the traditional Japanese tea ceremony could be practiced as the highest expression of the art of cultivated leisure.

There is no indication that Annie, whose inheritance was being spent, in any way disapproved. She had a natural flair for architecture, and the plans for the tea house no less than the remodeling of the old farmhouses must have been shaped in part by her. Her ideas were even more in evidence when the Mitchells went on to build a summer home for their daughter and her children.

It so happened that Alfreda's husband, far from his Honolulu background and craving a reestablishment of his New England roots, fell in with his father-in-law's urge to revive his ancestral home. The Binghams had spent part of the first summer of their married life in a tarpaper cabin near the Woodbridge House, erected as housing for the carpenters who had been renovating the big house. They spent part of their next summer in the newly rehabilitated "House of the Reveries." The Mitchells offered to build them a more permanent summer home on a site they might select. The outcome in 1905 was the building of the "Camp," a quarter mile from the Woodbridge farm complex. Again the Japanese motif of low roofs in a bucolic landscape was dominant, but instead of narrow panels of paper, vast sliding doors of glass panes were installed in ways first developed for their New London house.

By the summer of 1905, Alfred's development of his Salem estate was complete. As a lavish final touch, he published a book about it. With no concern for expense, he had engaged a Norwich genealogist, Mary E. Perkins, to explore his ancestral lines and the history of the Woodbridge and Mumford farms. In the same year the Bingham Camp was built, he brought out the result of her researches in a handsome boxed volume, *Chronicles of a Connecticut Farm.*

A masterpiece of the printers' art, between its marbled covers the book's three hundred pages of handmade paper—interspersed with colored maps, fold-out genealogical charts, and reproductions of family portraits by Ralph Earle and others—recounted the history of the revolutionary confiscation of the original Browne estate, and traced subsequent land sales and transfers, down to and including the building of the Japanese tea house and the Bingham Camp. Only fifty numbered copies were printed, to be distributed to family members and libraries (including those of Yale and Harvard). There is no record of any sales.

In lieu of a publisher's imprint, the title page of the *Chronicles* was annotated: "For Mr. and Mrs. Alfred Mitchell, the present proprietors of the Woodbridge and Mumford Farms—Privately printed. 1905."

But Alfred's urge to make good use of Annie's Tiffany inheritance was far from exhausted by the acquisition and development of the Salem properties—and the publication of a book about them. He turned next to the Caribbean island of Jamaica, whose warm winter climate had first attracted him a few years earlier.

CHAPTER 15
Folly Point

Alfred Mitchell always hated cold weather. The chills of New England winters had entered into his bones in his orphaned boyhood, when he had been shunted between Connecticut relatives and boarding schools. His dropping out of college for reasons of health after brief stays at Amherst and Yale may well be attributed to his inability to tolerate New England weather. His years as a young man in Hawaii doing business with the whaling fleet had given him a love of the tropics. After his marriage, he indulged himself in frequent trips to warmer climes—Florida and southern California, Mexico, Madeira, Spain, Italy, Egypt—sometimes taking his family, sometimes alone or with a male friend.

His first contact with Jamaica was inadvertent. In the winter of 1901, returning from a visit to Bermuda with a friend, his ship was beset by a violent tropical storm. A huge wave swept him off his feet into a stanchion on an upper deck, and he suffered severe injuries, including a broken leg. The next port was Kingston, Jamaica, where he was carried ashore to a hospital. In the course of some weeks recuperating, he fell in love with the island and its respectful British colonial atmosphere.

Two years later, after Charles Tiffany's death, he returned to Jamaica with his wife. They stayed in Port Antonio on the north side of the island where a large new tourist hotel had recently been built, overlooking a beautiful harbor and against the backdrop of a mountain range. The United Fruit Company was at that time promoting tourist travel to the Caribbean, and since the building of the hotel, their passenger steamers and those of the Hamburg-Amerika line were making regular stops at Port Antonio as well as Kingston.

The Mitchells were charmed by the setting and by the refined English families that had settled there. Annie in particular was tired of continual travel in search of winter warmth, and with their new wealth they began thinking of acquiring a permanent winter home.

Across the harbor from the town was a peninsula known as Folly Point, with a lighthouse at its northern tip, otherwise undeveloped except for one or two modest houses. They found a perfect site. From a little rise in the middle of the peninsula, they could look out over the turquoise waters of the Caribbean. There was even a little island, just off the beach to the northeast, to which one could wade at low tide. In the opposite direction, beyond a grove of coconut trees, they could see the harbor and the town with the mountains beyond.

The Mitchells found that a large part of the peninsula could be bought for what in their new affluence was a trifling amount, fourteen hundred English pounds. When they returned north at the end of the winter, they consulted one of New England's leading architectural firms, Chapman and Fraser of Boston, which had recently won critical acclaim for a Mediterranean-style mansion built for Mark Twain in Redding, Connecticut.

The design that emerged, no doubt with Annie's imaginative suggestions, was of an expansive Roman villa, centering in a two-story columned atrium, open to the trade winds and the views of ocean and harbor on both sides. Wings extending out at each end of the central structure included not only spacious bedrooms and a small swimming pool but, beyond the kitchen and servants' quarters, at a lower level under the same roof, a horse stable and carriage house.

The architects recommended a New York construction firm, James Wilkerson & Company, as better able than Jamaican contractors to incorporate some of the more exotic elements the plans called for. The floors in the main part of the house were to be of Portuguese tile. The divided staircase to the second floor was to be of white marble, probably from Vermont. The columns around the atrium and along the wide porches were of moulded crushed marble, manufactured in New York.

The house was built during the winter of 1904–05, under the supervision of Walter Mitchell, the youngest son of Alfred's brother Donald. Alfred's connection with the Tiffany family enabled him to play the role of rich uncle to several of Donald's many children. Donald's effort to maintain a large family on a generous scale out of royalties on his books and fees for lecturing had always been difficult, and he once had to accept direct financial aid from his brother when he could not meet a mortgage payment. Alfred employed both of Donald's grown sons at times, and was able, after the Jamaica house was built, to recommend Walter to Tiffany & Co. as manager of its silverware factory in Newark.

The main structure was of poured concrete. Fifty years later, when the roof had fallen in, local myths grew up about the crumbling ruin, and how the American contractors had used sea water and salt sea sand in mixing the concrete, against the advice of the local workers. In the course of time, the salt leached out of structural elements allowing dampness to reach the reinforcing rods and rust them out. But according to the myths, the building began to crumble at once: when the millionaire jeweler welcomed his child bride to the dream palace he had built for her, it began to disintegrate under her feet; she fled in terror, and he died of a broken heart.

As a matter of fact rather than of legend, Annie Mitchell was a grandmother and not a child bride when the house was completed in the spring of 1905. And the structure outlived Alfred by some years before it began to fall apart. The Mitchells spent the winter months there until his death in 1911.

In the early years after its construction, Alfred Mitchell improved his property and was lavish in his expenditures. Gangs of local people—mostly descendants of African slaves and East Indian contract laborers—worked on developing the grounds. Gardens were laid out with trellised arbors. The most striking of the outbuildings was a pavilion in the form of a little domed Greek temple out on the coral rocks near the lighthouse, where Alfred Mitchell liked to sit and watch the Atlantic rollers crash against the reefs. As in Salem, he laid out roads so he could drive a horse and buggy around his estate.

Occasionally they had guests from the mainland, usually one or another of the Mitchell nieces. Their daughter Alfreda came with her children for lengthy stays while her husband Hiram was in South America exploring, but there was no room for the children in the big house. Instead they were housed in a nearby cottage already on the property. The Mitchells had preserved the old name of Folly Point, and with a touch of irony named their mansion "The Folly." The cottage where the Bingham family stayed was called "Little Folly."

And there some of my earliest memories come in. I remember the roof leaked over my bed at Little Folly. Only a faded photograph reminds me of the celebration of my fourth birthday at The Folly. It was in 1909, when my father was first learning about the Incas in Cuzco. Another photograph shows him on the columned portico of The Folly on his way back from Peru, tanned and handsome, briefly a member of the Mitchell family. I am posed in that picture on my namesake grandfather's lap, looking as uncomfortable as he obviously is at this unwonted intimacy.

Another old photograph reminds me of another minor episode, probably of the same period. In the picture Alfred Mitchell, in his customary impeccable white linen suit, is concentrating on a huge picture puzzle laid out on a card table, while one of his Mitchell nieces looks on. I remember him similarly absorbed, when my nurse brought me over to see him. I watched in timid silence for a while, then spying a piece of the puzzle that would fit in a blank space, I picked it up and put it there. My grandfather was displeased, and my nurse hurried me away in tears, back over the little gully, where the big land crabs scuttled into their holes, to where I belonged at Little Folly.

The great concrete palace by the sea is a forlorn ruin today, a subject for myths, wondered at by tourists. When I last saw it, it was being used for military exercises by the Jamaican army. Various efforts to rehabilitate it as a private or public showcase had failed, and the government had acquired it for nonpayment of taxes.

CHRONICLE VI

Charly's Share

CHAPTER 16

Charly and Fred

Correspondence recently made available at the Yale University Library throws a flood of light on the private life of a very private man, the shy professor known to his intimates as "Fred," ultimately known to the world as Sir James Jeans, mathematician, cosmologist, astrophysicist.

Most revealing is a letter addressed to Mr. Alfred Mitchell in Port Antonio, Jamaica, dated December 17, 1906, and signed simply "Yours, J. H. Jeans." The long letter, sent from Princeton University where he had been teaching for a little over a year, was anything but informal. It was a request to Mr. Mitchell, whom he had almost certainly never met, for the hand of his daughter Charly, whom he had known for almost a year.

Princeton, New Jersey
December 17th, 1906

Dear Mr. Mitchell:

In view of what I am going to ask, I very much wish I was better known to you. To be brief, I have asked your daughter to be my wife, she, to my great happiness, has consented, and I now write to ask for your approval.

Before I can ask this I ought to explain to you something of who and what I am. My present position is that of Professor at Princeton.

You may also wish to know why I left my own country—England—and what my circumstances were there. I believe my family to be of good origin, although I can give no convincing proof of this, even to myself. I mistrust, as you probably would also do, the genealogical researches of the family itself. My father, who is just retiring from his profession, is a Parliamentary journalist. He has not been very successful in life and behind this statement you will be able to read all that is implied, to a man of no private means, by want of success. The rest of his family, although not hopelessly obscure, have never achieved real success or distinction, although his only brother, T. Jeans, is tolerably prominent in London—you will be able to find a list of his activities in the English "Who's Who" if you care.

My reason for leaving England was not want of success —again I will refer you to "Who's Who" for my English career—but a belief that I should have better opportunities here. One of the main interests of my life—the main interest until the beginning of recent events—has been the advancement of my own branch of science, and I hope to do more here than I could at home.

Perhaps, as I feel somewhat on my defense, you will forgive me for saying that I believe I am regarded as in the front rank in this country, as indeed I was in England. I am at the present moment the youngest man who has held a Fellowship in the Royal Society for many years, and I believe that whatever position is possible inside my profession I ought, with favorable circumstances, to be able to attain it. I wish you to see that I have a right to be regarded seriously in this respect. I intensely dislike writing about myself at all, but you naturally expect me to do so, and I think I have a right to tell you of the good as well as the bad.

You will say the main question remains unanswered: "Is the fellow a gentleman, and can he be trusted?" To this I will not attempt an answer, I know you will trust your daughter's judgment. I will only assure you that I love her with my whole nature, through and through, and without reserve, and that I have the supreme happiness of knowing that she loves me. I believe I can make her life happy. I need hardly say that I shall try to do so.

After this explanation, may I repeat my request, will you accept me as your son-in-law?

With sincerest regards to Mrs. Mitchell and yourself,

Yours,

J. H. Jeans

If Jeans did not like his given name, it was as nothing to the aversion with which Charly Mitchell viewed hers. Before her marriage she was "C.T.M." Afterwards she was "C.M.J." Even as a young girl, not wanting to offend the parents who had given her so odd a name, and long before her open revolt against her father, Charly played with acceptable variations on the original, of which "Carlina"—she was then studying Italian—was her favorite.

Charly's mother Annie had already inherited one-quarter of her father's $10-million fortune. Charly, having only one sister, was an heiress of no mean expectations. Yet to her and the young man who wanted to marry her, her prospective wealth was only an embarrassment.

As Jeans wrote to his would-be father-in-law, in the one part of the letter quoted above where his grammar failed him, he was afraid Mr. Mitchell would equate want of financial means with want of success. No wonder he overcame his shyness enough to set forth his extraordinary achievements as a man still in his twenties. Charly no doubt had told him that her father would be hard to please. Mr. Mitchell was descended from the first families of the colonial aristocracy, and even though he himself was penniless when he won Mr. Tiffany's reluctant consent to his marriage with Annie, he would want his own son-in-law to be well-to-do as well as well-born.

Alfred Mitchell was an old man in poor health at the time he received Jeans's letter asking for his daughter's hand. When he had finally married the Tiffany heiress in 1871, he was almost forty, and glad to retire to a life of gentlemanly leisure. After years of traveling with his wife and two daughters, he had finally settled in Jamaica as his home for half of each year, with a base in New London for the remainder.

The collection of Jeans's letters that has been preserved includes only one other letter addressed to Alfred Mitchell, a grateful acknowledgment of Mitchell's no doubt grudging consent. Alfred Mitchell died five years later in 1911, no more reconciled to his English son-in-law than to the other impecunious young man who had married his older daughter. It is doubtful whether he would have accepted them even if he had known that years later one of them would be knighted and the other would become a United States Senator.

Annie Mitchell, on the other hand, did live to see her sons-in-law become famous, and long before that she and Jeans became fast friends. Over fifty of his letters to her were found among her papers at her death thirty years later, and these letters (as well as Charly's to her mother) provide the principal source for understanding his private life during those years.

Charly was a bright and spirited girl, and at the age of seventeen she rebelled against her eccentric father and his eccentric educational theories. With the help of a cousin of her father's, who had been principal of a girls' school, she persuaded him to let her seek admission to Bryn Mawr College, then already in the forefront of higher education for women. After a furious stint of intensive tutoring, having had no previous formal schooling, she won admission to Bryn Mawr in the fall of 1895.

For the next four years she blossomed intellectually and spiritually in the stimulating atmosphere of that center of learning and the women's rights movement.

Nothing could better portray the qualities in Charly that won the passionate devotion of the young Professor Jeans than a letter she wrote her mother shortly before her graduation from Bryn Mawr.

"Dear Mamma," the letter began. (She had been brought up to put a fashionable accent on the second syllable, as if it were Ma-máa.)

> I have been having a most exciting week. Thursday evening we went to Miss President Thomas' reception, and as the young ladies in this college are not very easy on such occasions, Juliet and I had to furnish all the conversation. I evidently made a very good impression on Miss Thomas for I was invited yesterday to lunch with her which is a great triumph for me, or in fact for anyone, as only a very few are ever granted that honour. I met there Mr. and Mrs. Sidney Webb, who are two of the most prominent social and political workers in London, both of them very well known for their books and work as members of the Fabian Society. They spoke this morning on the methods of social and political work and its great necessity in America, and fired us all with much enthusiasm.

She also mentioned another "extremely interesting outside lecturer, the philosopher, William James, who spoke upon what makes human lives significant." Then, remembering her father's connections with Hawaii, which the Webbs were now planning to visit on their travels, she asked if he would provide them with some letters of introduction.

He must have written a caustic reply, for her next letter to her mother, across the top of which she scrawled "Please do not show this letter to Papa," was full of bitterness against him. First she thanked her mother for some Honolulu addresses.

> I think cards will do as well as letters, especially as I hardly know the Webbs. Of course the Honolulu people will not be foolish enough to sneer at people that have an exceedingly high position in London. I hope I may never be myself so narrow-minded as to call this place a "crank-mill," nor so out of touch with youth and change that I shall have no comprehension of the advance from one century or one generation to another.

She went on about her dread of returning home after graduation, where she would have

> no occupation and no end in view or object for which to live. I do not like to look forward to a life of continual lazyness and inactivity. I don't like to think that I am bound down to nothing for the rest of time.

After her graduation, Charly spent eight restless and unhappy years. For a while she lived with her parents, or went traveling with them, but her father, as she had written, seemed to have "absolutely no regard for anything that is really me or any sympathy with youth and ambition." Then her parents let her go to Europe accompanied by an elderly cousin as a chaperone. It seems never to have occurred to her that she might seek a job—even if she had, what suitable employment was available for a graduate of Bryn Mawr?— or that she might develop a career of her own, perhaps a literary one. She found an outlet for her literary bent by writing poetry, later collected and posthumously published by Jeans, poems of loneliness and death, of the sea and the beauty of the iceberg "with gems of rainbow spun," of hope turned to despair and love to cruelty.

Then in 1906 she found a fellow "star-gazer"; her verses spoke of two stars in collision. She wrote a poem entitled "To a Scientist," beginning with the line "From far and humbly let me worship thee." She had met Jeans. She had fallen in love. In ecstasy she found he was in love with her, and she wrote a series of sonnets modestly entitled, when later published, "Old-Fashioned Love." She was no longer alone. In this young man—they were both twenty-nine years old when they met—whom she addressed as "My Beloved Lord," she had found an answer to her ambition: "Thy fame my fame." "Woman's fate" was no longer "abhorred."

Yet if one is to judge by her poems, it was a bittersweet love: "Our hands have clung together during rain," as one sonnet says. And when she wrote that they would "sleep together and forever side by side," she seemed to be thinking as much of a common grave as a marriage bed.

They had met at the home of Charly's married sister. Alfreda, two years older, was the incessant companion of her childhood, but as Charly wrote when she went to Bryn Mawr, "I am not like her, Freda is not ambitious. She has no desires such as I have, naturally she does not fret then against circumstances." Except for one winter in New York with an elderly cousin as chaperone, Alfreda had almost never before her marriage been away from home or traveled without her parents.

Charly called her sister "Id" (no doubt a childhood derivative of "Freda," for it was long before Freud), and in one undated letter written at the time of her sister's engagement to Hiram Bingham in 1900, she reveals some of her hostility and her own related sense of guilt.

> Dear Id—
>
> Your letter heaped coals of fire on my head, for it seemed so absurd for you to be accusing yourself of being a selfish sister when it has always been I who was the selfish and you the sweet and generous one. As for my nature being nobler than yours, that is an absurdity; only it is a very different one. I feel that I have been very disagreeable to everyone ever since I left college, and in fact much longer than that—not because I did not appreciate my surroundings, but because of my disagreeable disposition, I suppose.

She went on to say she was "glad of your happiness" and that she had "always liked Hiram." After Freda was married and settled in Cambridge, Massachusetts, where Hiram was earning his doctorate in history at Harvard and Freda was becoming a full-time mother, the two sisters saw little of each other. I was born, the third son, in February 1905, a few months before the Ph.D. was finally awarded. In September of the same year, my father became a "preceptor in history, politics and economics" at Princeton University, appointed by its president, Woodrow Wilson.

Jeans, a lonely bachelor, arrived at Princeton at the same time. He and Bingham were nearly the same age, both were newcomers, and Jeans soon became an occasional visitor in the large Bingham mansion on Washington Road, which the Mitchells had provided for their daughter.

Just when Charly and "Fred," as he asked her to call him, first met is not clear. Charly was spending part of the winter of 1905–06 in New York with "Aunt Jule," the elderly cousin who had supported her college ambitions. Aunt Jule wrote the Mitchells in Jamaica as early as January 1906 about the attentions of the brilliant young Englishman. Charly began to visit her sister more and more frequently, and in March told Alfreda that she wanted to move to Princeton herself.

"Her ways trouble me," wrote Alfreda in her diary. Maybe it was because "Hi enjoys her." The strain of jealousy ran strong between the two sisters. Alfreda already was pregnant with her fourth child, and Charly was almost thirty, unmarried. Yet when Charly and Fred went walking together unchaperoned, Alfreda commented, "A little too!"

Summer came. The Mitchells were back in their New London home overlooking the harbor, with Alfreda and her children installed next door in the "Umbrella Cottage." Hiram, ever restless and unhappy with his arduous but lowly position as a mere "preceptor," was angling for a better job at his own college, Yale. He was dreaming of distinction, if not fame, as a historical biographer, and having taken Spanish colonial history as his field, he began a biography of Simon Bolivar, liberator of South America, thinking of exploring Bolivar's battlefields as an escape from academia and a growing number of children.

In the fall of 1906, the Binghams were back in Princeton in a big house on Mercer Heights bought for them by the Mitchells. At least Alfreda was back, with her boys—there were now four—with nurses and a staff of servants. But Hiram, having obtained a leave of absence on account of health (he had had a difficult appendectomy earlier in the year), left in November for a hazardous trek through the jungles and over the mountains between Venezuela and Colombia, following the route of Bolivar's army, and he was not to return until the following June.

With her parents in Jamaica, Charly was again spending the fall and winter in New York with Aunt Jule, but Princeton was little more than an hour away by train, and Freda could not deny her hospitality.

The courtship went on. Charly was in poor health, suffering from some nameless infection, and taking heavy doses of a dangerous drug. But by December they were engaged, and both transformed by love.

About the same time that Jeans was formally asking for Charly's hand, Aunt Jule was writing Annie Mitchell from New York:

> Jeans has arrived. Charly came from Princeton yesterday and he came with her, and they are both in a state of cooing bliss. He deliberately kissed her before me and led me to congratulate him—cool as a cucumber. I rub my eyes and look again to see the critical and scoffing Charly very very much in love, and not only unashamed but proud of it. She never looked so pretty or seemed so well as she does now. I think she has found a cure for all her ills and is a very happy woman.
>
> She is utterly and entirely bound up on Jeans. I cannot get used to it, sure as I have been of it ever since last winter. Love has beautified him too, he looks better than I ever saw him, is well dressed and well mannered.

Other letters followed. Aunt Jule admitted she was getting

> quite fond of J.J. myself, though he is quite unlike anybody we had had in the family. I think him very honest and straightforward, ambitious in his work, undeniably clever and entirely modest. He is heels over head in love—and so is Charly. Her doctor was astonished at the great gain she had made in health. So much for the curative power of love.

CHAPTER 17
Guilty Secret

M y grandfather, at least in his old age, seems to have depended heavily on his ancestors. Perhaps he needed them to bolster a low opinion of himself. For most of his life, as I found out many years after his death from a packet of letters preserved by my grandmother, he must have harbored a terrible guilty secret. Had he in his youth committed a sin for which his descendants "unto the third and fourth generation" had to suffer?

Alfred did not make a fortune on the Honolulu waterfront. When he left the islands in 1861 to join the Union Army, his capital was gone. His only acquisition was an infection that was to blight not only much of his own life but also the lives of others who came after him, even to the third generation. Perhaps on some wild night on the town, in the company of his cousins and other young men, he had been tempted by the attractions of a Honolulu brothel. That was his guilty secret.

How many others ever knew it? Surely not my parents. I only learned it myself late in life when my own interest in my ancestry prompted me to rummage through family papers in the Yale Library.

Among them was a letter to Annie Olivia Tiffany dated 1870 from her dearest friend May Goddard. Annie, then twenty-five, was being courted by Alfred Mitchell, and had apparently confided to her friend not only her own growing attraction to Alfred despite the disparity in age but also that she had heard rumors of some dark secret in his past. May obviously adored Alfred who had been like an older brother to her, and she wrote effusively to Annie to pay no attention to any mischievous gossip. May was sure her Uncle Alf had led a blameless life, and she herself would be blissfully happy if her beloved Annie and Alf were to marry.

In due time they were. Alfred's cousin and one-time partner, Gus Williams, from whom the rumor might have come, presumably attended their wedding; with business connections in both New London and Honolulu, Gus Williams was constantly adding to his wealth. By contrast Alfred, reduced for some time to living off relatives, had won Mr. Tiffany's grudging consent to his marrying Annie only after he had struggled desperately to obtain a job, finally finding one in Charleston, South Carolina. There the young couple went to live.

The job lasted only briefly, and my grandfather settled into a life of gracious living, much of it spent in travel. It was an era of male dominance. Though Annie's pet name for Alfred was "Baby," she was quite willing to be ruled by him. Early on he took her on a nostalgic trip to Hawaii. Most of the memories and connections he had in the islands were ones he could share with his delicately nurtured young wife. His indiscretion twenty years before was all but forgotten. Syphilis, like AIDS today, may lie dormant and undetected for years. When Charly eventually learned what her father had done to her before she was born, she came to hate him.

Among the revealing letters I came upon many years later were those written by Fred to his prospective mother-in-law. He had won a grudging approval of his courtship of Charly from her father, and the young couple were engaged and impatient to be married. But Charly had been suffering for some time from a persistent infection, mostly affecting her eyes. The specialists she consulted told her she had congenital syphilis, presumably inherited from her father. Her symptoms grew worse during the winter of 1906–07 while on a visit to her sister in Princeton. The Mitchells were at their winter home in Port Antonio, Jamaica, in the vast concrete palace overlooking the Caribbean.

Fred wrote Mrs. Mitchell of his despair. He was deeply in love with Charly and committed to her, but her doctors now advised that she should wait until all symptoms had disappeared before getting married; if she should get married, she should never have any children—for they might well be defective.

The treatment for syphilis was then a mercury compound. By midwinter Charly had developed new symptoms—extreme depression and nervous prostration—apparently due to mercury poisoning. Fred was at her side almost daily, and reported her progress and his unwavering commitment to her in his letters to her mother.

She improved and was symptom-free by summer. They were married in Salem, in the ancestral house Charly had been given by her father. The ceremony, attended only by a few close relatives of the Mitchells, was strictly private.

It is clear that their marriage, though no one ever said so—and it lasted for thirty years—was blighted before it began. They held off having children for almost five years. When a little girl was born on February 29, 1912, named Olivia after her grandmother Annie Olivia, they watched with anxious eyes for signs of some inherited defect. They had already moved to England where Jeans, relieved of having to earn a living—thanks to Charly's share of the Tiffany inheritance—could devote himself to the research and writing that made him famous.

Charly, always shy, became pathologically retiring as she grew older. Her daughter, my only first cousin, cared for by nannies, grew up to despise her parents. When Charly died in 1934, in her fifties, Olivia did not even attend her mother's funeral. She was briefly married and divorced. She died in 1951 at the age of thirty-eight of anorexia nervosa, starving herself to death, at the home of a lesbian friend.

Sir James escaped the blight, and went on to have a happy second marriage. Long after his death, his second wife confirmed for me the notion I had derived from those old letters of his. The second Lady Jeans told me what her husband had once told her, that the first Lady Jeans had suffered from congenital syphilis, "inherited from her father." Inheritance can only come by way of an infected uterus. So my grandmother must have had the disease. Then how had my mother Alfreda—Charly's older sister—escaped? Presumably the disease was in remission when my grandfather was first married and at the time of my mother's conception. It may well be that neither he nor my grandmother knew—at the time of Charly's birth—of the blight that had been passed on to their second daughter.

I am also inclined to believe that neither of my parents, in their zeal for a eugenically superior family, knew how barely they had escaped pollution. And I would never have known why the old man after whom I was named seemed so morose and ill-tempered, in the few memories I had of him before he died, if I had not been rummaging in old family closets.

Chronicle VII

The Explorer

Chapter 18

Restless in Academe

Young Hiram Bingham was too adventurous and too ambitious to settle down to ordinary domestic life as a Latin American history teacher and work his way up through the usual channels of advancement in an academic community. It was to escape such a humdrum life that he became an explorer. But it was not for lack of trying the more conventional route to the fame he craved.

The first five years of his marriage, 1900 to 1905, were spent at Harvard securing the doctor of philosophy degree without which he knew he could not achieve distinction in the academic world. To earn a doctorate he would have to take a certain number of courses and write a dissertation in an unexplored area of his field. Since Harvard had few resources for the study of South American history, he took courses in European and U.S. history and international law. Soon after beginning his program of study, he was exhorting himself with a quotation he had written in a pocket notebook: "Nine-tenths of all successful achievement in life consists of drudgery."

He had been a student for most of his twenty-five years, and he chafed at the requirements of his course work. Yet he was a voracious reader and had one of the important attributes of the scholar, a dedication to the printed word.

His feeling for books stemmed in part from his family background. His grandfather Hiram I had brought a printing press with him when he came to Hawaii and later had written a much acclaimed history of the "Sandwich Islands" and his mission there. His father Hiram II, in addition to his translation of the Bible into Gilbertese, had produced a Gilbertese-English dictionary, and a number of shorter religious works. Young Hiram III, brought up to think of a book as a sacred object, was determined to be a writer of books himself.

The major gift to his bride on his wedding day was a tiny printed volume in a satin-lined box, inscribed "Aloha—A Mystery. Edition limited to one numbered copy." It contained the story of his courtship in the form of a fable about a "wanderer" and a "vision" written in a stilted style and eked out with an assortment of quotations from romantic love poems.

Within his first year at Harvard, he edited and published a small book entitled *Five Straws Gathered from Revolutionary Fields*. The straws were five letters of American Revolutionary soldiers that he had found in the Harvard Library. The book was beautifully, if rather preciously, printed in an antique style. He had a taste for fine printing and rare books, and soon after coming to Cambridge he joined a club of fellow bibliophiles, the Club of Odd Volumes.

Bingham's principal concern, however, was with books in his own chosen field, the history of South America, and he searched the university library for any relevant material. He made suggestions for the purchase of books, and his active interest led to his being named "Curator of Latin American History and Literature." Little more than an honorary title, it gave him a status in recommending books for purchase. He preserved the official designation even after he had left Harvard and used it to good effect in connection with his first expedition to South America in 1906, when one of the ostensible objectives of that trip was to buy books for the Harvard Library.

Meanwhile he was acquiring a significant library of his own. He loved books of travel and accounts of early explorers and discoverers. Searching the catalogs of dealers in old books, he picked up what he could of South American history. As his knowledge of Spanish was limited, most of what he acquired was in English. When he left Harvard, he gave the library several hundred of the items he had purchased himself, and they were duly acknowledged as a gift from the "Curator."

Hiram's purchase of books was obviously an extravagance. But he and Alfreda had been given five thousand dollars each as a wedding present by her ninety-year-old grandfather, Charles Tiffany, and Hiram decided this could properly be invested in books related to his chosen profession. He did not have to worry about his family living expenses, thanks to the generous allowance Alfreda was given by her parents. His personal expenses and the cost of his tuition as a graduate student were covered for most of his years at Harvard by part-time work as a "teaching fellow" and a "teaching assistant."

Hiram's relative affluence made possible an active social life. Well aware of the value of social contacts in furthering a career, on enrollment at Harvard, he joined the Colonial Club of Cambridge. Before long he was a member of Signet in Cambridge, the St. Botolph Club in Boston, and the University Club and Grolier Club in New York. He bought his clothes with care and dressed meticulously. A crayon portrait made of him at this time by an artist friend depicted him in a smart riding habit and boots, with crop and gloves. His father-in-law had given him a horse, which he rode from New London to Cambridge and kept stabled there. Broad-browed, square-jawed, six feet four inches tall, Hiram Bingham was strikingly handsome. The combination of imposing stature and natural dignity with a boyish charm and respectful modesty could be quite winning, and he was able to make friends of some of his less affluent professors.

Bingham's academic progress inevitably suffered from the multiplicity of his interests and activities. At the end of his second year, with most of his course requirements completed, he failed the oral examination testing his general knowledge of history, and it was not until two years later that he dared try again. Meanwhile he took a year off to pursue his studies alone and begin work on his dissertation—and to travel.

Ever restless, Hiram's trips away from home began early in his life as a family man. Ten weeks after his first child was born, he left wife and baby for a winter holiday on the farm his father-in-law had recently bought in Salem, Connecticut, where he took long hikes, went fishing through the ice, and wrote letters to his "Beloved" about his exploration of the countryside. Two months later, health again seemed the excuse for a brief trip by sea to Cuba and Jamaica. Alfreda and the baby had two maids and a nurse to care for them when he was away from home.

Alfreda accompanied him on his next ocean voyage. They had planned a honeymoon trip abroad for the first summer after their marriage, but Alfreda's pregnancy had intervened. Finally in 1902 they spent the summer traveling in Europe, leaving their six-month-old son Woodbridge with his nurse at the Mitchells.

In London they shopped for furniture for the new home the Mitchells had bought for them. Wanting their daughter to have a settled home of her own, comparable to theirs in comfort and dignity, they bought for Alfreda an old mansion on a secluded street, across from the residence of the treasurer of Harvard University. Actually Alfreda had never much cared for her parents' style of living. One of the happiest periods of her married life was the few weeks she and Hiram had spent during their first summer together in a two-room tarpaper cabin on the Salem farm. There Alfreda had no servant problem and even did some simple cooking, although the evening meal was served in the big farmhouse by the couple her parents employed as caretakers. Whatever her craving for the simple life, Alfreda acceded to her parents' wishes and let them buy the imposing house on Reservoir Street in Cambridge, which the Binghams would occupy rent free. The Mitchells offered to pay for the furniture, as well.

Alfreda had grown up with no experience in handling money. Even the mention of money was considered poor taste. After her marriage, Hiram, who had had to count pennies all his life, found it difficult to teach her how to keep household accounts and balance a checkbook.

Alfred Mitchell, however, kept track of the support his wife was providing the Binghams. During the three years the couple lived on Reservoir Street, it was at the rate of about twelve thousand dollars a year, not counting the rent-free house and six thousand dollars' worth of furniture and furnishings. A full professor's yearly salary at Harvard was then perhaps four thousand dollars, and Hiram was still only a teaching assistant and graduate student.

Hiram's financial dependence on his in-laws irked him. Alfreda, until then always submissive to her father and still torn in her loyalties, came near revolt for the first time and complained that her parents were trying to control their lives, as indeed they were. But Hiram enjoyed his new affluence too much to protest—or to settle down. The Mitchells may have thought to curb his restlessness by giving the family a permanent home, but during the first winter in the Reservoir Street house, the young couple escaped the damp chill of the Cambridge climate by moving to Florida, taking one of their maids and a nurse with them, and spent two months in a rented bungalow in Palm Beach.

In the summer of 1903, after the birth of a second son, Hiram IV, the family moved again, this time to a house on the Mitchells' New London estate where Alfreda's mother could keep an eye on her, while Hiram went by train and ship to Honolulu to visit his parents.

He was horrified by what he found. His mother was dying of a "shaking palsy" (probably Parkinson's disease), from which she had suffered for ten years. Her "beloved" face, as he wrote Alfreda, was wasted to skin and bone, and she was barely able to whisper. His father was ill and distracted by her incessant demands. Both clung in despair to their lost son. All the old conflicts of religion, duty, and ambition were painfully revived, but his independence was then easily justified by the needs of his own family. He did what he could to ease his parents' misery, and on his return he dipped into his new "capital" and sent a trained nurse all the way from Cambridge to Honolulu to give his mother better care and ease his father's burden.

When his mother died a few months later, he did not attempt to make the long journey again to attend her funeral. He felt his father was adequately cared for by a sister, Hiram's Aunt Lydia. But he did arrange to take his father with him on a trip to Scotland the following summer, a trip connected with research for his doctoral dissertation.

The subject of his thesis was a colonization project undertaken by a Scottish trading company in the late 1600s. In colonizing South America, Spain and Portugal had been the great colonial powers, but the English, French, and Dutch had followed. A group of Edinburgh investors felt there was room for a Scottish colonial venture. They organized a company and, after investigating other still unappropriated sites, established a settlement on the north coast of Darien, where the isthmus of Panama joins the continent of South America. The venture proved a failure, Spain moved in, and the site of "New Caledonia" came to be known as Punta Escoces. If he were to dig up the forgotten history of the Scots Darien Company and its settlement, Bingham would have to go to Edinburgh to look for the records of the company.

Again Hiram seemed relieved to escape from home. He found the material he needed for his dissertation, but the trip was not a great success. His aging father, who had spent most of his life in the tropics, suffered in the Edinburgh chill even though it was summer, and his querulousness made young Hiram impatient to get back. The old father-son conflicts had endured.

Later, with his father safely back in Honolulu, Hiram was moved to a final extravagant act of filial piety. He dug into his own limited capital and paid Wilton Lockwood, a distinguished portrait painter who had just painted portraits of Alfreda and her parents, to travel to Honolulu and paint his father. The old man protested but to no avail.

Meanwhile Hiram completed his dissertation, passed his general examination on a second try, and received his Ph.D. The Mitchells, gratified and reassured, made him a present of ten thousand dollars, which he added to his depleted capital.

With his training complete, Bingham was ready to begin the practice of his chosen profession. He had given little consideration to staying at Harvard, nor was he encouraged to apply there by his professors. Yale, on the other hand, had a powerful hold on his affections, and his greatest hope was for a Yale appointment. As a loyal undergraduate he had shared the intense feelings of rivalry between Yale and Harvard that made a holy war out of a football game. Even as a graduate student at Harvard, he felt himself, at least during the football season, in enemy territory, and even attributed some of his academic difficulties to prejudice against him as a Yale man.

He had been in touch with the new president of Yale, Arthur Twining Hadley. Hadley, who was an economist and an expert on the development of railroad systems, was aware of the fact that American capital had ignored South America while British and German investors were building the continent's railroads. He believed that Yale should take the initiative in preparing young men for careers in the economic development of South America and should offer courses in South American history and culture. But the college history faculty, which controlled its own appointments, was not interested; in spite of Hadley's interest, Bingham found Yale closed to him.

In February 1905, Bingham was surprised to get a letter from Woodrow Wilson, the new president of Princeton University, asking him to consider an appointment as a tutor or preceptor in history and politics. Wilson was undertaking a bold experiment that involved establishing a new category in Princeton's teaching hierarchy. He was concerned that traditional lecture courses, which lacked personal contact between professor and student, failed to stimulate students' intellectual growth. The function of the tutor or preceptor would be to encourage students through frequent conferences in intimate groups to take a more active interest in their courses and in intellectual pursuits. To fill the new posts, Wilson was looking for "men of scholarly tastes but still young." Their salary, starting at fifteen hundred dollars a year, would be low, but they would have the rank of assistant professor.

When Bingham accepted an invitation to meet Wilson at lunch in New York, he was captivated by Wilson's idealism and charm, and the bold challenge to established tradition in the projected reform appealed to him. Wilson made him a definite offer, but before he could accept he felt he had to get the Mitchells' approval.

His family now included a third son, Alfred, born in February 1905. Alfred Mitchell may have been pleased to have a grandson named after him, but he was disturbed by the Binghams' proposed move to Princeton, not only because they were leaving the expensive home so recently purchased for them, but because Princeton had once been a refuge for religious fundamentalism. Hiram countered, in a letter to his mother-in-law, that the house on Reservoir Street had been improved and could be sold at a profit and Alfreda had found the Cambridge climate cold and damp and the social life of Cambridge uncongenial. Hiram said, however, that he would not accept the Princeton offer if Mrs. Mitchell disapproved. Then, apparently taking her silence as approval, he went ahead with his plans, found a spacious fifteen-room house to rent near the Princeton campus, and prepared to move his family.

They did not move in at once. One of the attractions of the academic life was its long summer vacations, and Hiram took full advantage of them. The Mitchells wanted their daughter and her family near them in summer, and their properties in New London and Salem offered a wide choice for a summer home.

Alfreda had made use of two of the cottages on the New London estate at times when her husband was abroad. But when he was home they preferred the remoteness of Salem—not so immediately under the eye of the Mitchells. They were given the use of one of the four old farmhouses acquired by Alfred Mitchell as he expanded his Salem holdings.

One of the untenanted houses was offered the Binghams as a permanent summer home in 1904, and they spent a month there in September. But it was too cramped for the growing family, and Hiram kept bumping his head in the low doorways. The Mitchells finally offered to build them a summer home of their own wherever they wished on the newly acquired Salem farmland.

It was an era when wealthy families were building "hunting lodges" in the mountains or lakeside "camps." Annie Mitchell had a talent for architectural design. She and her husband had been charmed by traditional Japanese houses on their travels in the Far East in 1899, and the house they built for the Binghams in 1905 had a distinct Japanese look. A one-story structure of unfinished boards, built around an interior courtyard, with no cellar and no provision for hot water or electric light (electricity did not reach that remote farming community for another twenty years), the house appealed to Alfreda's love of simplicity. Yet despite its simple construction "The Camp," as it came to be called, turned out to be a rather spacious residence. In addition to seven bedrooms and two baths for the family, it contained a large living-dining room with a magnificent view over the Mitchells' farmlands, a kitchen and a pantry, a laundry room, four servants' bedrooms, and a servants' dining room.

There the Binghams spent the summer months of 1905. In preparation for his tutorial role, Hiram read Wilson's *History of the American People*, but he was given a horse to ride, and he took time to help the Mitchells' work force develop a new kitchen garden and a tennis court. The Camp was there-after the Binghams' permanent summer home.

In September, the family moved to Princeton and Hiram took up his first full-time work as a college teacher, with a three-year appointment as precep-tor in history, politics, and economics. For the present he was willing to forgo work in his own field of interest, and he threw himself with enthusiasm into Wilson's experiment.

He soon found his assignment almost impossibly difficult. He guided the reading of only twenty-five students, but some of their courses were as unfamiliar to him as to them. He met with them in small conferences of four or five men at a time, but keeping ahead of them and leading their discus-sions fifteen times a week called for endless hours of preparation. The plan did not require giving examinations or grading his students' work, but he could bar a man from taking an examination if the student had not fulfilled his reading and reporting assignments, which would mean failing the course. Bingham ran into trouble when he attempted to apply this rule to the son of a prominent and wealthy alumnus. Wilson himself summoned Bingham to his office and told him the student must be passed.

Bingham's enthusiasm began to wane, and the pressure was affecting his health. In the middle of the academic year he took a brief trip to Florida to recuperate from an illness, but he was hardly back at his duties when he came down with acute appendicitis. Recovery from surgery was slow, and he had to be relieved of teaching for the rest of the term.

In fact, Bingham never did resume his teaching at Princeton. He had been engaged for a three-year period, but he asked for and was given a leave of absence on grounds of health for the entire second year. By the end of that year, he had discovered a new career as an explorer and he had also succeeded in getting Yale to take him back.

CHAPTER 19

The First Expedition

Bingham's shift from teaching to exploring was almost inadvertent. The slowness of his recovery from an appendectomy may or may not have justi-fied taking a whole year's leave of absence after only a few months of teach-ing. No doubt both disillusionment with the position and a lingering hope that he might yet secure an appointment at Yale contributed to his decision to ask for a leave. But he still considered himself a member of the Princeton faculty and he planned to maintain his home there even if relieved of teaching.

The Binghams had found a larger house on Mercer Heights that had a country atmosphere and more congenial neighbors than did the house they had rented during their first year. Alfreda was expecting a fourth child, and in view of her condition and Hiram's need for further convalescence, they accepted an invitation to spend the summer of 1906 at one of the Mitchells' cottages in New London rather than at the Camp in Salem.

Sailing on New London harbor in the small boat provided by his in-laws, Hiram reviewed the direction his life was taking. His first year as a college teacher had not been auspicious. The Tiffany fortune assured his family of financial security; if he were willing to depend on the Mitchells' continued good will, he knew he did not have to earn a salary. But his pride and Puritan conscience would not allow him to accept the life of leisure his father-in-law Alfred Mitchell led.

The year ahead—on leave from Princeton—seemed a fine opportunity to do some writing to further his professional career; he planned first to expand his doctoral dissertation into a book. He had visited Scotland to examine the original records of the Scots Darien Company, but could he write authoritatively about its New World colony without having investigated the actual site?

Restless, he considered using some of the months ahead for a sea voyage around the Caribbean. With stops at Puerto Rico to visit the island of Vieques (a proposed site of the Scots colony) and St. Thomas (where some of the Scottish ships had put in for supplies), he projected an itinerary that included Barbados, British Guiana, and Trinidad, as well as several South American ports before finally reaching Panama and the Darien site. Such a sea voyage would be good for his health and would enable him not only to gather material for the book on the Scottish settlement but also, by visiting Venezuela and Colombia (however briefly), to collect material for a projected biography of Simon Bolivar.

Bolivar's leadership in the struggles by which the Spanish colonies gained their independence in the years 1810 to 1827 made him a major figure in the history of South America. Bingham's special interest in Bolivar had been stimulated shortly after leaving Harvard; he had retained his appointment as curator of the library's South American collections, and in that capacity was asked by the university librarian to evaluate a collection of letters between Bolivar and his generals that had been offered to the library by a dealer for twenty-five hundred dollars. In checking their significance, Bingham was struck by the lack of materials available on Bolivar. There was not even a good biography, and he began to think of writing one himself.

If he included visits to Venezuela and Colombia in his Caribbean cruise, he might be able to buy books and documentary material on Bolivar in Caracas or Bogotá. He wrote his former professor and friend Archibald Coolidge, suggesting that he be authorized to buy books on South American history for Harvard while on his travels. Coolidge could only persuade the librarian to send Bingham one hundred dollars but added another hundred of his own. Bingham then arranged authorization from Princeton to spend five hundred dollars on additions to its collections of South American materials.

By the end of the summer of 1906, Bingham's plans for the trip had crystallized, and he was impatient to get away. November 17 was to be the day of departure, but first he had to get his family settled in the new house in Princeton. The birth of a fourth son at the end of August had not been easy for Alfreda, and she required surgery for a lacerated cervix. Hiram took her to New York for the operation. She spent over two weeks in a hospital, while he stayed at the Yale Club and pushed ahead with his plans.

Up to that point he had had no thought of recruiting others to form an expedition. But while in New York, he met Hamilton Rice, a young doctor who had achieved some renown as an explorer. After graduating from Harvard in 1898, Rice had made an adventurous journey across South America from Guayaquil in Ecuador over the main range of the Andes and down the River Napo and the Amazon to Para. For his addition to the geographical knowledge of a relatively unexplored area, Rice had been elected a Fellow of the Royal Geographical Society of Great Britain and could add the prestigious letters F.R.G.S. to his name.

In his talks with Rice, Bingham was fired with the idea of going overland from Caracas to Bogotá instead of the usual route by steamer between their port cities, La Guaira and Cartagena. Since colonial times, some trade between Venezuela and Colombia had gone overland, but by a trail for pack animals of almost a thousand miles—and usable only in the dry season. It required crossing many tributaries of the Orinoco and then climbing a high pass in the Andes. This route would add weeks to Bingham's projected travel time, but Rice's story of his one-man expedition over mountains and jungle stirred Bingham's imagination. And when Rice offered to accompany him, he promptly changed his plans.

Rice's journey had been recognized as adding to geographical knowledge. As Bingham's field was history rather than geography, he felt a historical emphasis was needed to justify the projected exploration. He explained his first expedition, in the book he published after his return, as "a study of the country where Bolivar lived and fought, and a visit to the scenes of his most important battles, Carabobo and Boyacá, but also an exploration of the route of his most celebrated campaign."

A different explanation of his becoming an explorer, probably closer to the truth, appears in a letter he wrote his father:

> I feel the Bingham blood stirring in my veins as I start for little known regions, as nearly all my Bingham ancestors for ten generations have done before me.

To his wife, left with the care of four small children, he justified the absence that stretched out for months by the claim of duty. He wrote long letters to her while he was away, describing the incidents of his journey in sufficient detail to be useful for the journal he planned to publish and also filled with expressions of his love and his longing to be with her. In one letter, halfway through his journey, he urged her to rejoice

in the fact that I am coming home as fast as the work will permit, that I am doing faithfully the things necessary to be done and that I love you with a love that increases from day to day. Let us not complain at our long separation but rejoice in the opportunity to accomplish a good piece of work.

Sailing from New York, as planned, on November 17, 1906, and stopping at Puerto Rico, Bingham spent a full month in the Venezuelan capital. He was ill with a tropical fever when he arrived and considered abandoning the rugged overland journey, but Rice, eager to be off, reassured him. Once under way, Bingham seemed to thrive on the hardships he encountered, and his health remained excellent.

In Caracas he stayed at the American legation as the guest of the minister, thanks to a letter he carried from Secretary of State Elihu Root, directing diplomatic and consular personnel to give him every assistance.

The expedition finally left Caracas on January 3, 1907. The first hundred miles was by train to Valencia, where Bingham and Rice obtained five saddle mules and a two-wheeled cart with a driver and his assistant. They had been told that the first few hundred miles of the road might be passable by wheeled vehicle, and they had half a ton of baggage, including their photographic equipment, Rice's surgical instruments, books, maps, clothes, and finally an arsenal of firearms: "two Winchester rifles, a Mauser, and two Winchester repeating shotguns, beside three revolvers and a sufficient supply of ammunition." The country they were going through was expected to have enough wild game to supply them with meat, and self-defense against savages might be necessary. As it turned out, there were times when Bingham's skill with a rifle was all that kept the party from starving to death. Bingham's personal transportation was a small mule named Blackie, who carried him nearly a thousand miles across Venezuela, Colombia, and over the Andes.

They managed to get the cart as far as the border at Arauca. But in Colombia, with many swollen rivers and then the Andes to cross, they had to rely on pack animals. They started the most hazardous part of the journey with their baggage loaded on four oxen. In a letter to his wife, Bingham described that stage in his expedition.

The worst was in the wilderness between Arauca and Tame, where we were detained four days by a little swollen river that had inundated the country and rendered the way impassable and game scarce. We were reduced to dire straits, and a few hours before help arrived had eaten the last of our salt. Everything else was gone except enough dried soup to keep us alive for three days more, but of which we had so sickened as to make the very thought of it repulsive.

Bingham shot two wild turkeys, but he and his party found the meat so rank they couldn't eat it.

The party's troubles were not over. The rainy season had begun, and there were more flooded rivers to cross. In climbing over the thirteen-thousand-foot pass, known as the Paramo de Pizva, to the Colombian highlands, two saddle mules gave out and had to be abandoned, but horses were obtained when the party reached the fertile Sogamosa valley. Bogotá was still two hundred miles ahead, and the road ran through small towns and villages where the principal hazard was the suspicious hostility of local innkeepers. Brief stops were made at Pantano de Vargas and the bridge at Boyaca to identify the battlefields where Bolivar's army had routed a larger Spanish force. The last thirty miles of Bingham's overland journey was made by train. Finally, on April 27, the expedition reached Bogotá, and Bingham reveled, as he wrote his wife, in the "comforts of the clean, quiet American Legation." He was months behind his original schedule.

Letters he received from home told of Alfreda's struggles with loneliness and illness through the winter. Anxious to get home, he realized he would have to give up one of the major objectives of his trip, the visit to the site of the Scots Darien settlement in Panama. Still in Bogotá, he bought an important private library of two thousand books, adding substantially to Princeton's collection of books on South America.

Bingham seemingly had had his fill of the dangers and discomforts of tropical exploration. He had a book to write about his adventures, but at this stage he gave no hint of an urge for further exploration. Yet he was obviously not looking forward to a return to teaching at Princeton. His future seemed almost as open to alternatives as when he had first decided against a missionary career. In the long letter he wrote his wife from Bogotá, he sought her reactions to various options.

> Here are some things for you to be thinking over while I am on my way home.
>
> Where do you personally, without any outside talk, want to live? Princeton, New Haven, Cambridge, Milton or England?
>
> My feeling is that the best place in the world to bring up boys is in England. I also feel that my chosen work could be done better in London than anywhere else. I should far rather have my boys brought up with the average little English boy than with the average little American. I should like to try living in England for the next three or four years. The work I look forward to is writing and research—and possibly later teaching or lecturing but of that very little.

The urge to explore the unknown was now to be satisfied in libraries rather than in the wilderness. As for his interest in living in England, the explanation that it was a good place to bring up children sounds like rationalization. What is clear is that he did not want to go back to being a preceptor at Princeton.

Within a week of his return at the end of May 1907, his dilemma was on the way to resolution. He went to see President Hadley of Yale, who repeated what he had told Bingham on a previous occasion, that he wanted to introduce the study of South American history at Yale and believed in Bingham's qualifications, but that he did not have the power to make an appointment. Because he had been unable to persuade those whose support was necessary (each department of the college faculty controlled its own appointments, and the history faculty was clearly not interested in Bingham or his field), Hadley suggested two alternatives, an appointment as an assistant professor of geography or as a lecturer in South American history. This latter position would be a means of introducing the subject into the curriculum and would give Bingham an official title, even though he would not be a member of the history faculty. Lecturers were paid an honorarium on occasion, but not an annual salary.

Bingham decided to accept the second alternative. Although he must have felt a certain humiliation at an appointment without a salary, it meant he had his foot in the door at Yale, working in his chosen field. He took the gamble, and it paid off. Within eight years and before he was forty years old, he was named a full professor in 1915—a rare achievement. Yet by that time he no longer cared for the academic title; he listed his occupation in *Who's Who in America* not as historian or professor but as "explorer."

CHAPTER 20
"Something Lost Behind the Ranges"

From the first, Bingham's career on the Yale faculty was out of the ordinary. Teaching was never more than a part-time occupation: within a year of his first appointment, he was planning a second expedition to South America. The unsalaried position, almost that of a volunteer, gave him freedom to devote as much or as little time to his duties as he chose. He arranged to teach two courses, one focused on the geography of the southern continent, the other on its postcolonial history. But that was far from a full-time teaching load.

All through the academic year 1907–1908, he worked steadily on his first full-length book, *The Journal of an Expedition Across Venezuela and Colombia.* Published by the Yale University Press, the book sold less than a thousand copies, but it won him his first recognition as a scholar and explorer. At the end of the academic year, his appointment as lecturer was renewed, with the addition of a four-hundred-dollar salary as a token of advancement, but also with an immediate leave of absence for the whole year to allow Bingham to travel or explore at will.

As if to indicate his confidence in having a permanent status at Yale, he began planning to build a house he could consider his home base in New Haven. He and Alfreda heard of some newly divided acreage in the best residential section in New Haven. One three-acre lot at the corner of Prospect and Ogden Streets commanded a magnificent view in three directions. The price, fifteen thousand dollars, was correspondingly high. But the Binghams set their heart on it. Unfortunately they could not afford it, and Hiram had to swallow his pride and ask his mother-in-law to buy it. She was indignant. There had been arguments over money before, but this was the most serious. She asked Hiram what had happened to the large sums he had been given previously.

In the end, the Mitchells did buy the lot and, during the next two years, paid for the building of the house as well, insisting on the final say on all specifications. The house turned out to be a vast mansion, finished in yellow stucco and red tiles in a Spanish style and containing almost thirty rooms, including a gymnasium. Although the title remained in Mrs. Mitchell's name, Hiram came to take great pride in the house. In his entertaining and social life, he was not averse to giving the impression of a man of substance.

Meanwhile Bingham was appointed as a delegate to the December 1908 Pan-American Scientific Congress in Santiago, Chile. He saw this as an opportunity to explore more of the continent he had appropriated as his own. Chile, the host country, invited the United States to send a delegation. Secretary of State Root persuaded Congress to appropriate funds for a delegation to be appointed by him and asked a number of universities, including Yale, for recommendations. President Hadley submitted Bingham's name.

At thirty-two, Bingham was the youngest member of the delegation. But having had some talk with the Secretary of State the year before, he was not overawed by his older and more distinguished colleagues. When the group was taken to the White House to meet President Theodore Roosevelt, he impressed the president sufficiently to establish a contact that he cultivated during the rest of Roosevelt's life.

Bingham decided to fit the brief Pan-American Congress in Chile into a six-month tour of the continent and set his departure date as September 30. He had much on his mind beside travel plans, however, that summer of 1908. Alfreda was in the final stages of pregnancy and gave birth to her fifth son on September 2. A more pressing concern was the illness of his father, who had arrived from Honolulu for a visit; the old man nearly died of pneumonia in midsummer. At the end of September, as his son was sailing from New York, he was slated for major surgery. He died in a Baltimore hospital a month later, while young Bingham was in mid-Atlantic between Portugal and Brazil.

163

The most direct route to Chile was by way of Panama and a Grace Line steamer down the west coast of South America. But Bingham decided on a transcontinental journey from east to west. To reach the east coast of South America, the quickest route was by way of Europe. He had a leisurely journey, first crossing to England and spending two or three days in London getting credentials and introductions from the Royal Geographical Society. After traveling by rail from Paris to Madrid, he sailed to South America from the Spanish port of Vigo on October 18 and arrived in Buenos Aires by the date planned. He had as a traveling companion one of his students from Yale, Huntington Smith, Jr., known as Coot, whose well-to-do father paid for this addition to his education. Bingham found him "respectful...a charming high class fellow of good family and very well bred."

In spite of Smith's congenial company, Hiram frequently mentioned homesickness and lonesomeness in his letters to Alfreda, writing "I don't believe I can ever go away from you again on a long trip unless compelled by Duty and your inability to accompany me." At Brazilian ports of call he bought postcards for his boys and asked their mother to tell the two older ones, "I expect them to learn a lot about South America.... Ask W. how the 'man of the family' is getting on, and if he is as manly and brave as possible."

The book that Bingham wrote after the journey, *Across South America,* was the most successful of his travel books. In it he explained his plan to retrace the old trade route that linked the Spanish settlements on the east coast, in what are now the countries of Argentina and Uruguay, with the center of the Spanish colonial empire in Peru. He could make most of the journey by rail, except for three hundred miles in southern Bolivia and somewhat more than that between Cuzco and Lima in Peru, where animals were still the only means of transport.

Bingham broke the journey at Oruro in Bolivia, going by rail and by ship to Valparaiso to attend the scientific congress in Santiago. He found the meeting uninspiring, with many dull papers presented by specialists on a broad spectrum of economic and social as well as scientific topics. His knowledge of Spanish, the language of the congress, was still rudimentary, and the delegation of the United States was playing an ingratiating rather than a leading role.

Clarence Hay replaced Coot Smith as a travel companion on the second stage of the expedition; a recent Harvard graduate, he had attended the congress as the secretary to the American delegation. The two men made their way back to Bolivia by rail from the Peruvian port city of Mollendo to Arequipa and on to Lake Titicaca. After picking up Bingham's equipment at Oruro, and visiting La Paz and Sucre, they returned to Peru and continued on the Peruvian rail line to its terminus in Cuzco.

Cuzco was the taking-off point for the long trip to Lima—a month's journey by muleback over the mountains. Cuzco had been the capital of the Inca empire and was linked to its distant territories by a marvelous network of roads. Pizarro had used those roads four centuries earlier when he conquered the empire with a mere handful of men. But Bingham was not yet interested in the Incas or Pizarro; his training as a historian had led him to be more concerned with Bolivar's exploits. The route Bingham had chosen would enable him to visit another of the battlefields associated with Bolivar's military genius—Ayacucho on the Cuzco-Lima road, the final defeat of Spanish power in 1824.

Bingham was greeted as an important personage on his arrival in Cuzco. Word had spread that an American delegate to the Pan-American Scientific Congress was exploring the country. The prefect of the Department of Cuzco sent his personal aide with mules and horses for an excursion to the stupendous Inca fortress of Sacsahuaman above the city. Bingham was impressed, but the Incas and their works were not yet his concern. And though pleased with the hospitality shown him, he was struck by the backwardness of this provincial capital, which seemed to have no other sewage disposal system than the fouled and slippery streets.

He and Hay rode out of Cuzco on February 1, 1909, to begin their overland journey across the great ranges and mile-deep valleys of the eastern cordillera. Traveling through the heart of the Inca empire, they passed many Inca remains, walls of worked stone, doorways, terraces. Bingham remained only mildly interested.

At Abancay in the Department of Apurimac, the prefect J. J. Nuñez, who had been informed of Bingham's expedition by the president of Peru, persuaded him to break his journey to Lima and visit the Inca ruins of Choqquequirau. Choqquequirau ("Cradle of Gold" in the Quechua language) was long thought to have been the last capital of the Inca empire, the fabled "lost city" to which the emperor had fled with his retinue after the Spanish conquest. Nuñez channeled Bingham's adventurous energy in a direction that would lead ultimately to the important discovery of Machu Picchu. The ruined city was on a steep ridge jutting out from the Cordillera Vilcabamba, the tremendous range of snow-covered and glaciated peaks rising to elevations of over twenty thousand feet that lie between the Urubamba and Apurimac valleys.

The two-day journey to the site, at the height of the rainy season, was vividly described by Bingham both in the book he wrote after this expedition and in his books about Machu Picchu. The trail over high passes to the two-mile-deep canyon of the Apurimac was a slippery nightmare. They crossed the roaring Apurimac River, the "Great Speaker," by a makeshift suspension bridge two hundred fifty feet long that was hung from telegraph wire, and then began a grueling climb of six thousand feet up from the river.

The mountain setting was spectacular, but Bingham discovered that the "city" consisted of only three small groups of badly constructed houses connected by stairways and a few storehouses—hardly the capital of an empire, even a rump empire.

In Lima a month later, when he recounted to government officials and professors at the University what he had found at Choqquequirau, one Peruvian historian, working with a newly discovered chronicle of the time of the conquest, told Bingham that he believed the "lost city" lay not in the Apurimac valley but down the Urubamba on the other side of the Vilcabamba range.

CHAPTER 21

Shaping an Expedition

The side trip to Choqquequirau was the high point of Bingham's second expedition. There he had penetrated the wilderness and made the first survey of an important archeological site. The breathtaking grandeur of the mountain setting and the hardships and dangers of the journey were meat and drink to a romantic young explorer.

All his life Bingham struggled with a sense of inadequacy. Danger and hardship helped him prove himself, and his expeditions did much for his self-assurance. The new self-assurance was evident when he stopped in Jamaica on his return journey and joined his family at the Mitchells' winter home, The Folly. His father-in-law, long dubious about the penniless young man his daughter married, had been critical of his shifting domiciles and employments. Hiram was still penniless, but he had staked out the beginnings of a career of distinction and he was no longer kowtowing to his rich inlaws. They, in turn, began to show him a new respect.

Two years before, when Hiram was in Venezuela and Colombia, Alfreda had come to Jamaica to visit her parents and escape her loneliness in Princeton. In the winter of 1909, she came again, bringing her baby and the four other little boys and two nurses to care for them, planning a rendezvous with Hiram on his return from Chile and Peru.

When Hiram arrived at The Folly, he had been away from his family for six months, the second such long absence in a comparatively brief period. His letters to Alfreda were always full of ardent protestations of his love and eagerness to get home: "You have been brave beyond words to take charge of all family matters for so long alone," he had written in his most recent letter from Peru. "I hope and pray it may never happen again." He wanted to spend the coming summer with her and his boys. "Only let me be with you and I shall be happy, the happiest man in the world." And for a good half year he did not plan a new expedition. Instead, he again tried to determine just what to do with his life and listed six books he planned to write, all on South

166

America, including his biography of Bolivar and books on the Scots Darien colony and a history of Argentina.

He had much to occupy him during the academic year after his return. As a "lecturer" he was still only a marginal member of the Yale faculty, but the two courses he taught were demanding. One was a general survey course on South American history, the other an advanced course on "Latin America," for students aiming at careers in foreign trade or the diplomatic service.

Though his professional life was now more demanding, Bingham took his role as the head of a large and growing family seriously. A strict disciplinarian, his word was law, and he required absolute obedience. Any willfulness or rebellion, if he knew about it, was met with swiftly administered corporal punishment—the application of his bare hand on a bare bottom. But the effect on a small child was powerful enough to achieve total compliance by the age of six or seven. Yet it was not a harsh discipline. Occasionally the lord and master would come down from his pedestal and delight in being a small boy himself with his older sons, roughhousing and wrestling on the floor and playing games. During this period, Alfreda gently worshiped her husband and her children. She was home- and family-centered, and remained shy and lacking in self-confidence. The frequency of moves from one home to another since her marriage made the establishment of close ties outside her family all the more difficult. Her husband had replaced her father as a dominant male presence, but never able to identify with his chosen career or his restive ambition, she fell back on her own career of motherhood, in which he was quite ready to encourage her.

After Hiram's marriage, there had been occasions when his gaiety and enjoyment of a pretty face had stirred his wife to agonies of jealousy. Yet for all his rebellion against his parents' religious and moral values, he had a strict code of his own. During all his journeys as an unattached male, he carefully avoided any temptation to stray from his marriage vows. By the time he returned to his "Beloved," his "Queen," the "noblest woman in the world," his ardor was great. Unfortunately, as he complained many years later, it was seldom reciprocated.

Alfreda belonged to a late Victorian generation of women for whom the only purpose of the marriage bed was procreation. After the reunion in Jamaica, when, with her fifth baby not long since weaned, she found herself again pregnant, she accepted her condition as a reaffirmation of her calling to motherhood and another period of welcome relief from the burden of wifehood. For once, however, her calling failed her. Early in November 1909, six weeks before term, her sixth baby died at birth. Both parents were grief-stricken, and for a while there was an unaccustomed tenderness in her husband's care.

That winter of 1909–1910 Hiram began to plan yet another expedition. Where he went was less important than that the locale be unexplored and far from home. But not until January 1911 was Hiram Bingham sure where his next expedition was to go. He felt he had a duty to expand human knowledge, and the field of knowledge he had taken as his own—Latin America—was wide. However, one scientific fact—determining the elevation of Mount Coropuna in the coast range of Peru—had now come to seem more important to him than any other. To establish its height meant that he would have to climb it.

A woman explorer and mountain climber, Annie S. Peck, had announced two years earlier that she had climbed Mount Huascaran in the Cordillera Blanca of central Peru and thus reached "the apex of America." Other mountain climbers had disputed her claim, asserting that she had not climbed to the top of Huascaran and that, in any case, it was not as high as she said. Hiram Bingham had read about Annie Peck's vaunted climb up Huascaran in *Harper's* magazine and was quite uncomfortable with the idea that a woman could be an explorer, performing a difficult and dangerous feat. That, he felt, was a man's prerogative. If Coropuna was indeed the highest peak on the continent, then Miss Peck's claim that she had reached the summit of Huascaran, even if substantiated, would not justify her boast of having reached the "apex." Moreover, he hoped to climb Coropuna before she attempted it herself.

He was more than ready for another expedition. But how could he justify an expedition to climb a mountain if he was not a mountain climber? The ascent of Coropuna would have to be combined with some other objective.

One field of study had always been a possibility, although up to this point not a primary goal—to investigate the land of the Incas. In locating Coropuna on the map, Bingham had been struck by the fact that the mountain lay due south of the "lost city" of Choqquequirau, which he had investigated on his last expedition. He formulated an "expedition to central Peru for archeology north of Cuzco and a geographic survey of Coropuna," and abandoned several alternative projects he had weighed earlier. The connecting link between an ascent of Coropuna and a search for Inca ruins was to be a geographic survey along the line connecting the two.

In the first five months of 1911, Hiram Bingham's plan for another venture into the wilds of South America became the Yale Peruvian Expedition, with semiofficial status approved by the governing board of Yale. He had only until the end of the academic term in early June to assemble a team and raise money to finance the undertaking. In these months, the expedition grew to seven members and its budget reached almost $12,000.

Financial support was offered by Yale alumni Edward Harkness and classmate Herbert Scheftel, both willing to pay expenses for one member of the expedition; Bingham's other wealthy classmates declined when solicited directly; perhaps his Yale contemporaries knew too much about his present affluence.

A Yale graduate, President William Howard Taft, when contacted by Bingham, arranged for a topographer, Kai Hendriksen from the U.S. Coast and Geodetic Survey, to join the team. Classmate William Erving, a doctor in practice in Washington, D.C., who had achieved some renown as an explorer by paddling a canoe from Cairo to Khartoum, agreed to join the party if his expenses were covered.

Bingham worked with tenacity in making preparations, often relying on his Yale contacts; he interviewed Yale faculty as prospective members of the team, arranged to write articles for *Harper's* to help pay his own expenses, enlisted backing from United Fruit Company to arrange reduced passages on its steamers to South America, and asked each member of the expedition to sign an agreement defining his own responsibilities.

In presenting his objectives to Yale for the university's sponsorship, Bingham put the search for Inca ruins in the Urubamba valley in first place, followed by the geographic survey ("the profile of the Andes") from the Urubamba to the Pacific, with the climb of Mount Coropuna to establish its elevation, listed third.

Meanwhile early in April Alfreda felt she would have to go to Jamaica to be with her distracted mother and her eighty-year-old father who was near death. Hiram was reluctant to interrupt his preparations but he felt he could not let her go alone. On reaching The Folly, they found the situation apparently stable, and Hiram left as soon as he could get passage, only to hear two days later that Alfred Mitchell had died. Again Hiram sailed to Jamaica. His father-in-law was buried near the end of Folly Point where he had liked to watch the breakers send their spray over the lighthouse. Hiram found Mrs. Mitchell in a state of near hysteria, thinking she too was about to die. Alfreda, with her mother now on her hands and her husband about to depart for many months, was not in much better shape.

Hiram had set June 8 as the date he was to sail for Peru. Torn between his cherished expedition and his family loyalties, he nearly abandoned the whole project. Alfreda entered an ecstatic note in her sketchy diary: "Plan given up!"

They brought Mrs. Mitchell to a hospital in New York, where she had Tiffany relatives, and Alfreda returned to her children. Hiram's preparations were all falling into place. He was going ahead with his plans. He still needed money for Dr. Erving's expenses, and in spite of his assurances to Mrs. Mitchell that he would not use Alfreda's funds, he accepted Alfreda's offer of the last $1,800 he was still lacking.

On May 25, William Erving and Kai Hendriksen, the advance party, sailed from New York with most of the expedition's equipment and supplies. Two weeks later, on June 8, Hiram and the rest of the party followed on another United Fruit Company steamer. On the dock to see him off stood Alfreda, holding her little boy Harry (Hiram Bingham IV) by one hand and waving frantically with the other.

CHAPTER 22

The Yale Peruvian Expedition

Hiram was never more fond of Alfreda than when he was away from her. As he set forth on the expedition that was to make him famous, he felt liberated from family cares while at the same time unable to put her image out of his mind. A stream of affectionate letters passed between them when he was off on an expedition. No doubt he felt guilt at his abandonment of her—a guilt assiduously cultivated by her parents—but he was genuinely fond of her, too, even if his love fell short of the romantic heights his rhetoric implied.

His first letter, written in Kingston, Jamaica, where his United Fruit Company ship made a scheduled call, contained the usual expressions of love and devotion:

> I shall never forget how you looked as you stood on the wharf with Harry—so brave and courageous and yet so little and so appealing. It was all I could do to keep the tears back.... It did seem too cruel for words that I should be leaving you all alone. Oh, I wish you could have come with me.

He reached Panama and crossed the isthmus, trying to catch up with Annie Peck, the sixty-two-year-old feminist, whose boasts of having outclimbed any man had first roused him to make the attempt on Coropuna. She had left New York just ahead of him, trying, he felt, to beat him in a race for the summit. She had written him a few months before, when she read of his plans:

> I was much interested to observe that you are soon to set out on an expedition to *my* particular country, Peru, and to investigate a mountain which I have planned this season to climb.... I wonder if it would be possible for us to cooperate in any way....

Bingham rejected her offer, chiding her for not publishing an announcement of her intention to climb Mount Coropuna, and asked her to postpone her climb:

> Under the circumstances, do you not think it would be more sportsman-like, now that this expedition has been definitely announced and approved by the Yale Corporation, for you to postpone your investigation of Coropuna until we have finished our work? It does not seem to me that it would be at all wise for us to attempt to cooperate. If we fail in climbing the mountain, your triumph will be all the greater the following year when you succeed.

She did not answer, but he soon learned that she was going ahead with her projected climb. She had accepted the fact that she had not reached the "apex of America" on Huascaran and must try again. She hoped no less than Bingham that Coropuna would deserve that title.

Bingham had decided to leave the climb to the end of his itinerary. When he heard of Miss Peck's plan to get there first, he was too proud to change his plans. But he did not want her to reach Peru ahead of him; he hurried ahead of his team and traveled on the same boat as Miss Peck—to prevent her, he wrote to Alfreda, from "calumniating us in Lima. She is a terror."

In Lima, waiting for his companions, Bingham made good use of the time. He called on President Leguia, whom he had met as a delegate to the Pan-American Scientific Congress on his previous visit in 1909. As part of his advance planning, he had written Leguia about the new project and told him that President Taft had taken a "personal interest" in the expedition and had released a "distinguished member of the U.S. Coast and Geodetic Survey" (Kai Hendriksen) to be the expedition's topographer. President Leguia was sufficiently impressed to give him credentials that provided free passage through customs for his baggage and assignment of a military escort wherever his journeying took him.

Bingham also sought out Peruvian experts to obtain information on the field he was setting out to explore. One of these was Dr. Max Uhle, the German director of the Peruvian Museum of Natural History, at that time generally considered the first scholar to apply scientific methods to Peruvian archeology.

The most knowledgeable expert Bingham found was Don Carlos A. Romero, a scholar associated with the National Library, who, as Bingham wrote, "has gone most carefully over the accounts written by the early Chroniclers, and knows more about Vilcapampa than anyone else." Vilcapampa (or Vilcabamba) was the legendary site where the last Inca emperors had found refuge and maintained their rump empire. To locate it was one of Bingham's objectives. The clues that Romero provided led Bingham, a few weeks later, to discount the importance of Machu Picchu as not conforming to what had been written, and prompted him, therefore, to press on to the subsequent discoveries that did fit.

Bingham also consulted the Lima Geographical Society and took what maps he could of the regions he proposed to explore. From Lima, Bingham and his party continued by sea to Mollendo and by rail to Cuzco, a four-day train trip with several stops, including Arequipa and Juliaca near Lake Titicaca. At the last station before Cuzco, the two members of the advance party, Hendriksen and Erving, who had come out from Cuzco to meet them, climbed aboard, along with the young American rector of the university, Albert Giesecke, whom Bingham had met in 1909. The information he had given Bingham then about ruins in the Urubamba valley provided Bingham the first hint of the existence of Machu Picchu.

And so on the afternoon of July 2, 1911, the expedition, united for the first time, reached its final staging area in Cuzco. Bingham was faced with a complex managerial problem. He had to fit his six colleagues of varying capacities into a program that antedated the selection of several of them.

For the survey of the Andes along the 73rd meridian, he had a top-ographer, Hendriksen, and a geographer, Isaiah Bowman. Bowman had submitted an elaborate "Outline for Geological and Geographical Work" that included investigation of fossil remains, glaciation, alluvial fans, soil samples, density of population, types of vegetation, and other aspects of physical geography.

So far as the search for Inca ruins was concerned, Bingham was content to assume full responsibility. With some experience as a topographer and as a mountain climber, Herman Tucker had been designated as "archeological engineer," ostensibly to assist Bingham in the archeological work and later on the mountain climb.

Harry Foote as naturalist decided he could hardly cover all plant and animal life, and would have to limit himself to small specimens in limited fields; in his plan of work, he wrote: "I propose to collect (1) insects of all orders, (2) mosses and hepaticae. The plan to limit myself to these two lines of work is in accordance with the advice of the botanical and zoological departments of the University." Foote, a professor of chemistry at Yale, was an ardent outdoorsman. If the expedition was to be a scientific study of a little-known part of the world, he thought its flora and fauna should be as important as its geology. Dr. Erving, responsible for the health of the party, was to study the physiology of the descendants of the Incas and endemic diseases. Erving's and Foote's duties were, however, considered peripheral to the expedition's main thrust, and for much of the time they would have to assist the others.

After the first few days, when the entire party was in Cuzco, the seven men were never again all together in the same place. But Bingham as director kept all the strings in his own hands, which meant asserting his authority through written communications. With frequent changes in the plans and difficulties of transmission out in the field, coordinating operations was no mean task. Bingham also assumed full responsibility for the financing and provisioning of the work, including providing mule transport for all members of the group. Most transport in Peru was by mule because mules are steadier, tougher, and more patient than horses. The llama, of course, was the native beast of burden, but it could not carry a man or even half a man's weight in freight.

Photography was to be an important part of Bingham's project. His experience on the Venezuela-Colombia journey, when tropical conditions spoiled many of his photographs, had led him to plan to develop pictures in the field on this expedition. He consulted George Eastman, president of the Eastman Kodak Company, and persuaded him to donate some of the necessary photographic equipment. All members of the expedition were expected to carry cameras, and Bingham provided them with written instructions as to the use and the developing of film. All photographs were to belong, ultimately, to Yale University.

With the rest of his expedition out in the field except for his friend Foote, Bingham stumbled on what for a while he thought might be his most important discovery. Some fragmentary bones he picked out of a gravel bank near Cuzco, within a few days of his arrival, seemed to establish a human presence in South America at a surprisingly early date. A letter home told of this find, only two days after his arrival:

> This morning Harry Foote and I took a stroll in the suburbs before breakfast and found some extremely interesting things including quantities of ashes, bones and pottery in the sides of a newly cut gulch ten feet below the surface. From my knowledge of geology I should say they have been buried there for a couple of thousand years. I believe they antedate the Incas by a thousand years or so. I shall await Bowman's verdict with intense interest.

In the letter he wrote eleven days later, having discovered Machu Picchu in the meantime, Bingham's primary interest was "the *very precious* photos of the glacial bones" he was sending home. Even a year later, in the first published report on the results of his expedition in the *Bulletin of the American Geographical Society*, he gave seven lines to Machu Picchu and over two pages to the bones.

The subsequent history of the bones was one of gradual anticlimax. After being carefully photographed, they were soaked in melted vaseline, packed in cotton batting, and shipped to the Peabody Museum at Yale for examination by its curator of osteology, George F. Eaton. Eaton identified some of the bones as human and substantiated their apparent antiquity by identifying one of the animal bones found with them as belonging to a possibly extinct species of bison, never previously known to have existed in South America.

From the geologic setting, Bowman estimated in the *American Journal of Science* (April 1912) that the bones were between twenty thousand and forty thousand years old, despite his skepticism about Eaton's prehistoric bison. If the animal bone proved to be that of a cow—cows came to South America with the Spaniards—he admitted he might have to change his opinion, but he could not see how the bones could have been buried under eighty feet of gravel unless they were of great age.

When Bingham organized his follow-up expedition later in 1912, with support from the National Geographic Society, a major objective was a final check on the antiquity of the "glacial bones." Eaton was prevailed upon to accompany the expedition and search for further bones.

One of Eaton's first discoveries was that the cattle slaughtered for the Cuzco meat market had the same kind of bone as he had identified with that of a bison. He made a thorough study of the gulch itself and found more bones in what were clearly graves hollowed out of the side of the cliff, some with animal bones as well as human remains. He concluded that it was not unusual for Indians, even after the Spanish conquest, to bury meat and other food supplies with a body to supply the departed in the next life.

After Bingham's return from that follow-up expedition, he was invited to address the annual meeting of the National Geographic Society, and he included a brief mention of the Cuzco bones as one of his discoveries, although they were no longer to be assigned to the glacial epoch. A few days later he wrote the society begging that the editors of the magazine omit that part of his speech when they printed the proceedings of the meeting.

A final irony: years after both Bingham and Eaton were dead, accumulated evidence has suggested that humans may indeed have been present in both North and South America thirty thousand years ago. One of the sites where diggings have produced evidence is in the Peruvian Andes not far from Cuzco. A definitive check of the antiquity of Bingham's find might now be made by carbon dating, but the Cuzco bones, so carefully packed and sent to New Haven, can no longer be found in the Peabody Museum. Either Bingham or Eaton may have disposed of them.

Delayed by the unexpected discovery of the glacial bones, Bingham now pressed on to carry out the long-planned objectives of the Yale Peruvian Expedition.

CHAPTER 23

Machu Picchu

Under the heading "Yale Peruvian Expedition, Office of the Director," Bingham spelled out in handwritten "orders" what he expected of each of the three "parties" into which he had divided his expedition. Bowman was to lead "Party No. 1" to the lower Urubamba valley and on to the edge of the Amazon basin, as part of the "profile" of the Andes along the 73rd meridian, which was the expedition's second objective.

"Party No. 2," under the direction of Hendriksen with Herman Tucker as his assistant, would proceed more slowly down the Urubamba River to its confluence with the Vilcabamba River and then up that river to Paltaybamba. They were to make two-hundred-foot contour maps of those valleys as well as ground plans of any ruins they might find.

Meanwhile, Harry Foote was assigned to "Party No. 3" with Bingham; they traveled together from mid-July until the beginning of September, when Foote had to leave and return to his teaching. Despite his quiet, self-effacing manner, he was rigorous, as any good wilderness man must be, in taking his own exactly equal share of whatever there was, whether food or supplies or tent space. Bingham liked that. Some of the rugged terrain they were entering would put their mutual forbearance to the test. But they were warmly attached to each other, and remained friends for the rest of their lives.

At first Bingham saw his own function as coordinating the three parties and keeping in close touch with all of them. But as it turned out, he was rarely in direct contact with the Bowman and Hendriksen parties. He relied on messages left at certain rendezvous points to direct his scattered expedition while he went his separate way doing what he liked best, exploring the unknown. As a result, even while Foote was sharing his tent, all the significant archeological discoveries of the next few weeks were his alone.

He and Foote were the last to move out into the field. On the morning of departure, July 19, Bingham's muleteer, Felipe Pinto, took hours to rearrange the loads and pack his animals. Bingham was furious. The boxes had not been designed with Peruvian packsaddles in mind, but Bingham attributed the delay to Pinto's sulks at having to leave a day earlier than expected. It was afternoon before he finally got off in what he called the "worst start I ever made," and after dark when he reached Urubamba.

The next morning, July 20, he made a better start, although he jotted in his diary while waiting to get off, "Felipe takes forever to load." For the twelve-mile ride to Ollantaytambo he had a military escort of two, Sergeant Carrasco and another soldier, Gumersindo Ore, an escort provided by President Leguia.

Bingham arrived at Ollantaytambo, the gateway of the Vilcabamba region, in a jubilant mood. All the aggravating delays and logistical difficulties had been overcome. Ollantaytambo was a famous center of Inca remains, which Bingham took a day to examine and photograph. The ruins had been described by many earlier travelers, and he decided one day was enough, though on his two subsequent expeditions he made the place a headquarters and gave it much further study.

By the morning of July 22, his party set out once again. Searching for Inca ruins was the expedition archeologist's responsibility, and Bingham, though without training in archeology, had taken that assignment for himself. Ever since his arrival in Cuzco three weeks before, he had been making a practice of interrogating everyone he met about places where he might find the remains of Inca settlements down the Urubamba valley and in the Vilcabamba region.

His most specific information had come from Albert Giesecke, the young American-born rector of the University of Cuzco. Called to Cuzco a few years before as an educational consultant to advise on its school system, he had married a local woman and subsequently was named rector of the ancient but struggling local university. He had met Bingham on Bingham's previous visit to Cuzco in 1909. When Giesecke heard of Bingham's return visit in July 1911, he went out to meet his train at a station down the line so he could ride with him the last few miles.

Giesecke was more than ready to help in the search for Inca ruins. He told Bingham about a horseback trip he had taken down the Urubamba River road some months before. When he stopped at a primitive tavern near the San Miguel bridge in the canyon, he had learned from the proprietor, a man named Melchor Arteaga, that there were extensive ruins on top of the cliffs above the bridge. Arteaga had offered to show them to him if he returned in the dry season. The dry months had arrived, and Giesecke had been think-ing of accepting Arteaga's offer but was glad to pass along the information to Bingham instead.

Bingham himself met Melchor Arteaga when he stopped to camp at a level spot beside the road on July 23, and made inquiries at a little hut nearby. In addition to keeping a tavern at the bridge farther down the road, Arteaga apparently operated a little farm just where they had stopped—where the canyon widened enough to provide some arable land. He said the place was called Mandor Pampa, or the Plain of Mandor.

The lower Urubamba valley was the richest agricultural area of the De-partment of Cuzco. Many of the wealthy owners of its vast cattle ranches and sugar and coca plantations also maintained homes in Cuzco. They made fre-quent use of the road Bingham was on, as did the pack trains that carried out their produce and brought in their supplies. The road, by Peruvian standards, was a good one, generally wide enough for two mule trains to pass. Some fifteen years earlier, the hacienda owners had persuaded the national govern-ment to blast a passage out of the cliffs at the bottom of the canyon.

It was by the new road, only two days out from Ollantaytambo, that Bingham had reached Mandor Pampa and met Arteaga, who told Bingham about the ruins across the river, up on a ridge between two peaks—"Machu Picchu" and "Huaynapichu"—whose names Bingham carefully wrote in his notebook.

When the rain let up, Bingham emerged from his tent and persuaded Arteaga, with the promise of a whole silver dollar, to show him the ruins. At 10:07, as he duly recorded in the notebook, they set off on foot. Sergeant Carrasco, under orders to accompany Bingham wherever he went, followed. Foote, who already had found many species of insects, was off again with his butterfly net looking for more and did not go along; Erving remained be-hind at the camp. Bingham therefore was the only one of the expedition to make the steep climb to investigate the possibility of extensive ruins.

The route for the first couple of miles was up the road Bingham had traveled the day before. After a half hour's walk, they approached a bridge, a primitive structure made of a few logs lashed together, running from boul-der to boulder. Arteaga and the soldier took off their shoes for better foot-ing, but Bingham, unwilling to go barefoot, crawled across on hands and knees.

He followed his guide up a steep but not too difficult trail. About noon, after a climb of an hour and a half, they came to a grass-thatched hut. Its occupants, an Indian family, were startled to see the tall American and the soldier, but Arteaga reassured them. As it happened, three Indian families had recently chosen to live high above the river, using old Inca terraces to plant their crops.

Hungry and thirsty, Bingham gratefully accepted a drink of water and some cooked sweet potatoes. When he was ready to proceed, Arteaga told him the Indian family's little boy would show him the way, and Arteaga would wait for his return. Bingham set off, with his new guide trudging ahead down the path. The boy, perhaps eight years old and hardly half Bingham's height, was barefoot; he wore a brightly colored wool poncho over his shoulders and what appeared to be an almost new felt hat. Carrasco, ever faithful to his assignment, brought up the rear.

Bingham's own account of the discovery follows, as told in *Lost City of the Incas*, 1948:

> Hardly had we left the hut and rounded the promontory than we were confronted by an unexpected sight, a great flight of beautifully constructed stone-faced terraces, perhaps a hundred of them, each hundreds of feet long and ten feet high. They had been recently rescued from the jungle by the Indians. A veritable forest of large trees which had been growing on them for centuries had been chopped down and partly burned to make a clearing for agricultural purposes. The task had been too great for the two Indians so the tree trunks had been allowed to lie as they fell and only the smaller branches removed. But the ancient soil, carefully put in place by the Incas, was still capable of producing rich crops of maize and potatoes.

Such well-made terraces were "nothing to be excited about," he commented, and could be seen at several other Inca sites in the upper Urubamba valley.

> So we patiently followed the little guide along one of the widest terraces where there had once been a small conduit, and made our way into an untouched forest beyond. Suddenly I found myself confronted with the walls of ruined houses built of the finest quality of Inca stone work. It was hard to see them for they were partly covered with trees and moss, the growth of centuries, but in the dense shadow, hiding in bamboo thickets and tangled vines appeared here and there walls of white granite carefully cut and exquisitely fitted together. We scrambled along through the dense undergrowth, climbing over terrace walls and in bamboo thickets where our guide found it easier going than I did. Suddenly without any warning under an overhanging ledge the boy showed me a cave beautifully lined with the finest cut stone.

Bingham soon came across ruins with walls made of unexpectedly immense granite blocks; some of the individual stones were taller than Sergeant Carrasco, as can be seen in Bingham's photographs taken on that day (see Alfred Mitchell, *Portrait of an Explorer*, 1989). He continued:

Then the little boy urged us to climb up a steep hill over what seemed to be a flight of stone steps. Surprise followed surprise in bewildering succession. We came to a great stairway of large granite blocks.... Suddenly we found ourselves standing in front of the ruins of two of the finest and most interesting buildings in ancient America. Made of beautiful white granite, the walls contained blocks of Cyclopean size, higher than a man. The sight held me spellbound.

He went on to describe the two structures facing the clearing, and told of his amazement at the size of the stones in the "principal temple."

I could scarcely believe my senses as I examined the larger blocks in the lower course, and estimated that they must weigh from ten to fifteen tons each. Would anyone believe what I had found? Fortunately, in this land where accuracy of reporting what one has seen is not a prevailing characteristic of travelers, I had a good camera and the sun was shining.

In a previous book, *Inca Land* (1922), he had mentioned finding the name of Agustin Lizarraga and the year 1902 on some of the masonry, thus acknowledging an earlier "discovery," but in this final version Bingham omitted any mention of his name. A local inhabitant, Lizarraga was of mixed Spanish and Indian stock and made his living by serving travelers' pack trains.

On the actual day of the discovery, Bingham was so little impressed with what he had found that he spent only a few hours at the site. His diary and his letters make it clear that he left the area the very next day. Bingham had been on the road less than a week. Unknown to him, the discovery that was to win him fame was already behind him. But the last Inca capital was, he thought, still ahead. The explanation he gave for continuing his "search" without further investigation of this site was that he was looking for "Vitcos," the last Inca capital, and the clues he carried in his pocket to identify it did not fit what he had just found.

The clues had been given him by the Peruvian historian Carlos Romero when Bingham sought him out in Lima a month before. A pamphlet by Romero that Bingham had read two years earlier was one of the factors that led Bingham to establish as a major purpose of his 1911 expedition a search for the last Inca capital in the Urubamba and Vilcabamba valleys.

Bingham persisted with the objectives of the Yale Peruvian Expedition—the search for other significant Inca ruins, the mapping of the 73rd meridian, the climb of Mount Coropuna—but all were eventually overshadowed by the significance of Machu Picchu. Annie Peck succeeded in climbing Coropuna that summer of 1911 but, as on Huascaran, she did not climb the highest of its peaks. Nor did Bingham, although the peak he chose to ascend—and climbed successfully—measured substantially higher than hers. In any case, neither of them reached the highest point in the Western hemisphere, which turned out to be Aconcagua on the Argentine-Chile border at 22,763 feet. (Aconcagua had already been successfully climbed fourteen years earlier.)

If Bingham is remembered today, it is as the "discoverer" of the "lost city." An intact Inca settlement untouched by European civilization, Machu Picchu has been acclaimed as one of the archeological wonders of the world. Its magnificent setting, combined with ease of access by rail, has made it a Mecca for tourists. Reaching the site, visitors read his name on the tablet at the head of the "Carretera Hiram Bingham." Another plaque at the entrance to the ruins cites him as the "scientific" discoverer, thereby avoiding the still irritating issue of whether he or Lizarraga was in fact the first to see them.

The touching beauty of the sheer walls perched on the mountain ridge, the half-obscuring vapors that drift up from the canyon, inevitably suggest mystery and romance. Who built Machu Picchu, and why?

Although Bingham had at first view so underrated its significance that he devoted only a few hours and a couple of rolls of film to it and did not make it the focus of his subsequent expeditions to Peru, its appeal finally gripped him, and as its fame grew, he desperately tried to give it a historical importance to match its visual and emotional appeal. He might have saved himself the effort. Enough to have Machu Picchu what it is, a superb example of Inca architecture in a superb setting. Historical scholarship since his day has given no support to his theories of its past, and no modern scholar supports his estimate of its great antiquity. The potsherds and the masonry, though of various styles, are all apparently of the late Inca period. (By contrast, his initial identifications of the other two great Inca discoveries he made later in the expedition, Vitcos and Vilcabamba Viejo, have been fully confirmed.)

If Machu Picchu was, among other theories, neither the cradle nor the grave of the Incas, neither their last refuge nor the "lost city" of Vilcabamba, what was its history?

Philip Means, the Harvard student who was assistant archeologist on Bingham's 1914 expedition, believed that it was built in the middle of the fifteenth century by the Inca Pachacutí, the ninth of the rulers known as Incas and the greatest of the empire builders. Means argued that it was built as one of a string of fortress towns to defend the eastern frontiers of the empire. This theory has until recently been the one most generally accepted by Peruvian and American scholars.

John Howland Rowe of the University of California in Berkeley, a leading American student of the archeology of the Incas, also believes the site was part of the vast lands of the Inca empire-builder Pachacutí but that Machu Picchu was his personal property, the royal residence of a much larger estate to which it belonged.

Regardless of theory, its Inca builders left at Machu Picchu perhaps the most moving reminder of pre-Columbian civilizations.

CHRONICLE VIII

The Heritage

CHAPTER 24

The Trusts

The Tiffany fortune would have been dissipated sooner if it had not been preserved by the dead hand of trusts. Alfred Mitchell himself, after his first riotous expenditures, took the initiative. No doubt, as a trustee for Burnie's trust, he had come to appreciate the importance of preserving capital from the spendthrift inclinations of a beneficiary.

Annie had turned over to him the fifty shares of Tiffany & Co. stock given her by her father, and in 1908 he decided to put them in a trust to assure that his daughters would benefit from this part of their inheritance. As his lawyer pointed out to him, it seemed unlikely that his sons-in-law—the explorer Hiram Bingham, the cosmologist James Jeans—would ever make enough money to support their families by themselves.

Hiram seemed particularly unlikely to earn enough to support a family that by 1908 already included five little boys. The Mitchells had provided Alfreda with a handsome allowance of $12,000 a year, more than enough to cover her household expenses. In the affluence that Alfred and Annie had come into upon Charles Tiffany's death, they had taken pains to see that Alfreda was housed in the style they had taught her to expect. They had bought the young couple a house on Reservoir Street in one of the most select neighborhoods of Cambridge, Massachusetts. They were somewhat disconcerted when Hiram, shortly after gaining his doctorate, moved to Princeton for his first teaching assignment; nevertheless they bought their daughter another big house. Two years later the Binghams moved again, when Hiram persuaded President Hadley of Yale that there was a need for Latin American studies at his old alma mater, and Hiram was offered an unpaid lectureship as a starter. This time he assured his father-in-law that he was where he wanted to be and belonged, and he would not move again. Unable to find a satisfactory house to buy, the Mitchells offered to build the Binghams a house. Hiram wanted to pay for a building lot out of his own and Alfreda's savings. But by this time accustomed to the best, Hiram found that the only lot that would do, on the crest of Prospect Hill out near the city line, was priced at $15,000, beyond what they could pay. He wrote his in-laws, who were in Jamaica at the time, asking if they would pay for the lot as well as the house.

An acerbic reply came back from Annie Mitchell. I suspect that her husband was too angry to be trusted with writing the letter himself. What had happened to the $12,000 allowance the Mitchells had been sending their daughter every year since the Binghams' marriage, more than enough for them to live on? What had happened to the wedding presents of $10,000 each, given by Annie and her father? For the first time, she asked her son-in-law for an accounting.

Hiram explained lamely enough that some of the wedding present money he had used to provide nursing care for his dying mother in Honolulu, and some had gone to pay for a portrait of his father for which a celebrated portrait painter had been brought to Hawaii. He also admitted that he had lost some money in the stock market, which left him with no capital funds of his own, though he had learned a valuable lesson about investments.

The Mitchells paid for the choice two-acre building lot, but kept the title in their own names. They employed the architects who had designed their Jamaica "Folly." When Hiram first saw the plans for the thirty-room mansion (with a gymnasium for the boys on the third floor), he objected that it would be unsuitable for a young instructor on a minimal salary, but he was told in no uncertain terms that the Mitchells were building it for their daughter and not for him. The only concession they made to him as a specialist in Hispanic America was to give the house a Spanish look with a red-tiled roof and wrought-iron balconies.

The Binghams moved in, with a staff of maids and nurses, in the summer of 1910. The first year in the new house was a stressful time for Alfreda. The house was too big for the furniture they had accumulated, and the only furniture they felt they could afford to buy, to make the big living room look less like a barn, was a collection of wicker chairs. Managing the large household was a strain Alfreda never felt easy with. She was pregnant for the seventh time, and gave birth in November to her seventh son, Mitchell (a sixth had died at birth a year before).

Hiram was readying the Yale Peruvian Expedition on which Machu Picchu would be discovered the following July. With his family living expenses taken care of and his teaching duties limited, he could well afford to go exploring, but he needed money for the expenses of his expedition. He had hoped his rich relatives might contribute. But at this point, both the Mitchells were ill and did not approve of his leaving his family to go exploring again. As he wrote his mother-in-law, he was meticulous about not drawing on his domestic bank account to finance the expedition. He did manage to raise a small fund from Yale University and a few friends, which, with an advance from *Harper's* for some articles to be written about his expedition, was enough to get it under way.

When Alfred Mitchell died in Jamaica in April 1911, at age eighty, Hiram and Alfreda were on hand for his burial in a tomb within sight of The Folly. Annie herself had not been well, and her husband's death was so devastating that she thought she was going to die. She had relied on Alfred since her father's death in 1902 to watch over her share of the Tiffany fortune, and now that Alfred was gone, she felt overwhelmed by the complexities of all the wealth now hers to manage alone. That wealth included not only the fortune left her by her father and the big New London estate she and her husband had acquired, but also the half a dozen houses and thousands of acres that Alfred had been reclaiming in Salem, and the great Jamaican plantation.

Alfred had felt the burden himself in his last years and had relieved himself of many management details by hiring two of his nephews, sons of his famous but impoverished brother Donald. He had persuaded the older son, Donald, Jr., to give up his only mildly successful engineering career and become his agent, managing the Salem farms and looking after the New London properties when he was away. Donald's younger brother Walter, who was also trained as an engineer, had been engaged to supervise the building of The Folly in Jamaica and later the Bingham Camp in Salem. It seems likely that both these Mitchell nephews had been helped through college with Tiffany money provided by their uncle.

Whether it was Donald Mitchell, Jr., or Hiram Bingham—both of whom must have felt their own future financial security at stake in the handling of Mrs. Mitchell's wealth—who advised the distraught widow is not in the available record. Hiram was eager to be off to Peru with his Yale expedition, but he had an even greater stake in seeing that his mother-in-law did nothing foolish. He accompanied the family back to New York after the funeral, and it seems more than likely that he recommended she see a lawyer without delay about putting her property in competent hands.

Hiram was so concerned about the family crisis that he considered canceling his whole expedition. Alfreda desperately hoped he would. But he was committed. The expedition's supplies and equipment and three of its members were booked to sail for Peru within the month, and he was to follow with the rest of the personnel two weeks thereafter.

On May 24, less than a month after her husband's death, and the day before the first contingent of the expedition was to sail from New York, Annie O. Mitchell signed a document putting all her property in the care of three trustees, who signed their names after hers. One of them was Louis's son, her nephew Charles L. Tiffany II, now in the top management of Tiffany & Co. The other two were lawyers, Robert Thorne and Winthrop E. Dwight. It seems probable that Hiram Bingham recommended Winthrop Dwight to Mrs. Mitchell. His father, Timothy Dwight, had been president of Yale during Hiram's college years, and had been the officiating clergyman at the marriage of Alfreda and Hiram in New London in 1900. Robert Thorne may have been recommended by Charles Tiffany II.

It was an awesome responsibility these three trustees assumed. The agreement signed that day provided in magisterial legal language that Annie O. Mitchell, "party of the first part,"

> has granted, bargained, sold, assigned, transferred and set over, and by these presents does grant, bargain, sell, assign, transfer and set over unto the said Charles L. Tiffany, Robert Thorne and Winthrop E. Dwight, as trustees, parties of the second part hereto all and singular the stocks,

bonds, mortgages and other securities of whatsoever name and nature, belonging to her, the said party of the first part, and wheresoever the same may be...

And as if that were not enough, the document went on to include "all moneys now on deposit" in certain named banks, and

also all and any other moneys, securities or other property which she may now or hereafter be or become entitled to receive from the estate of her late husband, or from any other source whatsoever.

The agreement then went on to add the saving words "IN TRUST, NEVERTHELESS" and to set forth the terms of the engagement. Aside from the repetitive legal language, they seemed simple enough. The trustees were to hold the assets put in their charge and see to their proper investment, and dispose of the net income.

A first charge, aside from the expenses of the trust, was the "care and maintenance" of Annie's real estate. Besides her ownership of the New London and Jamaica homes, she had a life use of the Salem properties. On its face this was no small charge for the three New Yorkers.

Annie was herself, of course, the primary beneficiary, and the trustees were to pay to her or her account "all necessary and proper charges for her own suitable maintenance and support." Who was to determine what was necessary and proper, or even suitable, was not spelled out. It seems to have been assumed that Annie would tell them.

They were specifically given "absolute discretion" in the next provision charging them to continue "such gifts, annuities and allowances" as she had been "accustomed to make and to pay in the past." But this referred mainly to what she had been giving her daughters. And here there is evidence of hasty draftsmanship, probably due to Hiram Bingham's eagerness to have the matter settled before his expedition set sail. Regardless of "absolute discretion," the trustees were specifically directed not only to continue what the daughters had been getting but to "increase" the amounts. Alfreda was now to receive $52,000 a year and Charly $40,000. The difference was no doubt due to the fact that Alfreda at that time had six children and Charly none.

The trust was to last "during the period of the natural life of the party of the first part." Annie thought she was going to die soon. Actually she was to live for another quarter century, but she had been complaining of her poor health even before her husband's death (a cousin of his who had visited them in Jamaica wrote of the couple's inordinate fear of dying), and after his death she no longer felt life was worth living. She began giving her daughters some of her most valuable jewelry, pieces given her by her father.

The securities and "moneys" she turned over to her trustees were duly inventoried, according to their first public accounting, at $4,733,679.98, and when the assets from Alfred's estate were added, the total of Annie's wealth for which they were responsible came to well over five million dollars. Included were 331 shares of Tiffany & Co. stock, which had increased in value to $5,700 a share, and thus constituted almost two million of the five million total.

Most of the rest was made up of railroad bonds and a variety of gilt-edge stocks. Apparently the Mitchells' extravagances had not diminished the inheritance Annie had received from her father.

The trust agreement provided that at her death the trust assets were to be distributed as she would direct in her will. Clearly she considered that everything she had put in trust was still hers, and what she had given the trustees she could take back.

CHAPTER 25
Building Boom

Following the custom of the day, Annie dressed wholly in black for a year after her husband died, then went into half-mourning in lavender, and finally into white. She began to wear a garb that remained standard for the rest of her life: immaculate and expensive white cotton and silk dresses that remained close to floor-length year after year even when fashion was prescribing shorter skirts. Also she began wearing a little lace cap suggestive of British royalty.

Along with this progression in her outward appearance went a change in mood, from desolation and an expectation of imminent death to enjoyment of the new life she began making for herself, spending her wealth on building and renovating houses for herself and her family.

With her husband gone, and her daughter Charly more than ever an ocean away, she wanted to be nearer Alfreda. Deciding to spend at least part of each year in New Haven, Annie bought a large empty tract of land directly across Prospect Street from the Binghams' house (to which she still held the title) and built another elaborate mansion for herself, almost as large as the one she had built for Alfreda and her family.

She had a natural flair for architecture, and on this occasion she indulged her whims with little restraint. Innovative features included an archway connecting a two-car garage and chauffeur's quarters with the main house, thus providing a view for a vehicle entering the driveway from Prospect Street through the house to the distant West Rock ridge, as well as offering a porte-cochère for the main entrance. Another unusual feature was a window cut through a chimney to provide light for an upstairs hall. The dining room was octagonal, and one of the living rooms was decorated with carved oak panels and furniture bought by the Mitchells in Europe years before. The general effect of the house, finished in gray brick, was more bizarre than beautiful. (It may still be seen on the campus of Albertus Magnus College, which acquired this and neighboring mansions some years later.)

About the same time she was persuaded, perhaps by the prospect of helping to design another building, to make the single most generous philanthropic gift of her years as a millionaire: she undertook to pay for the building of a hospital for infectious diseases in New London, to be located on Jefferson Avenue, half a mile from the city's main hospital on Ocean Avenue. After a few years, the hospital to which it was given found it too expensive and inconvenient to maintain, and it became a private nursing home.

Donald Mitchell, Alfred's nephew, who continued to manage her various properties, reported to Annie, in February 1915, that her philanthropy had cost her $70,867, advanced by her trustees. He also reported that they had advanced $149,598 for the new house in New Haven. These amounts made hardly a dent in her capital.

But these were not her only new ventures. She began improving and adding to the properties in Salem that her husband had acquired. With three older grandsons already given title to the Woodbridge, Mumford, and Beebe farms, Annie now provided for her three younger grandsons with neighboring farms.

Charles, now in medical school and recently married, was given the forty-acre Brown farm to the west of the Woodbridge lands. Annie had the farmhouse moved up from the roadside to higher land, and modernized and winterized. (Charles and his wife never occupied it, and sold it after his grandmother's death to the son of the family dentist in New Haven.)

Brewster, next in line, was given the two-hundred-acre Tillotson farm to the south of the other family properties, and again there was extensive modernizing and improving of the old farmhouse. Next she acquired the Frank DeWolfe farm to the east of the Mumford place, and once again extensively renovated the farmhouse. This property was subsequently added to the Beebe farm and put in my name. About the same time the small farmhouse on White Birch Road bought by Alfred Mitchell from William Tiffany (a remote cousin of Charles Tiffany) was given to my brother Mitchell, the sixth of the Bingham brothers.

Annie went on acquiring other adjoining Salem farms; the Niles, Williams, and Morgan properties up the valley to the north of the Beebe farm were given to her son-in-law Hiram Bingham, who kept the occupants on as tenants.

At its greatest extent, the Mitchell empire in Salem and parts of East Haddam extended two miles from Witch Meadow Road on the north to the Salem town line on the south, and two miles from North Plain in East Haddam on the west to the upper Shingle Mill pond on the east. Roger Daboll had surveyed each acquisition for the Mitchells over thirty years, and in 1932 he combined all the surveys in a single map, identifying the various parcels allocated to various Bingham and Jeans descendants.

It was an almost feudal domain of some three thousand acres. And from the old family mansions—the Mumford and Woodbridge houses—and from the porch of the Bingham "Camp," an entire valley with its surrounding wooded hills could be viewed as a single vast estate. Yet what differentiated it from a feudal barony was that it was not supported by its tenants' labor but the whole was subsidized by income from a New York jewelry store. Alfred Mitchell's first acquisition, the Woodbridge farm—two hundred acres with a house and farm buildings—had been bought for $5,000 in the early 1900s, and as late as 1940 I bought the Darling farm across the valley, with a house and barn and two hundred and fifty acres, for $6,000.

Even continuing Alfred's empire building, then, Annie was not exhausting her inheritance. Nor was she exhausting her own creative energies. She had given up her Jamaica mansion as a winter home during World War I, prompted by fear of German submarines on the Atlantic passage, and had begun spending the winter months in Miami. After a few seasons in rented mansions fronting on Biscayne Bay on the former Brickell estate, she bought a house and four-acre lot farther down Brickell Avenue. In remodeling this property, her architectural sensibilities were engaged to the maximum.

The existing house at 2025 Brickell Avenue, built on a coral cliff at the water's edge, she modernized but left virtually intact. But across a trestle bridge she built a new house, with sliding glass panels opening out under coconut trees to the blue waters of Biscayne Bay, and a winding outside staircase descending to a patio below.

Even that did not exhaust her energies. Behind the main house but still with a view of the bay, she built a two-room guest cottage and, at the street end of the lot, a garage and servants' quarters. Finally, carved out of a bit of the hammock jungle that had once covered the entire lot, she erected another more conventional house of two stories and six rooms, ostensibly for her daughter Alfreda.

The previous owners had operated a roadside stand selling jams and jellies, some from home-grown fruit, and had named the place "Sweet Way." Annie kept the name. And here in her old age—she died in 1937 in her ninety-third year—she was mistress of a kind of court where her descendants came to pay homage and enjoy a winter holiday.

Her brother Louis Tiffany and her sister Louise began to spend the cold months nearby. Louis built his own eccentric home, also on the waterfront a few lots to the north. It was a three-story tower with trunks of palm trees for columns. The two Tiffany houses, screened by coconut trees, were pointed out to tourists on a sightseeing boat that regularly plied the stretch of water in front of what was known as Millionaires' Row.

CHAPTER 26
Preserving a Heritage

When Charles Tiffany died in 1902, his estate was subject to a New York State death tax of approximately $40,000, but there was no federal estate tax for his executors to worry about. In 1911, when Annie put her entire share of her inheritance in trust, there was still no reason to worry about heavy taxation on her estate in case of her death, and she retained effective control of her fortune. In 1916, thanks to a coalition of Wilsonian Democrats and Progressive Republicans in power in Washington, a steeply progressive estate tax was enacted. The millions that Annie's trustees managed for her, and which under the terms of the trust agreement would form part of her estate if she died, would be heavily taxed.

Just when Annie was persuaded to do something about that threat to her fortune is not clear. She was no longer under fear of imminent death. But she was approaching her eightieth year, and was angrily conscious of the limitations of old age.

In the summer of 1921, she received a long letter from her son-in-law Hiram. He was recuperating from a series of illnesses—bronchial colds, sinusitis, gall stones, pneumonia, even a touch of tuberculosis—that had made · him a semi-invalid for two years after his return from serving in France during World War I. To speed his recovery, he had rented a ranch home on the island of Maui in the Hawaiian islands, where all his family had joined him. He addressed his mother-in-law affectionately as "Dearest Little Mother." He wrote that Freda was away on a side trip to Molokai with five of the boys; with more quiet at home he had leisure to write; and he proceeded to write at length about his sons.

No doubt he had been thinking about their future. They were all in private schools or in college. He had no salary. The only income for which he was not dependent on the Tiffany fortune was a meagre trickle of royalties from one of his travel books, *Across South America.* The books he had hoped to write about his Peruvian discoveries were as yet unwritten. He realized that his sons' continued education and their setting out on careers of their own were wholly dependent on his mother-in-law's whims.

How much such a train of thought may have prompted the letter is impossible to know. But he took the time to describe each of his seven sons and their current development. It was as if he wanted her to share in his affectionate understanding of each one of them. There was no suggestion of concern for their financial future or his own, but it may well have been in his mind. Moreover the $52,000 allowance Annie had provided for Alfreda in her 1911 trust was being stretched to the limit as inflation added to his growing family expenses.

Back in New Haven in the fall, with his mother-in-law now living across the street, and with his health apparently restored, Hiram began work on the books he had planned to write about Machu Picchu. He was also cultivating his long-deferred career in politics. Harding was now the president, and the trend in Washington was, as the president put it, "back to normalcy." There was no reason to fear any new taxes, but the federal estate tax was still on the books.

Hiram was on good terms with his "little mother," and she had come to trust him and rely increasingly on his advice. On some occasion he must have suggested that she put her property or a substantial part of it out of reach of the federal estate tax, and at the same time assure her children and grandchildren a more definite financial future.

At any rate, during that fall of 1921, she worked out a new arrangement for handling her wealth. She consulted with her nephew and trustee, Charles Tiffany II, and with her husband's nephew, Walter Mitchell, who was now an officer of Tiffany & Co. She decided to give a substantial part of her fortune to a new irrevocable trust assuring her daughters a comfortable living as long as they lived and providing for her grandchildren until they all were grown up.

Two new trust agreements were drawn up for her by her New York lawyers. One amended the existing trust agreement by removing securities, mostly railroad bonds valued at about two million dollars, from the trust fund, and by eliminating the provisions for paying income to Alfreda and Charly. The other agreement put these securities into a new trust fund specifically for the benefit of Alfreda and Charly and their children. Unlike the 1911 trust, under which Annie had the power to change its terms and to dispose of the funds by will at her death, the new trust divested her of all further rights of ownership over the trust assets and provided that it would continue beyond her lifetime and until the death of both her daughters.

It also provided a new formula for distribution of the net income, based on the number of children in each family. Since the previous trust agreement, Charly had had a daughter, Olivia, and Alfreda had brought her total of children to seven. They were now both beyond the child-bearing age. The new formula provided that Alfreda would receive 60 percent of the net income, and Charly 40 percent. In elaborate language running over several pages of legal-size paper, the document went on to cover various eventualities, providing for payments for the support of grandchildren in case of the death of their mother before the expiration of the trust, and even providing for the support of the "issue" of any grandchild who had died. A special provision for Olivia's benefit guaranteed her a minimum income of $20,000 a year in case her mother died.

The value of the securities put into the new trust, according to a formal accounting by the old trustees, was $2,158,229.78. But this was less than half of what had been in their hands. The old trust, which Annie could still change at will, still held almost three million dollars' worth of securities, with over a million dollars' worth of Tiffany & Co. stock.

The value of the company's shares had been rising steadily. During the founder's lifetime, a good portion of the profits each year was plowed back into inventory and reserves so that the value of shares was continually increasing. At Charles Tiffany's death, each share with a par value of $1,000 was considered to be worth $4,000. The company had a policy of buying back any shares any shareholder wanted to sell, and these occasional sales provided one measure of their potential market value. When a shareholder died, a value had to be established for probate and tax purposes, and this provided another measure of their value. In 1916, when a member of the Moore family died (the Moores had been associated with the firm since the 1830s), his estate valued Tiffany shares at $7,683 each. In 1920 Tiffany shares were split five for one, and the new shares continued to rise in value.

This 1922 trust arrangement gave Hiram a new sense of financial security. He was no longer directly dependent on his mother-in-law. The trust income was to come directly into the family treasury. Meanwhile the national economy was emerging from a post-war recession and heading into the great boom years of the 1920s. As if to add to his good fortune, the opportunity came at last for an entry into politics.

Even before the war, he had been cultivating the Republican party leadership—Ike Ullman, the New Haven chairman, and J. Henry Roraback, chairman of the state Central Committee. They had helped put his name before the party organization when he was named a member of the Electoral College in 1916. As a means of broadening his contacts beyond the rarefied social atmosphere of the Yale faculty and Prospect Hill, he had joined a Masonic Lodge—fortuitously named the Hiram Lodge—and worked his way through the order to the 32nd degree. In the summer of 1922, he was nominated as Republican candidate for Lieutenant Governor of Connecticut, and easily elected in the Republican sweep in the November elections.

His political career advanced swiftly. Not only a professor but an explorer and a World War I aviator, his six-foot-four stature and prematurely white hair made him a strikingly handsome figure on a campaign poster or a speaker's platform. Two years later, he was nominated and elected Governor. Then, before his inauguration to the new post, by a combination of political accidents and astute maneuvering, he was nominated to fill a seat in the U.S. Senate that had suddenly become vacant when its occupant, Frank Brandegee, committed suicide. Winning a special election in December, Hiram resigned the governorship after one day in office and went to Washington the next day to be sworn in as a senator.

His salary as senator was larger than any salary he had ever earned before. But the expenses of maintaining a home in Washington and fulfilling the new social obligations that he and Alfreda felt incumbent on them, while still keeping up the New Haven establishment, swallowed up a substantial part of the income the family was now getting from the new 1922 trust.

Hiram could hardly ask his mother-in-law for more money to meet his growing expenses. But he conceived the idea of getting her to assume some of his boys' educational expenses. Tuition charges were only a small fraction of what they would be a generation later, but the cost of private education of seven sons was still considerable, even for beneficiaries of the Tiffany fortune.

Hiram had tried to train his sons in handling money. His wife had had no such training, and he was appalled at her unworldliness when they were first married. From an early age, his sons were taught how to keep a cash account with receipts and disbursements on opposite pages. He set up savings accounts for them, and then checking accounts, and explained the difference between principal and income, and between stocks and bonds.

During the last of my boarding school years and on through college, he paid me an allowance of $2,000 a year, out of which I was expected to pay tuition, buy my clothes, and pay other expenses when not at home. Before receiving the semiannual installments of $1,000, I was expected to display my account book to show how I had spent my income. As each Christmas vacation rolled around, I sweated over trying to make my accounts balance for the year: a substantial amount of expenditure always had to be entered in the books as "Lost."

In the spring of 1925, I was in my second year at Yale. My brother Woodbridge had graduated the year before and had started on a teaching career by enrolling as a student teacher at Yale-in-China in Changsha. Clearly if he was to go on as a teacher he would need postgraduate training. Harry was graduating in June, uncertain of his future. It was becoming evident to my father that his sons might have to be supported for some years if they were to be trained in a profession.

Annie by this time had overcome some of her early doubts about his financial reliability, and had even named him an executor in her will. He easily persuaded her to make a contribution from her fortune to her grandchildren. Under his guidance she established a scholarship fund for the postgraduate education of his sons, in the form of a "single premium fifteen-year decreasing endowment" insurance policy, in the amount of $54,000, with $2,000 to be paid to each son for the first five years after graduating from Yale. (Hiram seems to have assumed that all of his sons would go to Yale, and all did except for Mitchell, who chose an independent career as an artist and forfeited his share of the fund.)

My father's elevation to the U.S. Senate in the year 1925 marked a turning point in his life. As I have told in my book *Portrait of an Explorer*, the demands of politics and the social life of Washington tended to alienate him from his wife and family, and he fell in love with the wife of a Maryland congressman. Still, he could not forget that in the long run he was dependent on the Tiffany fortune and the whims of his mother-in-law. If his marriage should break up, he would be a poor man again. If his wife died, he might become dependent on his children.

The scholarship fund was only a temporary stopgap. Limited to the years of his sons' postgraduate education, it did little for his own financial security, except to make a little more of his wife's income available for his own uses.

In the fall of 1927, he suggested to his mother-in-law that she make further provision for her grandsons, and in January 1928 she set up another trust fund, transferring close to a quarter of a million dollars' worth of securities to the Union & New Haven Trust Company as trustee for the benefit of her grandsons. The officers of the bank, friends of Hiram, were already trustees of the so-called Scholarship Fund. The new "Trust for Grandsons" would provide each of her grandsons with income that initially was about a thousand dollars a year for many more years. These payments were to be paid out of the income from the fund, and the principal was to be distributed to them upon their mother's death—except for one curious provision: if Alfreda died before her husband, the income was to go to him for the rest of his life. In the words of the document establishing the trust, the payments to him would be "for the purpose of maintaining a family home and residence for himself and such of my said grandsons as may desire to live with him." It was not an unreasonable provision considering that the grandsons would be handsomely provided for upon their mother's death, under the terms of Annie's will and of her 1922 trust.

Having made this substantial gift for her seven grandsons' benefit, Annie felt obliged to do something comparable for her other grandchild, Olivia Jeans, now sixteen years old. So another trust fund was set up for her benefit with securities worth about one-seventh of those in the Trust for Grandsons.

The stock market collapsed in October 1929, setting off the Great Depression worldwide, and the Tiffany fortune was not unaffected. Tiffany & Co. depended on selling luxury goods to the rich, and its profits, which had been soaring in the boom years, now turned to heavy losses. Yet it weathered the Depression remarkably well, continuing to pay dividends right through the Depression years, though at a greatly reduced rate, out of reserves accumulated during many years of prosperity.

The beneficiaries of the Tiffany fortune suffered no hardships in the Depression. Annie, my grandmother, saw her annual income drop precipitously, but she did not have to change her way of life. Neither did any of the Bingham family, though my father later said the family income was cut in half. But for my father the onset of the Great Depression brought other woes.

The very week of the stock market plunge in 1929, Hiram Bingham, scholar, patriot, tall and white-haired, the very image of what an upright senator should look like, was "censured" by his fellow senators. He had knowingly if innocently introduced a lobbyist for the Connecticut Manufacturers Association as an expert adviser to the Senate Finance Committee, then writing a tariff bill, and he had stubbornly refused to admit that he had made a mistake. His political image was badly tarnished. Only twice before in history had a senator been "censured." For the most part his family accepted his version of the affair, that he had been unjustly victimized by progressives and radicals in the Senate in a complex political battle. His mother-in-law, Mrs. Mitchell, continued to trust him.

CHAPTER 27
Lone Pine Lawn

Annie's business sense that had led her father to wish she had been a son, able to take over the family company, stood her in good stead in managing her various properties.

Donald Mitchell, her husband's nephew, agent, and administrator, served as her chief executive officer. He gave her monthly financial reports on her various establishments in New London, New Haven, Salem, Jamaica, and Miami. During the 1920s, his accounts indicated expenditures under those geographical categories totaling as much as $66,000 a year. He was conscientious about trying to preserve her capital and to make her properties income producing so far as possible. Some of her houses were rentable, and he collected rents to offset up to a tenth of his outlays.

In the case of the Salem farms, which his uncle had wanted to be productive, he employed a farm manager and additional farm workers to grow corn and hay for a herd of cattle, in a dairy farm operation known as the "Mumford Dairies." The business marketed its milk products at retail in the New London area. Making use of old farm buildings on the New London properties as a distribution center, it delivered milk to a substantial clientele that included Connecticut College. Occasionally a small profit from the "milk account" would show up in Donald's monthly reports to his "Aunt Annie."

As she entered her late eighties, she became increasingly concerned about the future of her properties. After years of unsuccessful efforts to sell it, the Jamaica estate was virtually abandoned. The future of the Salem properties had, she felt, been assured by placing them in the names of her children and grandchildren. The New Haven house was rentable and could presumably be sold. Her Miami home she could leave by will to Alfreda. What most concerned her was the future of her New London property. Despite all her other acquisitions, it had long been her home base—and the only home her husband had ever had. It had been the home where her daughters were brought up and where one of them married. It was packed with sentiment.

She consulted her son-in-law Hiram. He referred her to his New Haven lawyer and political adviser, Fred Baker, who suggested setting up a family corporation to take title to the Pequot Avenue property; and by a wide distribution of shares, the corporation presumably could provide collective wisdom to the property's management and division of its benefits.

My father suggested the name Lone Pine Lawn, which described his conception of the property (actually it had not one but two conspicuous pine trees on the lawn), and in the summer of 1931 the Lone Pine Lawn Corporation was organized in Fred Baker's office. To it Annie Mitchell transferred most of her New London property, reserving a life use, along with $250,000 in securities and $45,000 in cash as an endowment fund to assure its maintenance. The four thousand shares of the corporation's stock, with a par value of $100 a share, she immediately transferred to her two daughters and her eight grandchildren, four hundred shares to each. She was told that if she lived three more years, under the provisions of the federal tax laws, the gifts would not be treated as made "in anticipation of death," and therefore would not be taxable as part of her estate.

The portion of the property not transferred to the Lone Pine Lawn Corporation, a ten-acre wooded tract cleared of brush and made into parkland by my grandfather, she had recently given to the Alfred Mitchell Woods Association, a nonprofit charitable corporation organized in New London to hold and maintain the land as a public park. The property had been enhanced by the construction of tennis courts and a handsome stone field house, with living quarters for a resident park superintendent, bringing its value to over $300,000. With it went $110,000 worth of bonds as an endowment fund. As the bearer of my grandfather's name, I was named the chairman of the board of trustees, though I was traveling abroad at the time and was not consulted.

The Lone Pine Lawn Corporation rested in Fred Baker's files while my grandmother lived not only the tax-required three years more but another three years. At her death in January 1937, at the age of ninety-two, the corporation proved its usefulness.

Of the original stockholders, my Aunt Charly Jeans had died in 1934, and her shares were now held by Sir James. Neither he nor his daughter Olivia was in a position to play an active role in deciding what to do with the New London property. The other stockholders were my mother and her seven sons. None of us wanted to live in New London or make use of the rambling old mansion that climbed up the hill from Pequot Avenue, or the three smaller dwellings on both sides of the avenue. Only the old barn and outbuildings on

Montauk Avenue that provided a retail outlet for the Mumford Dairies were of concern to those of us who wanted to see the Salem farm operation continue. The rest of the property could be sold.

But I had a social conscience about just cashing in. In 1937 Franklin Roosevelt was beginning his second term, after the resounding support given his New Deal in the 1936 election. My own revolutionary dreams of the early 1930s had been abandoned, and the pages of *Common Sense*, the magazine I had cofounded with Selden Rodman, were devoted to supporting and enhancing the liberal aspects of the New Deal. Public housing for low-income families was in high favor. I envisioned the green lawns with their gardens, orchard, and fine shade trees overlooking New London Harbor as the site of a low-cost housing project.

Though the New Deal measures had helped start the country on the road to recovery, unemployment was still high and the real estate market still depressed. A sale of the property as a whole would mean a heavy loss from our estimate of its real value. To subdivide and develop the land ourselves would require an investment none of us was interested in making. I persuaded my mother and my brothers to hire an architect and city planner to advise us on the disposition of the property.

Our adviser, Julian Whittlesey, a college classmate and friend of mine who had made an international reputation as a city planner, had little trouble coming up with a recommendation. He found that a group of growth-minded New London citizens, under the leadership of a promoter and developer, was already in the field looking for a site for a junior college.

Waldo Clarke, an engineer turned insurance salesman, had already boosted the lagging economy of his hometown by helping to bring the Coast Guard Academy and other educational and industrial enterprises to New London. He had recently been in touch with New York University, his alma mater, about the possibility of establishing a branch in New London.

Instead, Clarke's interest was diverted by a doctoral student in the University's department of education, Richard Saunders, to the more promising establishment of a two-year junior college to round out New London's educational facilities. Saunders persuaded the head of the New London Savings Bank, the publisher of the *New London Day*, and other civic leaders to join him in a promotional committee. They already had their eyes on the Mitchell property as a possible site for a college when Julian Whittlesey was introduced to them by the Chamber of Commerce. He told them the property was now owned by the Lone Pine Lawn Corporation, which was less interested in making a profit than in preserving a beautiful site for some worthy use like public housing.

The committee told him it had no money to buy the property, though it hoped to raise enough to start the college. It evidently was looking for a gift of a site.

I was won over by Whittlesey's recommendation, and persuaded my mother and my brothers to approve it. In the end we were moved less by philanthropic considerations than by the practical fact that promptly getting rid of the real estate would permit dissolution of the corporation and distribution of the nearly $300,000 endowment fund to the stockholders. The New London committee, probably aware of the endowment fund, indicated that they could not accept the gift without some seed money toward launching the college, and it was finally agreed that $10,000 from the endowment fund would accompany the transfer of the land and buildings.

The conveyance to the newly organized New London Junior College took place in the summer of 1938. At the end of that summer, on September 21, occurred the most devastating hurricane ever to hit New London. One of the houses on the property, near the beach, was so badly damaged it had to be abandoned; all the buildings suffered some damage; a large section of the brick wall around the Pequot Avenue tract was blown down; and most of the handsome shade trees, including the "lone pine" (pines?), were blasted. But each of the Bingham brothers and the other family stockholders in the Lone Pine Lawn Corporation were richer by some $30,000 of what had been Tiffany money.

Duly appointed president of New London Junior College, Richard Saunders took over the hurricane-ravaged campus. The committee, now a Board of Trustees with me as a member, was only half successful in a fund drive, but Dr. Saunders, with what he had and what he could scrounge, not only repaired the buildings (turning parlors and bedrooms into classrooms, and transforming the old stables and carriage house into a rudimentary "engineering" building) but also assembled an enthusiastic young faculty, recruited students, and opened the college for the academic year beginning September 1939.

Classes began just as Hitler was invading Poland. Three years later, when most of its students were facing the draft, the college had to close. But it reopened with a new president in 1946, taking advantage of the GI Bill program of student aid. Its subsequent growth, especially the enlargement of its physical plant (including dormitories built with "post-Sputnik" government grants) and the gradual expansion of its student body (to over a thousand day and evening students), took place under the dedicated and vigorous leadership of Robert Weller, who served as president for thirty-five years.

The science building, Bingham Hall, with its physics laboratory named in honor of Sir James Jeans, commemorates the role played by the Tiffany fortune in what is now Mitchell College. The adjoining park facilities of Alfred Mitchell Woods, to which have been added a playground, ball fields, a skating pond, nature trails, and picnic grounds, now under the college's control, all still serve the neighborhood.

CHAPTER 28
Cashing In

In the spring of 1932, Annie, then eighty-seven years old, decided to distribute her remaining shares of Tiffany & Co. stock. She had been told by her son-in-law, Hiram Bingham, then a U.S. Senator, that a new gift tax was about to go into effect. Just why she decided to put her Tiffany stock out of the reach of the Internal Revenue Bureau, rather than other of her holdings, is not clear. But it is more than probable that sentiment played an important role: shares in Tiffany & Co. meant shares in the enterprise that had been her father's life work, and she wanted to be sure they stayed in the family. She had given some of her holdings to her daughters in the 1922 trust, but now she decided to give the rest and to include her grandchildren in her largesse.

After a five-for-one split of Tiffany shares in 1920 and the 1922 distribution to her daughters' trust, Annie's holdings were an even thousand shares. She decided to give one-third to each daughter, and to split the remaining third evenly among her eight grandchildren, seven Bingham grandsons and one Jeans granddaughter. The nearest approximation to these fractions worked out to 336 shares each for Alfreda and Charly, and 41 each to the grandchildren.

In 1932, in the depth of the Great Depression, the value of Tiffany shares was hard to determine, but such shares as were redeemed by the company that year were priced at $600 each. At that figure, the gift to each grandchild was worth $24,600, and the total distribution amounted to $600,000. A few years before—or a few years later—the distribution would have had a value of two million dollars, more or less, and the gift to each grandchild would have been estimated at $50,000.

However valued, this distribution of a substantial part of the Tiffany fortune had a profound influence on at least two of the recipients. I was one of them. My father was the other.

In my case, I had already received a special gift of $10,000 from my grandmother when I graduated from the Yale Law School in 1930. This had enabled me to indulge in two years of travel—in India, China, the Soviet Union, and other parts of Europe and Asia.

The world was then in the throes of revolutionary change exacerbated if not brought on by the Great Depression. I came back from my travels in the summer of 1932 convinced that the capitalist system was in its final collapse, and that the world revolution predicted by Karl Marx was at hand. But I found it hard to believe that the uprising of the working class Marx forecast as the instrument of the revolution would be effective in middle-class America.

Instead I had come to the conclusion that middle-class discontent, such as was producing Fascist revolutions in Italy and Germany, could in this country, if properly understood and guided, become the engine of a transition to a planned socialist economy. I decided to try to launch a magazine to help promote a movement I believed was already under way.

Before my radical conversion, I had planned to go to work in a New London law firm on return from my travels, and to use the New London area as a base for the political career I really yearned for. I knew that I would have to start to earn my own living since the second Mitchell scholarship fund was coming to an end. But now, like a gift from heaven, came forty-one shares of Tiffany & Co. stock.

I did not know how much they were worth, but I gathered that I could turn them in to the company for cash and that they might be worth as much as a thousand dollars apiece. Even in that depression year, Tiffany & Co. was still paying dividends from a large surplus accumulated in the fat 1920s. In 1932 the dividend was $60 a share, down from a high of $165 in 1929. I could live on that even if I had nothing else.

In July of 1932, I met another enthusiastic rebel who wanted to start a magazine. Selden Rodman as a student at Yale had started an iconoclastic journal, the *Harkness Hoot*. He was now eager to start a new national magazine and fell in readily with my plans. We complemented each other admirably. I had definite social and political goals, which he accepted readily. His radicalism was focused on literature and the arts.

We drew up a prospectus for a weekly magazine to be called *Common Sense*. We had learned that the *New Yorker* had been started with only $100,000 a few years before, and we set out to raise a like amount. If necessary, my new capital could make up at least a quarter of that amount. I was not so rash as to think of cashing in all forty-one of my Tiffany shares at once, but I did turn in twelve, for which I received $600 a share from the company. I found out later that the company arranged with my grandmother for her to buy them. A few months later, I sold the company another fourteen shares. The first issue of *Common Sense* appeared in December 1932, bearing on its cover a lurid cartoon of Andrew Mellon, the Pittsburgh banker who had been Secretary of the Treasury under Hoover. I had hoped the magazine would be so successful from the start that it would soon be able to pay me a salary and restore my investment in it. That hope lasted only until the first printing of 100,000 copies came back from the newsstands largely unsold.

In the course of time *Common Sense* did become a significant journal of opinion, but it made scarcely a ripple on its first appearance. In one place, however, it did cause a stir: my father glanced through a copy, flung it across the room and, so far as I know, never looked at another copy.

If he knew that I had used Tiffany shares to help finance it, his anger at its blatant radicalism may have been magnified by a sense of guilt, for he had persuaded my mother to transfer to him the 336 shares she had received from her mother in the same distribution. He probably suggested that there would be a tax saving if the shares were in his name.

But other motives were certainly in his mind. He had for years been carrying on a secret affair—secret at least so far as his wife and family knew, if not the Washington gossip mill—with Suzanne Hill, wife of a Maryland congressman. His marriage to Alfreda was by this time little more than a hollow shell, and he could well see it ending in divorce. His taking advantage of her continuing confidence in him was something he must have been deeply ashamed of—in the inner recesses of his conscience.

There was one factor that would have helped him ease his conscience. He did not of course disclose his acquisition of the stock to his mother-in-law, and Alfreda did not consider it important enough to mention to her mother. Yet when he had first urged upon his mother-in-law the distribution of her shares, he must have assured her that it would make it easier to take care of his sons' needs, when and if they needed financial help. Specifically he seems to have undertaken to see that each of his sons received a wedding present of $10,000 when they married. Annie was anxious to have her grandsons marry and had spread her largesse to the first two when they were married.

A year later, in 1933, Brewster, then a student at the Union Theological Seminary, announced his plan to marry fellow student Frances Beach. His father, somewhat skeptical of Brewster's financial sophistication, set up a $10,000 trust fund for his benefit, contributing six of his newly acquired Tiffany shares, along with some other securities, to the fund. Later, when some of the investments turned sour, he added another four shares from his Tiffany holdings to restore the fund to its $10,000 level.

Brewster's marriage was followed within a few months by Harry's and then mine. Our father felt committed to provide each of us with a comparable wedding gift. This time he sold twenty of his Tiffany shares back to the company to raise the cash.

Whatever the understanding between Hiram and Alfreda at the time she gave him this $300,000 slice of the Tiffany fortune, he treated it as his own. He may well have persuaded himself that he was holding the stock for the benefit of his sons. But within a year of his acquisition, he turned in fifty shares to the company for cash. He had been defeated for reelection to the Senate in November 1932, and no longer had a significant income of his own.

Two years later, Alfreda sought a divorce. She had fallen in love with a pianist and composer, Henry Gregor, whom she had first gotten to know as a paid accompanist to her violin playing. She then asked Hiram to return the Tiffany shares. He claimed that his mother-in-law had meant them for him, and cited the similar allotment to Charly Jeans, which had passed to Sir James upon Charly's death.

It was, of course, a matter of transcendent importance to him, and it seems likely that he had persuaded himself that the gift had really been intended for him. Perhaps he also viewed it as a kind of alimony. Alfreda had supported him for thirty-seven years, and now she wanted a divorce. She should therefore accept responsibility for his continued support. She may have thought of it that way, for she made no great issue over his refusal to return the shares.

When his mother-in-law learned of it, however, she was horrified and incredulous. She first got word of the transaction in a letter, dated February 28, 1935, from Donald Mitchell, her late husband's nephew, who had watched over her financial affairs during her long widowhood. He wrote that he had been to New York, had stopped in at Tiffany & Co., and had seen her nephew Charles L. Tiffany II, then vice-president of the company. In a passage that she underlined in red pencil and kept in her most personal files, Donald Mitchell had written:

> Charles asked if you knew that Hi [Hiram] had sold eighty-five shares of T stock. This stock has been bought from him by T & Co.

She was uncomprehending. In answer to her inquiry he wrote again:

> The shares Hi sold were part of those you transferred to Freda and which she in turn made over to Hi. Charles talked quite a bit on the subject, but it is just as well not to write this, for the conversation carried on verbally might not be understood if written out, and it is better not to try to repeat. I gathered that Charles was not altogether pleased with any part of the transaction, i.e., in his having sold part or in having him still as a stockholder.

Annie remained bewildered, and this time Charles Tiffany wrote to clarify:

> This is to refresh your mind on the transfer of T & Co. stock which still seems to disturb you. I was not present and got this all from conversation with you after the transfer was made.
>
> On your way from Miami to New London [in May 1932] you stopped in Washington and were advised by Hi (then in the Senate) that there was a bill pending (sure of passage) in Congress making deeds of gift *Taxable*, and he advised that you should make distribution of your T & Co. shares before the bill was enacted.
>
> On your arrival here you told me of this and how Thorne had opposed the suggestion, but you told me that as Hi had advised it very strongly you were perfectly satisfied and the shares were divided as per my letter of March 22. Alfreda's share was 336 shares which she immediately made over to Hi.
>
> Of course this was absolutely within her rights, the shares were hers and she had a perfect right to transfer them to whom she pleased.
>
> I am rather surprised that you did not know of this transfer, but I do not see how it could have been prevented.

Annie changed her will. She no longer wanted Hiram as an executor. More than that, in her bitter disillusionment with her son-in-law, she developed paranoid thoughts that he might murder her daughter for her money. She died in January 1937, still concerned about Alfreda's safety.

CHAPTER 29

Trickling Down

A nnie's five-million-dollar share of the fortune left by her father at his death in 1902 was still virtually intact, if not all still in her possession, at her death thirty-five years later. The extravagances in which her husband encouraged her came mostly out of surplus income. When he died in 1911, she was still worth about five million dollars. This comfortable fortune she immediately put in the hands of trustees to assure its prudent preservation, but she retained control. Then in 1922 she transferred approximately two million to a trust for the benefit of her daughters, but she still controlled three million. The distribution of her Tiffany & Co. stock in 1932, and other gifts for the benefit of her grandchildren, brought the 1911 trust fund down to $1,717,009.42, as her trustees reported after her death in 1937.

The distribution of this sum, by the terms of the 1911 trust agreement, was to be in accordance with her will, and her will left it to her seven grandsons. Now after her death, for the first time, I felt really rich. My share in her estate, when it was put in my hands, was a quarter of a million dollars. There had been relatively little inflation or loss of the value of the dollar since Charles Tiffany's day, so this, together with the Tiffany shares we had received a few years before, was enough to assure me—and my brothers, who received a like amount—at least a modest living for the rest of our lives. I had given most of my Tiffany shares to the "cause" represented by *Common Sense*. But at the age of thirty-five, rejoicing in spite of my radical views in my new affluence, I felt financially secure enough to add two more to the two children I already had.

"Shirtsleeves to shirtsleeves in three generations," as one popular writer had put it, did not seem to apply in the case of the Bingham brothers. And there was more to come. Our inheritance was soon augmented from another direction.

Burnie was not the only one of his children who Charles Tiffany feared would dissipate his hard-earned fortune. Louise, Annie's younger and more delicate sister, was also thought by her father to be unable to manage her own share of his fortune. She was not reckless like Burnie, but so timid and fragile that she might be easily victimized. She became deeply dependent on her more assertive older sister Annie, and only survived her by a month. She also was dependent on her servants—a "lady's maid" and a chauffeur; they married while in her employ and took care of her for many years. In her old age, they acquired a house in Scarsdale, and she became their tenant. At her death she left them a good part of her property. But her share of the Tiffany fortune, being in trust under the terms of her father's will, went to other branches of his family, half to the children of Louis, who had died in 1933, and half to Annie's family. Since Charly had died, her one-quarter share went to her daughter, Olivia Jeans Smith, and the other quarter went to my mother. The original trust had been well over a million and a half dollars. My mother's share came to almost three hundred thousand dollars.

Alfreda had never had much capital to dispose of, being dependent on the trusts set up for her by her parents. But with this new wealth under her personal control, she turned over a substantial portion of it, about $100,000, to her new husband, Henry Gregor. She had married him shortly after her divorce from my father early in 1937.

The gift was intended to give him some financial independence. He had been, after all, her paid accompanist, and it would hardly make for a stable marriage if he remained wholly dependent on her. True, my father had always been dependent on her income, and their marriage had lasted thirty-seven years. But it had been only her income to which he had access until the distribution of the Tiffany & Co. stock in 1932, and his dependence was more on his mother-in-law than on his wife. Alfreda had been protected from financial responsibilities all her life and, after her marriage to Hiram, had always trusted him to make financial decisions.

I first met Henry Gregor in the summer of 1935. My mother had invited him and a cellist to spend a week at the Salem Camp to play classical trios together. I gathered that Henry was music director in a private girls' school in Washington.

The following winter I came to Washington with my family to spend Christmas in my parents' newly rented house on the edge of Rock Creek Park where they had bought a lot and had planned to build a house. On Christmas day, after the usual morning distribution of gifts, my father left to go "to his club," and Henry showed up for some music. Watching them together, I realized that Henry had become more than a paid accompanist to my mother's violin playing. They spoke German together and seemed to be on intimate terms. So it was no surprise to me when some months later my mother told me she and Henry were in love, and she wanted a divorce from my father.

I learned that Henry, though German, was born in Moscow of a Russian mother. He had early shown musical talent and had studied piano, organ, and composition at the Berlin Conservatory. He had come to this country in the 1920s. As a composer he had little success, only a few short pieces achieving publication. His name was originally Heinrich Schmidt, but his compositions had been published under the name of Schmidt-Gregor, adapted from his mother's patronymic, Gregoriovna, and he now used the name Henry Gregor. He had been married to a German opera singer, but they had no children and were now separated.

I felt some responsibility for my mother. I had been aware for years of my parents' estrangement. My mind went back to an incident that had shocked me at the time they were moving into the lavish duplex apartment on Sixteenth Street in Washington, after his election in 1926 to a full six-year term in the Senate. My parents were deciding about the placing of furniture in their new home, and my mother objected to his placing of an Oriental rug.

"You have no taste," she told him, "and never have had." It was as if she had slapped his face.

"What about Father?" I asked, when she told me she wanted to marry Henry. She seemed smug. He would be all right, she told me. She thought he might be interested in a certain "Mrs. Hull." (This was eleven years after he had first fallen in love with Suzanne Hill. As I learned later, it was at the home of a Mrs. Hull, a friend of Suzanne, that he and Suzanne had often rendezvoused during the intervening years.)

When I next had an opportunity to talk to Henry, I asked him if he truly loved my mother. I had had a letter from the cellist who had first accompanied Henry to Salem, warning me that Henry was an "adventurer" out for my mother's money. Henry quietly replied that he was uncomfortable with the word "love" but that he and "Dousha," as he called my mother, were very fond of each other and had much in common.

I became Henry's partisan. And remembering the humiliations to which my father had occasionally been subjected in his dependency, I urged her to turn over enough of her fortune to Henry so he would not have to be wholly dependent on her. The distribution of Aunt Louise's trust two years after their marriage gave her enough capital for the first time so she was able to endow Henry.

Their marriage was a happy one. Most of her share of the Tiffany fortune was locked up in her mother's 1922 trust, but Henry made good use of her large income and shrewdly invested the capital she had given him. He had no expensive tastes. The funds he now had access to were used to bring members of his German family—a sister with her daughter, and a half-sister with her husband and children—to this country after World War II, and helped them establish homes and find jobs in the Miami area.

At Henry's death in 1964, his relatives were astonished to learn that he had acquired a fortune of over half a million dollars, and had set up a trust fund in his will to take care of the education of his American nieces and nephews. How had he become so rich? He had used as much of the Tiffany fortune as he controlled to buy and sell land in south Florida's booming real estate market. No one was the poorer for it, and his gentle and sensitive personality endeared him to most of the Bingham family hardly less than to his German family.

In 1945, eight years after my mother's marriage to Henry, her uncle Burnett Tiffany died, and another distribution of Tiffany money took place. Under the terms of the million-dollar trust his father had set up for Burnie, the assets were distributable half to Louis's descendants, and half to Annie's. Charly had died in 1934, and her one-quarter share went to her daughter

Olivia. The remaining quarter went to Alfreda, and she distributed it—seven-eighths to her seven sons, and one-eighth to Henry Gregor. (Thirteen years younger than she, Gregor apparently was treated on this occasion as another son.) After all the subdivisions of Uncle Burnie's trust, I was the richer by about thirty thousand dollars. And this was when prices were still under control, and the tenfold inflation that has occurred since was just beginning, so it would be more like three hundred thousand today.

Another windfall came my way six years later, in 1951, with the death of another Tiffany heir, Olivia Jeans Smith, my only first cousin. This time the beneficiaries were not only her Bingham cousins but also, thanks to some complicated litigation, a considerable number of lawyers.

Olivia was born under a cloud and her life was a sordid tragedy. Her death was attributed to anorexia nervosa: she had starved herself to death. Named for her grandmother Annie Olivia Tiffany, she was deprived even of a normal birthday, being born on Leap Year's Day, February 29, 1912, and therefore able to celebrate anniversaries only every four years. Her mother, my Aunt Charly, had also been born under a cloud, having "inherited" syphilis from her father. Presumably Alfred Mitchell had been infected in a Honolulu brothel as a young man, and many years later, in a recurrence of the disease, had infected his second daughter in utero. Olivia was brought up in the vivid apprehension that she herself might carry the disease, or even be defective. This meant special schooling, mostly at home. Apparently normal, healthy, and bright, she made it through childhood and adolescence in England and entered one of Oxford's women's colleges.

She revolted against her oversolicitous parents, and became so estranged from them that she did not attend her mother's funeral in 1934. She was briefly married to a man named Smith, but the marriage did not last, thanks to a lesbian relationship. Olivia wanted a family and adopted two children. But her life became intolerable when her lesbian partner was conventionally married. She had long struggled with obesity, but now she refused all food, and eventually died, in February 1951, at the home of her former lover.

Olivia had been the beneficiary of her grandmother Annie Olivia's 1928 trust and of her 1932 distribution of Tiffany stock, and she had inherited a large slice of the Tiffany fortune when her mother Charly died. At her own death, she left such a large part of her fortune to her woman friend as to spark the theory among some of her Jeans relatives that her friend had contributed to her early death or had done nothing to prevent it. But she did make generous provision for her adopted children.

The question that required a court trial to settle was whether those children could be considered "issue" to bring them under the provisions of her grandmother's 1922 trust. The trust had been set up with over two million dollars' worth of securities to provide income for Alfreda and Charly so long as they lived, and if one of them died, then to her children or to the "issue" of any child who died. After Charly's death in 1934, Olivia had been getting an income of $20,000 a year from the trust.

Now, after Olivia's death, were her adopted children entitled to the $20,000 a year? If not, that sum would be added to the large income my mother was already getting from the trust. The trust funds were held in New York with the Bankers Trust Company and Walter Mitchell as trustees. They brought suit in a New York court asking the court to tell them what to do.

My mother was in her late seventies when the question came up, so how it was answered was of greater concern to her sons, who would be the beneficiaries of the trust at her death, than to her. Two of her sons, Jonathan and I, were lawyers, and she left it to us to handle the case. Jonathan suggested we engage a friend of his, Daniel Tenney of the prestigious Wall Street law firm Milbank, Tweed, Hope and Hadley, to represent her and her sons.

I felt uncomfortable about the position I was in, seeking to deprive two little English girls of a share in the Tiffany fortune. But I comforted myself with the belief that these children must have benefited by direct inheritance from their adoptive mother. Olivia had, after all, received a large share of the Burnett Tiffany and Louise Tiffany trusts, as well as a share in her grandmother's distribution of Tiffany stock, and presumably had taken care of her adopted children's financial future.

The children's legal guardians and the executors of Olivia's estate were represented in the litigation by other New York lawyers, and there was a flurry of pleadings and legal memoranda. On behalf of the adopted children, it was argued that the original trust agreement had explicitly stated that it was to be governed by Connecticut law, and that under the Connecticut law an adopted child was entitled to inherit from the "adopting parents or their relatives as though he were the natural child of such adopting parents," and it was further argued that the words *child* and *issue* had been used interchangeably when Annie Mitchell had signed the trust agreement. Our lawyer argued that Annie would not have intended these English children, who had been adopted after her death, to have a share in her inheritance.

The New York Supreme Court judge before whom the case was argued ruled, in a brief paragraph, in our favor. For the rest of her life, my mother received $20,000 a year more income than if the decision had gone the other way, and when she died a dozen years later, my brothers and I received all the principal of the trust.

CHAPTER 30

Family Affairs

My life was profoundly affected by the Tiffany millions. I was born in 1905 in a big house on Reservoir Street, in an elite neighborhood of Cambridge, Massachusetts, across the street from the home of the Harvard University treasurer. The house had been bought for my mother by my Mitchell grandparents shortly after the distribution of Charles Tiffany's estate. All the spacious houses in which I lived as a child, and the ample staff of nurses and house servants that surrounded me, were financed with Tiffany money.

Not that my family was totally dependent on Tiffany & Co. Even in his lifetime Charles Tiffany had diversified the wealth he acquired from his business, and at his death barely a quarter of his wealth was in Tiffany & Co. stock. The various trusts by which his wealth was preserved always contained a variety of corporate stocks and bonds. But the company that had been the source of the affluence continued to play a central role in all the Tiffany descendants' financial affairs until my fiftieth year.

During all that time, I was a silent and largely unknowing recipient of benefits springing from the Tiffany heritage. But when Tiffany & Co. ceased to be a family business in 1955, I became aware of a dramatic struggle for its control.

I still owned a few shares of the Tiffany stock my grandmother had given me in 1932. In July 1955, I received a letter addressed to Tiffany stockholders from Irving Maidman, a New York real estate developer who owned the largest single block of Tiffany stock. The company, he wrote, had been losing money for years, and dividends, paid out of capital reserves, were now reduced to one dollar a share. It was clear he wanted a change in management.

About the same time, I attended a family conference called at the request of Bill Lusk, an officer of Tiffany & Co. He was a grandson of Louis Tiffany and therefore a second cousin of mine. He told us that the company was in danger of being taken over by the Bulova Watch Company. For over a hundred years, under the leadership of the Tiffany and Moore families, the company had been a symbol of quality and integrity. Now it was faced with the possibility of becoming a subsidiary of an upstart watch company. He seemed to suggest that those trying to take over the company were not gentlemen. For him, I felt this was almost a class struggle.

He was willing to admit that the direction of the company by the Moore family had been stuffy and too conservative, and the company had fallen behind. But he had a plan to block the takeover and revivify the company: he was in touch with Walter Hoving, owner of Bonwit Teller, the expensive women's clothing store next door to Tiffany's on Fifth Avenue. Hoving, a patron of the arts, and at one time the city's Park Commissioner, was now acquiring shares of the company's stock. If we would sell our shares to Hoving and so help him obtain a majority of the stock, the good name of Tiffany and the interests of the Tiffany family would be preserved.

We agreed to go along. The stock had been selling as low as $30 a share, and Hoving was offering $55. "Blood is thicker than water," and our cousin Bill Lusk was to become president of the company if Hoving won control. Later it appeared that Hoving had offered another large stockholder $70, and Mr. Bulova himself had tried to buy out Hoving at $95 a share.[1]

Hoving did not buy all the scattered holdings of Tiffany stock in the hands of members of the Bingham family, and he did not immediately gain full control of the company, but none of the Binghams any longer had a substantial interest in the company. Even my father had sold the shares my mother had turned over to him.

My father had used the proceeds from his Tiffany shares in a program of careful investment, and during the 1940s and 1950s had seen his capital grow. For the first time in his life, he was making money. As a United States Senator and a member of the Senate Finance Committee, he had moved among the rich and powerful. After his defeat for reelection in 1932, he continued to live in Washington and became a member of the board of directors of a large Washington-based bank. After his divorce and remarriage in 1937, he moved into Suzanne's spacious town house at 1818 R Street. He brought with him the cook and butler that had been part of my mother's household staff. In a distribution of assets that had been amicable enough (except for the block of Tiffany shares), she had kept the chauffeur and housemaid. He devoted himself increasingly to the study of investment strategies, and became a member of his bank's investment committee. Suzanne entrusted her own not inconsiderable inheritance to him, and he had the satisfaction of seeing her capital funds, as well as his own, double in value.

The Washington climate in summer is so heavily oppressive that all who can escape to cooler resorts. Hiram and Suzanne first established a summer home in Old Lyme, on the Connecticut shore not far from Salem, but the staid society of old families did not welcome the notorious Binghams. After other summers in a rented house in Newport, Rhode Island, or traveling abroad, they bought a beachfront mansion in Magnolia on the north shore of Massachusetts Bay.

My father's health began to deteriorate in the 1950s. He had long been subject to respiratory illnesses, and he developed emphysema. He arranged for a reunion with his seven sons on his eightieth birthday, expressing some

---

[1] The story of this and a subsequent battle for control of Tiffany's is told in Joseph Purtell's *The Tiffany Touch* (New York: Random House, 1971).

pride in having lived longer than his father. In the winter and spring of 1956, his emphysema worsened. In May, I had a call from him; he was in a Washington hospital and wanted me and my doctor brother, Charles, to come to see him. He would put us up in his club, the Metropolitan Club. He had set up a special account at his bank for me to draw upon for my expenses.

Charles and I found him gaunt, dependent on an oxygen tank, seemingly near death. Charles, using his prerogatives as a doctor, checked his medical chart and was horrified to find that the doctor in charge had prescribed almost lethal doses of narcotics.

Calling for the first time for my professional help as a lawyer, my father asked me to get his will from his Washington lawyer. He wanted to make some changes. The lawyer, Richard Wilbur, refused to surrender the original will but gave me a copy, assuring me that any change made in its terms now would be challenged. I read the copy and found that my father was leaving practically everything he owned to a trust for the benefit of his "beloved" wife. At her death the trust assets were to be distributed to his grandchildren "per capita and not per stirpes." His sons were each to get a thousand-dollar legacy apiece, as were Suzanne's three daughters. There were other legacies: ten thousand dollars to Rose, wife of my brother Harry and mother of nine children at the time the will was written; and ten thousand dollars to Groton, the boarding school in which Rose's sons were enrolled.

Though my share of his estate would be only a thousand dollars, I could find no fault with the will. In the past, my father had made sure that the Tiffany fortune controlled by his mother-in-law would benefit his sons during their educational years, and that they would benefit even more—even obtain a moderate financial independence for life—at their mother's death. He could reasonably skip over one generation to the next for the final disposition of his wealth.

I told him as much. He made no further move and never told me what he had in mind to change. But when he died a couple of weeks later, and his executors listed an estate of almost a million dollars, it was clear that he wished he had been more generous to his sons.

He had been hurt, as he had indicated more than once, that none of his sons had consulted him on the management of their inheritance, although he was for years a director of his bank and on its investment committee, and was parlaying his fraction of the Tiffany fortune to two or three times what it had been.

Yet he was also hurt by the indications Suzanne had given that his death would not be unwelcome. In my last bedside conference with him, he hurried me out of the hospital room obviously afraid that Suzanne would find me there.

On our return to Connecticut, Charles and I were half inclined to charge the doctor and the lawyer and Suzanne with conspiracy to murder, if not murder itself. This was, to be sure, before the days of "living wills" by which a dying person can be spared the horrors of a protracted death or a life continued as a vegetable. From my present point of view as an octogenarian, if Suzanne did in fact conspire with the doctor to give him a lethal dose of sedatives, it was as much an act of love as of greed.

My father died June 6, 1956. His burial, in Arlington National Cemetery with military honors, was arranged by Suzanne, but presumably as he wished. His seven sons and a few of his twenty-nine grandchildren gathered at the entrance of the cemetery, and followed the horse-drawn caisson, with its flag-draped coffin and a military escort, up the hill to the beat of a muffled drum. As we stood at the grave site, behind Suzanne and her three daughters, all veiled in black, and behind a group of black-coated pallbearers, Suzanne's friends whom we did not know, we felt more like spectators than mourners. We never saw Suzanne again. She lived another five years, dying of cancer in January 1962.

The trust fund established in my father's will for her benefit was in due course distributed to the twenty-nine Bingham grandchildren. As laid down in the will, the shares of those under twenty-five years of age remained in trust till they reached that age, while those over twenty-five received their shares in cash. The last distribution came in August 1979 when the youngest of the grandchildren, William S. Bingham, Harry's eleventh child, reached twenty-five. The amount of principal each received was close to $22,000. This was about one five-hundredth part of what their great-great-grandfather had left to his descendants. But the bulk of the fortune inherited by his daughter Annie was still intact, safely preserved in family trusts.

CHAPTER 31
Filthy Lucre

As a girl, Alfreda Mitchell never heard talk of money. For her mother Annie, talking about money was as indelicate as talking about one's bodily functions. And her father must have constantly guarded against any suggestion that he had married the Tiffany heiress for her money. All her life Alfreda was shielded and protected from financial concerns.

Told that money was dirty, she was taught to wash her hands after touching a dollar bill, already touched by a myriad of unclean hands. Most of the money spent on her behalf never even existed in visible form. It was no more than bookkeeping entries in checkbooks and bank statements. She left the understanding of those figures first to her father and then to her husband.

Under conservative management, Alfreda's inheritance had not multiplied but neither had it been dissipated. And she seldom had much of her inheritance under her direct control. When her mother distributed her Tiffany stock in 1932, Alfreda quickly put her shares in her husband's name. Later when she came into possession of the remaining funds of the Burnett Tiffany and Louise Tiffany trusts, she passed most of them on to her sons and her second husband.

Even the houses she lived in during much of her life were not hers. The house at 787 Prospect Street in New Haven, built for her by her parents in 1909, was not put in her name until ten years later. In 1925, when her husband became a U.S. Senator, she moved to Washington to live in rented quarters. The great Prospect Street house stood empty. For a couple of years it was leased to the president of the New Haven Railroad. Then for a season it was occupied by old friends from Hawaii, the James Judds. Part of it was later leased at a nominal rental to the youngest of the Bingham brothers, Jonathan, and a group of his Yale Law School classmates.

Put up for sale in the late 1930s, the house became a white elephant. Like so many of the oversized mansions of the rich that ended up in the possession of charitable institutions, two of the nearby big houses on Prospect Hill had been taken over by Albertus Magnus, a Catholic women's college. The college seemed to be the only possible purchaser of the Bingham house, but it would take it only as a gift.

Another group calling itself the Women's College of New Haven saw possibilities in the property and was willing to pay $12,000 for it. Thirty years earlier, the empty lot had cost the Mitchells more than that, but a sale seemed better than a gift so, in the summer of 1939, my mother sold it for that amount.

My brothers and I divided up its furnishings, storing most of them in the Woodbridge House barn in Salem. I acquired the grandfather clock that stood in the hall, the big leather armchair that I had thought of as my father's when it stood on one side of the library fireplace, a carved oak library table that had been my father's desk, some Oriental rugs, and the furnishings of what had been my bedroom. With the dismantling of the house my parents had called Casa Alegre, I felt as if I were at last leaving my childhood behind me.

The Women's College of New Haven ran out of funds the next year, and Albertus Magnus at last acquired a new dormitory, probably for the amount of debt the property then carried.

Meanwhile my mother was building a new house for herself and Henry Gregor in Florida. She had inherited her mother's house, Sweet Way, on Brickell Avenue in Miami, with its charming waterfront view of Biscayne Bay. But when Henry discovered the possibilities of a new career for himself in the music department of the University of Miami in Coral Gables, they decided to build a house near the university campus.

Sweet Way was then made available to my brothers Brewster and Mitchell and the Moral Re-Armament movement (MRA), which had for some years been absorbing their energies and other resources. The movement's message of absolute moral purity (and its call to commitment to four moral values—honesty, purity, unselfishness, and love) seemed to have a special appeal to some wealthy individuals, and MRA depended to no small extent on inherited wealth. The Brickell Avenue complex became a southern headquarters for the movement, emulating its northern headquarters, Dellwood, the great Westchester County estate turned over to MRA by Mrs. John Henry Hammond.

Dr. Frank Buchman, the founder of the MRA, may have hoped that Sweet Way would eventually be deeded to his organization. He spent some months of his last years as a guest of Brewster and Mitchell. Mitchell transformed part of the house near the entrance on Brickell Avenue into a little theater where the movement's promotional films could be shown, and installed an elevator to the second floor for the use of the increasingly crippled Dr. Buchman.

Even though my mother had not liked living near the shore, she was glad to have Brewster and Mitchell make it their home, and she liked to have her grandchildren enjoy vacations there. She put a few thousand dollars in my hands out of which I was to pay the travel expenses of any of her descendants who wanted some Florida sunshine.

She lived to be ninety-two. In her last years she was crippled by osteoporosis, but she continued to shuttle back and forth between summers in Salem and winters in Coral Gables. After Henry Gregor died in 1964, she gave up the Mantua Street house and moved into a smaller and more manageable house nearby that had been acquired by my brother Charles. One whole wall of his living-dining room was covered by a large painting by her Uncle Louis Tiffany. It portrayed a "queen of the May" idyll in which Alfreda had posed as a twelve-year-old queen seated on a throne, her younger sister Charly and her little Tiffany cousins, gauzily attired as wood nymphs, bringing her gifts of spring flowers.

In June 1967, for the last time, she made the trip north from Florida to Salem. Now needing round-the-clock care, she was accompanied by two registered nurses, as well as tiny Blanche Smith, who had been her cook and maid-of-all-work for some years. The nurses were installed in the Camp's guest cottage while Mrs. Smith and my mother occupied the north wing of the Camp.

Early on in her marriage to Henry Gregor, my mother had remodeled what had been the servants' wing. Two of the small bedrooms had been combined to make a larger music room for Henry's piano. A big picture window was carved out, and a new chimney and fireplace installed. With a small kitchen added, the wing was transformed into a self-sufficient apartment of some charm.

After Henry's death, further alterations had provided a separate bedroom and bath for the newly widowed Mrs. Smith.

Like the rest of the Camp, the north wing had never been insulated or winterized and had no cellar so that it was virtually uninhabitable in cold weather. Electric heat was finally installed.

In her last months, my mother, almost totally crippled, lay uncomplaining on her bed in the tiny room of the old servants' wing, from which she could look out over the farmlands that had been in her family off and on for two hundred years. The sight of miniature cows in a distant meadow gave her pleasure, she said.

She was having difficulty breathing, her vital functions were failing, and Dr. Ely, the old family doctor from Hamburg, said she didn't have many days to live. She had wanted to be present at the wedding of one of her twenty-nine grandchildren scheduled to take place in mid-August. But on the morning of August 18, in the bed next to the window, she quietly stopped breathing. The wedding guests were to assemble for a family party in the Camp's main dining room that evening, with the wedding reception in the main living room of the Camp the next day. By common agreement the wedding plans went forward, even as my mother's frail remains were taken charge of by the funeral director.

A few days after the wedding, a memorial service was held at the Camp. With chamber music and singing provided by grandchildren, each of the seven sons took some part in a touching program of reminiscences, and then walked over to the family cemetery, downhill from the Woodbridge House, where a simple burial service was conducted by my mother's fifth son, the Reverend Brewster Bingham.

Along with the sense of loss, my brothers and I felt relief that her suffering was over. And we could not but be aware that we would benefit from her death. The annual income she had been receiving from the family trusts, around $70,000 a year, would now be available to her sons—$10,000 more or less for each son.

Most of that would come from the termination of the trust established for her benefit by her mother in 1922, forty-five years before. The value of the securities originally put in the trustees' hands for the benefit of Alfreda and Charly was close to two million dollars. The trustees had been Charles Tiffany II, Annie's nephew and an officer of Tiffany & Co.; Walter Mitchell, Alfred Mitchell's nephew; and the Bankers Trust Company of New York.

The trustees had filed three formal accountings to a New York court; the first in 1948 after the death of trustee Charles Tiffany II showed that the value of the trust assets then on hand, $1,956,256, was almost exactly the same as the value of the securities received in 1922, $1,969,585. In terms of purchasing power after the inflation caused by World War II, the fund had shrunk. Family trust funds handled by big banks are necessarily managed ultraconservatively.

When trustee Walter Mitchell died in 1962, a second accounting was filed by the Bankers Trust Company as "surviving trustee." Despite the inflation that had spurted during the Korean War, the trust funds had shrunk further, and the total fund, at inventory value, was only $1,754,135.

However, the "third and final account" submitted by the Bankers Trust Company showed the net assets available for distribution as $2,423,477. Under the terms of the trust, the "remaindermen," Olivia Jeans Smith having died, were the seven Bingham brothers, and in due course I received one-seventh of the securities, valued at $346,211.

Nor was that all. Two other trusts terminated with my mother's death. The first trust Annie and her husband had established for the benefit of their daughters in 1908 had originally consisted of $91,000 in bonds. Over the years the Union & New Haven Trust Company, the trustee, had shifted into stocks, and the value of the trust assets had increased by 1967 to $163,000. The one-seventh share distributed to me was valued at $22,000.

The other trust distributed at that time (also by the Union & New Haven Trust Company) was the Trust for Grandsons established by our grandmother in 1928, with $218,000 worth of securities. By 1967, when the principal fund was distributed, it was worth close to half a million dollars, and my share came to $67,000.

In addition to the three trusts that were liquidated at my mother's death, she owned real estate left under her will. Of the Salem properties she had been given by her parents, the Camp property she left in trust, along with $100,000 as a maintenance fund, to five of her sons as trustees. They were to maintain it for the benefit of her living descendants (then sixty-nine in number) for summer vacations and family gatherings. Its three self-contained living units, together with a guest cottage, would now be available to members of her extended family free of charge or at low rental fees.

The rest of her Salem land, including the Marvel farm and several hundred acres of overgrown pasture and forest land, had been previously transferred to the Salem Valley Corporation, a family corporation organized to continue dairy farming on family lands and thereby preserve a beautiful valley.

My mother had also inherited her mother's even more valuable property on Brickell Avenue in Miami. This she left to Brewster and Mitchell for their lifetime use (they still were using it both as a residence and as a Moral Re-Armament headquarters), and then it was to be sold for the benefit of all her sons. A few years after her death, Brewster and Mitchell decided to give up their life use and sell the property. Comprising two acres overlooking Biscayne Bay, its value had skyrocketed. Of the two million dollars for which it was sold to a developer as the site for a high-rise apartment building, about half went to Brewster and Mitchell as the value of their life use. The other half was divided among the other brothers, a last windfall from the Tiffany fortune amounting to about $140,000 for each.

CHAPTER 32

Bottom Line

With the sale of the Brickell Avenue property, all my Tiffany inheritance was now in my hands. All older Tiffany heirs were dead, and I could expect no more windfalls. The ancestral Salem lands that had been acquired by the Salem Valley Corporation might still be sold to developers, but I had given my shares in the corporation to my children, and there seemed no likelihood that the property would be sold during my lifetime. How much then had I—and my brothers—inherited?

Briefly put, we were virtually assured of lifetime financial security. During our childhood and youth, our parents supported us with Tiffany money in a style that, while never ostentatious, included an amply staffed palatial home, a country estate as a summer home, nurses, governesses, tutors, music lessons, dancing lessons, private schooling (all the way through postgraduate courses), foreign travel, and the best medical care available. As we grew up, portions of our Tiffany inheritance came to us at such opportune times that none of us at any time was dependent on his own earnings. As detailed in the foregoing pages, each of us had received the following amounts, without effort on our part, merely because we were great-grandsons of Charles Tiffany:

1932	Tiffany & Co. shares	$25,000
1934	Wedding present	10,000
1937	Bequest from Annie O. Mitchell	250,000
1938	Lone Pine Lawn Corporation dissolved	30,000
1945	Burnett Y. Tiffany trust distributed	30,000
1951	Olivia Jeans Smith trust distributed	30,000
1967	Mitchell Trust of 1908 distributed	22,000
1967	Mitchell Trust of 1922 distributed	346,000
1967	Trust for Grandsons distributed	67,000
1977	Sale of 2025 Brickell Avenue	140,000
		$950,000

The total is in some degree meaningless since the items are not in dollars of a constant value: prices today are ten times what they were in 1930, and if inflation were taken into account, the total might be a much larger figure.

The effect on a person of the inheritance of wealth is a problem going back thousands of years. That wealth corrupts is a part of the Christian tradition. The Bible declares that it is harder for a rich man to enter Heaven than for a camel to pass through the eye of a needle. Dives, the rich man, went to Hell for no better reason than that he was rich.

Yet it is hard to see why a person should be damned simply because he was born rich. The accretions of our cultural heritage, the splendors as well as the evils of our civilization, were the product of excess wealth beyond the requirements for survival of the species. On balance, what was the effect of the Tiffany fortune on its possessors?

Charles Tiffany himself was by all accounts an upright and hard-working man of impeccable morals, whose business standards made the name Tiffany a symbol of quality and reliability. His children reacted to his wealth in different ways. Louis took advantage of his inheritance to become a productive and innovative artist, though in his later life he became extravagantly self-indulgent. His younger siblings, Louise and Burnett, were pampered and spoiled, but it was their limited natural endowment rather than their wealth that restricted their lives.

As for Annie, Charles Tiffany's oldest child, she was born rich and took her riches for granted. Accepting the prevailing social attitude toward the "weaker sex," she was ruled in all financial affairs by her father and then by her husband. When they were both gone, she turned over management of her inheritance to the family bank, thereby preserving it almost intact. She became a disciplined but gracious Lady Bountiful to her friends and family.

Her husband, Alfred Mitchell, indisposed to tying himself down to a job, allowed himself to become wholly dependent on his wife's money. This made him restless and moody, and reinforced his tendency to benign self-indulgence. He was, however, born to a relatively affluent family, and if he was corrupted by inherited wealth, it was a process that had begun long before his marriage.

My father, the retired missionary's son, imbibed a strong sense of moral rectitude and responsibility as a child, and it never wholly left him. Even when he married a Tiffany heiress, he turned his new-found affluence to good account as a college teacher, explorer, aviator, and U.S. Senator. But the allurements of the glittering world that wealth opened up to him eventually proved stronger than his New England conscience.

His children, my brothers and I, exemplified the advantages and perils of inherited wealth in different ways. Woodbridge and Jonathan, the oldest and the youngest, both enhanced their wealth by marriage. They made good use of their good fortune and had effective lives. Woodbridge, choosing the academic world, became a professor of Chinese and Asian history at one of the country's greatest institutions of higher learning, the University of California in Berkeley. Jonathan had a varied and productive career in public service, variously serving on the New York State Labor Relations Board and on the foreign aid or "Point Four" program in Truman's administration; serving as executive secretary to New York Governor Averell Harriman, and as American ambassador to the United Nations under Adlai Stevenson in the Kennedy presidency; and serving for eighteen years as an able and conscientious member of Congress. Politicians are particularly subject to the corrupting influence of power and wealth. Being born wealthy and marrying wealth insulated my brother Jack from the temptations that beset all men of power and influence, and gave his career of public service a unique luster of integrity and intelligence.

The rest of us were less successful.

Harry (Hiram IV), the second in line and eighteen months older than I, served for seventeen years as a Foreign Service Officer in the consular and diplomatic service. His most notable achievement in that field occurred when he was stationed in Marseilles during the Nazi occupation of France in 1940–41; defying protocol, he granted visas to Jewish refugees and helped them escape over the border into Spain. With his Tiffany inheritance seemingly freeing him for unlimited procreation, he ultimately fathered eleven children, but his growing family complicated his diplomatic career, and he resigned from the Foreign Service. He brought his sizable family to live in the house he had inherited in Salem, and attempted to enhance his fortune in the promotion of some innovative business enterprises. Far from producing additional income, they drained his capital, and he was victimized by business associates, one of whom swindled him out of $100,000. Despite these losses, he managed to provide all his children with private schooling, even through college. But his last years were haunted by poverty.

In the case of Charles, my next younger brother, his inherited wealth helped launch him on a promising career as a physician. The fact that he did not have to depend on his earnings enabled him to defy the medical establishment when it was slow to adopt the findings of psychosomatic medicine, of which he was a pioneer advocate. As a result, he lost his hospital connections as well as his patients and retired early, to devote his energies and his capital to improving the Bingham family lands in Salem.

Brewster, the fifth brother, who had horrified his father as a small child by throwing away money given to him, was in the course of time ordained as a missionary to China. When the Communists took over the country, he devoted his energies and his capital to Dr. Frank Buchman's worldwide Moral Re-Armament movement (MRA). He never depended on his own earnings, and gave most of his inheritance to the movement. He was saved from penury by the sale of his life interest in the Miami property. Returning with his childless wife to New Haven, he lived, a benign figure in a wheelchair, crippled with osteoporosis, in an apartment on Prospect Street, midway between the sites of his birth and his youth, until his death in 1995.

Mitchell, the sixth of the seven brothers, never made a financial success of his chosen career as a painter but, like the rest of the family, he was able to live on his inheritance. In his thirties, he tried his hand at farming on the family lands in Salem. Despite the subsidies made possible by the Tiffany inheritance, dairy farming proved bafflingly unprofitable, and when his marriage broke up, Mitchell moved to Florida and joined Brewster in supporting the MRA. That movement absorbed half his capital but, like Brewster, he was saved by the sale of the Florida property. In his later years, he lived in southern California within sight of the Pacific, with a second wife, painting beautiful landscapes for which he was unable to find a market. He lived, however, a blameless and creative life, thanks again to his great-grandfather Tiffany's attention to business.

We were all shaped for good or ill by that inheritance. One may conjecture that we might have achieved more if less privileged. We would certainly have been tougher. But I doubt if we would have been more outstanding.

As for the effect of inherited wealth on myself, it is not for me to judge. It enabled me to pursue a varied career without having to worry about paying my bills. Late in life, it gave me an opportunity to help save one of my sons from imprisonment and a possible death sentence as a fivefold murderer.

Chronicle IX

My Beginnings

CHAPTER 33

My Birth

I am on death row. I have been sentenced, but the date of my execution has not been set. Before I die, I have an opportunity to make a statement. I may not be able to finish it before the day comes, but I can at least make a beginning.

Why should I bother, if I am to die anyway? Partly, I suppose, because I am a denizen of what the late Clarence Day called "this simian world." I am an evolutionary cousin of the chattering primates. Like them, we humans enjoy giving expression to our thoughts and feelings, and we continue to do so whether we are listened to or not. Unlike them we can record our chatterings, and thereby address assemblies in treetops far removed in time and space from our own.

From my present vantage point, I look back to see where and when I should start my personal history. One obvious place to begin is my birth. That, as it happens, is well recorded, not only with an entry in the index of vital statistics in the City Hall of Cambridge, Massachusetts, under the date of February 20, 1905, but in descriptions of the event written by both my mother and my father.

Apparently I delivered myself. The route I traveled had been cleared by two earlier children, and I came with a rush. It was 4:00 A.M. on the day in question. Labor had hardly begun. My father, to make more space for the doctor and nurse he had called, was dismantling his bed. It was a single bed, for double beds were then out of fashion. To the surprise of both parents, a tiny cry came suddenly from under the covers in my mother's bed. I had announced myself. My mother thought it a sign of character. My father only noted, in his record of the event, that I had a "well-shaped" head.

My birth was, to be sure, not my true beginning. My physical features no less than my character had been developing for some time. At what point before my birth I became a "person" is a matter for theologians—or lexicographers—to dispute, but obviously my existence as a separate individual began when two independent assemblies of atoms and molecules—and no doubt subatomic particles—came together in the infinitely chancy event known as conception.

Before that, I know, was an act of love. Yet, as I have reason to believe, it was a sense of duty as much as love that moved my parents to want a third child.

Much later, my father told me that my mother, from whom he was then estranged, had never relaxed and given herself wholly to him. For her, as for many of her generation, sex was a cross to be borne. Yet after pain came motherhood, and she had chosen that as her profession.

Then, too, she and my father both had been attracted by eugenics. The selective breeding of humans was a beguiling but dangerous offshoot of the science of genetics. It was later to give Hitler his rationale. My parents believed they came of superior stock and should therefore have many children. The idea that I was superior because of my genes was imbibed almost with my mother's milk.

My mother had never studied biology and probably knew little of genes and chromosomes. But she had an early interest in evolution. She was brought up on Darwin. For her father, Alfred Mitchell, who had become a gentleman of leisure after marrying the daughter of Charles Tiffany, the education of his two daughters was for years his principal occupation. Foreign travel determined the curriculum; French, German, and Italian governesses and music teachers were the faculty; but his wide-ranging interests in current ideas set the direction of his daughters' studies. Charles Darwin's theory of evolution and Thomas Huxley's agnosticism were as basic in my mother's upbringing as was the Bible in my father's.

Evolution and natural selection by the survival of the fittest may well have been a harsher creed even than the fundamentalism of her husband's missionary parents, but her romantic and artistic sensibilities softened her beliefs. Her religion had as its deity a benevolent "nature," more goddess than god.

No doubt I inherited her bent. I can apprehend a continuity of existence that stretches much further back than the chattering apes, who were themselves a way station. Back to the first stirring of the original life stuff in the primeval slime. Still further back to the evolution of the earth's elements in the explosion of a supernova. My ultimate beginning was in that moment when time began, when God clapped his hands and the heavens resounded. I belong in this universe. Lost in its infinite empty spaces, I have sometimes been overcome with panic. But in my more mystical moods I see it, from the moment of its creation, as bearing the seeds of love. My faith is not beyond reason.

Whatever my later perspective on the universe, my first view of it was obviously more restricted. From my mother's bed, I was briefly housed, as she reported, in a bureau drawer. From there I was lifted for the doctor's and nurse's ministrations, then gently laid in the family cradle. It hung from a graceful but sturdy frame of cherry or maple. On each side, a little railing atop a row of nicely turned spindles, all suitably cushioned, provided a snug security. This particular cradle was one that had gone back many generations in our family and was to be used for many generations to come. Thus I was from my first hours cradled by my ancestors. At the time, to be sure, I didn't care.

CHAPTER 34

Childhood Memories

A point of transition from the secure world of my cradled infancy, so painful that it remained buried in my subconscious for many years, was the birth of my brother Brewster. Another brother, Charles, first known as Tiffany, had preceded Brewster, but I was too young to be aware of his birth. I was three and a half years old when one morning I was taken by my nurse to the door of my mother's bedroom, and looked up to see my mother, propped up on the pillows of her bed, holding a new baby in her arms and smiling down at me. I started to run toward her, but was quickly snatched away by my nurse. That may have been the moment when I first realized that I was not the center of a nurturing universe.

To be sure, that bitter experience was not conducive to unselfishness. Something akin to murderous rage must have been the immediate response. For, some months later, I accompanied Bertha, wheeling the new baby in a baby carriage, around the block from Prospect Street to the top of Edwards, and there I indulged myself in a delightful fantasy: I saw the baby carriage, released from Bertha's grip, careening down the sidewalk into the path of a Whitney Avenue trolley.

My murderous feelings were stirred again that year when my mother, in the sixth of a swift succession of pregnancies, gave birth to a stillborn child: in some depth of my consciousness, as I discovered fifty years later on an analyst's couch, I believed I had killed it.

Outwardly I was taught to love my little brothers, and in time I think I did. An early lesson in consideration for others came with a visit one Easter time to my mother's cousin Sue in the quaint little English cottage built for her on Forest Street by her father, the then famous author Donald Mitchell. When candies were offered to my brothers and me, I chose the biggest on the plate. It was a marzipan rabbit, and I found the taste revolting. Somehow, perhaps chided by an older brother, I learned that reaching for the biggest might be counterproductive.

The China Doll

Much of my life has been spent in bathrooms. Today in my late eighties, the rituals of the medicine closet and the shower appropriate a disturbingly large number of my dwindling supply of minutes and hours. Even as a child of four the bathroom figured prominently.

225

One of my earliest memories is of sitting on a toilet seat. I was fondling a favorite toy, a tiny china doll. It slipped and fell, between my straddled legs, into the toilet.

The flush toilet was so new a product of the industrial revolution as to have had no proper christening. Its inventors called it a "water closet." That was too suggestive for the Victorians, and even in countries where the alphabet had no "W," certain doors were discreetly marked "W.C." Today we have entered a new era in which the flush toilet, with its enormous waste of the nutrient products of human digestion—older cultures call it "night soil"—and its extravagant squandering of a diminishing supply of water, is seen as a double threat to the environment.

When my doll slipped through my fingers, however, the toilet into which it fell was a primitive device. The seat was a wide flat board with a roughhewn hole far too big and far too rough for my small and tender bottom. To have to maintain my awkward posture of straddled legs until I had "done my duty" was sometimes torture. Added to my physical discomfort was the nameless fear of falling through, and being flushed down into another world of unspeakable horror. A long chain led up to a tank near the ceiling, and when the chain was pulled, the water came down with a frightening rush into the bowl, sloshing out of sight whatever lay on the shallow shelf onto which my doll had fallen.

My wails brought Emily, the thin impatient nursemaid to whose care I had graduated the year before from the warm embrace of Bertha, now in charge of the new baby. Emily fished out the little porcelain figure—I did not want to see how—but it had broken in its fall. My wails redoubled when I saw it was in pieces.

Uncle Ernest

Uncle Ernest mended my china doll and became my lifelong friend. He was an angular Englishman with a scraggly cigarette-stained moustache. From the scraps of memory of this first remembered crisis, I can surmise that he had come for dinner, and that the incident in the bathroom had happened as I was being readied for bed by Emily and Bertha. I was almost immediately comforted on being told that Mr. Brown—he was not yet known as Uncle Ernest—would take the china figure home with him and make it whole again.

He lived on Everit Street, half a mile away, in a house that my family had rented when they first came to New Haven. I can visualize the interior of the house only from a visit when I no longer lived there, perhaps to pick up the mended doll. Mr. Brown was a bachelor, but his unmarried sister Mildred had come over from England to keep house for him. I remember being confused about their relationship when it was explained to me that she was to be called Miss and not Mrs.

Across the street was a part of East Rock Park, and in it, not too far for my nurse to take me, a playground with swings. I liked the big swing that had two facing benches where I could sit with my nurse, swinging gently and safely, without the awful vertigo and nausea, the sense of falling into an infinite void, that assailed me when I was put on a real swing, alone, with hands no longer supporting me.

The Everit Street house, overlooking the park in the best residential district of the city, was modest enough, a plain two-story dwelling with a front porch, its clapboards and trim painted in neutral browns. I have the impression that my mother thought it very ordinary. Certainly her parents, as I later learned, considered it unsuitable for their daughter. Perhaps my father realized that it would be inappropriate for so humble a member of the Yale faculty—he was at that point an unpaid lecturer—to live in too grand a style. But the Mitchells, insistent, even offered to build a house for my parents that was up to the Mitchells' standards, and while it was being built, under pressure from my grandparents, the family had moved to a larger rented house on the crest of Prospect Hill.

It was called the Whittlesey House, after some previous owner. The number on the red sandstone gatepost was 367. A big brick mansion in an early Victorian Gothic style, it was graced with a turret, almost a steeple, the upper windowed chamber of which I explored once with my father: we could look out on the treetops of the mansion's spacious grounds, and more exciting, in the dust and cobwebs, we found the shriveled remains of a bat.

Another memory of peering out one of the mansion's windows was more frustrating. I was woken from a sound sleep to look at Halley's comet. At the head of the stairs was a big window facing west in the direction of the Forestry School. I was sleepily aware of a sky full of stars, but I could not see the one with a tail. I looked and I rubbed my eyes. The grownups, who may well have included Uncle Ernest, an astronomer as well as a mathematician, told me how important this was and exhorted me to remember it all my life. But I could see nothing special in the sky. Perhaps the comet was too smudgy for me to know it when I saw it. Finally I was allowed to go back to bed, only dubiously comforted by being told I might be able to see it next time. This was 1910, and next time would be seventy-five years later. When 1985 did actually roll around, Halley's comet, too faint to be visible in the northern hemisphere, was an especial disappointment to me.

No Smoking

My conscious life really begins with my family's moving into the new house. Before that, only slight memories of memories remain. My conscious development as a human being is closely linked with 787 Prospect Street.

The only recollection I have of its construction was of a walk there from the rented Whittlesey House at 367 Prospect—whether with nurses or parents is not clear—and being aware of scaffolding and hollow brick and dust.

Sometime later I learned about the hollow brick construction, an innovation, I believe, at the time. The walls of hollow brick, stuccoed on the outside and plastered within, were supposed to make the building to a large degree fireproof.

Fear of fire was clearly on someone's mind in the planning stage. An interior fire escape was provided by the back stairs that led up from the cellar past the kitchen to the servants' quarters on the third floor—inhuman iron stairs surrounded by blank walls as if in a factory—and there were little iron balconies, rudimentary fire escapes, outside three of the bedrooms. But what I most remember about that visit to the half-built structure was a big sign over the doorway that led from the terrace into the living room: NO SMOKING.

It was certainly not an unusual sign then or now: a construction site is always a fire hazard. But my interpretation of it as a five-year-old was unusual. My father never smoked, at least I never knew him to, though he once told me it was only because my mother so strenuously objected. Our family doctor, Dr. Arnold, who had "pulled me through" pneumonia, always smelled of tobacco smoke, and "Uncle Ernest" Brown was a chain smoker with yellowed fingers, who ultimately died of lung cancer. But aside from those two, the smell of cigarette smoke was not a part of my childhood. What "No Smoking" meant to me then, and for an embarrassingly long time thereafter until I learned better, was that the fireplaces in the new house would not smoke, that is, they would have proper drafts.

Fireplaces with open fires were an important part of my childhood. Presumably the fireplaces in the Whittlesey house did not draw well, and the thought of having an open fire without smarting eyes was to me one of the wonders that the big new house would bring into my life.

Many years later when I was remodeling an old New England farmhouse for my own family, I gained a better understanding of the significance of open fires in home heating. My eighteenth-century house was built around a central chimney with three fireplaces on the ground floor—one a huge affair with a brick-vaulted oven adjoining—and another fireplace in an upstairs bedroom, all giving into a central flue and clearly the only source of heat through the cold New England winters. But during the nineteenth century, the century of iron stoves, all these fireplaces at some point were boarded or bricked up to keep the heat from being sucked up the great chimney. Then when I installed a twentieth-century central heating system with hot water radiators in the old house, and rebuilt the central chimney with separate flues and dampers for each rediscovered fireplace, open fires came into their own again.

They are, of course, a luxury; however, some country dwellers with firewood easily available may thereby save on their fuel bills. They certainly were a luxury in the new Prospect Street house, designed with nine fireplaces, four on the ground floor and five in upstairs bedrooms. Few of them were ever used; most were more decorative than otherwise. Only the one in the library, which became the family sitting room, was in anything like constant use during cool weather.

The lavish provision of fireplaces in bedrooms was probably the idea of my mother's mother, always known to me as Granny. She had done most of the planning of the house. Granny's full name was Annie Olivia Tiffany Mitchell, and I was rather proud of myself when I could recite it, but it was clear from the "A.O.M." monograms on all the linen, silver, and china in her own house that she had dropped her father's name when she married my grandfather. Not that she was trying to hide the fact that she was a daughter of Charles Tiffany. After all, it was his fortune that enabled Annie to build a handsome house for her daughter, and provided the yearly income for Alfreda's by now sizable family to live in it.

As for fireplaces, the rambling and twice remodeled house the Mitchells lived in on Pequot Avenue in New London had even more of them than the house they were building for the Binghams: there was even a fireplace in the master bathroom.

At a time when central heating systems were inefficient, there was, to be sure, some utility in an open fire. As it turned out, the large coal-burning furnace with which the new Prospect Street house was equipped was unable to keep the whole big house comfortable in winter, and some years later a second furnace was added. When I was still having difficulty dressing on cold mornings—it took me years to learn how to tie my shoes so they would stay tied—a fire would often be lit by my nurse in the southeast bedroom that I occupied with my next younger brother.

The room had a cozy embrasure flanked by built-in benches on each side of the fireplace. One held firewood under the lid, the other was for toys. There was no mantle, but the fireplace was decorated with antique Delft tiles set into the wall on each side, all with simply depicted Biblical scenes. From them came my first knowledge of Bible stories—Adam and Eve, Jacob's ladder, Noah's ark, Samson and the lion, and so on.

When I last visited the house, now a women's dormitory of Albertus Magnus College, the fireplace had been blocked off and the embrasure was a clothes closet, but the tiles were still in place telling their simple stories at the back of the closet.

Casa Alegre

A child knows no other world than what he or she sees and feels. The norm for me at age seven was the big thirty-room house on Prospect Hill.

For all its size, it was a cheerful sunny home. My parents had named it Casa Alegre. The name appeared on my mother's stationery in the robin's-egg-blue box from Tiffany's, and on rare engraved invitations to a dinner party or musicale, but did not supplant "the new house" or "the Prospect Street house" in ordinary usage, or "787 Prospect Street" as our given address. The name, as it was explained to me, was Spanish for "Happy Home," which was the name my father's parents had given to the tiny mission house on a Pacific atoll where they had lived before he was born. I had only a vague notion why the name was in Spanish: was it because of my father's interest in Peru, or because the house with its red-tiled roof was supposedly in a Spanish style?

It faced south, and the sun streamed into the big living room through a conservatory filled with greenery. Outside the conservatory was a tiled terrace, protected by the slightly jutting wings of the dining room and the library. The living room with its high ceiling was no doubt designed for formal entertaining, and on rare occasions it was so used. But in most of my early memories of it, especially after the acquisition of three large yellow Oriental rugs, it was a playroom littered with building blocks and toys.

The library, lined with books to the ceiling on all sides and richly furnished with Tiffany lamps and a carved oak desk, was the family sitting room. Two sofas and my father's big leather armchair were grouped around the fireplace where in cold weather a fire seemed to be always smouldering on a big bed of ashes. There in the most idyllic of my memories I can see my father playing a riotous game of crocinole with a couple of my brothers and myself—until the Tiffany clock sent us dutifully off to bed at our several bedtimes, spaced a half hour apart in order of age, the older brothers enforcing the schedule on the younger ones.

It seemed indeed a happy home. I never saw my mother cry except once. Her loneliness during my father's long absences in Peru, and her sense of inadequacy as the mistress of a huge establishment of servants, nurses, and underlings, she confided only to her diary.

At times she had a housekeeper, or a combination housekeeper and governess, to help her manage a household staff that at its maximum numbered fifteen.

The cook, who was usually assisted by a kitchen maid, and the laundress, who came in from outside and did her work in the cellar, were not much in evidence to a small boy who was told not to bother them. But Mary the waitress and Nelly the chambermaid—two young Irish girls who were with us for years—I remember vividly. I was once chided for being too playful and familiar with them, and for the most part kept a respectful distance. Nelly came into our household a frightened teen-ager fresh off an immigrant boat, and was dealt with by my mother in such a gentle affectionate way that seventy-five years later the story was passed on by a granddaughter of hers to a granddaughter of my mother's.

The tasks my mother taught Nelly, in addition to making beds and cleaning the upstairs rooms, included helping Mary wait on the table at family meals. Mary also did double duty. Besides being in charge of the pantry and waiting on table, she served as "parlor maid," dusting and straightening out the downstairs rooms.

The yard man who raked the leaves and mowed the lawns was also responsible for indoor chores—tending the furnace, bringing in firewood, doing heavy cleaning. For much of my childhood, the post was held by Joseph, a dignified colored man. No one was called a black in those days. But once, as he was engaged in one of his daily chores, changing the water in a big goldfish bowl that stood on a marble pedestal next to the conservatory, I deeply hurt him by calling him a "nigger." I meant nothing by it. I was in a playful mood and had brought the word home from school as a meaningless epithet. He stopped what he was doing and turned on me with such a look of pain and misery and anger that I never forgot it.

"Alfred," he said, "don't ever use that word."

I was horrified at what I had said. I wanted to sink through the floor. I was fond of him, and I knew he was fond of me. Many years later when I saw Fugard's great play *"Master Harold"... and the Boys,* the recollection of that look in Joseph's eyes came back to overwhelm me, and I wept uncontrollably.

Joseph had ennobled his servitude, as many black men and women undoubtedly did in the days of slavery. When my parents acquired a new set of dining room chairs, I remember him unpacking them with a glow of pride, something handsome and well made, to be admired and cared for as part of an establishment that was his as well as ours. And when he invited me to be the first to sit on one of the chairs—as it happened I had just begun to wear long pants—he showed me how to pull up the legs of my trousers before I sat down so as not to spoil their crease. Years later, when he was no longer working for us, I heard he had killed himself after some domestic tragedy.

A Broken Chair

To furnish the big new house adequately took time. The Mitchells had paid for the house, and for some years the title remained in my grandmother's name, but she had not provided additional money for furnishing its thirty rooms. Furniture was added gradually only as my parents were able to save money from the generous allowance the Mitchells provided my mother.

The big sunny living room was almost barn-like in the first few years. My mother made a virtue of its simplicity. A scattering of wicker chairs, probably bought in Jamaica on one of my mother's visits to her parents' winter home at Port Antonio, is all I remember.

Some time after I had watched Joseph unpack the new dining room chairs, we heard in the nursery about a very important dinner party that was being planned. Former President Taft was to be a guest. He had moved to New Haven after his defeat for reelection in 1912, having accepted a teaching post at the Yale Law School, and we had heard he and his family were living in our old house at 367 Prospect. In those days, my family was not concerned with politics, and I remember nothing of the 1912 presidential campaign in which Woodrow Wilson defeated both Taft and Theodore Roosevelt, who was the candidate of the "Bull Moose" Progressives. But we did know that William Howard Taft, with a reported weight of three hundred pounds, was the fattest president the country had ever had.

We speculated whether he would break a chair. The new dining room chairs were probably strong enough, though it was clear he would not be able to squeeze into one of the armchairs that stood at the head and foot of the table.

On the evening of the dinner, two or three of my brothers and I in our pajamas were taken by a nurse down the back stairs and through the pantry to the glassed-in sun porch next to the dining room, and allowed to peek through curtains at the glittering dining table and the great man sitting on my mother's right. Apparently his chair had held.

The next morning, however, we were told, to our great delight, that he had indeed broken a chair. One of the wicker chairs in the living room had been very generously built with a wide seat and flaring armrests, and this had been offered as the biggest chair the house afforded. The seat had not let the ex-President down, but one of the armrests had given way when he had tried to rise to go in to dinner.

Later the wicker chairs were supplemented with stained glass lamps and furniture from the studios of Louis Comfort Tiffany, and the walls, which had at first been graced only with crystal light fixtures, were hung with plaster casts of friezes from the Parthenon. My mother prided herself on her taste.

Progress

I grew. Every living thing grows. The essence of life is growth, sprouting from the seed, leaves lifting, hands reaching up. The upward direction seems essential, at least with higher forms of life than worms, and I think inevitably of growth as upward. Progress is another word for growth, and it too has an arrow pointing upward.

Memory does not embrace infancy, the period of most rapid growth. Plot a graph of the growth of a human being from a fertilized egg cell, doubling in size and complexity day after day: the line on the graph paper is almost vertical. The rate of growth of the fetus continues steep, though the doubling begins to fall off at once and the line begins to curve however slightly. The doubling may be week by week or month by month, but the progress is still sharply upward. There are bursts of growth and periods of consolidation, even of retrenchment, before growth resumes. Weight may fall off after the trauma of birth but soon begins doubling again. Gradually, of course, the curve of life levels off.

It is really a complex of curves. Physical growth levels off at eighteen or so. The number of cells in the brain is said to have reached its maximum in the womb, but its contents, the mind, with its all but infinite intricacy may go on growing during almost the whole of a life.

I will not dwell at this point on decline. In the complex curve of growth, to be sure, there is always an inherent element of decay. Almost from the beginning some cells die and are replaced. The time comes when the elements of decline and death overbear the factors of growth, and the composite curve turns downward. I know only too well that in my late eighties my mind and body are not what they were. But I am now concerned not with my end but my beginning.

Like other forms of life, I grew. Unlike some, I was aware of growing. Sometimes I had growing pains, my bones aching with the strain. But I was aware of the growth of my mind, the process of learning. I learned my letters from a governess. I think I knew her as Miss Damon. I remember nothing of her but her last name, and the fact that she was kind and patient and there was a bond between us, probably as strong as the bond between me and my mother who was always having another baby.

A, B, C, and the other letters all had separate personalities in my imagination. The letters that came first were friendliest. Not that X, Y, and Z were hostile; they were more like strangers who joined the alphabet late. The order of the letters was important. To this day I find satisfaction in an alphabetical index, and I take pride in the speed with which I can find a word in a dictionary. The letters that came first were in some way superior. I felt myself to be superior in that my name Alfred began with A and Bingham was only one letter removed from the top.

Learning letters was an early stage in the sprouting of my intelligence. A different kind of mental growth came with a Montessori step, learning to pass a button through a buttonhole, either to button up or to unbutton. A strip of cloth, perhaps cut off an old garment, had a row of buttons sewed on it, and another matching strip had the matching buttonholes, and the pleasure of fitting these together and taking them apart is still with me.

That was the beginning of my formal education. Counting came next. It was another affirmation of progress. From one, two, three, I went on to a hundred, and bigger numbers began to fascinate me. In this learning process I depended more on my brothers than on a teacher. I recall lying in a brass bedstead in the nursery, one of my brothers in the bed beside me. Brass for bedsteads was then in fashion. We found it fascinating to count not only to a hundred but to a thousand. The sense of the large size of a thousand is with me still. But we were lured on further. It must have been an older brother in the other bed, for I learned about a million, and went on to consider a billion and a trillion and a quadrillion, and so on to a "millillion," and even that was not the end: the frightening notion of infinity came next.

Dr. Arnold

In my early life, no one had a more lasting influence on me than Dr. Arnold. He may or may not have saved my life as a small child, but I know his medications set the tone of my digestive system for the rest of my life. His shiny bald head and beak nose, and the twisted mouth that was both cynical and sympathetic, appear again and again in my childhood memories.

He became the family doctor when the family moved to New Haven, and from the time he "pulled me through" a bout with pneumonia at the age of four, my mother put her full trust in him. Doctors made house calls in those days, and as my brothers and I went through all the childhood diseases, his visits to our house were frequent. His prescription for any cough or cold was invariably a cathartic to clear out the system. Calomel—two pills at night followed by Seidlitz powder in the morning—was the most favored. He was also a great believer in surgery. Tonsils and adenoids were routinely snipped out at an early age, and there were times when the smell of ether pervaded the house. I did go to a hospital for what I believe now—having no recollection of prior abdominal pain—was a totally unnecessary appendectomy recommended by him, but otherwise his ministrations were always at our house.

Although my mother had complete faith in Dr. Arnold's medical skill, she was both repelled by and attracted to him. She considered his raucous laugh and his manners not altogether refined, and she disliked the smell of tobacco smoke that lingered after his visits, but his sensitivity and essential gentleness appealed to her, and she found a common bond in music. Since he was an accomplished cellist, and she had continued to play the violin after her marriage, they occasionally made music together, accompanied by a pianist from the Yale Music School. Their tastes were equally classical though he preferred the trios of Beethoven and Brahms to those of Mozart.

When my father was home and not himself a patient, Dr. Arnold would join him in the library after a sickbed visit upstairs, and soon (if I were the patient) I would hear the doctor's bursts of thigh-slapping laughter from down below. Usually I could not hear what they talked about, but I gathered that they traded stories of the foibles and pretensions of the Yale establishment they were both close to, but not wholly a part of. Harry Arnold was cynical about academic pomposity, and my father resented the fact that, despite his social prominence and his renown as an explorer, he had never been accepted as a scholar by the history faculty.

Dr. Arnold was such a frequent visitor in our household that I learned a good deal about him, but it was all at second hand from inadvertent remarks of one or the other of my parents, or from snatches of conversation overheard. I knew he was a bachelor when he first became the family doctor, and then I heard he had married, in his forties, a young and pretty wife—and wasn't it nice for him after struggling through so many lonely years. But then I began hearing they were unhappy together, and Harry's outbursts of joyless humor over the miseries of matrimony, which I could not help but overhear, were a shock to me.

All I knew of the marriage state was my parents', and that always seemed one of perfect harmony. I never saw them quarrel. I never heard them raise their voices. I never knew of the loneliness and feelings of desertion that my mother confided to her diary during my father's many long absences from home exploring in South America. She would occasionally read us parts of the long love letters he wrote her from Peru, extolling her as the noblest of womankind, and I never knew until many years later that it was as much to escape from her cloying embrace as for love of adventure that he became an explorer. So far as I knew then, their marriage was ideal, and to hear Harry Arnold rail against the married state was more than a little upsetting.

Divorce was all but unthinkable in the Prospect Street society in which my parents moved. It existed, much as cancer existed, but almost never to be spoken of except with bated breath. Actually, Harry and Justine Arnold settled down, raised a family in the suburbs, and stayed together until Harry's death at a respectable age. Justine went on for thirty years of widowhood, recalling at times her husband's commentaries on the Bingham boys as something more than patients. In his wry way he had loved us.

Ma'moiselle

When I was eight, a French governess was added to the household staff at Casa Alegre. A new class distinction became necessary, for a governess was not to be considered a servant. She did not occupy one of the servants' little rooms up under the eaves on the third floor, but was installed in a small bedroom next to the nursery on the east side of the house. I don't think she ate with the servants either, though where she had her meals remains a mystery. The kitchen was for the most part off-limits to us boys. Presumably the servants had their meals there, and it was impressed on me that it would be an improper invasion of their privacy for me or my brothers to enter that domain.

There was, however, an intermediate zone, a point where the front and the back parts of the house met, a place where all paths crossed and no one had exclusive rights. It was part hallway, connecting the kitchen and the front hall, part office where a housekeeper (when we had a housekeeper) would sit at a desk telephoning, and part dining room for the intermediate help (the housekeeper, a nurse, a governess). Yet at times certain members of the household staff were recognized as having professional status, particularly in the case of a trained or registered nurse, and they might be seated at the family dinner table.

The French governess was usually accorded this more privileged rank— and particularly for breakfast. Ma'moiselle then came into her own. My mother usually had breakfast in bed; my father, when he was home, was served in lordly style alone, at a table in the sun porch beyond the dining room, with a newspaper propped up against the coffee pot in front of him. The boys' breakfast on school days would be earlier than his in any case. And this was the time for speaking French.

Ma'moiselle was no disciplinarian, and when she first arrived, she found it hard to enforce on three or four small boys the rule that no English was to be spoken at breakfast. Theoretically a fine of a penny a word for every word

235

of English spoken was to be imposed, though I don't remember its ever being collected, and one could always circumvent the rule by introducing whatever one wanted to say in English with the French for "What is?"—"Qu'est-ce que c'est?"—not necessarily waiting for an answer.

Leonie Bernard was a Parisian lady of impeccable but modest background. She was instructed to speak only French in dealing with those in her charge. My next younger brother Charles and I, occupying the big sunny southeast bedroom next to her little room, were her original charges.

On cold mornings she had been instructed to build a fire for us to get dressed by, and we would wake up to her complaints about the painful cracks in her fingers as she extracted firewood from the bench next to the fireplace, protecting her fingers as well as she could by wrapping the rough logs in newspaper.

Her fingers were further victimized as she was given the additional duty of darning the children's stockings. It seemed to me in those days that my stockings always had holes in them and the darned parts got bigger and bigger. Ma'moiselle would go into paroxysms of frustration when she saw Charles or me walking around the nursery in our stocking feet. Presumably that was when the holes developed.

"Ah, que c'est agaçant," she would explode. "Combien de fois je vous ai dit, ne marchez pas dans vos chaussettes."

She had had a good education, knew French literature, and loved to read. Her one indulgence on her days off was to go to the public library downtown and bring back such French books as she could find. She was encouraged to read aloud, and I reveled in hearing her read books by Madame de Ségur and Jules Verne from the *Bibliothèque Rose*, and hearing her tell of the writings of Victor Hugo and Anatole France.

She was a Catholic, regularly attending Sunday mass with the maids in the chauffeur-driven car, though I had a suspicion she was not a real believer. Her churchgoing was no doubt a following of tradition, and perhaps a means of brief escape from the confinement of her room.

She stayed on in our family year after year. I became very fond of her and she of me. I was dimly aware of the fact that she was lonely and sad. She always wore black, and I gathered she had never given up mourning for her mother whose wedding ring she wore. I heard about a sister back in Paris with whom she corresponded, and about a nephew who was the apple of her eye. When he was killed in the early months of World War I, her grief was unbounded, and it seemed as if she never smiled again.

The end of her employment came when I was away at boarding school. My mother, recovering from an operation in St. Raphael's Hospital, had apparently told my father that she dreaded going home to face once more that mournful presence in the household. For his part, my father had found the gloom intolerable on occasions when he was forced to dine alone with Ma'moiselle. Returning from the hospital and desperately forcing himself to be cruel, he gave Ma'moiselle notice to be out of the house within forty-eight hours.

Cousin Kate

Cousin Kate Reynolds was an important member of our family from about the time I was ten, when she came to live with us as housekeeper and general helper to my mother. In our well-behaved family, I was never made aware of—and later could only guess at—the tensions between my mother and this angular poor relation of my father's. She was his first cousin, and the arrangement was no doubt my father's idea.

They had once been close. At the time he left Honolulu in the 1890s to begin school at Andover, she was studying music at the New England Conservatory in Boston. She had felt somewhat responsible for her awkward cousin, unfamiliar with his new surroundings, and had played the role of an older sister. When he later came into affluence with his marriage to my mother, he began to feel responsible for her.

Their common Bingham grandparents, Hiram I and Sybil, the redoubtable first missionaries to Hawaii, had sent their two oldest children, Sophia and Lucy, back to New England for their first schooling, entrusting the little girls to kindly whaling captains for the long and perilous voyage around Cape Horn. Both survived, and in time found themselves husbands and bore children of their own. Lucy's husband, Charles Reynolds, was a minister and settled in Florida. Two sons made their way, if unspectacularly, in the world of business, but for daughter Kate a business career was out of the question. While awaiting a husband, and with a natural talent as a musician, she studied music. She may have had dreams of becoming a concert performer, but at the very least, giving piano lessons was a respectable occupation for an unmarried gentlewoman.

How close to marriage she came I never knew. When I was old enough for her to confide in me and she was long past marriageable age, she would drop a hint, with just a suggestion of a catch in the voice, about a shadowy young man who had come into her life when she was at the Conservatory and just as quietly had gone out of it. Hiram, my father, may have dutifully introduced her to school or college classmates at a graduation or other academic ceremony, but at that stage a four-year age difference was a dreadful barrier, and she covered up her shyness with a playful imitation of baby talk, which was never a successful gambit. By her late twenties, she was undoubtedly a hopeless spinster, bravely trying to make a living as a piano teacher in Boston.

From Boston, she went to Honolulu to care for my father's Aunt Lydia. Caring for the dying was eventually to become her principal occupation. My father had apparently persuaded her a few years before, after his father died, to give up the small clientele of piano pupils she had managed to gather in Boston, and move to Honolulu to look after Aunt Lydia—who was also Kate's aunt—at "Gilbertinia," the old family home, underwriting Kate's expenses until she was able to build up a new clientele there. Aunt Lydia died, however, in 1915, and not long thereafter Kate joined our household in New Haven.

My mother had often felt deserted during my father's frequent expeditions to South America—from 1906 to 1912, half his time was spent exploring—and providing some companionship for her was undoubtedly in my father's mind, as well as a home and some financial security for Kate. Even after his last expedition in 1915, he was not ready to settle down to a domestic routine. War was raging in Europe. He joined a National Guard unit, learned to fly, and was commissioned in the budding Air Service shortly after the United States entered the war in April 1917. An overseas assignment meant another long absence from home.

Perhaps my father thought Kate's musical training would add to her acceptability, for my mother continued to play the violin, and from time to time she needed a pianist to accompany her. But I never heard Kate play the piano while she was with us. Nor was she ever recruited to give music lessons to any of us boys. The family doctor Harry Arnold, an accomplished cellist, and a pianist from the Yale Music School would arrive for an impromptu performance with my mother of a Beethoven or Schubert piano trio. But no doubt to my mother Kate seemed not up to their musical standards, nor was her taste as strictly classical.

I never heard Cousin Kate complain about my mother's treatment of her, and for the years she was in our household, the inevitable pangs and frictions were kept out of sight. The only complaint of my mother's I recall is that Kate was too proud to accept the cast-off dresses my mother offered her. My father, I gathered, did not encourage Kate to consider herself a member of the family when guests were invited to dinner, and she would absent herself on these occasions. Instead, she would be served her meals in a bleak and ill-lighted room on the north side of the house, known as the "office," where she joined other indeterminate members of the household—such as Ma'moiselle.

When Kate's older brother became a widower, she left our household to keep house for him. I was away at boarding school at the time and knew none of the circumstances, but I gathered later that Kate's brother promised to leave her his property when he died. In the event she got nothing. For a while she was with my Mitchell grandmother as a housekeeper and companion, but their personalities could not have been congenial.

My father continued to subsidize her from time to time, and he had no doubt promoted her serving in my grandmother's household. But after my grandmother's death, when she again tried to take up her career as a music teacher, this time in New York, my parents' marriage was breaking up and my father no longer felt as affluent. He suggested that my brothers and I should help provide for her support, considering all she had given us. I collected what I could from my brothers from time to time and sent her a few dollars, but it was not much.

She went to New Jersey to live with another brother who was in failing health, and once more was left stranded when he died. Again she found a few pupils and gave piano lessons. But, as if she had not suffered enough, she broke her hip and became a hopeless cripple. She died uncomplaining to the last.

Aloha Oe

In 1914 I traveled with my parents to Hawaii.

For as long as I could remember, I had been hearing stories about Hawaii. My father was born in Honolulu and had spent his boyhood there—a grim boyhood marked by the poverty and fundamentalist piety of his retired missionary parents. But the scenes of his youth still held an allure for him, and he had not been back since his mother's death eleven years before. For my mother as well the islands had a romantic attraction. She had visited them with her parents as a girl and again as a young woman when she was courted by and became engaged to my father. I needed no travel posters to tell me that Hawaii was the Paradise of the Pacific.

The trip was a memorable adventure—many scenes still remain vivid in my mind. First was the four-day trip across the continent by rail. I had been on a train before but never on a sleeping car, and there was something magical about its green plush seats, heavy green draperies, and mahogany trim, with the black porter in starched white jacket hovering at hand. We watched the Palisades roll by from the windows of the Twentieth Century Limited, changed trains in the middle of the night in Chicago, got cinders in our eyes on the back platform of the observation car as the Great Plains unrolled beneath us, and looked out from our curtained berths to see the twinkling lights of a city far below as our train climbed into the mountains. Then there was the train ferry at Contra Costa, the Oakland-San Francisco ferry, the Fairmont Hotel on Nob Hill, and the Seal Rocks at the edge of the Pacific—one excitement after another.

My father manipulated his large family party with the managerial assurance he had gained on his Yale Peruvian Expeditions, never permitting a sign of friction or tension. There were eight of us, my two older brothers and myself under Mr. Wing's supervision, my baby brother Jonathan, only a couple of months old in the care of a nurse, and my parents. We embarked on the *Matsonia*, flagship of the Matson Line, for the uneventful ocean passage to Hawaii, remembered only in a blissful haze.

We stayed in a breezy cottage of the Halekulani Inn on the beach at Waikiki. The leonine profile of Diamond Head in the background was an old friend, for a huge photomural of the mountain and its fringe of coconut trees, enlarged from a picture taken by our Mitchell grandfather in the 1880s, graced a wall of our dining room at Prospect Street.

The Mitchells had spent a month in another cottage on this same beach at that time, and my mother, then twelve, remembered a birthday party shared with the Princess Kaiulani at the royal estate next door. Later, in her twenties, on another of her many travels with her parents, Alfreda had played hostess on this same beach to a group of slum children from the Palama Mission whom my father, then a settlement house worker, had brought for a beach picnic.

Compared to other famous beaches, Waikiki is narrow, and its long crescent is today overwhelmed by monstrous hotels, but to my nine-year-old eyes, it had a magical allure. The surfers riding in on the Pacific rollers with such daring and grace were a constant delight.

My father took my brothers and me out in an outrigger canoe, and we tried to ride back on the surf as the surfers did, but for all my father's masterful paddling, abetted by the older boys, the canoe never got moving fast enough, and each breaking wave, after a moment of uplift and expectation, slipped by without carrying us along.

After a few days of splashing in the surf, I was surprised to find myself swimming, as my father proudly said, "like a fish." I felt a stage of childhood being left behind. One day, alone with Father in the shower room after a swim, he showed me how to wash gingerly under my foreskin so that I would not again have to go through the agony of genital hygiene to which he and Dr. Arnold had periodically subjected me. The taboo on touching my genitals had been so deeply imbedded in my consciousness that even after years of exploring the unconscious I cannot remember how or when the stricture was imposed. But now it seemed there might be a legitimate occasion for what was otherwise forbidden, and this exception to the taboo led in the course of time to the widest exploration of the delights of masturbation.

Another sexual memory illumines the Hawaiian trip—my first view of the naked female form. I had never seen my mother naked, much less any other female in this family of boys. The occasion came about as a result of my father's nostalgic yearning to have his sons share some of the scenes of his childhood. He wanted me and each of my older brothers to spend a night at Gilbertinia, his boyhood home, sleeping in the attic room that had been his for most of his first sixteen years. The house, named after the Gilbert Islands where his parents had served as missionaries, had been provided them on their retirement by the Mission Board, and after their death it had been inherited by his Aunt Lydia. Now a semi-invalid, she still lived there, in the care of her niece Kate Reynolds, my father's cousin. I was surprised to find some of my father's childhood books, shabby and old-fashioned, still on a shelf in the little bedroom. I slept well enough, with no sense of my father's presence. On waking up the next morning and looking out the window, my heart jumped as I saw a little naked girl, five or six years old, casually coming across the backyard as if in the Garden of Eden. I did not tell my father, and there is no record that he had a similar vision from his attic window as a boy.

Another boyhood experience he wanted his sons to have was the view from the Pali on horseback. By 1914 the streets of Honolulu were all paved, and the automobile was in charge. But my father arranged to hire four suitably equipped horses for his sons and himself. We drove by car to the horses' stables and mounted them there. Most of the way was a gradual ascent; it was only as we emerged from the last residential development into open country and looked back that we saw the city below us, and the harbor and the ocean rising up behind it. Near the head of the valley where perpendicular cliffs began to lock it in, we gazed up at wispy waterfalls, and were astonished to see that sometimes the water never reached the ground, blown up and away as fast as it fell. Where we were riding, no breath of air stirred, and we were hot and sweaty and thirsty. The road began to zigzag steeply upward, and ahead we could see the sky and hear a roar of wind—though where we were the air was still dead. After a warning from Father to hold onto the pommels of our saddles, we were suddenly hit by the strongest blast of wind I had ever felt. My horse struggled to keep his footing, and I hung on for dear life.

Today the motorist drives through a tunnel far below and misses the dramatic blast of the trade wind, here funneled through the narrow pass, and misses too the full view of the promised land that lay before us. As we and our horses fought the wind, we looked out at an enchanted panorama: immediately below was tropical jungle and then came miles of rolling pineapple plantations, tinged a soft gray-green; beyond, framed by mountain ranges, the land flattened out, merging at last in the distant blue of the ocean, and this merged in turn—without horizon—into the blue of the sky.

The magic of that ride was still with me when our holiday came to an end. As the *Matsonia* pulled away from the dock at Honolulu to the sobbing strains of "Aloha Oe," I clutched the end of a fluttering confetti streamer, half smothered in fragrant leis, and wept with romantic emotion.

God the Father

Ideas that crystallize into religious beliefs no doubt begin in early childhood. Certainly mine did. But it seems as if they began in confusion, and the confusion has never been resolved.

When I first heard about God, I could make no clear distinction between God and my father. A higher power that both punished and loved—that was clearly my father. He was immensely tall not only compared to me but, at six feet four inches, compared to everybody else as well. He was to be feared, but also to be admired and glorified. The first time I was asked what I wanted to be when I grew up I answered at once: "a father."

Father was absent for months at a time in my childhood, exploring in Peru, and the threat "Wait till Father comes home and hears about this" seems to have been common when I misbehaved.

I was a willful and stubborn child, and I could throw a marvelous temper tantrum to get my way—or so I was told when I was older. Actually I can remember only one temper tantrum, and it may have been my last. I remember it happening in Salem. Father had recently returned from one of his lengthy expeditions, and I had forgotten his presence in the house. I had become used to expressing my frustrations audibly, and was astonished when he burst into my room in a fury. Regardless of what my grievance was, he told me to stop my kicking and screaming and to behave, and seizing me roughly and pulling down my pants, he began to spank me to make me stop. He told me later that he had never spanked any of his boys as hard as he did me that day. It was with the bare hand on the bare bottom, and he continued spanking as I continued to scream until, as he later confessed, his hand hurt. It must have taken me a little while to realize that this time I could not win. In the contest of wills I finally conceded defeat.

He wanted me to grovel and I did, and then his conscience hurt him and he wanted me to love him, and it ended with my tear-streaked face next to his in a comforting embrace.

Newspaper editorial writers today declaim against child abuse, and occasionally an enraged parent is hauled into court on charges of murder. I have felt murderous myself in dealing with my own children, though I never gained the upper hand as effectively as my father did with me. I suspect that half the fathers and sons of the world have known similar outbursts of violence, and from what I can gather from my own later years of psychoanalysis and psychotherapy, I suffered no lasting trauma.

I did learn to respect and fear my father, and to love him, and did resolve to "be good." And as I identified him with God, it was natural that God should seem to have the same attributes.

My questions about God were directed, I believe, to nurses, maids, and governesses rather than to my mother or father. Mother was refuge of last resort. If I was very unhappy, I always felt I could run and bury my face in her lap and she would reassure me that "everything is going to be all right." But in my daily life before I went to school, it was the paid staff that I was left to deal with and talk to and ask questions of.

Perhaps that gave me a simpler, less intellectual apprehension of religious issues than if I had taken them up with my parents. My father had studied theology with his father for a while after graduating from Yale. Although brought up to be a missionary himself, he found he had to reject some of the fundamentals of Christian belief as a matter of logic. Years later he told me of a crucial discussion he had had with his father.

"You have taught me," he had said to the old missionary, "that God is a loving father. A loving father would sympathize with his child if he so much as touched a hot stove by mistake and raised a blister on the end of his finger. A loving father could not deliberately inflict pain on a little boy—except perhaps as a brief punishment to teach him to be good. You have not 'spared the rod' with me, but you always said when you punished me that it hurt you more than it did me. How is it possible then for a loving father to send some of his children to hell to burn not just the end of a finger but their whole bodies, and not just for a while but forever and ever?"

His father sadly replied that he could not give a clear answer. "We have to accept it as a mystery. But we must not question what God tells us in the Bible."

My father conscientiously avoided indoctrinating his children one way or another. He let us develop our religious ideas on our own, only making certain, by taking us to Sunday services at the Yale College Chapel and later sending us to a Congregational Sunday school for a while, that we would be exposed to traditional religion. He himself retained enough of his early piety to find a Unitarian Church congenial in his later years, but so far as I know, there was no Unitarian Church in New Haven when I was a boy.

My mother was even less a believer than my father. Her own father was a free thinker and had given her Darwin and Huxley to read rather than the Bible. But she had promised her mother-in-law when she married that she would teach her children about Jesus. I learned to sing "Jesus loves me this I know, 'cause the Bible tells me so," and to say bedtime prayers, asking "Gawd" (always so pronounced in our family) to "help us be good and kind and brave." But the idea of God she left with me was less clear than her concept of "Nature," which I gathered provided us with flowers, sunsets, and all things beautiful, and might have been described as a kind of mother goddess.

So I picked up what I could of the stories in the Delft tiles. They were clear enough. And I could believe that Jesus loves me. But how to relate God and Jesus—and which one was the Lord—were questions my nurses could not answer.

Yet from such explanations as they did give me, I felt a tie to traditional folklore that stood me in better stead than would have instruction in the catechism, or being asked to struggle too early with such metaphysical concepts as the Trinity.

God the Mother

Our minds crave simplicity. One God, father of us all, is a comforting idea. The mind rebels against three gods or a god who is both three and one. Mother Nature is another comforting idea, but Nature in her infinite complexity does not seem as One.

Existence can seem simple and secure only in the womb. Birth brings complexity, and life out of the womb begins with a cry of pain. Still, the mind's capacity to take in the new complexity is limited. The baby goes to sleep, and the sense of comfort and security is renewed.

My mother nursed me till another pregnancy began, encouraged by my father in a cult of motherhood. As a girl she had dreams of being a concert violinist, a poet, or an artist. But fantasies of a career of her own were quickly abandoned when she fell in love with my father, and she probably saw herself in the role of perfect companion if not of lover. He found her companionship less than perfect, however. When he fled from her worshipful embrace to go exploring, he began to recreate her as an immaculate image. His letters are full of his adoration of her as the perfect woman. She found herself on a pedestal.

It was lonely, but it gave her a *raison d'être*. Motherhood became her career. In practice, her mothering focused on the newborn, or perhaps it would be more accurate to say the newly conceived. For with so many pregnancies in quick succession, each baby in turn was consigned to nurses when weaning stopped.

I have told of my sense of abandonment when I looked through a bedroom door and saw baby Brewster in my mother's bosom. But I came to realize that Woodbridge and Harry had themselves been abandoned earlier. And at some time, even before the last child was born, I sensed that I was back in the center of my mother's attention.

It may have been in the period after Mitchell was born—in the first interval of as much as two years between pregnancies when, as my father later told me, my parents practised birth control—that my mother, having no baby to nurse, turned back and focused her mothering once more on me.

The baleful look my older brothers gave me on one occasion I remember vividly. Mother and I were sitting in the soft velvety sofa beside the library fire. I may have had an arm around her waist, and we were holding hands. It was not a new closeness. For some time, it seems, I had been privileged to hold or stroke her hand, and she stroked mine. This time she could not help but feel the hostility directed at us by the two older ones. She said something that only added to the injury, perhaps asking them why they did not love her as much as I did, and I knew that she did not love them as much as she loved me. That feeling, for good or ill, never left me.

No doubt I took advantage of being the favorite and was at times quite shameless. Once, when Father was again away exploring and I was being willful and provoking, Mother was infuriated with me for resisting some demand of hers and said she would have to punish me. She picked up her hairbrush to use as a paddle, knowing her hand was not strong enough to inflict pain, and took hold of me to spank me—in my mind's eye it was in the same room where my father had so thoroughly thrashed me a few years before. But now I was as strong as she was, and I pulled away smirking and laughing, half in derision and half in embarrassment. This unnerved her, and she began to giggle too. The issue was soon forgotten, and we both tried to put from mind an incident that had been an embarrassment for us both.

Still I was a good boy, probably too good.

A Good Little Rich Boy

What does it mean to be "good"? What does it mean to be "too good"?

As every young parent knows, a "good baby" is one that doesn't cry, sleeps through the night, smiles when you smile at it, and when discomfort or hunger makes it fretful, is easily satisfied and restored to peaceful acceptance. And yet any knowledgeable parent is likely to begin to worry if a baby is "too good."

From reports of my violent temper as a small child, I could not have been "too good" at that stage. The terrible beating my father gave me when I threw my last tantrum seems to have had a decisive impact. I decided, whether then or later, that it would be better for me to behave the way my father wanted me to.

When, in my sixth year, my older brothers went off to school and I had a governess all to myself, I received strong positive reinforcement. I was bright and responsive, and Miss Tait—and Miss Damon who succeeded her—must have found me an engaging pupil. I learned fast. I wanted to please and I did please. I was loved, appreciated, admired.

Yet I was not totally unaware of the seamy side of life. I knew what pain was. Little hurts are common enough so that childhood is never a bed of roses, and when I had my tonsils and adenoids removed under general anesthetic at home, I knew more grievous pain. In a vague sort of way, I knew too that there was poverty, and I felt uneasy when I was confronted by it. Italian immigrant women would invade our lawn every spring to cull dandelions for food, and I can see them now advancing and stooping as they worked their way across the lawn with a knife in one hand and a capacious apron held in the other, emptied periodically into a basket. And at the foot of the hill across the street where my brothers and I went coasting in winter, when the snow got packed down enough to enable us to reach the wire fence at the far end, there were slum children from the Winchester Arms factory district peering through at us.

In the stories that were read to me, or that I read myself as I was able, there were accounts of battles, killings, and bloodshed. But that was long ago, and the world was now a safe and happy place. In some story a forest fire raged, and it struck me with peculiar terror. But that too was long ago, and I knew I need fear no forest fire in the fortunate time in which I had been born.

Good boy that I was, I excelled in my school work when at age seven I was admitted to the First Form at Hamden Hall, the equivalent of the third grade in the public school. I wanted to please my teachers and I did. I was always first in my Form. There were, to be sure, only three other boys in my Form in that first year, which was also the first year of the school. But my classmates were bright too, and hardly less privileged.

I had started that first school year not in the safe surroundings of Hamden Hall, which was an extension of Dr. and Mrs. Cushing's own home, but at the public school, the Worthington Hooker School on Canner Street, out in the cold and dangerous world, where Woodbridge and Harry had gone the year before. That fall of 1912, my father was again in South America, and it must have been my mother who bravely set me on my way. I was terrified.

I was put in tow of a bigger boy who lived nearby, the son of another Yale professor. He guided me by some short cuts down the hill to the school, and the third-grade teacher was welcoming and reassuring. I was given a yellow scratch pad to write on to do sums. (To this day, I don't like yellow paper, and in my years as a lawyer I shunned the legal-size yellow pads used by other lawyers.) I felt safe enough in the schoolroom with the teacher present, but at recess I was appalled by the cacophony of voices and the boisterous play that surged around me on the asphalt playground. I knew I did not belong.

The school was located just off Whitney Avenue in the most favored residential area of New Haven, and many of the children may well have been of solid middle-class background. But a nearby factory district was responsible for an invasion of Italian immigrant children, and they played the same role as minorities in inner city schools today. For me, emerging from the rarefied atmosphere of the great mansion on Prospect Hill, all were the children of an alien and hostile world, and I was afraid of them.

Class consciousness was bred into me almost from birth. I could not help being upper class. Class distinctions are repugnant to the American ethos, and even my mother, who had always led the sheltered life of inherited wealth, did not consider herself or her family at the top of the social pyramid. Perhaps her modesty stemmed from her Tiffany grandparents: her grandfather had become a millionaire by catering to the extravagant tastes of New York's newly rich, but he had come from a small town in eastern Connecticut and never sought the trappings of great wealth.

My father, as I learned later, was more socially ambitious. During my childhood he wanted to belong to the best clubs. Though he had objected to the unsuitability of the magnificent mansion the Mitchells had built for his family, he could not help but glory in the grandeur of its marble staircase and its splendid site on the crest of Prospect Hill. His missionary family had been poor, but the ministry was a high calling, and all his ancestors so far as he knew were, as he once told me, of the gentry.

So I could not help but feel that I was special, and my family was special. I did not believe it was a matter of wealth. Other people might be "rich" but that word was not to be applied to the Binghams. Yet wealth was obviously a major factor.

I remained afraid of the children of the poor. It was not only because of those three days at a public school. St. Francis Orphan Asylum, incongruously located in one of New Haven's finest residential districts, occupied an entire block not far from our house, and I dreaded the sound that came from its playground at certain times of day, a sound much like a huge flock of squabbling blackbirds—the shouts and cries of innumerable ragged children.

The noise of the Canner Street school playground was similarly troublesome. But after three precarious days at the public school, I learned when I arrived home—to my infinite relief—that Hamden Hall had decided to take me, though I was a year under its minimum age. So I could go to school with my older brothers. Hamden Hall was where I did belong.

I was there for four years and became part of the school establishment. I think I related better to the teachers than to my contemporaries. Dr. Cushing in particular was a surrogate father. Although he was careful not to show favoritism, there was no doubt he liked the Bingham boys. For one thing, they were important financially. In the school's first year, only eighteen boys were enrolled, and three of them were Binghams. I learned much later that my father might have had a hand, maybe even a dominant one, in founding the school. I suspect that all he did was to indicate to Dr. Cushing that, if the school were started, he would send his sons there. At the time he had six sons, and ultimately they all attended, as did a seventh born two years later in 1914.

At any rate Dr. Cushing established his school at the former Steinert property. Steinert was reputed to have grown wealthy as proprietor of a music store and vendor of pianos, and had built himself a fine mansion just outside New Haven on twelve acres of a wooded hillside opposite Whitney Lake. A patron of the arts as well as a merchant, Steinert had the large music room in his house designed as a concert hall with a stage and anterooms, and this became the assembly hall and the setting for dramatic performances in Dr. Cushing's school.

My first appearance on that stage—or any other—was as "Flute, a bellows-mender," with my older brothers in the more important roles of Quince and Bottom in a performance of "Pyramus and Thisby" from *A Midsummer Night's Dream.*

A curious feature of the assembly hall was that it was duplicated, complete with stage and anterooms, on the basement level below it. I never knew what Steinert had in mind in providing this additional room for performances; perhaps he had planned a music school. After Dr. Cushing took over, the room served only very occasionally as a makeshift gymnasium, but the low ceiling and steel columns supporting the floor above were obstacles to any such serious use.

One use I do remember, and with peculiar delight as a feature of spring fever, was as a setting for games of marbles. Many of the floorboards had warped, perhaps because of dampness, and curled up into shallow troughs, down which boys could roll marbles as in a bowling alley. The game was to place an agate in a trough and challenge other boys to hit and capture it by rolling the cheaper kind of marble down a board from the other end of the room. On one occasion as a challenger, I raked in a whole bagful of marbles without losing my aggie. That was almost the only time in my entire life when I felt the exhilaration of rapid accumulation of wealth. About the same time, I succeeded in capturing the largest and most beautiful aggie on the floor—a monster of glass and colored stripes that I hoarded for weeks.

I was not so lucky in other forms of competition. There was a field for playing soccer, and I did the best I could, but Harry and Charles were both more athletic than I, and I accepted the notion that I was not good at sports. Woodbridge was even less athletic than I, and his censorious manner earned him the unhappy soubriquet "Prune." My nickname, at least in my first year when I was one of the smallest boys, and skinny too, was "Skeet," derived from "mosquito."

Early Lessons

What are memoirs but selected memories? And how does one select? And why?

I have been dipping into memories of my early childhood. It is pleasurable to rummage in that incredibly vast store of material. Thinking about the big house on Prospect Street into which my family moved when I was five, I find innumerable visual images appearing; every room, every wall space, every nook and cranny is still there in my mind to be resurrected and toyed with. People are less substantial, and don't as easily come to mind without an incident to bring them to imagery.

My family is large but finite: parents, brothers, only one grandparent by the time I was six, no first cousins till Olivia was born in 1912, but lots of second cousins on my mother's side, mostly Mitchells. But beyond family, and nurses and household servants coming and going, and Mr. Smith, the shy postman with red cheeks and bushy gray eyebrows, and Dr. Arnold with his bald head and smell of tobacco, and family friends like Uncle Ernest Brown and the Footes, mostly faces of boys from my first school begin to crowd in. No girls. Hamden Hall was a boys' school, and the only girls I had wary contact with were a couple of girl cousins and the sisters of a few schoolmates, and girls seen—and occasionally fearfully touched—in starched frilly dresses at a dancing school or at children's parties.

There was one earlier occasion, before I went to school, which seems to have set the stage for my fear of girls. I had been taken by my mother to visit the little private school that Woodbridge and Harry were then attending. She had some business with a teacher or member of the staff, and I was left alone in the front hall of what was clearly a modest private home, when down the stairs, probably at the end of a class period, came trooping a noisy claque of girls, enormous from my perspective. I screamed in terror till my mother came and took me away.

If almost no girls' faces appear in my early gallery, there are a fair number of older women, mostly relatives or servants. Among the men in this collection of early images, schoolteachers stick out. Hamden Hall, typical of boys' schools, employed all male teachers. My father believed firmly that boys should be taught by men, and except for the drawing teacher and Miss Daly, the monthly dancing school teacher, the teachers were known as masters and addressed as "Sir."

In my first year at school, there were only three masters: Dr. Cushing, the headmaster, who lived on the premises; Mr. Olds, balding and impish; and Mr. Barrows, younger and friendlier.

Dr. Cushing (his title came from a Ph.D.) was always on hand when we arrived, reeking of pipe tobacco smoke, genial but very much in command. He had been principal of a high school. In the studies he prescribed, the three R's were basic, as was geography and, almost from the beginning, Latin.

My first lessons in Latin come vividly to mind. We learned to conjugate *amare*, to love: *amo, amas, amat*, and when at an early stage, friendly Mr. Barrows encouraged us to put words together, *puer puellam amat*, "boy loves girl," was first to come to my mind, and we tittered.

I knew something about sex by that time. My father had taken solemn pains to tell me at a session in the library, when I reached the age of seven, that there was no Santa Claus—he was surprised that I hadn't identified him when he came down the stairs in a Santa Claus suit on Christmas mornings. He also explained to me, with the help of some pictures of nude women, the differences between the sexes—and I was surprised that he would think I needed to have that explained, considering the classical pictures and statues that were part of my environment. But he went on with what was indeed surprising news to me, about where a baby comes from. I had been quite certain that I had heard the swishing of the stork's wings when Mitchell arrived the year before. But he explained that a baby comes painfully out of a hole in the mother in the same way an egg comes out of a hen (also painfully, he said).

He did not explain how the baby gets into the mother, and I had not thought to ask. But my next older brother Harry told me not long thereafter what he had gathered from talk at the Canner Street school, that people did what we had seen dogs doing, and that one boy at the school had actually tried it with a girl, though without result.

However, I had no sense of the biological implications of the Latin phrase that I had offered to Mr. Barrows. And in the unaffected innocence of my age and the age I was brought up in, I had no awareness of anything other than slight embarrassment when the other master at Hamden Hall, Mr. Olds, romped naked with little boys in the locker room after the afternoon sports program. I was not unused to male nakedness, both of little boys and grown men, for in our summers at the Camp in Salem, swimming in the brook was always an all-male affair and always in the nude. And never in my recollection, either at the swimming pool or in the school locker room, was there anything more improper than a surreptitious inquisitive look.

A Profound Question

The Foote family had a more important connection with my own family during my early years than any other. Harry Foote was a professor of chemistry at Yale. He and his wife—her name was Martha but she was always known as Patty, and I never called her anything but Mrs. Foote—lived on Livingstone Street near the Everit Street house that my parents moved into when they first came to New Haven, and it was presumably as neighbors that the Footes first became family friends. They were having children at the same time as my parents. Their oldest son, William—he was always known as William and not Bill until he went to school—was just my age. Twins came next, Mary and Edward.

In 1911 Harry Foote went to South America with my father as a member of the Yale Peruvian Expedition, and was with him on the day Machu Picchu was discovered, though as the expedition's "naturalist" he was off collecting new species of insects on the morning of the discovery. As tent-mates on the six-week wilderness trek that resulted in the subsequent discoveries of the Incas' last capital at Vitcos and their jungle refuge at Vilcabamba, the two men became devoted friends. Each had, to be sure, reservations about their friendship. Harry Foote was a little older and academically senior to my father; my father, on the other hand, did not let anyone forget that he was "director" of the expedition. And when the Binghams moved from the Footes' neighborhood onto Prospect Hill, the difference in their life style made for awkwardness. William was in public school when I went to Hamden Hall, and my mother explained that the Footes, if not really poor, still could not afford some things that we took for granted.

Since we were in different schools and no longer neighbors, I would not have become William's friend if the Footes had not become summer tenants of one of the Mitchell family houses in Salem. The Camp would have been too isolated a summer retreat even for my family, and my brothers and I would have been left entirely to ourselves, if my father had not sought out congenial friends with children from the Yale community, and arranged to have them as summer tenants in one or another of the half dozen houses that my Mitchell grandparents had acquired in Salem about the time I was born. Through most of my childhood, the Footes spent summers in the little house at the bottom of the hill below the Camp.

William always came along when any of the Bingham boys were going swimming in the brook, or catching bullfrogs in the pond, or exploring old wood roads, or on rainy days playing hide-and-seek in the big hay barn behind the Foote house. Often enough as time went on, his younger brother Edward came along too, but not Mary, Edward's twin sister. My brothers and I had little use for a girl in our games; having no sisters ourselves and going to an all boys' school, we felt girls were an alien species. But we liked Edward. He was competent and eager. I suspected he was popular in the school he went to.

During the school year, we rarely saw the Footes and did not think much about them. But one winter's day I heard that Edward had been hurt in an accident. Sliding downhill on a sled, he had collided with a tree and was in a coma. After several days of hearing my parents speak of him and his parents in hushed voices, I was told he had died, and it was suggested that it would be nice if I wrote a letter to his parents.

I was awed by the fact of death, almost the first time it had seemed to come close; however, Edward was younger than I and not such a close friend. Still I had an oppressive sense of his family's grief; I was fond of Mr. and Mrs. Foote, and would have been glad to comfort them if I could.

I wrote a letter, the gist of which was that Edward had done so well in the school of life that he was qualified for early admission to Heaven. My father seemed doubtful as to how the Footes would take it, particularly Mr. Foote who, he had reason to know, was not religiously inclined. But my mother overcame his doubts, and the letter was sent.

I never heard whether it did give the sorrowing parents any comfort, though Mr. Foote seemed to me, for the rest of his life, a personal friend regardless of the difference in our ages. Mrs. Foote was somewhat more formidable—she later founded a school that still bears her name—but she too, if more distantly, was always a friend.

As for Edward's admission to Heaven, my father's skepticism about my letter raised doubts in my mind on the issue of a heavenly reward. Just where the idea originated—that if I were good I would go to Heaven—I don't know, but it was more likely from nurses than from my mother. Even before her marriage, my father's missionary parents had impressed upon her that she was dangerously uninformed in religious matters, and she gave me and my brothers little guidance in theology. And my father, having broken with his parents' fundamentalism, gave even less.

At bedtime at an early stage she taught me to say a simple prayer: "Dear God, please help me to be always brave and good"—to which were added in the course of time many other adjectives in a long list of virtues. But I don't remember her tying my behavior to what might happen to me in an afterlife. In my adult years the question of a life after death has never been a major concern of mine. But the great, overwhelming question behind it—What is life for?—for which the notion of an earthly schooling and testing prior to admission to some higher existence provides a comforting answer—remains of deep moment.

Money

I always did well in school. The report cards I brought home from Hamden Hall every week were liberally sprinkled with "VG"s, meaning "very good"— the top marking grade. I was not happy if the mark was only a "G" for good, and on the very few occasions when I brought home an "F" for fair—most likely for penmanship—I felt disgraced. The lower levels of marking—"M" for unsatisfactory, "P" for poor, and "B" for bad—were only theoretical possibilities, affecting other boys perhaps, but not me.

At an early stage in my schooling, my father began offering a financial incentive to academic success: he gave me and my brothers a nickel for each "VG" on a report card. This was in addition to a weekly allowance of twenty-five cents.

Money played a strange role in the Bingham household, mostly a hidden role. It was almost never mentioned. If my parents ever had financial worries, neither of them would have spoken of it in front of the children. They may have felt they could not immediately afford the furniture the new house called for, but they never said so.

It is clear in retrospect that they had very different attitudes toward money. My mother had grown up in the most protected of environments, thanks to her Tiffany grandfather. He had worked hard to amass a fortune, but her father was a gentleman of culture and leisure who looked down on money-grubbing. My mother knew nothing—and wanted to know nothing—about how money was earned and saved and spent. Enough money for all her needs was always available. People who had to "earn a living" were, it seemed to me, subtly disparaged by her.

In my father's youth, on the other hand, there never was enough money. The small pension his father received as a retired missionary hardly covered essentials, let alone such luxuries as a bicycle. All through his boyhood, every penny he could earn had to be saved for his education, and he worked his way through school and college with whatever odd jobs he could find. When he married my mother, it would have been a shocking and inadmissible thought that he had chosen her for her money, and he was always able to persuade himself that it was only for love. In any case the Mitchells kept a sharp eye out for any disturbing indications that their son-in-law was taking advantage of his position. They provided their daughter with a generous annual income but no capital. In the early days of his marriage, my father tried to teach Alfreda how to keep household accounts, but she lacked the incentive since there always seemed to be enough, and he soon gave up.

As his boys reached school age, he tried hard to inculcate in them a sense of the value of money, and a feeling that it was to be earned. Getting good marks in school was a way of earning it. He also wanted us to learn to save, and I remember being taken into the Connecticut Savings Bank in downtown New Haven, an impressive marble temple with a columned portico, where a small savings account was opened in my name. He took me awestruck into the bank's vault, where he said all the substantial people of the city kept their wealth.

When my father's Aunt Lydia died, leaving a modest legacy to be divided among his children, he bought each of us a few shares in Consumers Power Company, a Michigan utility company, and for years thereafter I received a check for three dollars each quarter as an introduction to the benefits of investment and inherited wealth.

Wanting his sons to understand the competitiveness of the market, he organized a little auction in which we bid against one another for odd items he provided from his surplus. Unfortunately, his boys had so little acquisitive sense, or perhaps my father was so unused to merchandizing, that the competition was anything but fierce, and I remember acquiring two beautifully bound little books, my great-uncle Donald Mitchell's *Reveries of a Bachelor* and *Dream Life*, still in my library, for something like seventeen cents.

Schools

In its first year Hamden Hall enrolled eighteen boys, three of whom were Binghams. I entered the First Form at Hamden Hall, which corresponded to third grade, having covered the first two grades with my governesses. Harry was in the Second Form and Woodbridge in the Third. The next year Woodbridge went off to boarding school at Groton, and Harry and I advanced to higher forms. Then Harry left for Groton, and my younger brothers began coming in. The school was growing, and new boys joined at each level.

In First Form my best friend was Norman Schwab, son of the Yale University Librarian. Curly haired, broad of face with a perpetually puzzled expression, as gentle and shy as I was, he and I found comfort in each other.

Carlos Stoddard, known as Toddy, was impish, mercurial, a friend one day, a tease the next. A dozen years later as editor-in-chief of the *Yale Daily News*, he successfully carried through a campaign for the abolition of compulsory chapel attendance.

Albert Thomas, small and eager to please, was the only son of a doctor. His family lived in cramped quarters connected with the New Haven Hospital.

In Second Form, Gordon Sweet became my friend and we occasionally visited each other's homes. Mannerly and self-assured, he lived alone with his mother in a walk-up apartment downtown; no father was in evidence, and this troubled me, but I gathered that a grandfather was rich and respected, and owned a fleet of oyster boats. When I went to Yale College, Gordon was the president of the fraternity I joined. Like Stoddard, he was a class ahead of me in college. Later he played a leading role in the redevelopment of downtown New Haven. In the 1960s and 1970s, we became friends once again. In my mind's eye, the image I see today is at once a boy and a wheezing senior citizen.

Hamden Hall was not much more than a half-mile from my Prospect Street home. It was on the far side of Mill Rock, a steep little hill at the end of Prospect Street crowned by a round concrete water tower. My brothers and I were expected to walk to school except in very bad weather. The accepted route was by way of Whitney Avenue where the road curved uphill past the dam that had once powered Eli Whitney's factory. A major streetcar line ran on Whitney Avenue, and we could, if we chose, ride this to school, but we preferred to walk. Naturally we found short cuts. All my life I have been fascinated by short cuts, and have wanted to try every possible alternative to any accepted route, whether on foot or by car, if it would save a few feet.

Hamden Hall was called a country day school. It was far enough from the city limits to have a remnant of "country" around it, a field for soccer games, a tiny pond that froze in winter for skating, and a grove of pine trees. Three pine trees embraced the letters "H H" on the school's coat of arms, which was emblazoned on the uniform caps we wore. As a "day" school, it offered an afternoon sports program, and on Saturdays, in addition to athletics, "manual training" was provided in a carpentry shop fashioned from pine logs cut on the place, or occasionally we were taken hiking on Mount Carmel a few miles away.

The school curriculum was designed to meet the standards of the best boarding schools, with an emphasis on Latin. At age twelve Woodbridge and Harry went on to Groton, then a six-year school. I assumed that was the natural order, and as my fourth year at Hamden Hall came to an end, I expected to do what my brothers had done. But I was only eleven, and my parents thought I was too young to go to boarding school.

I was disappointed. I had come to believe I was brighter than my older brothers. My governesses had given me confidence in my ability to do schoolwork ahead of my age bracket, and my experience at Hamden Hall only confirmed my belief in my intelligence. Now I was to be denied the rewards of being bright. I felt I was being handicapped.

My father arranged a program of private tutoring so that I would at least keep up with the schoolwork provided in the first year at Groton. Three times a week I made my way downtown to my father's office in Lampson Hall near the Yale campus; there or in a basement room of Osborn Hall, where the pottery shards my father had brought back from Machu Picchu were being catalogued, I met with the student tutors he had hired, to go over what I was studying in Latin and other subjects. I hardly knew where I belonged.

After the fall term of my being rather aimlessly tutored, my father, whose semester of college teaching had been interrupted by recurrent respiratory illness, went to Florida to regain his health and took me with him. We spent a few happy weeks in Miami, in a rented apartment near my grandmother's winter home, a rare episode in my childhood when my father and I, alone together, could relate simply as two congenial human beings. Then my father decided to learn to fly at a flying school on the outskirts of Miami, as his form of preparedness for the imminent entry of this country into the war raging in Europe. He heard about a small boarding school in nearby Coconut Grove, and there I was enrolled for my next bout of schooling.

The Adirondack-Florida School was an even more sheltered environment than Hamden Hall. With an enrollment of only thirty boys twelve to eighteen years old, the winter term was spent on the shores of Biscayne Bay, with sailing a major sport, while the fall and spring terms were spent in a group of log cabins overlooking a lake in the northern Adirondacks. Despite the luxurious implications of two holiday sites, and the refined big-family atmosphere given the school by Mrs. Ransom, the widow of the school's founder and its sole proprietress, the style was more spartan than sybaritic, and academic standards under Levering Somers, the headmaster, were rigorous enough. Still, isolation from the world, now in the throes of World War I, was extreme.

Not that I was unaware that a war had been raging in Europe for over two years. Remote from schoolboy concerns at first, the sinking of the *Lusitania* in May of 1915 had brought a sense of involvement on the side of the Allies. In our big house we played war games with toy soldiers and toy cannon on the floor of the gymnasium on our top floor, and we moved colored pins on a map of the western front when there was any change in the lines of trenches in northern France.

Reading about the horrendous casualties in the battles on the Somme and at Verdun put a strain on the structure of moral values I had previously absorbed. I did not question the distinction made between the heroism of British, French, and Belgian soldiers as opposed to the bestial ferocity of the murderous Germans. But I had been taught the Ten Commandments, including "Thou shalt not kill," at an early age, and it was a difficult adjustment, never altogether satisfactorily made, to accept the idea that it was good to kill Germans.

The United States entered the war in Europe a month or two after I entered boarding school in Florida, and I swelled with pride when I heard that my father was now in the Army, commissioned a major in the Air Service of the Signal Corps and soon to wear a pilot's wings. I did my best to accept his admonition, in a letter addressed to his seven sons some months later, as he was about to sail for France, always to hate the Germans. It would not have occurred to me to question the righteousness of the cause.

In the fall of 1918, after a year and a half at the Adirondack-Florida School, I went on to join my older brothers at Groton. The notion I had imbibed at home and in my serious schooling, that one's life should be moral and useful, was further reinforced at that Episcopal church school. Its Latin motto, *Cui servire est regnare*, was literally translated for the boys by the phrase "whom to serve is to rule," but it might as well have been "noblesse oblige." The "whom," we were told, referred to God, though the prayer with which the Rector concluded his sermons—"Help us, O God, so long as we live, to live nobly, to Thy glory and the good cheer of our fellow men"—suggested that the welfare of our fellow humans should be a parallel target of our service.

CHRONICLE X

Confessions of a Social Reformer

CHAPTER 35

Sources of My Social Conscience

The first step I took as a social reformer was not auspicious: I fell flat on my face.

On the morning I began work as a farmhand, I was told to harness up the team of workhorses. A harness to the uninitiated is a vastly complex contraption. I put the collar over the head of the startled horse upside down. The farmer gave me a second chance to show I knew something of farm work. Three days later he told me, gently enough, that not only did I know nothing, but I seemed incapable of learning. For a young man who had just graduated with highest honors from Yale, that was a hard first lesson in the real world.

I had told the man in the employment office in Springfield, Massachusetts, that I had had experience as a farm worker. I had not told him that my experience was limited to spending vacations at my family's summer home overlooking several hundred acres of farmland. The place was identified on my mother's stationery as "Woodbridge Mumford Farms, Salem via Colchester, Connecticut" (Salem was then too small and remote to have a post office of its own). The farms were worked by a salaried farm manager and his help.

My brothers and I had played hide-and-seek in one of the big barns when the hay crop was in, but had never lent a hand in the haying. To be sure, I had done some weeding in the family's vegetable garden, at a beginning wage of ten cents an hour, and had learned how to put the bit in the mouth and the saddle on the back of Roxy or Judge, the family's riding horses, but the leather straps on a saddle and bridle are as nothing compared to the harness of a working horse.

After this initial fiasco I tried again. Not wanting to face the employment office a second time, I answered a "help wanted" advertisement in the *Springfield Republican*. The pay offered was only a dollar a day, but I had no pride left and no bargaining power, and I took the job.

I stayed even when I found that no dollar was paid for Sundays, though the cows had to be milked night and morning and the barn cleaned the same as other days. I accepted the hard-faced farmer's explanation that after all I was getting free board and room. He was a tenant or employee of a rich absentee owner, and was keeping costs down by running his help-wanted advertisement every day and making do with the steady stream of homeless men and boys who responded but rarely stayed more than a week at that rate of pay. In one of my college courses, I had read a book called *How the Other Half Lives*. It had stirred my still embryonic social conscience.

A child accepts the world round him as a given. My world as a child was the affluent world of inherited wealth. For me, a thirty-room house staffed by a dozen servants, with views of distant hills and with a marble staircase and a vast music room flooded with sunshine filtered through a conservatory, was a standard of normality, and if most of the human race fell well below the norm, that was not for me to question.

Yet I did not think of my family as rich. There were two larger mansions than ours in New Haven, and their occupants, the Brewsters and the Stoddards, were indeed "rich," but not the Binghams.

Only dimly did I become aware that there were people less fortunate than we. My mother, brought up in an equally sheltered environment, educated at home with not even the experience of going to school, made me understand that the really poor were so placed by a divine providence to remind us of our blessings and encourage us to charity.

An occasion that made a great impression on me was a visit to a factory tenement. It was Thanksgiving time, and the private school I attended had made up some food baskets to give to the poor; I went along with a teacher—perhaps as a first lesson in "how the other half lives"—to deliver one of the baskets. I can still smell the fetid atmosphere in that third-floor tenement kitchen, full of silent dirty children, where we left the food and quickly fled.

So I was aware of poverty. I accepted it as one of the harsh facts of life, from which I could be duly thankful I was spared, but it was not my problem, and I felt no pangs of conscience at my better fortune.

Once, perhaps on my tenth birthday, a relative presented me with a ten-dollar bill, and I did not know what to do with it. My father told me his father had believed in tithing, giving a tenth of one's income to charity. For the first time I gathered that I might have a moral obligation to feed the poor and hungry. Wanting at this point to demonstrate my generosity, I decided to allocate half of the ten dollars to charity—my father said he would take care of that—and half to my savings account.

My father called the children of slum tenements who had frightened me at public school "muckers." In time I came to realize that in his sheltered boyhood as the son of a retired missionary in Honolulu, he too had been afraid of the rowdyism of his schoolmates, even though they had come from the favored white community of that outpost of America. In our great mansion on Prospect Hill, my brothers and I felt reasonably secure from any mucker invasion.

The nearest the slum children came to our fortress home was a large open field across the street where, after a winter snowstorm, the kids from the Winchester Avenue factory district came to coast. Not all of them had sleds, and when the snow was packed down and frozen, some made use of dishpans for sliding. My brothers and I watched this invasion from afar. However, a year or two after our house was built, my widowed grandmother, Annie Mitchell, bought the big lot and built another oversize mansion for herself. The fenced lot was now available to us to coast on, and if muckers from Winchester Avenue came wistfully to watch us from the other side of the fence, and asked how they could get in, we explained that this was now private property.

I began to feel some uneasiness at my privileged status, but that was the way things were and always had been, and my social conscience was not yet aroused.

Later, at Groton, social welfare was not particularly emphasized, except for a summer camp for Boston slum children maintained by the school on Squam Lake in the White Mountains: the older Groton boys were urged to put in a couple of weeks out of their summer vacations as camp counselors. I dutifully put in my stint, but found myself no better able to relate to those street kids as human beings than to the unruly orphans at the St. Francis asylum. I would have swept all human misery under the rug if I could.

My still embryonic social conscience was not greatly stimulated when I went on to Yale in 1923. It was the Coolidge era and the national mood was one of complacency. My father had begun his political career with his election to the post of Lieutenant Governor of Connecticut in 1922, and I had no inclination to differ from his staunch Republican philosophy. Left alone, the economy would in time assure a chicken in every pot, two cars in every garage. Poverty and war and civil strife were no longer matters of concern. It was the philosophy that returned to favor with Ronald Reagan two generations later: the less government the better.

I had ambitions to be a writer, perhaps even a poet. And for a while my natural bent for romantic idealism found expression in religion. My logical mind had rebelled against the creedal orthodoxy of Groton, and I had not been moved to join the Episcopal Church there as had my two older brothers, but the nondenominational college church appealed to me. Battell Chapel, where my parents for some years had a pew reserved, was familiar to me from early childhood. My father felt his boys should know the Bible and be exposed to religion. So with some regularity, when he was not exploring in Peru, he took his family to the Sunday services in the college chapel where we listened to the moral exhortations of Dean Charles R. Brown of the Divinity School, and such visiting preachers as Henry Sloane Coffin and Harry Emerson Fosdick. It would not have occurred to me then, or later as an entering student, to object to the college's traditional rule—shortly to be abolished—of compulsory chapel attendance. Not long after entering Yale, I consulted Dean Brown and was duly baptized by him—my father's missionary ancestors had not favored infant baptism—and was admitted as a member of the college church.

I was also touched by the more evangelical atmosphere of Dwight Hall, the campus center for religious activities. At a student religious conference at Silver Bay on Lake George at the end of my freshman year, I quailed before the soul-searching exhortations of Samuel Shoemaker, then a spokesman for the movement that came to be called Moral Re-Armament, but was not sufficiently persuaded of my sinfulness to hit the sawdust trail. However, in my increasingly pious mood, I began as a sophomore at Yale to participate in the only activity sponsored by Dwight Hall that dealt with poverty and the "social problem." It was the Yale Hope Mission.

The mission was run by a weather-beaten Scotsman named Angus Macdonald who had been saved from alcoholism by evangelical religion. His clientele were for the most part homeless vagrants with the same weakness that he had surmounted, and he told them that they could be saved only by giving themselves to Jesus. The mission provided free board and room to transients. Frequent gospel meetings gave them an opportunity to turn from their ways and embrace sobriety and the good life. Their stay at the mission might then be prolonged while they were helped to find employment. With his own experience behind him, Macdonald was quick to spot a false conversion or a repeater, and my impression is that he urged the men—I don't remember any women—out the mission's revolving door, after one night's shelter and showering, as fast as they came in.

A friend at Dwight Hall invited me to visit the place and then to join a student committee that helped raise money for its running expenses and provided speakers for the evening gospel meetings. Reluctantly I eventually accepted a call to speak. Not having hit the revivalist sawdust trail myself, I could not bring myself to urge conversion on the huddled group of sleepy vagrants newly fed, clothed, and washed, but Macdonald took care of the exhortatory part of the program. I limited myself to vague expressions of piety and good will.

This slight contact with the nether world of poverty served as little more than a reminder of its existence. I received no hint of the social and economic problems that made for unemployment and homelessness. Addiction to alcohol was a consequence of moral and spiritual failure. Yet I was uncomfortable. My social conscience had been pricked.

One other aspect of my college experience stirred my discomfort. Yale Station, where I picked up my mail and a copy of the *Yale Daily News* every day, was then located in the basement of old Fayerweather Hall, part of the Berkeley Quadrangle, now the site of Berkeley College. At the hours when students were likely to be flocking in and out, the adjacent sidewalk of Elm Street was often crowded with little shoe-shine boys from New Haven's slums competing for the students' extra cash. Each had a box for the tools of his trade with a footrest on top, and if he snared a customer, he would get down on his knees and proceed with a flourish to clean and polish one shoe at a time. In those days students wore three-piece suits, pants were regularly pressed, and the desirability of a high-gloss polish on one's shoes insured enough return on a tenement child's investment to clutter the sidewalk on football weekends. To have a little boy with unwashed hands and face go down on his knees before me so discomfited me that I seldom became a patron. But I could not be wholly unaffected by the raucous pleas from which I escaped to go back to my studies.

No one suggested I had any obligation to the little shine boys. A conscientious student, I did what was expected of me. I did well in my studies, becoming a "scholar of the first rank" in my freshman year, elected to Phi Beta Kappa in my junior year, and awarded a "philosophical oration" equivalent to a summa cum laude degree at graduation. Yet I was always careful not to be considered a "grind." I took up rowing as a sport and made the 150-pound crew. I joined Zeta Psi fraternity, which at that time had a good sprinkling of serious-minded and literary types, some of whom became lifelong friends.

I was as unsure of my future as most of my fellow students. I had majored in English and history, and my bent seemed to be a career either as a writer or in government. My father had been elected to the United States Senate in 1924 during my second year in college. I basked in reflected glory and hoped to emulate him. Though himself previously a professor and explorer, he emphasized to me that the best road into politics was through the legal profession. When I graduated from Yale College in the spring of 1927, I was already enrolled in the Yale Law School.

That summer, I set out to act upon the moral imperatives of my burgeoning social conscience. I laid out a program for myself. My summer vacations during my school and college years had been happily and not too unprofitably spent, mostly at my family's summer home, the Camp in Salem, with occasional visits to friends and some foreign travel. I was not impelled to seek a summer job either out of financial need or peer pressure: my family was providing me with an ample allowance of $2,000 a year, and it was not then the rule for the prep school crowd to get summer jobs.

But I had become uncomfortably aware of the disparity between my privileged status and what I had seen of poverty. I knew that the world of Groton and Yale, of Prospect Street and Salem, was a protected and isolated world. I felt both curiosity and a sense of obligation to learn "how the other half lives."

I would begin by seeking work as a farm laborer.

After graduation and a house party during the Yale-Harvard boat races in New London, I set out with trepidation on my quest. Before leaving, I bought a pair of overalls and a blue-collared shirt. Embarrassed by the crisp newness of my clothes, I took pains to get them dirty before packing them in an old suitcase, from which I had carefully removed the labels indicating foreign travel. I wanted to make it on my own, and set forth by bus for Spring-field. Since the name of Bingham was, as I thought, too well known in Con-necticut, I would make my first application for a job in Massachusetts.

Still, it was hard to escape from my past. I had written my mother about my failure to keep my first job, and about my subsequent whereabouts. One hot summer day, drenched with sweat, I was tossing forkfuls of hay onto a hay wagon in a field some distance from the farmhouse of my new employer, when I saw with horror a familiar automobile stopped on the shoulder of the adjacent highway. It was my mother's Locomobile limousine, and she was sitting in the back seat while Smith, the family chauffeur, was dispatched to call me from my work. I took a few minutes off to greet her suitably, hoping that my fellow worker on the top of the hay wagon would not see too much. Apparently my mother had stopped at the farmhouse and been told where she might find me. I learned later that the farmer's wife had assumed that the man in the chauffeur's cap was my father; apparently she had not been led to wonder why my mother was not sitting next to him in the front seat. My cherished incognito had not been breached.

CHAPTER 36

From Guilt to a Sense of Mission

In my three years at Yale Law School, my social conscience began to take shape. It was not to remain merely an uneasy sense of guilt at my upper-class privileges.

A little group of friends, enrolled in graduate studies in law and other fields at Yale, turned out to have liberal political and social ideas that led me to question my father's conservative Republicanism.

Winlock Miller was virtually a liberal Democrat from birth. He was from the State of Washington where his father had been a leading Wilsonian Demo-crat. Social reform had laced the conversation around his family's dinner table in his earlier years, and his agile mind was quick to point out the inadequa-cies of the protectionist policies of the Coolidge administration. He would be supported in a "bull session" in our boarding house by Ken Ryan, a burly Irish Catholic, everybody's friend, and also a confirmed Democrat from infancy.

A crisis in my Republican faith came in 1928, at the beginning of my second year in law school. Al Smith, an Irish Catholic, was challenging the Republican establishment and its candidate, Herbert Hoover. As governor of New York, Al Smith had demonstrated that government could be used to promote the welfare of working men and women and the poor.

In New Haven, the local Republican machine, perhaps prodded by my father, approached me to set up a Hoover-for-President Club at Yale Law School. I agreed and organized a political rally. For a speaker, I went to see the president of the university, James Rowland Angell, and was gratified to find him willing. The law school auditorium was full for the occasion, which further gratified me. But my self-satisfaction was not to last. In introducing President Angell, whom most of the students had never seen before, I became tangled in my rhetoric: I said we were particularly glad to have him with us on this occasion as we saw him at the law school "only too often—I mean seldom." The laughter struck me as not too friendly.

The president's remarks were not memorable, but at his conclusion he was given polite applause, and then my friend Ken Ryan rose and began to sing the "Sidewalks of New York," Al Smith's campaign song. Most of the audience rose at this apparently prearranged signal, joined the defiant singing, and marched out of the hall behind Ken. I apologized to President Angell as he fled, and no more was heard of my Hoover-for-President Club.

A poll of the law school faculty and student body at that time would have shown overwhelming support for the Democratic party. The prevailing philosophy of the school was iconoclastic. Robert Maynard Hutchins was then nearing the end of his brief tenure as dean. He was responsible for bringing William O. Douglas from the West Coast as a step in a career that would soon put him on the Supreme Court. Felix Frankfurter was lured down from Harvard one day a week for a seminar on constitutional law.

The standard courses on contracts, property, torts, and trusts I found intolerably dull. Douglas's course on business organization appealed to me even less: he was a shy and awkward teacher in those days before he became a national figure, and I even had the presumption to complain to Hutchins about him and his course.

The casebook method of instruction was strictly adhered to at that time at the leading law schools. Whatever the field, students read appellate decisions exclusively. In class discussion of the cases, the main thrust seemed to be to get behind the words to determine the prejudices and foibles of the judges who wrote the decisions: the law was what the judges said it was, and what they said was determined, as we sometimes put it, by what they had had for breakfast. Such high-sounding phrases as "equal justice under law," soon to be inscribed on the new Supreme Court building in Washington, were never heard.

I was bright enough to adapt to the critical analytic approach. At the end of my first year, I qualified to compete for a place on the editorial board of the *Yale Law Journal*. But my faith in the established order was being subtly undermined.

That summer I wanted to continue with my investigation of the realities of American life away from both academia and Prospect Hill. I decided to look for a job in a factory. It was the summer of 1928—the high tide of Hoover prosperity and the stock market boom—but there were already signs of unemployment. The actual experience of factory work seemed more important to me than how I found the job, so I used one of my father's new political connections and went to see Edward Goss, executive vice-president of the Scovill Manufacturing Company in Waterbury, fabricators of brass products. The only opening he found for me was on the night shift, from 6:00 P.M. to 6:00 A.M., with a thirty-minute lunch break at midnight, five days a week.

I found a room at the local YMCA within walking distance of the sprawling plant. On showing up at the factory gates the next evening, I was directed to a machine shop where the foreman put me on a machine for shaping brass rivets. I was to take short cylinders of metal one at a time from a bin, insert them into the jaws of the machine, pull a lever that would trigger the machine to squeeze them—in a deluge of hot oil—to the proper tapered dimensions, and eject them into another bin. After a few minutes of the foreman's instructions, shouted over the grinding roar of the machine, I was left to myself. I knew it was piecework, and the faster and more consistently I applied myself, the more I would earn.

After what seemed an eternity of repetitive action, suffocated by the smell of hot oil, deafened by the noise, I stole a glance at the clock over the foreman's desk and was horrified to realize that only half an hour had elapsed. Five and a half hours lay ahead till the midnight lunch break, eleven and a half hours before the day would bring release.

I stood it for about two weeks, enduring the monotony each night with elaborate reminiscences and fantasies evoked from my past. It was a hot summer and before the days of air conditioners. Sleep at the Y, after a shower and breakfast, came easily enough despite the heat and the sunshine outside. But I began to wonder if my sanity and my health would stand the strain. I persuaded myself that I had learned the lesson I wanted to learn, and could go on to something else with a clear conscience. I went back to Mr. Goss and told him I wanted another job; he sent me to the same machine shop as an "inspector" on the day shift. I was to circulate around the shop and test samples of each product with a micrometer to see that the dimensions were correct. If an item did not meet specifications, I was to call a mechanic to make an adjustment in the machine. Compared with my earlier job, this was blissfully easy. The foreman must have guessed I had some pull with the management but made no comment.

In circulating among the machine tools in that shop, I became aware how interchangeable human beings and machines were. Most of the workers were doing what I had been doing with the rivets, feeding small units into a machine tool for a single processing operation. One machine gave a spiral twist to the metal footing that would become part of an electric light bulb. Another stamped a thimble with MADE IN USA. Other small metal parts that were stamped, ground, drilled, or otherwise shaped were unidentifiable as to their ultimate purpose. But in every case, the insertion of the item for processing might just as easily have been done by machines, only requiring human intervention if the system broke down.

Occasionally, if the machine was not too noisy, I would pass a few words with the workers while I was testing their products. To my surprise, they were not resentful of the dehumanizing work to which they were bound. One elderly woman who had worked in the Scovill plant for twenty-five years was happy because the company now gave her a week's paid vacation every summer. Others seemed glad to have a job at a time when factory workers were beginning to be laid off.

It seemed to me that all but the foreman and the mechanic in the shop were superfluous. It was only a question of time before automatic feeding devices would be perfected and replace all the routine mechanical jobs. I welcomed the prospect of the liberation of these workers from the noise, smells, and intolerable monotony of their present work. I was not then prepared to speculate as to what would happen to them when they lost their jobs.

I had taken one course in economics at college and knew something of cost effectiveness and the workings of the market. I was not disposed to question the system, but I was convinced from what I had seen of factory labor that it blighted the lives of those dependent on it. At the same time I had a glimpse of the machine as not only a slave driver but a liberator.

Returning to my studies, I felt a growing distaste for the aridity of legal scholarship. The cases I read in corporate reorganization of industrial enterprises seemed far removed from the flesh and blood of the workers I had seen at the Scovill Company. I fled to courses on the fringes of the curriculum—with Walton Hamilton, a sociologist who did not even have a law degree, with Edwin Borchard on international law, with Arthur Goodhart on jurisprudence, the philosophy of law.

Only at two points did the law school program touch on the actual practice of law. The "moot court" provided for the preparing of briefs and the arguing of hypothetical cases before an appeals tribunal made up of three faculty members. More down to earth was the "legal aid" program in which students were expected to devote a certain number of hours to volunteer work at an office in City Hall providing legal assistance to the poor. There I found myself talking to and ostensibly advising women from the working-class districts of New Haven, confronted with the intractable problems of abusive husbands, delinquent children, unlivable tenements, and the like. I had had no training in how to proceed and left my sessions at City Hall with feelings of total inadequacy, but with a new awareness of social problems just under the surface of the secure world I had been brought up in.

I decided for my second summer vacation to try to learn more about the rest of my country. I took a train to Pittsburgh as a starter and looked in the Help Wanted pages of a newspaper for a possible job. I wondered what, after my years of superior education, I was fitted for. An advertisement told me a good income could be made selling magazine subscriptions on commission, no experience necessary.

I became one of a crew of half a dozen salesmen, peddling group subscriptions of the *Saturday Evening Post, Redbook,* the *Ladies Home Journal,* and other popular magazines. We would go by streetcar to an outlying residential district where I would be assigned to work one side of a street. These were small one-family houses, the homes of industrial and white-collar workers; in those days wives were often found at home doing the housework. The trick was to get one foot in the door to gain enough time to make an ingratiating opening spiel and so, if only occasionally, gain entrance to a kitchen or living room where I could spread out my sample copies and explain the savings that came with group subscriptions.

Here was no grinding poverty, but the drabness of lower-middle-class life depressed me. And it was with revulsion that I forced myself to try to extract a slice from a meager family budget for the questionable wares I was peddling. At the end of my first day, I had made one sale, to a timid little housewife recovering from surgery, who seemed glad to have somebody to talk to.

After a few days of knocking on the doors of houses that were always the same, I decided to move on to what I hoped would be wider horizons.

I had left home with barely enough money to travel by train across half the country and to support myself for a couple of weeks. I wanted to find out what it was like to have to earn my own keep.

Oklahoma City was my next stop. Here truly, I felt, was Middle America, fresher and newer than Pittsburgh. The only employment I found immediately available was another magazine subscription crew, and I tried that for a few days with little more success. The kitchens and parlors I insinuated myself into seemed identical to those I had seen in Pittsburgh. From my sophisticated eminence as a product of Prospect Street, Groton, and Yale, I found the cultural poverty of the average American home depressingly dreary. I had read the Lynds' *Middletown* and Sinclair Lewis's *Main Street,* and now I saw the reality behind them.

I sought to expand my experiences. I had heard there was work for the unskilled in the oil fields, but I could find none. The lines of grizzled men outside employment offices indicated in this hot summer of 1929—a few months before the stock market crash signaled the beginning of the Great Depression—that all was not well with the American economy.

Running out of money myself, I began to cut back on my restaurant meals. I moved from a cheap hotel to a cheaper one where I could get a cot with a blanket and one sheet of dubious whiteness in a room with three or four others for fifty cents a night. There I found it hard to establish contact with my fellow roomers.

Finally, beginning to feel actually hungry, I gave up. I was not going to be able to earn my own way. I wired home for money.

By the next day, I was once more a member of the leisured class. But I was not ready to take on the trappings of my restored privileged status or to give up on my quest to see the country. I had heard that migrant workers followed the wheat harvest north at this season and decided to try my luck as an itinerant harvest worker.

For a hundred dollars, I bought a battered old Chevrolet, an open "touring car" with a fold-back top, and headed north. The car had a special feature in that the back of the front seat could be folded down to make a short bed, and with some of my baggage supporting my feet, I slept more than one night in my car under the sky.

I picked up a young hitchhiker, younger than I, and for two or three days we traveled together, making occasional stops at farmhouses along the way looking for work that was never available. My cheerful fellow traveler proved a godsend when an alarming hammering began to sound from the engine block one day: he diagnosed a failed bearing and offered to help me replace it. We limped to the next town, bought the needed replacement, and then, parked beside the road on the outskirts of town, we took the engine apart and put in the new bearing. I glowed with pride at our achievement when the jalopy took off again without the squeaks and rattles in the body I was accustomed to, and with only a purr from the engine.

The next day an armed posse stopped us, ordering us out of the car with our hands up while they frisked us. We were not the men they were looking for and they let us go, but I got a new sense of being out in the real world.

Somewhere along the way, my companion decided to head back where he had come from and left me. I drove on across Kansas and Nebraska. At one town I nearly lost my car in a flash flood. It was a sunny day with no sign of rain, but somewhere upstream a small creek that ran through the town had been the target of a cloudburst, and when I returned to my car after lunching at a hot dog stand, I found water welling out of the storm drains and already up to my hubcaps. I managed to drive the car to dry ground and watched while the water quickly became waist high where it had just been parked moments before. Later I found a route out of town up onto the prairie and went on my way.

At that point, I felt I had seen enough of the hazards of life that beset a migrant worker. I headed for a Wyoming mountain resort where I had an open invitation to visit the vacationing sister of a college friend of mine. After first being directed by the doorman to the servants' entrance, I was finally welcomed back into the world of clean clothes and expensive food that I had come from. The next day I was able to find a taker from among the hangers-on at the ranch for the old jalopy that still had mileage in her.

That fall I returned to my law studies, but more with a sense of an uncompleted job that had to be finished than with any enthusiasm. My brilliant academic record began to flag. I was so disaffected with the carping cynicism of the faculty and the desiccated language of the cases I was reading that I could not bear the thought of going immediately into a law practice.

Both in school and college, I had occasionally thought of myself as a poet and had written verses that were published in school and college publications. Now I found release for my thwarted romanticism in writing a poem. A few lines should be sufficient to indicate its tenor.

> Must your fine fire be consumed
>   In chaffering day by day,
> Not even for gold, but only crisp, cold
>   Promises to pay?
> Will you hunch those Homeric shoulders,
>   As winters pass away,
> Over books where fools are told
>   How other fools unwisely bought or sold?

I did not submit the poem for publication in the *Yale Law Journal* of which I was then an editor, and it remains unpublished.

In November of that year came the stock market collapse and the beginning of the Great Depression, the most severe of the cyclical downswings that capitalist economies—not only in this country but around the world—had ever experienced. But it meant little to me at the time. And the notion of having a means of livelihood as a lawyer had no appeal. I had always had enough money to pay my bills, and I assumed that I always would. Whatever I chose as my career would, I felt confident, provide me with an adequate income.

My father had conscientiously sought to instill in his sons, so much more favored by inheritance than he had been as a boy, practical and prudent habits with regard to money. By the time I went away to school, I had a checking account in the Union & New Haven Trust Company and was pressed to pay for any purchase of a dollar or more by check. I was provided with an income of $2,000 a year, partly in cash, and partly in the form of dividends from stock put in my name. The $2,000 was considered adequate to cover all my expenses, including tuition at school and college, though of course on vacations at home I had no expenses and all doctors' and dentists' bills were paid for me. For many successive years, I was required to keep an account of my income and expenses in a ledger, and show it to my father twice a year before I could receive my cash allowance.

My father's boyhood as the son of a retired missionary had been marked by a painful sense of deprivation, almost of grinding poverty, and it seems likely that his missionary father had required strict cash accounting of his meager earnings and expenses. He was no doubt determined that his own sons, born to privilege, would not become spendthrifts. Actually the lessons he taught me about prudent management of the money that came my way— about capital and income, savings and expenditure, a balanced portfolio of investments—tended to strengthen a natural conservatism, even to the point of penuriousness. But he was not able to impress on me the necessity of earning a living. He had, of course, escaped from that necessity himself.

As I took my bar exams at the end of my formal education, I was unable to appreciate my classmates' concern for entering at once on the practice of our profession. I still expected to be a lawyer, but I was not ready to begin. I did not look on it as a means of livelihood but as a base from which to enter on a political career.

Under my father's guidance, I had already taken my first steps as a politician. Not that he urged me to go into politics. His hopes for me were that I would be a writer, perhaps a journalist, or if I went into law, that I would become a judge. He told me I had literary ability and a good mind, but he no doubt felt I lacked self-assurance and the common touch—the marks of an effective politician. Still, if I were determined, I should begin by establishing a home base.

I had followed his advice, and sometime in 1926, after my twenty-first birthday, I appeared at a voter-making session of the selectmen of Salem. I was duly made a voter, swearing to uphold the Constitution of Connecticut as a "free and independent state," and I was then enrolled on the Republican party list. I had never been a true resident of Salem, having only spent summer vacations there, but if questioned, I could say with a measure of truthfulness that I intended to make my permanent home there. And, after all, the First Selectman was a tenant farmer on some of the family property.

Also at my father's suggestion, I had sought appointment as a delegate from Salem to the state Republican convention in 1928, the year of the Hoover campaign. Even as late as that, after a year of the iconoclasm of Yale Law School professors and my Democratic friends, I was still quite willing to follow my father's lead as a conservative Republican. But two years later, when I attended another state convention of the party as a delegate from Salem, I showed the first signs of rebellion.

The issue was prohibition. The ground swell of opposition to the ban on alcoholic beverages was mounting. My father had come to believe the Eighteenth Amendment had been a mistake, and I was not inclined to disagree with him. At the convention, which was to select candidates for state office and adopt a platform, I was named to the platform committee as a courtesy to my father. The committee met some hours before the convening of the convention and drafted a platform that called for repeal of the Eighteenth Amendment and the Volstead Act.

But late that night, after the opening session of the convention, and while the delegates were partying with plentiful supplies of bootleg liquor provided by would-be candidates, a subcommittee of the platform committee met to edit the planks adopted to ensure logical order and appropriate grammar and rhetoric for presentation to the convention. I, having served as secretary of the full committee, was automatically a member of the subcommittee. To my surprise we met in the private office of J. Henry Roraback, president of the Connecticut Light & Power Company and state chairman of the Republican Party. Indignantly he told the subcommittee the repeal plank would have to come out.

"Alfred," he said to me, "your father and I have decided the state is not ready for repeal, and we drafted a plank calling for law enforcement and further study of the issue. Here it is. I don't know why the platform committee didn't know about it. It will have to be adopted now."

Appalled at my own temerity, a tyro among old professionals, I objected that we were merely a subcommittee, empowered only to improve the language but not the substance of the platform.

"Well, then," said the red-faced chairman, waving his cigar in the air, "reconvene the full committee before the convention meets in the morning and make the change."

With only one other dissent, his orders were carried out. When the revised platform was read to a wholly inattentive convention the next day, it was steamrollered to unanimous adoption, and only a few of the delegates may have noticed me on my feet, vainly and quixotically seeking recognition from the presiding officer to voice my protest.

As it turned out, Mr. Roraback had made a mistake from which he never recovered. The Republican nominee for governor, Lieutenant-Governor Ernest Rogers, was a conscientious "dry" while his opponent, Wilbur Cross, and the Democratic platform were unashamedly "wet." Cross was elected that November and for several terms thereafter, and in 1933 the Eighteenth Amendment was repealed.

In my small way, I had challenged the establishment. In this case, I was in tune with my generation. Yet on the moral issue of respect for law, I had already experienced a sense of alienation from my peers.

All through my college and law school years, I had struggled with my conscience on the issue of alcohol. I concurred with the growing opinion that prohibition of the manufacture and sale of alcoholic beverages was a bad law. Aside from the question of the benefits or harms in the consumption of alcohol, the prohibition law could not be enforced; gangsterism and crime flourished to meet the demand for alcohol; and a cynical disregard for law infected much of the population. As an undergraduate, I was revolted by the vomit that fouled the campus walks on the morning after a football weekend. I decided, for reasons not entirely clear to me now, that I would not drink. Not that drinking bootleg liquor, or even the purchase of liquor from a bootlegger, was in itself a violation of law, but it seemed to me to contribute to the spreading lawlessness corrupting American society.

Yet I hated myself for seeming a self-righteous prig and a purist. In taking an active stand for repeal, I was rejecting the role of moralist. Instead I became a social reformer.

CHAPTER 37
Celebration of Self

I suspect that everyone born to riches has at times a tendency to romanticize poverty. Marie Antoinette played at being a milkmaid. I built myself a log cabin in the woods, and spent part of the summer of 1930 living in it alone.

The remote site, almost inaccessible, was on a large tract of woods put in my name by my grandfather Mitchell when I was born. My share of land included a dairy farm, operated by a tenant, and a hundred acres of rugged woodland.

In my student days I had explored the land and had discovered, in a ravine at the far end of the woods, the remains of a never completed mill dam of huge boulders. On occasional holidays in my college and law school years, with the help of friends equally drawn to the wilderness, I had repaired the dam enough to turn a large upstream swamp into a lake. On a level spot halfway up a steep rocky hillside overlooking the lake, where I had at times pitched a tent, I began assembling logs for a cabin.

For a month one summer, I hired two local workers. One was enough of a mason to build a fireplace and chimney from stone close to the site; the other did the necessary carpentry work to make a door and windows, and fitted logs around them. Lumber for flooring and roofing and other building materials were brought in over an arduous route. A truck could be driven over an old wood road to the edge of the lake, a quarter mile from the site. There I launched a folding canoe, and cleared a channel through the brush choking the upper reaches of the lake. The materials could thus be floated to a landing just below the cabin site and carried the last hundred feet up a rocky trail. By the same route I eventually brought in an iron cot and a few other simple furnishings.

I had built a habitable dwelling of my own, and there I installed myself with some books, including Thoreau's *Walden,* and a typewriter. I had graduated from Yale Law School, taken a cram course for the Connecticut bar examinations, been admitted to practice by the Superior Court of New London County, and then, while my classmates began their professional careers in various law offices, I vanished into the woods to sort out my ideas about life.

I had decided to take two years off to complete my education. In spite of my years of school and university study, I felt strangely uneducated. During my vacations spent variously as a farm worker, factory worker, salesman, and job seeker, I had learned a little of the realities of American life outside my own protected environment. However, America was not the whole world, and I wanted to see what life was like in the rest of the world. I was vaguely aware, as the decade of the 1930s was beginning, that vast changes were taking place overseas.

Before I set forth on my great two-year adventure to see the world, I wanted to set down my basic beliefs. And at a crude desk set up in my forest retreat, and with an Underwood portable typewriter on which my college and law school papers had been written, I hammered out what I called "A Young Man's Creed." It was in the form of a Socratic dialogue among a group of students, roughly modeled on a group of my own friends as if in a college dormitory "bull session."

There were no dormitories for students in Yale's postgraduate professional schools at that time. I had lived for three years in a rooming house at 242 York Street, across from the Gothic quadrangle that was soon to be reconstructed to house Saybrook and Branford Colleges. John McDill, who was studying for a doctorate in English literature at the Graduate School, was my roommate. In the dialogue I wrote, I gave him the name of Paul, and had him give expression to a tolerant and romantic idealism that was really my own.

In my second year of law school, a couple of brilliant graduate students, one in law and one in medicine, lived upstairs in the same building. Bob Huntington, the medical student, had, I believe, been a philosophy major in college. His elephantine manner and genial skepticism I tried to recapture in the person I called Theo. One of his roommates, Spike Kennedy, a reluctant and rebellious fellow student at the law school, I renamed Dirk and, when my utopian views sounded too bland, made him the mouthpiece for cynical comments. The real Dirk killed himself a few years after I wrote my imaginary dialogue. The fourth of my protagonists, whom I called Harry, was a friendly Irish-Catholic law student who occasionally brought our high-flying philosophizing down to earth.

With the faint if presumptuous suggestion of an Old Testament king, I called myself Asa, and steered the group discussions to the moral and religious views I wanted to formulate. The problems I sought to explore were not the social problems that later came to preoccupy me. They were the problems of my own soul, of God and the meaning of life, of youth and old age and death.

I proclaimed that the pursuit of happiness was illusory. In words I put in Paul's mouth:

Happiness is only an imaginary state of continual pleasurableness. It's imaginary because life doesn't know any states; life is dynamic, not static.

Deciding that happiness no more than pleasure was a worthy goal in this life, I rejected any religion based on the notion of pleasure in heaven as a reward of virtue. A generous altruism was not a sacrifice of self but a fulfillment of self.

I based my religious beliefs on a scientific philosophy that had gone beyond Newtonian determinism. Here is a sample of the discussions that went on for a hundred pages:

ASA: I don't think I could call myself a humanist. In the first place a humanist is not a mystic. And secondly he clings to the old fetish, happiness, however skeptical of its attainment. But I do call myself a humanist if that means worship of man.

DIRK: But man is so insignificant, he isn't—

ASA: He isn't insignificant. The universe is his, as he sees it, with himself at the center, at the "conflux of eternities," as Carlyle had it. He is heir of all the past, ancestor of all the future. But I don't like to put it in the general form. It is not man, but I myself that am lord of my own universe, and you yourself of yours.

DIRK: Well, having put yourself on your magnificent pedestal, what next?

HARRY: Yes. What on earth—or off of it—are you driving at, Asa?

ASA: Why it all follows from the change in the scientific attitude; Henry Adams, you know, called it the most significant event since the spread of Christianity.

HARRY: What change do you mean?

ASA: The adoption of metaphysics by physics, the change from order to anarchy, from the absolute to the relative—all this makes man the only standard and the only reality. We've at last mastered the universe, and we find that after all we are at the center of it. It gives us vastly more importance and a new dignity.

HARRY: Shucks, who cares about dignity? You can call me lord of the universe if you want, but I really prefer a home and family.

The interruptions were intended to suggest the many facets of the good life I was projecting: "Man has such infinite possibilities that he can never feel he has done justice to them." I was obsessed with the idea of living life to the full. I argued for "an ideal of greatness, which means striving to fulfill all one's possibilities, especially the creative; it means constant growth, constant development."

When his imaginary interlocutors reminded Asa of his privileged status, he insisted every individual had infinite significance.

ASA: There would be no sense in protecting the weak if they did not have intrinsic worth. In a chaotic world where all is relative, we admit in spite of ourselves that all have an equal right to live and to enjoy and to develop. The trouble is that our social ethic is based on altruism, which means pity or condescension, rather than on respect. We try to make people comfortable or happy instead of giving them the fullest opportunity to live worthily, as we want to live ourselves.

That was almost the only recognition of my still undeveloped social conscience.

I was more aware of the lack of development of other parts of my psyche. I knew my intellectual development had far outpaced my experience with the more earthy facts of life. I was still a virgin.

In my protected childhood, I had accepted as a given, without knowing its source, the impropriety of sexual intercourse before marriage, and had had no occasion to be tempted otherwise. My knowledge of the opposite sex, having had no sisters and having gone to all-male boarding schools and an all-male college, was minimal. As a prelude to mating, I had dutifully attended holiday dances, but whatever erotic impulses might have been aroused by bodily contact had been thoroughly damped down at an early stage in the dancing classes at Hamden Hall, where the little girls' frilly starchy dresses revolted me.

When in my late teens I fell in love for the first time—it was at a house party in Lenox, and I went for a sleigh ride with a beautiful girl named Sylvia Brewster—I was puzzled when the flow of unaccustomed juices made me feel unaccountably ill.

A succession of nice girls from Vassar and Smith, whom I invited to football weekend parties at Yale, only fleetingly attracted me. It may well be that my juices had been blocked in a bout with mumps in my sophomore year, the infection spreading from my neck to my pancreas and my testes. I was told by a specialist at the Yale infirmary that I would probably never be able to have children, a prognosis that then gave me only marginal concern.

Once, when I was in Oklahoma City looking for summer work, curiosity more than libido prompted me to follow a streetwalker to a squalid room in a brothel. In accepting her solicitation, I told her I only wanted to look, and, just as she said, there was nothing much to see, and I was not attracted further. When I asked her about her trade, she looked frightened and told me that she wasn't paid to talk to me and that my time for occupancy of the room was up.

Occasional masturbation seemed to meet my sexual needs, though it made me ashamed, and I deplored my lack of self-control.

By the time I had finished delineating my idealized self as Asa, I was equally ashamed of my virginity. I was now eager to drain life to the dregs, though it would be some months before a suitable occasion arose. In the meantime I reminded myself that at twenty-five I should not wait too long for marriage and the possible procreation of a family. They too were necessary to the full life I projected.

And so I was ready to set forth on a journey that would give new directions to my life.

276

Hiram Bingham III and Alfreda Mitchell Bingham, 1919.

Alfreda Mitchell Bingham, center, and Hiram Bingham III, far right, with their seven sons. The author Alfred Bingham is fourth from the right. Far left, Annie Tiffany Mitchell. Florida, 1919.

Hiram Bingham III, photographing at Ollantaytambo, Peru, on the Yale Peruvian Expedition of 1911, during which he came upon the Inca ruins at Machu Picchu.

"Casa Alegre," 787 Prospect Street, New Haven. Annie Tiffany Mitchell built this home in 1910 for her daughter Alfreda and son-in-law Hiram Bingham III. Five of the Binghams' sons pose in front of the house, about 1912.

Left: "Sweet Way," Annie Tiffany Mitchell's home on Brickell Avenue, Miami. The new house, center, built about 1922, connected by a bridge, left, to the house originally on the property.

Below: "The Folly," built by Annie and Alfred Mitchell as a winter home in Port Antonio, Jamaica, about 1904. The house is now an abandoned ruin.

The Mitchells' home on Pequot Avenue, New London, acquired in 1870 and enlarged in stages. It later became Mitchell Hall, the administration building of New London Junior College, now Mitchell College.

Above: Alfreda Mitchell Bingham, on an outing in her chauffeured Locomobile, with her mother Annie Tiffany Mitchell and six of her sons, New London, 1911.

Right: In his twenties, the author built a log cabin, as a retreat for writing, on land he had inherited in Salem, Connecticut, 1930.

Top: The fifteenth wedding anniversary of Sir James
Jeans and Charly Mitchell Jeans (third row, center).
Their young daughter Olivia Jeans sits directly in
front of them. At Mumford House, Salem,
Connecticut.

Above: The author with his grandmother Annie
Tiffany Mitchell in New London, about 1920.

Right: Alfreda Mitchell Bingham and her son
Mitchell in the music room, Prospect Street, New
Haven. A Louis Tiffany lamp is visible on the table
behind them.

Left: Hiram Bingham III with his second wife Suzanne Hill Bingham, revisiting Machu Picchu in the late 1940s.

Above: Alfreda Mitchell Bingham Gregor plays chamber music with second husband Henry Gregor, in Coral Gables, Florida.

Below: The author's four children, Stephen, Douglas, Christopher, and Alfreda, in front of their home on Darling Road, Salem, Connecticut, 1943.

The author in the 1930s as editor of Common Sense, a left-wing magazine he founded with Selden Rodman.

Above: The author and his first wife Sylvia Knox Bingham, with their four children, 1942.

Right: The author as a captain in the Civil Affairs Division of the U.S. Army during World War II.

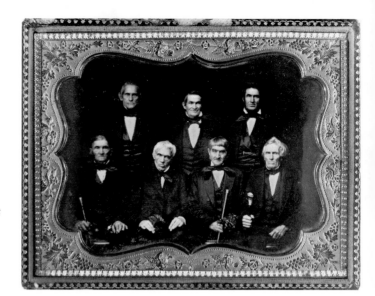

Daguerreotype of Hiram Bingham I, back row, left, and his six brothers, 1855. His seven great-grandsons adopted a similar pose for the photograph below.

Portrait of the Bingham brothers in the 1970s, at "The Camp" in Salem, Connecticut. Front row, from left, Woodbridge, Hiram, Alfred, and Charles. Back row, Brewster, Mitchell, and Jonathan.

CHAPTER 38

Odyssey

On October 17, 1930, one day out of New York on the French liner *Lafayette*, I began a travel diary.

> At eleven o'clock to the minute yesterday we got under way. I felt strangely unmoved as I left. All the morning before getting to the dock and all the rest of the day I kept saying to myself "You are leaving your home and your country for two years, and your past self forever. This is one of the greatest days of your life. Appreciate it." And I could not. Only for a moment as the faces on the dock, and particularly Mother's face, drew away with increasing speed was I moved. Rising tears and a choking sensation made me hope I was not quite cold and callous. But the next moment I was myself, only with a new sense of freedom.

My diary made no mention of the young woman standing beside me at the rail. Sylvia Knox was a fellow passenger. I had met her at a debutante dance in New York some months before. Then and on subsequent less formal occasions, I was attracted by her keen and independent mind. When I learned she was going to begin postgraduate work in psychology at the University of Berlin about the time I was planning to begin my Grand Tour, we arranged to cross the Atlantic on the same boat. Her mother, like mine, was on the dock to see her off, and must have wondered, as no doubt did my mother, what we were to each other.

I was indeed looking for new experience on my travels. As I laid out the objectives of what I called my "adventurous quest" in the first pages of my journal:

> I must live. I am a child, inexperienced, innocent, ignorant of much that is most elemental. I would know what it is to fear, to love, to hate. I intend to give myself every opportunity to escape from the emotional lethargy and barren conventionality in which I have been reared.

Here surely on an ocean crossing was opportunity enough to break the taboo I had set on my sexual activity. But the congeniality of mind and personality I found in Sylvia involved no sexual excitement. We dined and drank together—the drink taboo was left behind as we left American waters. We shared our thoughts and hopes. We even talked about marriage. And we read our books together in the lounge. Four years were to pass before we set sail, on another ship, on a honeymoon voyage.

A major reason for postponing my entry on a professional career, as I told her then, was to round out a liberal arts education that, after four years

277

in college and three in law school, had come to seem sadly inadequate. I set forth my objectives in my journal:

> So now I am going to devote two years (not that that is enough, but only a compromise with necessity) to my further education out of books. This means as wide reading in world literature as I can manage, with particular emphasis on the history of society, including anthropology, and on philosophy.

I could, of course, have read the books at home. But if I was to "understand human society," as I wrote, I must travel, "to see and study the peoples of the world." I felt I had gained at least a sketchy knowledge of my own country, and I wanted to know what the rest of the world was like. I had made two previous trips to Europe, once with my parents and once on my own, but then I was only a vacationing tourist looking at scenery and visiting museums. I now wanted to spend enough time in various centers of civilization, not only in Europe but in Africa and Asia, to gain some sense of how people lived—not the other half, but the other nine-tenths.

I had little awareness of the perilous state of the world I was setting forth to explore. The economic depression that had been signaled by the New York stock market crash a year before was causing large scale unemployment and making millions desperate in one country after another. Colonial empires were crumbling in the parts of the world I planned to visit—North Africa, the Middle East, India, the Far East. Nationalist and Communist revolutionary movements were threatening the established order on every continent. Parliamentary democracy was failing to cope with new forces surging onto the scene. Stalin and Mussolini, to be followed soon by Hitler, were modeling new techniques of totalitarian dictatorship.

I was only vaguely aware of the global stresses and strains that would lead to World War II within the decade. But I knew the world was in turmoil. And I planned to write about it. Writing was, in fact, another of my journey's goals.

> My future, I deeply hope, is more bound up with writing than law or politics. What I write is not so important. This journal will give me a regular outlet for expression and experimental writing. I intend to try my hand at many things. If any one of them turns out to be worth publication, well and good, if not, it is never time lost.

I had in fact definite hope of publishing some of my observations in three Connecticut newspapers whose editors I had contacted before I left.

I pictured myself as an observer of the contemporary world rather than as a participant. Yet almost from the moment of my arrival in England, I began to feel a new sense of involvement in the social forces now stirring in the world. My personal inner life was for the moment forgotten. I had parted from Sylvia at Cherbourg where she was to board the train for Paris on the way to Berlin. Across the Channel, on the boat train for London, the wider world confronted me in the person of a talkative fellow passenger. I described him in my journal the next day.

> Thirty years a Londoner, but born in Moscow, and making frequent trips (in the fur business) to America, this mercurial Jew, with vivid expressiveness in his restless hands and his restless eyebrows—two bushy clumps spaced wide apart—was thoroughly "old world," cosmopolitan in his views, a European with a world perspective.
>
> His views were not slow in coming out. In broken English I heard successively about the amenities of ocean travel, civilized life in England and America (with all the civilization in England), the lot of the unnational Jew who is always a pariah, and the future of communism. His was a strangely worldly idealism, tolerant of the weakness of human nature. I sensed a ruthlessness that would override the individual in the pursuit of the social good, sending capitalists to the scaffold with as passionless unconcern as nobles a century and a half ago. Russia, he told me, is only a little ahead of the rest of Europe.
>
> And his goal? Apparently it is for the children of this disappointed generation, "children who vill be shtrong [with clenched fist], intelligent [sweeping gestures from the forehead], healthy, and vill enjoy the world and shports and the good air, like the sons of the capitalists [with a half gesture toward me]." He was a man with an international business who considered the *Lafayette* a "cattle boat," but he knew what it was to be "hongry."

I spent ten days in London. I was primarily concerned with establishing connections and getting introductions that would help me in Asia where I planned to spend the first year of my travels before returning for a year in Europe. An important London contact was Lady Astor, the first woman elected to Parliament. I had met her previously when I was traveling in England with my parents as a boy, and when I wrote her on my arrival in London, she invited me to tea at the House of Commons and later to a formal luncheon where the guest of honor was Lord Salisbury, the frock-coated Conservative leader of the House of Lords.

I was not too greatly awed by my glimpse of the elite of the social pyramid. After all, with my father a United States Senator, I had been to diplomatic receptions at the White House in white tie and tails, and was used to shaking hands with the great. In my plans for seeing the world, I wanted to explore the top as well as the bottom of human society, and I had included a tuxedo and tailcoat as well as riding breeches and boots, in the huge wardrobe trunk that was part of my baggage, together with a hatbox containing a top hat and a tropical topi. There were occasions when I was glad I had.

I attended a Communist rally in Trafalgar Square. Scores of policemen stood ready on the outskirts of the crowd, but as I worked my way toward the Nelson monument from which the speeches were coming, the crowd—shivering in a cold wind—seemed anything but ominous, and most of the red banners were carried by children. Rather than fear, I felt something like compassion for these poor people forlornly trying to rouse the dull conservative British mind to revolution. A year later when I returned to England, I would be ready to take such demonstrations against unemployment and poverty seriously as something that might involve me. But not now.

I had decided to make the Middle East the first major focus of my "quest," with Egypt the immediate target. Leaving London armed with sufficient introductions for Egypt and India, both still part of the British Empire, I stopped briefly in Paris to look up my brother Mitchell, then a fledgling art student, and some college friends. One of these, whom I considered a "gilded youth," took me and Mitch out to dinner. I described the evening in my journal.

> First a little restaurant with the flavor of an American speakeasy, then a cafe, then a nightclub, all harmless but with the savor of wickedness. I got a strange impression sitting in the last, sipping a liqueur, watching the people and listening to occasional singing, an impression of Sodom and Gomorrah. Man is rich and idle and too sophisticated to be moral. His own pleasure is his chief god. Corruption and perversion may well be the result. For the rest he is courteous and kind, would not hurt a dog or a child, but would think nothing of stealing the love of another man's wife. So I imagined as I watched those painted men and women, with their fragile loveliness, absorbing nicotine and alcohol and coffee and, often enough I suppose, dope. It is the decadent West, one day to be overturned and crushed by the invading East in the shape of a young Russia, a day that will not regard beauty or intelligence or kindness, but only the power of youth. And on that day will America be on the side of youth or age?

I had been reading Spengler's *Decline of the West* and was half persuaded, on vague cultural and moral grounds, that Western civilization was nearing its end, whatever that might mean.

The Simplon-Orient Express took me from Paris to Venice, where I embarked for Egypt and the East. At times on my travels, still only beginning, I had felt lonely, depressed, and unsure of myself, but now on the Adriatic I was drunk with the beauty of nature and the works of man and the excitement of my journey. The magic of Venice, particularly as a seaport, had overwhelmed me.

> And now the Adriatic, swift following wind, great misty clouds, through which the sun comes down in a gloria to light some remote white town on the shore. These were the crisp frothy waters through which Ulysses and Aeneas and Pompey and Caesar made their way. Out of the subdued distances one is almost ready to see a great trireme appear, or some strange bark with bellying sail.

I felt engulfed in the vast drama of human history. After a talk with a fellow passenger, a Zionist on his way to Jerusalem with a millenarian view of a future in which all men would love one another and live together peacefully, wild fantasies gripped my imagination. He yearned for a great leader who would come from America to rescue a distraught Europe from its miseries as Wilson had once tried to do with his visionary League of Nations, and I began to think of myself as another Wilson. Grandiosity and self-depreciation were evident in what I wrote in my journal.

It is not necessarily vanity or stupidity to think of my possibilities as the great leader. Circumstances are all with me: I am an American and he must come from America. I am a dreamer and an idealist, which is essential. I am headed for politics with every sign pointing to practical success and a position of power, all of which, if the arena is international politics, is as it should be. I have a religious belief in the worth of the individual human being, and that is the world's articulate ideal of the future as it has been the inarticulate faith of the past.

But I am not the man now. I do not believe in God or destiny: hence all depends on me and my success in making myself the man. All the chances but one are against me, but there is that one and I must play for that. This trip takes on a new significance, for without it that one chance would be gone. I have now (and if not now then never) to become the man. I am not even a man at present. I am a timid child. Courage, guts, will, drive, even the courage to be kind, I need.

Meanwhile the bright spray goes by my porthole, dazzling as flying mountain snow, and hides the wine-dark sea, and even the great brown mountains of Crete.

CHAPTER 39

East Is East

At a sidewalk table outside a "Brasserie-Restaurant" in Alexandria a day or two after my arrival in Egypt, I faced a different world from any I had known. In the street before me streamed a motley crowd, dodging streetcars and taxicabs: scrawny Arabs in dirty white robes, Turks in fezzes and business suits, Greeks in straw hats, barefoot children begging, some with an arm or an eye missing, turbaned vendors of articles from shrimps to neckties, whose cries competed with the strains of Italian opera from an orchestra inside the restaurant. A mangy cat prowling among the tables, its hunger constantly at war with its fastidiousness, seemed a parody of the grim realities of human life on the planet.

I spent a month in Egypt. Such poverty and misery I had not seen before. I was not unmoved by the pyramids and temples of ancient Egypt, but it was the social and political currents of the present that absorbed my attention.

I had an introduction to a friendly and scholarly American judge, serving on the Mixed Court that had jurisdiction over all cases involving foreigners, and he persuaded me to focus on the rapidly changing Egypt of the moment. British imperialism, long dominant, was now on the defensive. A growing middle class of Egyptians, in revolt against centuries of foreign rule, was struggling to make a democratic parliamentary system work in a country with no experience of self-government. An immediate crisis was at hand as a reactionary king had just abrogated the ten-year-old liberal constitution in the name of stamping out corruption.

Making the most of the introductions Judge Brinton and the chief of the American legation in Cairo gave me, I talked to government officials, foreign businessmen, and travelers I met on the way. An officer in the British army of occupation told me he had never met an Egyptian he could trust. A student supporting the populist Wafd Party told me he had never met a Britisher he could trust. I came away still admiring the civilizing role of British colonialism, but convinced that its end was near.

One night before leaving Egypt, I went to the movies and watched a showing of the American film *All Quiet on the Western Front*. Based on the German novel, the film was in English, with French and Arabic subtitles, and a program provided synopses in Italian and Greek—a truly international dramatization of the folly and horror of war. I was moved to tears. That night I dreamed a dream that I described in my journal:

> A woman was being tried for murder, and the story came out that she was a schoolmistress who by long training had taught all the little boys and girls in her care that to torture and kill each other was all that was right and noble and natural; then she furnished them with the most horrible weapons she could devise for the infliction of pain, divided them into groups, and set them to fighting. In the orgy that followed none of the children thought of running away from school, but all stayed and exterminated each other.

My mind was being turned inside out by the intensity of new impressions. I spent a week as a solitary tourist on the upper Nile, sightseeing at Luxor, Karnak, and Thebes. A bout with fever and diarrhea ("gyppy tummy" as foreigners called it) put me for a few days in a state of alienation akin to a mystical trance.

> *Dec. 3, 1930:* I have caught a feeling of a strangeness wholly Oriental. This comfortable world that we build about ourselves in the West in the shape of trim lawns and country churches and New York hotels and science, a breath of the utterly strange makes it all grow tenuous with unreality, and behind it we can see such formlessness that even chaos is too friendly a word for it.
>
> These fellahin [Egyptian peasants], those staring Pharaohs, they know life not as we do. They see evil eyes or ibis-headed gods that we cannot see.

282

Knowledge itself is a different concept. There is no world, only a million worlds that have no relation to each other.

A donkey braying—what was a mere hairy machine for carrying, now a creature of the void seeking expression—a roar, a mighty choking reproach, a deep guttural lament, rising from some unknown and unknowable reach of the limbo of souls, that are not of us yet of the earth we tread.

We are cursed with consciousness. What a sardonic laugh a Creator might indulge in who saw his creatures ask themselves what they are, and whence they came, and finally in agony bury their faces in some absolute of their own desperate making, mother- or father-god, sidereal universe, well knowing they are only the dreams or phantoms of their own imagining.

It is well to keep at home. To try to embrace a human brotherhood is as treacherous as trying to enter into the consciousness of a buzzing fly. The Egyptian is only a step nearer than the donkey and the fly. I cannot seek to understand strange ways, strange people, without a formless thing leaping out to torture and kill my own gods. Its weapon is only doubt of their existence, of existence itself. For there is no existence if it is not part of me and my mind.

Yet I am not to be frightened off so easily. I may be able to keep my Western soul safely and add to it some of the feeling and the wisdom of the East. But matter of fact must be willing to give space to vision of things unseen.

My feeling of the strangeness of the East was partly derived from two books I was reading, E. M. Forster's *A Passage to India* and Count Keyserling's *Travel Diary of a Philosopher.* Since one of the tasks I had set myself was to write articles for Connecticut newspapers, I used my credentials and my introductions as a free-lance journalist to interview Egyptian politicians and foreign observers, and wrote three articles that were more factual than mystical. In them I drew conclusions as a quickie expert on contemporary Egypt to the effect that Egyptian nationalism and a growing competence in self-government were making Britain's imperial role an anachronism.

Yet I was more impressed by the positive than the negative aspects of British imperialism, both in Egypt and in Palestine, which I visited next. Britain was then governing Palestine under a League of Nations mandate. "In Palestine," I wrote—somewhat fatuously—in my journal, "it appears that British rule has been wholly altruistic in sentiment."

I saw Britain's role, under the mandate of an international body, as "reconciling and safeguarding conflicting interests" in a setting that made normal nationalism impossible. For "Palestine is the center of three great religions, and it should be policed as a park is policed for the enjoyment of the world."

Upon further reflection, I added: "Yet an international supervisory agency would seem essential." The trouble with giving one nation such a mandate, rather than having the international community itself take charge, is that no nation can be sufficiently disinterested. Britain had supported the Zionist dream of a national home for the Jews for domestic political reasons during

World War I, but in assuming the mandate it was motivated, to an extent I could not then realize, by concern for the oil-rich Arab landowners whose interests obviously ran counter to Zionism.

The three religions came to a focus at the site of Solomon's temple. Inside the beautiful Dome of the Rock that dominates the old walled city of Jerusalem, I was shown a rough rock ridge that rises out of the floor. Here, on what may have been a place of sacrifice for centuries, I was told that Abraham, the patriarch of all three religions, prepared to sacrifice his son Isaac. In the temple that replaced Solomon's after its destruction, Jesus taught and healed and overturned the tables of the money changers. Centuries later, it was from this rock that Mohammed was said to have ascended to Heaven to receive the Koran. A mosque was built over the sacred spot only to be replaced by a Christian church when the crusaders ruled Jerusalem, and again replaced hundreds of years ago by the present magnificent mosque.

Even more moving to me was the dingy and crowded Church of the Holy Sepulchre not far away. As every tourist knows, it houses not only the tomb where, according to tradition, Christ was buried, but, a few yards away, the site of the crucifixion. My first reaction to the place, as I wrote in my journal, was dismay:

> That the place where the Galilean carpenter was executed ignominiously for blasphemy only to transform the world centuries later and become truly the king of kings, should be in a musty little church reeking of decay and petty sectarian quarrels, piled with tawdry ill-assorted odds and ends of piety, that the place should be open to the gaze of any curious eye and be talked about by any mercenary drab dragoman, and be tended perfunctorily by a few muffled priests who eye each other's rival ministrations jealously, while a policeman lolls nearby to prevent quarreling, that the great original of all the crucifixes that have comforted and blest and terrified and changed the world should have stood here in this miniature vanity fair, is hard to accept.

My visit to Palestine focused more on religious than political or social issues and helped to fix some of my basic beliefs. I had always thought of myself as a Christian, and in my teens, moved to piety, I had prayed regularly and earnestly to a dimly conceived God. But my scientifically disposed and analytical mind had balked at accepting the established Christian theology, despite four years of reciting the Nicene Creed in the chapel services at Groton School. I found Albert Schweitzer's *Quest of the Historical Jesus*, which I read in the school's "Sacred Studies" class, more congenial than all the Gospel readings I listened to. So my self-identification as a Christian was only in the broadest sense of cultural affiliation. And my visit to the Holy Land turned into a historical quest of my own.

One of the impressions I wrote in my journal was of the difference between my "Western" mind and "Eastern" mysticism.

My Christianity is thin enough, but even such as it is, it is associated with New England church spires, and the moral teachings of a humble Jewish peasant, not with such Oriental mysteries as a Word that became flesh and a sacrificial lamb that took our sins upon him and ascended to sit on the right hand of God.

I visited Bethlehem and found the cave considered the traditional site of the birth of Jesus as tawdry and profaned by sectarian quarrels as the Church of the Holy Sepulchre. But I was moved by the beauty and the smallness of this barren land.

I walked back from Bethlehem, part of the way across country from hilltop to hilltop. Behind me straggled the churches and low houses of the little hill town. To the right the land dropped and dropped into a great hole where was the Dead Sea, only to rise high again beyond. In front was Jerusalem, golden in the sunset long after I was in shadow, with a brilliant sunlit rain cloud behind it.

From Jerusalem I went on to visit Nazareth.

Around Galilee it was the hills that were most full of the thought of Christ. But they made him seem small, wandering in bare feet up and down this little land, asking poor fishermen to follow him, creating a tiny stir among a simple folk for a day. How is it that I have called myself a Christian?

I concluded, rashly perhaps but with enough conviction to last a lifetime, that the image of Christ that has dominated Western civilization is a human construct.

I stood on the Great Pyramid just before I left Cairo and was not disappointed. It is the oldest and the greatest of human works, gigantic stones heaped halfway to heaven. But these holy places are not so simple. The Christ we worship is not merely the Galilean who died on the cross, he is what centuries of the greatest of all civilizations have made him, he is the product of all that is great and beautiful and powerful, yes even of all that is wicked in nineteen hundred years. The builders of Chartres not only built *to* him but actually built *him.* Worshippers of all ages, architects, poets, carol singers, Popes, priests and humble people, missionaries to China and domestic revivalists, all these have given of their lives and their virtue to add to the great figure of Christ.

Viewed thus, worship of Christ is replaced by a worship of man. Or if the first does not vanish, it is swallowed up and swells the measure of the second. As one stands on the Great Pyramid and looks over the green Nile valley to the mosques of Cairo, one is led to exclaim of the greatness of the material works of man. As one surveys Christianity, it is the greatness of the spiritual temple man has built that overwhelms one. Great are the works of man! His wisdom and his power and his goodness are great! Let us magnify the name of Man!

The language sounds high-flown, but it was heartfelt at the time, and it remains now, more than sixty years later, as a valid expression of my beliefs. I had always been put off by the creedal aspect of organized Christianity, and its rituals had only appealed to my aesthetic sensibilities. My visit to Palestine made me more aware of the historical reality of Jesus as a man, and of the power of the image of godhead that his followers had created, but I was not moved to a new faith in his divinity. In my travels in India and the Far East that soon followed, with some exposure to Hinduism and Buddhism, I gained a new sense of the mystery of existence. This enhanced the religious, even mystical, element in my worship of humankind.

Some of my church-going relatives have called me a secular humanist. I prefer to call myself a religious humanist. In magnifying the name of humankind, I am thinking of the human being in a generalized and idealized concept, as greater than any of the gods humans have conceived. But this is not to abandon secular concerns. If there is nothing more sacred than human life, then there is no higher calling than the service of one's fellow human beings, and as humans are social animals, then the welfare and progress of society are of prime concern.

One of the books I was reading at this stage of my travels was W. E. H. Lecky's *History of European Morals*. I was impressed by his argument that Christianity's obsession with the next world had diverted attention from the social and political problems of this world, thus contributing to the collapse of the Greco-Roman civilization and the coming of the Dark Ages. Dedication to social reform seemed to me implicit in a religious attitude centered in humankind.

In Beirut, next on my itinerary, I visited the American University. Its campus was, I noted, on a site "worthy of a New England prep school." I was struck, as I had been in Cairo in my contact with another American university, and in Jerusalem at the American colony, by the civilizing role of American philanthropy. Here the idealistic goal of "service" was more in evidence than the materialism and imperialism implicit in American influence abroad. Even the more evidently exploitative role of British and French imperialism—Lebanon and Syria were under a French mandate at the time—seemed to me to bring far more benefits to these Arab lands than losses.

Motives, I concluded, are never pure, and I was ready to accept the sincerity of those Westerners who had written of the "white man's burden" even while I recognized that the white man had grown rich in developing the poorer parts of the world.

In India, my next and more important field of inquiry, the conflict between Kipling and Marx was to become even more glaringly evident.

My passage to India was by way of Damascus and Baghdad. I hired an American car in Damascus for the trip across the northern reaches of the Arabian desert. I had shipped my heavier baggage from Cairo to Bombay and was traveling light. My driver knew enough French for essential communication. The first night was spent in a chilly little inn in a village next to the vast ruins of the Roman city of Palmyra. Then two nights as the guest of a Yale archaeologist at the site of another Roman city, Dura Europos, under excavation by a Yale expedition.

> On to Baghdad, this time in a rattling old Chevrolet that shuddered in agony at every bump, which meant every foot for three hundred miles of irregular rocky desert. Night and Christmas Eve came down and we were nowhere. I sang carols to myself, touched by their tenderness in this cruel land. An Iraqi soldier stopped us, then let us go on in the dark with an escort. At Hit we were allowed to go no further, presumably for my own safety, and my driver and I curled up on musty beds in a caravanserai, to the sound of an Arab phonograph and cats yowling. Dawn saw us on the march again. But it was not till noon that the flat city of Baghdad appeared.

The name had a romantic appeal, but the city on a cold winter's day seemed unutterably dreary. I drove out to see the ruins of Ctesiphon but found them unappealing. I was weary of ruined cities and ancient history. The next day I hurried on by train to Basra to catch the boat for Bombay.

CHAPTER 40

India

On the five-day sea voyage down the Persian Gulf and across the Arabian Sea, the inner conflict between my conservative background and my budding liberalism was sharpened by two traveling companions. Yet despite the inner conflict they brought to the surface, life on the S.S. *Varsova* seemed a blissful interlude after the rigors of land travel. On December 31, 1930, my journal entry began:

> The last few days have been days of delectable pale rose, days without care or labor, of mild skies and seas, of ample rest and quietness.... The boat is almost all mine, mine and Maurice Hope's, Lieut. R.F.A., and an American girl's. The turbans and fezzes and strange garbs that live between decks might as well be only scenery.
>
> Hope and I share a second-class cabin to our mutual edification. He is a straight, tall, pink-cheeked lad of twenty-nine, six years an officer but as fresh as twenty, and a thoroughbred. I have learned much of the traditional dignity and power of Old England from this ingenuous son of hers. Yet he is, I am afraid, somewhat of an anachronism today.
>
> He is a strange contrast to "Annabelle Lee" Norwood, a kittenish Southern girl with a passion for serious movements and conferences and ideas, the more radical and impractical the better. Most of her ideas I

would have if I were bolder. Still I do not admire this false liberalism that denounces Nordic superiority and American racial pride, that hobnobs with Negro educators, Russian reformers and Indian nationalists, however correct all their opinions may be. For all that, she is reasonably pretty, though without sex appeal as Hope says, and quite good-humored in her naive views for the salvation of the world.

I never saw Annabelle again after docking at Bombay, but she remained as an irritating voice of conscience even while my first look at India tended to reinforce my Anglophilia.

I was approaching India with the perspective of Lieutenant Hope. My contacts in England had been with its charming and beautiful upper crust, and the advice I had received as regards travel in India centered on two points. First, for health in the Indian climate, an Englishman, and presumably an American like me, should take a little whiskey every day—*chota peg* or two fingers before dinner—advice that I found very pleasant to follow. The second item was that I should hire a "bearer" or personal servant to carry my baggage and take care of my personal needs. The former British official who gave me that advice had been quite insistent and had cabled ahead to his former bearer to meet my boat.

When I arrived in Bombay, it was the former bearer's brother who appeared at dockside and took charge of my hand baggage; he looked up my huge wardrobe trunk and the hat box that had been shipped ahead from Cairo, and found conveyances to transport me and all my baggage to the Hotel Taj Mahal. All that was convenient and helpful. But when he hovered about my room wanting to unpack my things and dress me for dinner, I was horrified. I wanted to get rid of him. As I wrote in my journal:

> It is incongruous in view of my theories of the wrongness of all servitude, but it was rather in spite of myself that I acquired this man, and it soothes my conscience to think it will be a good experience to test my theories. He is an awful nuisance most of the time, hanging vaguely and solicitously about and neither of us knows what he is to do next. Minsamy, age 23, inexperienced and deferential—I have to keep him for he came three hundred miles to meet me.

What he asked in pay was pitifully little, and I knew he needed the job. In the course of my three months in India, there was little he did for me that I could not have done better for myself, but I tried to play the role of master he expected of me. In most of the places I stayed, he would wake me in the morning with early morning tea, and I would often find that he had been sleeping on the floor outside my bedroom door like a faithful dog. When I traveled by rail, he would get me and my baggage to the station, buy my tickets, find me a compartment, and then he would disappear into the fourth-class compartment, reserved at the end of first-class cars for personal servants.

My first rail trip out of Bombay was to visit my former shipmate, Lieutenant Hope, at his army post in Poona. There for once I felt Minsamy gave me status, and I was accepted as an equal in a setting where each officer had his own Indian servant.

Lieutenant Hope put me up in a guest house near the parade ground. That evening in the officers' mess, I was introduced to the other officers in his Royal Field Artillery regiment. All were dressed for dinner in splendid uniforms of scarlet and gold, some decked with medals. Fortunately I had brought along my dinner jacket for such formal occasions. I was struck with the beauty and charm of these splendid animals, all seemingly in a common mold including their trim little moustaches. At the proper moment they all rose and drank a solemn toast to the King.

The next day began with an early morning ride on a polo pony provided by my host. Then after breakfast I was left to my own devices while the regiment engaged in some daily training program. Afternoons were devoted to athletics, for fitness seemed to be a prime requisite for these Greek demigods. Hearing I had been an oarsman in college, they enlisted me to join a four-man crew on the river. "Thence to the polo club for a few drinks among the solemn kind people," I wrote in my journal, "too kind perhaps, for the drinks were too many."

So I had a glimpse of one segment of the ruling power, and how a conquering race, still believing itself secure, behaves. These young men with their disciplined self-confidence were part of the structure of empire. They were not yet aware that their empire was crumbling.

I came to know another segment at the boarding house in Bombay where I roomed for a couple of weeks: they were what uniformed officialdom called "box wallahs," Britons involved with merchandise and trade, definitely of a lower class than the military but still rated in their own eyes as superior to the highest of Indian castes.

Of the Britons I met, they were the most vocal in their advocacy of brute force as the only way to deal with the independence movement. They dealt with the natives every day, and they assured me all Indians were "beastly" and none could be trusted. "The only thing these people understand is force," they told me.

I had arrived in India at a crucial time, when the nationalist revolt against British rule was reaching a climax, and the figure of Gandhi, though silenced and in prison, was dominating the revolt. Some months before, he had launched a national campaign of civil disobedience by leading thousands of followers in a dramatic march to the sea to make salt in protest against the British salt tax. He had been imprisoned, but the nationalist movement—committed to passive resistance and "non-violent non-cooperation"—was gaining momentum.

With my newspaper credentials, I sought an interview with the editor of the English-language *Times of India*, and with his help I met and talked with some of the Indian nationalist leaders in Bombay. They told me the same story in reverse: they had never met an Englishman they could trust. I soon came to sense an almost total lack of understanding between the dominant British and their Indian subjects.

One of the introductions I had obtained in London from a former high-ranking official of the Indian Civil Service was to Sir Geoffrey de Montmorency, K.C.S.I., K.C.I.E., K.C.V.O., His Excellency the Governor of the Punjab. For a couple of days I lived in style as his guest at Government House, a vast remodeled Moslem tomb, in Lahore. His family was in England and his only housemates were a couple of handsome aides-de-camp. He took me with him to an official function. We were driven in an open car between rows of policemen—he had been shot at and wounded some months before on a similar occasion. He was gracious in greeting Indian officials and distinguished guests, but I gathered he had none but official contact with any Indian, and if the dinner I ate at his table with the two respectfully silent ADCs was any indication, no Indian, however distinguished, would ever be invited for a purely social occasion.

Another introduction I had obtained was to a District Officer, the highest British official in a largely rural district of the United Provinces with a population of three million, and he invited me to go with him and his wife on one of his regular tours of the villages in his district. We traveled on horseback with a large supporting train of servants and pack animals in an area of jungle and primitive villages where there were no motor roads.

"Four nights I spent in Canal Department bungalows, one under canvas," I wrote in my journal.

> But always there were baths before dinner, and sherry and fresh sweet peas from Shahjahanpur in silver vases, well-cooked, well-served meals, books, easy chairs, wood fires, all the amenities of civilized life.
>
> Mr. Hobart took great pains to show me all the intricacies of his job. The amount of organization and red tape is amazing: lists of fields, landowners, payments, crops, sales, arrests, "breakings by night" and "by day," "with force" and "without force," reports, counter reports, marginal commentaries, and annual summaries. British rule has meant system and honesty and peace and many advantages like railroads and canals. But the poor wretched villages are ever the same, unspeakable. The interiors of the houses are often swept clean. The people obviously do not like to live in sties. But how hard it is for them to live otherwise. The naked children run like monkeys but less picturesquely. Their eyes and noses are unclean. They empty their bowels on the street. They make pies with fresh cow dung. And their elders, lean and ragged, salaam almost to the mire when the great white man rides by, with his reports in his saddle bags.

The District Officer and his wife were charming and kindly hosts, and I could not but admire their dedication and sympathize with their isolation, half a world away from their children in England. Yet their days were not all taken up with bearing the white man's burden. They had an arsenal of hunting weapons with them, and they organized hunts of wild game—"black buck" and waterfowl—for my benefit. And one day we went tiger hunting, this time riding elephants into the jungle to a platform in a tree, while a hundred villagers with noisemakers beat the bushes to drive game in our direction. Unfortunately the beaters started too soon; we were late to our platform and saw no tiger.

Revolt against British rule seemed not to have reached into the countryside, although another District Officer with a more urban population had recently been assassinated. Gandhi's emphasis on non-violence was, however, dominating the movement in the cities.

Released from prison early in the year to attend a Round Table Conference in London, Gandhi was now in Allahabad conferring with Nehru and the other leaders of the Indian National Congress Party on whether to accept the latest British offer of limited self-rule with dominion status within the Empire. I decided to go to Allahabad and see if I could interview these shapers of India's future. I had by this time immersed myself in the dramatic struggle then seemingly reaching a climax. I had come to the conclusion that no real understanding between the Indian nationalists and the British was possible, yet I could see no possibility of a smooth transition to independence.

In a hotel in Allahabad, I met a bright young Indian reporter, Chaman Lal of the English-language daily *Hindustan Times*, himself an ardent nationalist, who encouraged me to try to meet Gandhi, and suggested it would be easy if I joined the great man on his daily early morning walk. Gandhi was staying, along with Nehru and other Congress leaders, in the home of a wealthy supporter.

On February 12, 1931, I wrote in my journal:

> I got up before six. It was quite dark. My tanga did not come till half past so I was not able to get to Anand Bhawam till sunrise. Mr. Gandhi had already left for his walk. I was sorry I could not have got there in time to go with him. I waited on the porch as the low beams of the sun threw long shadows across the lawn. Three or four poor Hindus came up the path from the gate to wait under the porte-cochere. I talked to a young physics instructor from the university who had come to see him.
>
> Finally a small group appeared at the street gate, a little bald-headed, bare-legged, white-robed figure marching determinedly ahead of the others. The Hindus in front of the porch and the physics instructor all prostrated themselves while he stopped long enough for them to kiss his sandaled feet. Then he saw me and we sat down together in two of the wicker chairs on the porch.
>
> He spoke in a soft low voice, in good British English, looking now on the floor and now at me. His eyes were disfigured by yellowish-rimmed bifocal glasses; they were very dark, so dark that pupil and iris were hardly distinguishable; there was a grayish circle around the iris. His ears were hidden by his thick robe. His front teeth were gone, and perhaps that is why his lips seemed to protrude. His little moustache was not an ornament.

291

I had brought along a recent issue of *Time* magazine to show him, thinking he might not know of his being featured in a cover story as "Man of the Year." The portrait on the cover I had assumed was a caricature, but his homeliness was such that no caricature was needed to emphasize it. He brushed the magazine aside, but it gave me an opening. The article had dwelt on the fusion of religion and politics in his movement. I asked him about it.

"Yes," he replied, "religion must be involved in all we do."

"How is this possible in a country with two separate religions?" I asked.

"There are not two religions. All religion is the same. There are just different expressions of it. In India all can work for the country under the guidance of God," he replied.

He went on to speak of India's spirituality as opposed to the materialism of the West. It might be well if India and Britain could cooperate, but they were headed in different directions. Whatever the outcome and whatever the cost, there could be no compromise.

"It is not in our hands. I never look far ahead. In the words of Newman's hymn, 'One step enough for me, I do not need the distant scene.' All I can do is decide that the present step is right. The rest I can leave safely to God," he said.

After a few more words, he rose, a fragile old hand emerged from his robes to shake mine, and he indicated the interview was at an end. His secretary had been standing by and now said I would have to submit anything I wrote for approval, but Gandhi said it was not necessary and turned to go in the house.

I also had a brief talk with Jawaharlal Nehru, who was to become India's first prime minister when independence finally came seventeen years later—in 1948. Like Gandhi he made it plain that there could be no compromise with Britain: independence must be complete, however much he might still welcome cooperation on a basis of equality. His fine presence and deep conviction made a powerful impression. He was dressed in the white homespun that had become almost a uniform for the nationalist movement. I learned that he had persuaded his father, Motilal Nehru, a rich and successful lawyer, to burn his expensive Bond Street suits and dress in the same simple uniform. Both father and son had been to England for their university education, as had Gandhi, and I sensed how much the political philosophy and the goals of their movement derived from the English model.

The Indian debt to Britain struck me all the more a few days later when I attended a session of the elected but largely powerless Indian Parliament in New Delhi: fiery denunciations of British rule were addressed to a dark-skinned Speaker wearing a long curled white wig, and all the rituals and formalities were those of the British House of Commons.

The Parliament was meeting in one of the new government buildings in New Delhi (a few miles from old Delhi), only recently finished after ten years of work, as the capital of British India. The huge circular legislative building was overshadowed by the even vaster Secretariat buildings, and on a higher level still were the palace and gardens of the Viceroy. A ceremonial inauguration of the new buildings took place while I was there, and I obtained a press pass. There were marching bands, brilliantly uniformed military formations, turbaned maharajahs, pomp and ceremony, all intended perhaps to impress "the natives" but actually, it seemed to me, only impressing the British rulers and their dependents. The masses that crowded old Delhi were not invited. Thousands of them were attending an outdoor prayer meeting presided over by Gandhi in his loincloth.

One of the journalists I met commented wryly on New Delhi as being only the latest of a series of capital cities whose ruins dotted the countryside. I had toured three of these ancient capitals a few days before, and in the oldest of them I had climbed the Kutb Minar, a 250-foot tower dating from A.D. 1200. I wondered if it would still be standing when the vast new Secretariat buildings and the Viceroy's palace of New Delhi had crumbled.

A few days after the dedication of the new buildings, Gandhi accepted an invitation to confer with the Viceroy, Lord Irwin. He declined the Viceroy's offer of transportation in an official limousine, and chose to walk the ten miles from Delhi to the Viceroy's palace in his sandals and loincloth. Back in London, Winston Churchill, who opposed concessions to the nationalist rebels, thundered in the House of Commons that it was an affront to the King for this "half-naked fakir" to approach the representative of the Crown in this fashion.

In my reading during this period, the rise and fall of empires was a recurrent theme. I had brought along a suitcase full of books, and about the time I was witnessing the challenges to British rule in India, I was reading two monumental books dealing not only with the transitoriness of empires but of civilizations. In addition to Lecky's *History of European Morals,* I was absorbing Oswald Spengler's dire *Decline of the West.* In touring the crumbling capitals of the great Moghul empire near Delhi, and at Agra and Fatehpur Sikri, I felt the surge, as I had in Egypt and Palestine, of the tremendous tides of history. The British Empire was collapsing as other empires had collapsed before. But did this mean the end of Western civilization? And what of the even more ancient civilization of India?

I visited Benares whose Hindu temples and rituals were thousands of years older than the Islamic Moghul empire. "I have never been so revolted by any place as by Benares," I wrote in my journal. I described a walk through its "putrefying alleys" to the Golden Temple:

> Ordure, refuse, misshapen bodies, hideous old men, blear-eyed boys, naked beggars, naked priests, bloated gods with elephant bodies in dirty shrines, temples where everyone wanted money. I saw a woman with four twisted limbs, not legs or arms but such things as crippled insects crawled upon. I shrank from skeletons holding up begging bowls waiting till death could give them the boon of the Burning Ghat, ghastly dogs that might

have been flayed alive sniffing abjectly at piles of refuse, a holy man standing stark naked in the street scratching at his belly, another urinating in a crack of the pavement till jostled by a calf whose mange might have infected hell...

I was puzzled as well as revolted. This was India's holy city where devout Hindus came to die. It had beauty if one could see beyond the filth. Even the Burning Ghats, where I saw half-burned bodies thrown in the Ganges, were a riot of color with masses of bright flowers strewn on the water. I thought back to the unbelievable purity of the Taj Mahal, which I had visited by moonlight. I had been overwhelmed by the fantastic hanging gardens and floating alabaster palaces of Udaipur. My credentials had permitted me to be the guest of the ruling prince of that "native state" for a day or two, but I gathered that his rule would probably come to an end with an independent India. Was all that was picturesque and beautiful merely the remains of a civilization that had died?

The only expression of contemporary Indian culture I included in my itinerary was the "University of the World" established by the famous poet Rabindranath Tagore at Santiniketan, not far from Calcutta. Touted in its literature as a "forest school, set in an abode of peace and loveliness, where the young spirit may unfold in closeness to nature," I found only "squalor and unloveliness."

> The Guest House where I stayed was a place of decaying shutters, and mosquitoes from stopped drains, and broken window panes. The country was as little picturesque as any I have seen, with few big trees, no gardens, unkempt groves of scrawny little trees, strange corners where was rusting machinery and refuse. The "Halls of Residence" are miserable shabby hovels.

I called on "The Poet" in his palatial residence, a majestic figure in flowing white robes and beard. I was half inclined to think he and his "University" were all a pious fraud, but I knew that even Westerners thought of him as a great poet, and there was no reason to doubt his deep dedication to this dream of an institution synthesizing East and West. Still there was a make-believe quality about him and his surroundings. This had also bothered me in my impression of Gandhi. Perhaps the very magnitude of India's problems, with its enormous population mired in the direst poverty, required of its social reformers a great measure of make-believe if they were not to give up in despair.

Overall, my three months in India had been a deeply moving experience. I had hobnobbed with the great—movers and shakers of history—and had felt personally involved in currents of empire and revolution. Along with this manic intoxication, I had had moods of despair, of deep self-doubt. If I had been parochial before undertaking my odyssey, I now felt myself a member of the human race, concerned with its past, present, and future, a responsible citizen of the world.

As if to climax my emotional binge, I fell in love—in my last few days before sailing from Calcutta—with an American girl, sister of an American vice-consul to whom I had an introduction. I dined with her and danced with her and made love with her in my imagination. In my exalted emotional state, I was moved to poetry. But I had my passage booked and was eager to be on my way, and had too much conscience to take advantage of this shy and impressionable young thing, so there was no word of love or even a kiss, but only a transient ecstasy of feeling.

Oh, parting is not meeting,
Though hands feel much the same;
For hearts are harder beating,
Though words are quite as tame;
And though you're no nearer,
Your cheek is much dearer,
There's giving in your greeting,
And eyes are aflame.
We met and then we parted,
Our looks alone gave speech,
Our thoughts were not imparted
Beyond what smiles might teach;
Yet our lips were aquiver
At parting forever,
Disguised yet open-hearted
Each to each.

CHAPTER 41
To the Far East

I sailed from Calcutta to Hong Kong. With stops en route, I would be over two weeks at sea with plenty of time for more reflections on the meaning of colonialism. The first stop was at Rangoon, capital and chief city of Burma, where the ship lay over for a day, discharging and taking on cargo.

Burma was then part of the British Indian Empire though its culture and history were quite different from India's. One difference that struck me immediately as I looked down at the dock from my upper deck was the rickshaw, the two-wheeled vehicle pulled by a man that had come to Burma from Japan and China.

On the dock a tourist agency was making rickshaws available for passengers who wanted to go sightseeing. I lined up with other passengers and found myself next to a British officer a few years older than I. He asked if I was alone and suggested we join forces for a tour of the city. He introduced himself as Theodore Vaizey, Captain in the Royal Artillery. We hired rickshaws, and then, to my surprise, instead of climbing into his, Captain Vaizey ordered the man to step out from between the shafts and stepped into his place. He said he had not seen a rickshaw before and wanted to gauge how heavy it was and how hard it was to pull. I had never expected to see a British officer in uniform so demean himself as to take the place of a ragged coolie, but he was obviously a man of more sensitivity than those I had met in Poona three months before.

He also had a greater curiosity about "native" culture than I had seen in uniformed officialdom: when we visited the great Shwe Dagon pagoda, a Buddhist temple of such sanctity that no visitor is allowed within its enclosure other than in bare feet—a rule that I gathered kept out most Englishmen concerned with losing face in the eyes of the "natives"—Captain Vaizey was not to be put off. Together we scampered barefoot from one shady spot in the hot pavement to another as we visited the temple's many shrines, dodging pigeon droppings on the way.

Vaizey had found the rickshaw as light as a bicycle and easy enough to pull, but riding in it gave a new wrench to my social conscience. I wrote of my discomfort in my journal:

> To have a little brown-legged man trotting and sweating at your feet does not seem so wrong at first, for you are used to horses and this seems only a kind of little horse, until suddenly the horse turns around with human eyes and features and asks you which way to go next: that is a horrible shock. You feel to be consistent you should have a whip handy and flick those legs to keep them from slacking. But they do not slack. They trot on as steadily as the most eager pony. Those brown hands are little more than harness to hold on to the shafts—till one takes a cloth to wipe the sweat off a streaming face.

As our ship sailed on the next day, I was moved to question my right to ride in lordly style at the expense of another's sweat.

> We live off the toil and sweat of many slaves. Every rivet in this ship meant sweat to put in. This typewriter [the Underwood portable I had brought along], the furnishings, the cleanliness and comfort of this cabin, the Quaker Oats from the plains of Iowa that I had for breakfast thousands of miles from where they were sown and cultivated and harvested— everything money can buy means someone's sweat.
>
> I have absolutely no right to command these things. Not one cent of what I pay have I earned. Nor has anyone now alive earned it for me. It might have fallen from heaven. As a matter of fact it came to me as an heir of Charles L. Tiffany, of whom I know nothing except that he was my

great-grandfather and the founder of Tiffany & Co. Yet was it his sweat that earned it, or only an unusual ability to make a profit from others' sweat?

I discussed my doubts with my new traveling companion. Vaizey had been too long a faithful soldier bringing peace and order to Kipling's "lesser breeds without the law" to allow himself such doubts. We talked endlessly of the role of empire and a man's duty to his fellow man as we steamed along the Malayan coast.

We learned that we could see something of Malaya by leaving the ship at Penang, going by train to Kuala Lumpur, the capital, and on to rejoin the ship at Malacca. Malaya, still a peaceful Crown colony, rich in rubber and tin, with trim plantations, neat lawns and churches and asphalt roads, gave an impression of cleanliness and prosperity, and seemed the fullest justification for empire as the bringer of Western civilization.

At Singapore, I wrote that Britain was "triumphant without question or reproach." I had an introduction to a British businessman. "We *rule* here," he told us.

"No shilly-shallying with black men like Gandhi. Look at the country. Clean, orderly, peaceful. Any politician gets sent right out of the country. Native judges? Native officials? None of that here. We know our place and the native knows his, which is more than he does in India."

With Vaizey's military connections, we had an easy entrée to British officialdom and an invitation to the Swimming Club, and on Good Friday we attended services in the great Gothic cathedral of the Church of England.

Vaizey was a devout member of his church. For him the soldier's profession, with its ideals of service and sacrifice, went hand in hand with the church. Two days out on the South China Sea, he organized and conducted a decorous Easter service in the ship's first-class lounge, attended by a dozen fellow passengers.

Afterwards I was vaguely uneasy as I looked down on a mass of Chinese coolies on the open deck below. At Singapore, our ship had taken on two thousand workers returning to China, and they were jammed between the hot lower decks.

As we steamed north, a storm came up. I found the lashing wind, rain, and heaving sea a relief after the sticky calm we had sailed through ever since Calcutta, but I grieved for the crowded humanity below, at this point denied the open deck and without air or light.

One day the throb of the ship's engines stopped suddenly. I learned that one of the deck passengers had fallen or jumped overboard. A life buoy was thrown to him, and I could see its intermittently flashing light when it rose on the crest of a distant wave. A lifeboat was launched and retrieved the man's body floating nearby. It was hoisted up to my deck, and I heard someone say the man must have died of a heart attack, leaving the body buoyant. It lay limply on the deck, so much repulsive animal matter, fluid oozing from the mouth, forlorn white stubble on the chin. No relative or friend came up from below to claim it, and I was moved to think of the nameless millions of human creatures who live and suffer and die on this crowded planet, each essentially alone, making no history. Am I not one of them?

The body was disposed of with minimum ceremony the next day. Wrapped in canvas, weighted with lead, and dumped in the South China Sea, the slight splash it made was immediately lost in the ship's wake.

We reached Hong Kong later that day, April 9, 1931. My plans did not call for travel in China until I had been to the Philippines and Japan, and I was able to get passage to Manila on a ship leaving the next day. Vaizey reported to his new assignment, but we agreed at parting to try to meet later in the spring when he would be eligible for leave, and we might do some traveling in China together.

I had included the Philippines in my itinerary because American rule there was being challenged in the same kind of anti-colonial movement that I had been studying in Egypt and India. The colonial problem was particularly meaningful because of my father's involvement as chairman of the U.S. Senate Committee on Territories and Insular Possessions. On the very day of my arrival in Manila, the newspapers carried headline stories about a speech my father had made declaring the islands were far from ready for independence. Reporters at the dock spotted me as his son, and I was immediately a subject for interviews and official attention.

I made the most of my vicarious importance. I met leaders of the independence movement, including Manuel Roxas, speaker of the lower house of the elected legislature, and Senator Sergio Osmena. I was most hospitably welcomed by Governor General Dwight F. Davis, and on a quick tour of some of the southern islands (Iloilo, Mindanao and Cebu), the provincial governors Davis had appointed were attentive and deferential.

The future status of the Philippines was everywhere a subject of discussion. The Filipinos I talked to were universally in favor of independence, though in contrast to the bitterness against the colonial power so prevalent in India, here the mood seemed more appreciative of the benefits of American rule—schools, roads, public health services—and more aware of the hardships that might come with independence. On the other hand, among American officials and businessmen I met, there was not one who did not feel independence would be disastrous for all concerned: maybe in thirty or forty years the vague promises the United States had made of eventual independence could be fulfilled, but the islands were certainly not ready for it now. The prevailing view was that the Filipinos had neither the character nor the intelligence to govern themselves or the minority races they would dominate.

This view was expressed most forcefully at a party I was taken to by the Governor General's son Dwight Davis, Jr. The party began at the Manila Polo Club in the afternoon with many drinks and went on far into the night with a late steak dinner at the Army and Navy Club. The company consisted of two young married couples and half a dozen unattached young men, all American except for two polo-playing Spanish businessmen.

As I listened to the idle talk, I came to feel that at the heart of the problem of Philippine independence was the white race's invincible sense of superiority to colored races. I could not help but admit to myself that I was prejudiced too, for I had often found myself subtly condescending in my talks with Filipinos. Even the most liberal and tolerant Americans I had met, who socialized with Filipinos—in a more friendly fashion than I had seen displayed by their British counterparts in India—seemed to think of the natives as our "little brown brothers."

During my last week in the Philippines, my fascination with colonialism was pushed into the background by a sudden attack of lovesickness. Governor Davis had invited me to spend a weekend with his family in the mountain resort of Baguio in northern Luzon. The bracing climate at its high elevation would be a welcome change from tropical heat, and after my visit with the Davises, I would be able to drive over a new trail into a wilderness of mile-deep valleys inhabited by the primitive Igorot and Bontoc tribes. But what came to overshadow all other attractions was the governor's daughter Cynthia, then acting as his official hostess. I fell painfully in love with her.

I played golf with her and her brother the day after my arrival. I watched her. In my journal I wrote of

> her magnificent chin and throat, her playful short hair, her brown eyes, her smile, her freckles, her generous forehead, the white flower she wore behind her ear as she had seen the Bali women do. But it was not till the evening that the tinder caught and I began to feel a fierce fire in my chest. She had worn entrancing silk pajamas to dinner, with Japanese sandals, a vision of loveliness, yet an unconscious, modest, almost childlike vision. I watched her and pretended to converse with her father.
>
> I undressed early but before I went to bed, I stepped out on the balcony of my room in the cool night air. The stars were brilliant. Right in front, beside a tall pine, was the great Scorpion. The distant hills were dotted with fires. It was quiet except for the crickets. I began to shiver. Yet I knew it wasn't only the cold. I felt something great impending. Suddenly music began to come from a room two windows over, a faint orchestra. I shook all over. The light went out and a dim shadow appeared on the other balcony. I was afraid it might be her father. But I knew it wasn't. It was she.
>
> With a great effort I let her know I was there. For an hour we watched the stars and the night. I hardly stopped trembling. I was afraid she would hear me shake when I said a word or two or pointed to a shooting star.

Nothing came of my sudden romance. When I pursued her during the next two days, she brushed me off. When I told her I was in love with her, she seemed annoyed and professed disbelief. Perhaps she sensed my callowness, but I chose to believe she was too young and inexperienced to appreciate a grand passion. I never got beyond a touching of hands.

On the boat from Manila to Shanghai, I wrote some verses and enclosed them with a letter expressing the hope that someday she might change her mind about me.

A year later I looked her up in Paris, and we had a drink together at a sidewalk cafe on the Champs-Elysées. I hardly recognized her under her makeup and expensive clothes. We were both a year older, and there was no spark of that brief fire left in me.

CHAPTER 42
Japan and China

Japan was next on my itinerary. Most of my six weeks there was as a guest of my next older brother Harry, and thanks largely to him, it was a time of intense arousal of sexual and aesthetic feelings.

He had made good use of his Foreign Service assignment as a vice-consul to the American Embassy in Tokyo and had acquired a working knowledge of the language. Taking full advantage of his status as an eligible bachelor, he made friends in the foreign colony that included a fringe of Japanese elite society.

His living arrangements enchanted me. Teaming up with a young American reporter on the English language daily, he had rented a beautiful little Japanese house. I described it in my journal.

> From the front steps where one takes off one's shoes to the sliding paper walls and the garden at the back, it is a joy to the eye throughout. The soft warm browns of the woodwork, ceiling, and end walls, the luscious give of the straw matting floor, the pale washed light that makes the windows so many panels of a picture only in light and shade, the alcove dedicated to beauty where is a statuette and two vases of flowers arranged by the master hand of the housekeeper—it is all an abode of rest and beauty.
>
> His household is wonderfully complete and smooth running. There is the housekeeper, motherly, capable, jolly, yet unobtrusive, whose only fault is her use of too much neck powder. There is the maid who typifies unintelligent willing service. And there is the sweet, gentle, confiding Namiko, the final luxury of tasteful living, the crowning feature of this home of Japanese charm.

Harry had become a man-of-the-world and was eager to initiate his virginal younger brother into the delights of sex. I was more than ready, but I told him I did not want sex without love, without beauty and romance.

One night he took me on a round of cafe-bars. He wanted to get me tight, and I drank much more sake than I wanted. Namiko joined us to take us to a reputable geisha house. There she found a friend to be my companion, but when Harry turned his attention to my girl, Namiko began to make love to me. She was more attractive than her friend. Still I balked at intruding between her and Harry. Finally I went with her friend into an adjoining little room, with a bed on the straw-matted floor. I partially undressed. She kept on a light night kimono.

> She wanted to go right to bed. I dallied for a while. I must love her a little, and must make her love me a little. That was my only requirement. She was obviously overpowered with sleep from the sake. She wanted me to come right to her and get done with it. She took my hard cock and tried to draw me into bed. But I wanted to pet her and kiss her. She resisted. Finally I did have one good kiss but it didn't seem to interest her. There was no response of affection. I made her bare her breasts. She was beautifully formed, all but her face, a trim little Venus with silken skin, perfectly shaped. But nothing for romance to feed on. She couldn't keep awake. I told her I couldn't come yet, and she gave up trying and went to sleep.

The night ended with me still shamefacedly a virgin.

I was now a challenge to Harry and Namiko and later to some of Harry's friends.

One of Harry's friends was the sculptor Isamu Noguchi, not yet famous. Born in the United States of an American mother and a notable Japanese poet, he was on his first visit to Japan, and was savoring all it had to offer. Though I had met him in Tokyo, it was in Kyoto, Japan's ancient cultural center where he had established a studio, that he helped me overcome my reserve.

I had been naive in thinking love could be bought along with sex. But in this ancient capital with its temples, samurai traditions, and craft workshops, I found romantic charm an adequate substitute. A night on the town with Noguchi as guide and host did the trick.

> The evening began in a little cafe-bar done in a prehistoric Japanese style of slats, with old armor and straw raincapes on the walls. The proprietor makes sacred masks, practices black magic, and for direct inspiration wears his hair to his shoulders to increase the contact with the spirit world. He had apparently agreed to show Noguchi the workshop of a maker of brocades, a friend of his who turned out to be even more disreputable looking. I was told he kept a bawdy house on the side. His factory was in his home, and there we saw the most exquisite brocades being woven, their floral designs picked out with silver and gold and crimson threads.
>
> We went on to a little underground restaurant where I was introduced to raw fish and sea slugs and fish cooked and eaten whole, guts and all. We had been drinking beer, but after a long supper we went back to the cafe-

bar where pretty girls in the gayest of kimonos and obies served us rounds of whiskey and sake. The proprietor was honored to have the son of Japan's leading poet and an American vice-consul as his guests. A couple of tiny geisha girls joined us, little gaudy dancing girls of fourteen or so, as demure as mice, not yet full-fledged in their profession. Another artist craftsman, a maker of obies who was also, I was told, a famous Noh dancer, joined us. He was to take us to an ancient geisha house of special renown.

In a smoke-blackened upstairs room lit only by candles, I was shown dents in the old corner posts left long ago by the swords of fighting samurai. There were eight of us now, sitting on cushions in a circle with low tables for the tiny sake cups that were continually refilled as each guest toasted the others in turn. Two geishas were strumming plaintive notes on samisens in a corner as a musical background to the talk. We were waiting for something.

Suddenly, in a hush of awe, in the dim medieval light appeared a miraculously brocaded figure. I was told she was a dancer of taiyu, a dance above all ordinary geisha dances. Slowly she stepped into the circle, with a magnificent flowing cloak of brocade over her kimono. Her motions were slow risings and subsidings, slow shiftings of the great cloak, all gestures focused on a tiny lacquer dish. Her face in that dim light was the face of a priestess who felt the divine spirit resting upon her. The undulations, the risings and droopings gradually became more passionate. Finally as if in ecstasy, she swooped down to the lacquer dish, raised it up and held it out to us in total surrender. She was the goddess of love, making the supreme offering of herself. And then she was gone.

Noguchi turned to me and told me, dramatically, and I thought somewhat bitterly, "She's yours." The goddess of love herself! Apparently the Noh dancer who had here been our host was offering her as part of the entertainment, and Noguchi, who had arranged the evening, was giving her to me. As in a dream, the guests all disappeared. I was ushered through the silent house down a corridor. A door was slid back, and there in a tiny room with a bed laid on the floor was the goddess, waiting for me.

This time I no longer had scruples. There might be no love beyond the allegory, but the beauty and the romance of the whole evening had me by the throat. And so, however clumsily and unsatisfyingly, I had my first full sexual experience.

The rest was anticlimax. She went to sleep beside me, no longer a goddess, only a country girl. I slept fitfully for a couple of hours. When I woke, dawn was breaking. I woke her and told her I must go. She left to order a taxi as I dressed. When she returned, I began to see her, for the first time, as a person, and an appealing one. I wanted to communicate this new warm feeling inside me, no longer sexual, that made me yearn to reach her. When I talked gently to her, she was obviously uncomprehending, but responded, for the first time, with a faint smile.

She took me by the hand down the empty corridor, now no longer dark and mysterious, and at the door said good-bye, "Sayonara," a little sadly, still sleepily. The courtyard of the ancient house was full of golden morning light coming down through the old trees' foliage. A last glimpse and the little goddess was gone.

When I left Japan a few days later, I wrote in my journal that I had fallen in love with the country. My aesthetic and sexual feelings had been intensely stirred in my six-week visit: "Japan and the Japanese seem to me the most lovable nation on earth."

The fringe of cultivated, English-speaking Japanese Harry had introduced me to impressed me as sensitive, intelligent, and kindly. Even in the heart of Tokyo, wherever I had been, it was smiling faces, courtesy, charm, apple-cheeked children in bright kimonos that filled my memory. The traditional and the modern seemed to have blended happily.

The rising political and social tensions that had struck me in India and other parts of the colonial world were nowhere evident here. I was aware elsewhere of a prevailing anxiety about the worldwide economic depression, but Japan gave me an impression of security and peace.

As if to emphasize the shift in my own interests from political and social change to the inner life, I spent my last night in Japan at a Buddhist monastery on the holy mountain of Koyasan. I considered devoting the whole night to meditation. Outside my room in the guest house was an ancient garden bathed in moonlight.

I put on a shirt under my night kimono to keep out some of the damp cold, and in geta that cut my toes wandered about beside the frog-filled ponds, over little bridges, by a tiny group of ghost-like iris arranged as in a bowl, then up a little lawn and a rough path, past carved shrubs on the hillside to a seat on a step protected from the dew by a pine and a Japanese maple, whose foliage outlined against the moon was as in a thousand drawings. In the distance over lofty cryptomerias loomed the hills that ring the mountain cup wherein is Koyasan. Mists began to veil them. Below, the moon was reflected in a pond not too much ruffled by a fountain and occasional frog splashes. Off to the left, a couple of lanterns dimly lit the front of a temple. A deep bell struck at intervals filled the air with vibrant humming, indeterminate.

Mosquitoes distracted me. But I persevered, thinking that now in this perfect setting I might capture the essence of the spiritual. I asked myself: Does this garden, do the pale iris have a spirit? Am I any closer to God in this ancient place of devotion? I concluded that "God is unknowable."

Our own selves alone we can know and work with. Life is to be laid hold of and made the most of. Our only duty is to ourselves. Family, community, society can claim nothing as morally due, for we are no party to the contract. That leaves us free to do as well as we can, in good works as in good living.

Finally the mosquitoes and an overmastering desire to sleep drove me in from the garden. The next day I sailed from Kobe.

As the *Shanghai Maru* slowly moved away from the dock, I was gripped by the strongest kind of emotion. The passengers seemed to be all Japanese, and I felt strangely alone. Dozens of friends and relatives were on the quay to say good-bye, each attached by a colored streamer to a loved one on board. All were bravely smiling, and tears rolled down their cheeks and into damp handkerchiefs, as the streamers began to break. I cried too.

I have no reason to think my ecstatic reaction to what I saw of Japan was not valid. But within months of my visit, in September 1931, a Japanese army invaded Manchuria, in what was seen as the very beginning of World War II, and a series of assassinations of Western-oriented politicians showed that the samurai tradition could be cruel as well as charming. In those people I had met, I had not encountered the Japanese traits that were to lead ten years later to the blasting of Pearl Harbor.

What had moved me in Japan was the delicacy and sensitivity and gentleness of its women, and there was enough of those feminine traits among some of Harry's Japanese men friends to make me think the national character was that of a lingering childhood.

That impression was sharpened by my first reaction to China.

> After the wonderful and ever-present natural courtesy of the Japanese, here was proud self-assertion and rudeness. The taxi man would not go till I paid him, and when I demurred he put my bags on the road. The room boy here in the YMCA is sullen and irritable. The faces on the street are the faces of men, not children, and I can take nothing for granted.
> Another point, at once striking: the sudden cheapness of human life. Four or five men harnessed like struggling horses to a wagon, half-naked coolies everywhere carrying over-heavy burdens, swarms of people grimly and consciously facing the struggle of life. By contrast Japan had given me an impression almost of leisure and wealth.

I was again in a country seething with social discontent. For generations a weak and moribund China had been pushed around by aggressive European powers, and Shanghai, its principal seaport, was under foreign control. The International Settlement, with its YMCA (where I stayed), luxury hotels, country club, and skyscrapers, was under Anglo-American control. The French Concession adjoined it as an industrial and commercial outpost of empire. Surrounding the bustling foreign enclaves were the slums where most of the Chinese population lived. On one occasion when I was driven on a sightseeing tour through the Chinese city, I was aware of people spitting in my direction.

As in Egypt, India, and the Philippines, I was conscious of nationalist revolt against Western imperialism. And behind that anti-colonial movement,

I had an uneasy sense that the world's poor were in rebellion against the rich. As a scion of wealth and privilege, I began to feel personally threatened.

Actually these two aspects—the nationalist and Communist factions—of the Chinese revolution were already in conflict. Four years before, the Kuomintang or nationalist party, under the leadership of Chiang Kai-shek and his army, had broken with its Communist left wing, and the two forces were engaged in a civil war then beginning in Kiangsi province.

As I had in Egypt and India, I used my credentials as a journalist and exploited the connections I could make, as the son of a U.S. Senator, to meet and talk to knowledgeable and important people. The focus of my research shifted once more from myself to the contemporary political and social scene.

In Shanghai and Nanking (the then national capital), I had interviews with two cabinet ministers, both of whom had studied at Yale. One was H. H. Kung, wealthy banker and Minister of Industry and Commerce, a descendant of Confucius. As husband of one of the Soong sisters, and thus a brother-in-law of Sun Yat-sen and Chiang Kai-shek, he was a power in the Kuomintang. He wanted an end to extra-territorial rights for foreigners, but his lavish Western-style mansion where I interviewed him was located in the French Concession of Shanghai, presumably safe there from Communist "banditry," and he spoke of the need for Western capital to help develop the country.

I had two interviews with C. T. Wang, the other Yale man, who was Foreign Minister. He provided stock answers to my questions about Chinese foreign policies. He deplored the Western powers' limitations on China's sovereignty and the menace of Communist banditry, but it was Japan's aggressive moves in Manchuria that he considered the greatest threat to China.

I took a trip by Yangtze steamer from Nanking to Kiukiang and then by rail to Nanchang (capital of the interior province of Kiangsi) on the chance of being able to interview Chiang Kai-shek, head of the nationalist government and generalissimo of its armies. Chiang was then leading a campaign against the Red Army in the opening round of civil war. My first attempt to meet him was at a military funeral in honor of fallen General Hu. I arrived just as Chiang drove off and was greeted by the officer in charge as an important American dignitary. As newsreel cameras clicked, I was led to the dead general's bier where, coached by my Chinese guide, I bowed solemnly three times. The next day my guide, the director of an Episcopal mission school and hospital in Nanchang, arranged a three-minute interview for me with the generalissimo at his military headquarters. I was impressed by Chiang's piercing dark eyes and magnetic personality, but obtained only one quotable remark: he hoped to have finished with the Communist threat in a couple of months, and he would then begin to disband his armies and undertake the peaceful reconstruction of China.

I was back on the Yangtze the next day. The river was in full flood with much of the adjoining land under water. In a narrow defile where the boiling yellow current was kicking up enormous standing waves, we passed a junk that had just capsized, its crew clinging to the bottom and waving frantically for help. The Japanese steamer paid no attention. Human lives were obviously of little account in China.

In Nanking, much of which was under water, I managed to get a ferry to Pukow and the train for north China.

In Peking, I was helped in making personal contacts by the fact that both my older brothers had lived there—Woodbridge as a student, learning Chinese and gathering material for his doctoral program in Chinese history, Harry as a private secretary to the American minister, as a prelude to entering the American Foreign Service. I had introductions from them to add to my newspaper credentials and my father's status.

I spent the first two weeks of August 1931 in Peking. I had been joined by Theodore Vaizey, the British army captain I had traveled with from Rangoon to Hong Kong, and together we did some of the usual sightseeing. But I was beginning to think of myself as an authority on Chinese politics and contemporary social problems, and I continued to seek interviews.

Among the celebrities I talked to was Chang Hsueh-liang, known as the Young Marshal, commanding an army inherited from his father Chang Tsolin, the Manchu "warlord" who had ruled north China a few years before. He was in an American hospital recuperating from typhoid. Another prominent figure I interviewed was Hu Shih, liberal philosopher and intellectual, said to be the leader of a literary "renaissance." He had studied under John Dewey at Columbia University.

I was impressed with the amount of influence America exerted in China. The national government appeared to be dominated by graduates of American universities. American mission schools and hospitals had introduced Western ideas to an elite now wielding power. I went to a party of young Chinese professionals and their wives, and found that they all spoke English, not only to me but among themselves and in their own families. It seemed to me that traditional Chinese culture was confined to museums and antique shops.

In my journal I wrote:

> I am prouder of my own civilization than ever before. I have not seen China's own civilization being displaced but rather abandoned. What is being displaced is squalor, and by such Western institutions as Boy Scouts, good roads, cleanliness, philanthropy, democracy, public service. China seems far behind India in every way except for the potentialities for practical achievement of her people. She is fortunate to have Christian missionaries helping her to help herself instead of foreign rulers civilizing by force and condescension.

Such sentiments were soon to be overwhelmed by my entry into the Soviet Union.

CHAPTER 43

The Soviet Utopia

$\mathbf{F}$rom the beginning of my travels, I had felt the baleful appeal of Communism. The deepening crisis of the Great Depression was affecting all countries I visited, and many people I had talked to seemed to believe the capitalist system was collapsing and revolution was imminent. I knew little of Marx's prophecy that the contradictions inherent in capitalism would bring on a revolution powered by the working class and leading to socialism. But the Russian Revolution, with its hammer and sickle symbolizing rule by workers and peasants, was a fact of history, and the growing power and influence of the Soviet Union seemed everywhere to be felt as a menace or a promise.

In Egypt and India, I had been appalled by the misery of much of the population. I had inwardly cringed at the luxury enjoyed by the wealthy upper classes whose privileges I was able to share. Revolt of the poor against the rich was obviously a major element in the revolt against colonialism, and I found it easy to accept and sympathize with the anti-colonial uprisings, while struggling at the same time with feelings of fear and guilt in observing the misery of the lower classes. Occasionally, in desperation, I wrote in my journal that communism might be the only answer. So my projected visit to the Soviet Union had become the focus of my odyssey.

I had begun preparing for the visit in Tokyo by acquiring a primer of the Russian language and a pocket English-Russian dictionary; in Shanghai and Peking I engaged Russian émigrés as tutors for intensive practice in speaking Russian. I had a certain facility in learning foreign languages, thanks to childhood exposure to German nurses and French governesses. In Egypt, I had learned a few words of Arabic; in India, I had begun my travels with tutoring in Hindustani. So it was not too hard to acquire a smattering of Russian in the months before I entered the Soviet Union.

As further preparation, I had brought along a couple of books on the Russian Revolution. In *Utopia in Chains*, Edmond Walsh viewed the Soviet Union as the sworn enemy of Christian civilization, an empire masking its evil designs behind the propaganda of a perfect society. I had tended to accept his view, but the recently published *Humanity Uprooted* by Maurice Hindus made me question whether Russian Communism was all bad. I began reading it on the Chinese Eastern train, which carried me from Harbin in northern Manchuria to the Soviet border-crossing at Manchouli. There I switched from luxury to the rigors of the revolution and the Trans-Siberian Express.

In this supposedly classless society, travel by rail could not be designated first or second class but was either "soft" or "hard," and a knowledgeable traveler advised that if I really wanted to learn about the Soviet system I should travel "hard."

I had therefore provided myself with a bedding roll and a basket of emergency rations. Although I had shipped my wardrobe trunk and hatbox ahead by freight, I still carried a big suitcase and a typewriter.

In a compartment of the hard-class carriage, two facing benches were on each side of a central aisle. Above each of them hung two hinged slabs. The upper one usually remained down during the day, and there I could store my baggage. The car was wide, thanks to the broad Russian railroad gauge, and each bunk, though at right angles to the aisle, was close to six feet in length. The maximum capacity of a section was six persons, and the same on the other side of the aisle. On long train journeys I had a chance to communicate in a primitive way with many kinds of people.

In the pages of my journal, I began a dialogue with myself. For the next two months, the dialogue continued with increasing intensity, my mood vacillating between fear and exaltation. My first entry indicated the suddenness of my potential conversion.

On the Siberian Express, west of Irkutsk, August 26th:

> I am enthusiastic. I feel I may be starting on a complete internal revolution. Equality and fraternity seem to be realized as nowhere ever before, and in many ways liberty undreamed of...
>
> There seems to be enough to eat. I asked a doctor who was traveling with a sick soldier, and he said there was enough bread always but not enough meat. All the people I have talked to have laughed at the idea of not having enough to eat. But, they reminded me, the former bourgeoisie, of course, cannot get food cards...
>
> People are not afraid to talk. I asked about the GPU Secret Police and its terrible spy system. The young mining engineer who is traveling in this compartment laughed. He has a friend in the GPU. We have talked much in halting German most of the time, with an occasional Russian word looked up in my dictionary to help out. Last night we had a hot discussion in which an older man in the next compartment joined. The young fellow is a Communist at heart though not a member of the party. He does not like America because with all its wealth more people there than anywhere else do not work, which means exploitation. A Communist only works for the community, not for himself: he should not want any property, only food, clothing, a room. He said there was no further use for the family, but the older man, who is traveling with his wife and a thirteen-year-old boy, here argued at length in rapid Russian with the engineer and apparently differed on that point...
>
> The train is reasonably clean and comfortable. The two porters on this car are pleasant and keep it fairly neat...
>
> The country is beautiful, forest, stream, prairie, wheat fields, mountains, lakes, flowery meadows.

In the dining car that I described as "luxurious," I had a talk with an older man, fluent in French, who was a professor of zoology at the University of Moscow and had been studying the fisheries of Lake Baikal. More guarded in his response to my questions, he would say only that I should not take everything I was told at face value. He gave me the name of the zoological institute where he worked in Moscow, but when I later looked him up there, he was obviously fearful of continuing the contact.

I left the train at Novosibirsk, capital of Siberia and center of a new industrial and mining region. I had learned that a new railroad linking Siberia with Russian Turkestan, known as the "Turk-Sib," had recently been opened. It ran from Novosibirsk to Tashkent, and in an adventurous mood I decided to switch trains and take the new line south.

Three vivid memories dominate my recollections of Novosibirsk. The first is of a door handle coming off in my hand when I tried to enter my hotel room. The impression I received of the shoddiness of the new construction was to be continually reinforced.

The next vivid memory is of a dynamic young woman on the staff of the local newspaper who took me on a tour of a huge new factory complex under construction. In flimsy clothes and shivering from the cold, she pointed out the workers' housing and the school for their children, as the first buildings completed. Though only the foundations of the factory were visible in the muddy expanse, my guide described it in glowing terms as the world's largest factory for the manufacture of mining machinery, and went on to picture the wonderful new world—free of poverty and oppression—that the Soviets were building, while the old world I had come from was crumbling into ruin. Her sincerity and enthusiasm bowled me over.

My final memory of Novosibirsk is a scene in the railroad station the next day as I was trying to buy my ticket for Tashkent.

I was waiting in the head office of the station by special favor; outside the office the building was jammed with women and children and bundles crowding every inch of space. I couldn't make out who was in charge. It seemed to be an apple-faced sharp-nosed young woman who could smile at me but the next minute drive a poor woman intruder out of the office with a tongue-lashing. The office was in utter chaos. I never thought I would get my ticket on time. People drifted in and out, the favored ones sitting and smoking.

Through a tiny ticket window over a counter, I could see a harassed crowd outside trying to get information or tickets. There must have been a long line, but it never moved, for the people at the head of it never got what they wanted: always they were the same two distressed faces. When they were too insistent, the young woman would slam the shutter down with a laugh. But most of the time she munched her bread, joked with those about her, made telephone calls. It seemed perfect anarchy compared with any ticket office at home, efficient with mechanical white collar behind the wicket. God save the world from being run this way!

Finally I obtained a ticket and began the six-day journey to Tashkent in a crowded car with only a coffin-sized space to call my own. I had now to rely entirely on my meager but growing knowledge of Russian to communicate. I was going through an intensive course not only in the language but in the realities of life in the Soviet Union. For most Soviet citizens then, the rigors of daily life did not allow for much leisure, and talk with foreigners was always constrained, but on this long slow train journey I was, in effect, visiting half a dozen families, all with time on their hands and seemingly ready to talk. "Everybody," I wrote in a letter to my mother, mailed in Alma-Ata,

> is as kind as can be. One man who lives with his wife about two feet away, used his food ticket to buy me some borscht at a station. A soldier bought me a huge chunk of bread on his ticket. Watermelon, grapes and tomatoes have come my way.

A young member of the Communist party occupied the bunk above me for a couple of days; he spent hours trying to make me understand the virtues of this wonderful new society of freedom and equality the Party was building, and attempting to convince me that my capitalist world was on the brink of disaster. The power of his faith made me think of the early Christians. And in the railway carriage everybody—perhaps afraid of dissent—agreed with him.

I heard a different story in Tashkent from a casual meeting with a gaunt carpenter on a park bench who, with no one else to hear, apparently felt free to rail at the system: the only shoes he could buy were a size too small, and he could only relieve his agony by slitting them open. That was what the current slogan "The Five-Year Plan in Four Years" meant to him.

Tashkent, the capital of Uzbekistan, was the center of industrial development in central Asia under the plan, and I presented myself as a foreign journalist at the headquarters of the security police to get help in seeing some of the new factories. A puzzled and angry official told me no foreigners were allowed in this part of the Soviet Union, and I must leave at once for Moscow.

I gathered later that the reason for the ban on visits to Soviet Central Asia was the continuing resistance of the Moslem populations to Russian overlordship. Russia had conquered the area in the 1860s, and it was ruled as a colony by the Czars. It had been "liberated" by the Communists in the 1917 revolution, and thereafter a more enlightened policy was adopted, recognizing the linguistic and cultural differences of the region's many ethnic groups, and establishing a pattern of ostensibly autonomous republics and districts. But it was still conquered territory, with the Russians continuing to dominate, only now the controlling and unifying force was the Communist party dictatorship rather than the Czarist empire.

I saw no sign of overt resistance, and the situation was obviously not then critical, for I was able to persuade the security police to let me pursue my planned southern route toward Moscow by way of the ancient city of Samarkand and the Caspian Sea.

Leaving Tashkent, I had to force my way with my excess baggage on to a crowded hard-class railway car for three more days of rugged travel. Again and again, however, I was given friendly help.

First it was a group of students on their way to an engineering school in Ashkhabad. They crowded around me as I sat on the edge of my berth, my head protruding from under the bunk above—no room to sit up in these berths—and tried to converse with the aid of my dictionary. The group contained a Tartar, a Turkoman, and Uzbeks, besides Russians. They told me that since the Revolution the peoples of Central Asia were given equal opportunities for education with the Russians, and in their own languages.

Among the group was a fine-looking but bashful Uzbek girl studying medicine. She told me her parents were nomads still living in a tent, but the Revolution had given her a chance to become a doctor. The Communists have solved the problem of racial discrimination, I thought, and liberated women too.

Dumped with my baggage at an isolated railroad station marked "Samarkand," I had the good fortune to find an English-speaking professor of the Samarkand Pedagogical Institute, who had come to meet a colleague arriving from Moscow. The colleague was not on the train so he took me in tow, gave me lunch at his comfortable little house, and showed me the sights of the ancient town, including the tomb of Tamerlane. He avoided my questions about Communism, but as a physicist he bemoaned his isolation from scientific work being done in the rest of the world.

Another long train ride took me across the sandy Kara Kum Desert. Some Armenian students, all ardent Communists, were especially friendly. One was reading a book by Jack London. Some boys across the aisle were reading Russian translations of Kipling's *Jungle Book*, a Mexican War story by Mayne Reid, an American Indian story. I noted in my journal how every railroad station, even in Kazakstan, had its newsstand, stocked not with movie magazines and flashy cover girls, but with scientific and technical books, and literature. The Revolution, I decided, had brought literacy, learning, and culture to all the diverse peoples of the Russian Empire.

Crossing the Caspian Sea as a deck passenger on an overloaded little steamer, with only such deck space to sleep on as I could physically take possession of, I met further warmth. Two young army officers—one a blond Russian, the other a swarthy Tartar—both invalided to the Caucasus along with their wives and babies, occupied deck space next to mine. They helped me with my baggage, shared food with me, told me of the wonders that would be in their country.

Continuing my journey, I wrote in my journal:

And so to Baku and a hotel with spring beds, and a tourist bureau and concerts. After Turkestan it was civilization itself, though the comforts of the Hotel Novi Europa are meager enough. New buildings, even the best of them, give an impression of unkemptness and poverty in Russia. Windows are always broken. Furniture is of the plainest except what is of a decayed past. Toilets are almost always unspeakable. In new construction, previous provision of pipes and wiring is often ignored so there are always gaping holes and cracked plaster where these have been put in afterwards. Nothing is ever repaired except in the most cursory fashion.

The tourist agency, Intourist, now took me in tow. It showed me first a workers' club and cultural center (a huge building decorated in bright colors, housing two theaters, children's playrooms, a library). But it was largely empty and seemed dreary.

Next, I was proudly shown a vast new complex of apartment buildings with its own community hospital where, I was told, seven medical specialists gave free treatment to three hundred patients a day. I had to admit it was better than a slum, but from my standpoint, reared at 787 Prospect Street in New Haven, it was far from utopia.

What was more impressive was a symphony concert in an open air auditorium. The place was full, and I rejoiced in my journal that the "proletariat" was able to attend and support a daily program.

Leaving Baku, past forests of oil derricks, my train skirted the splendid peaks and green valleys of the Caucasus, a welcome relief after the deserts of Turkestan.

In Rostov-on-Don, where I broke my journey for a couple of days, I was taken by Intourist to visit a model *sovkhoz*, or state farm. This was the period when Soviet farms were being collectivized. The state farms were to be models for the *kholkozes*, which were ostensibly cooperatives. I was only dimly aware through posters and newspapers of the "war" on the *kulaks*—wealthy peasants—going on at this time, and only later came to wonder if some of the huddled crowds I had seen in railroad stations, and the occasional pitiful beggars in restaurants, were among the millions of victims of Stalin's fearful campaign. What I saw at the *sovkhoz* were rows of barrack-like buildings on a bleak prairie, and big assemblies of tractors, combines, and other farm machinery.

It seemed to make sense—the efficiency of large-scale mechanized farming, machines replacing the toil of the peasants, paved roads and bright lights, and the amenities of the city brought into the country to improve the quality of life in peasant villages. I tried to be optimistic in spite of the grimness of what I saw at the *sovkhoz*—no trees, no gardens, nothing of beauty—but I was ready to believe these would come.

The next day my Intourist guide took me to a new factory for the making of agricultural machinery. The symbols of industrialization—the factory and the machine—had met my eye on posters in every public place since I had entered the Soviet Union, and all the printed media were full of pictures of tractors, dams, and power lines, and the expected achievement of the goals of the first Five-Year Plan in Four Years. In this Rostov factory, for the first time, I had a sense not merely of expectations but of achievement. The great industrial complex was, as I wrote in my journal, "impressive":

> Three years ago planned, six months ago finished ahead of schedule, employing twenty thousand men and women housed in a specially built new city, it is all huge, alive. If we must have factories, this is the kind to have. I am always wondering if we must have them, and so I was as I walked down those endless corridors of noise that made me think of hell; but perhaps these people never wonder, perhaps they are all Thors and love the forge.
>
> Machines, monsters of machines, as unruly and fierce servants of man as the first wild horses: pouring liquid fire, pounding steel bars, slicing wooden beams, shaping, fashioning—spokes of countless wheels being banged into place by a mammoth arm, wheels upon wheels, iron wheels coming smoking out of the sand and the fire, din, smoke, shouting—and working the machines, pale and tired but seemingly not unhappy faces of women and men.
>
> And littering the broad avenues between the great white buildings are the machines produced, rakes, drills, harrows, plows, combines, wagons, all to get food more easily from the soil.
>
> The machines point so clearly to an easier future when no longer is there the stooping "man with a hoe." And here perhaps the cost is not too great. Already they are planting flower plots around the factory. How wonderful it would be if no one needed to work in the whole place except boys who love noise and dirt and machines.

I tried to believe in the reality of the image on the posters, of a proud, bare-breasted, heavily muscled giant—the proletarian worker beside his machine, confidently building the future.

Chapter 44

Moscow

September 17, 1931: I stood in the Red Square this evening as the sun was setting. It made the insane pinnacles of St. Basil's Cathedral and the exquisitely beautiful towers of the Kremlin stand out in red relief against a lowering sky. I felt almost as a Greek must have felt on first beholding Rome: here was now the center of the world. The vast square was strangely drab and bare: a few trucks and trams, a few soldiers, a long queue of people waiting to visit Lenin's tomb. Yet here is beginning—new Life, or

Death, I don't yet know which. And under the squat mausoleum lie the remains of the great prophet of Life—or Death—Lenin. There is a hard unloveliness about his mausoleum which perhaps is fitting, for as my enthusiasm for the new regime rises, my despair at its lack of charm grows deeper.

My ambivalence over Communism continued during the month I spent in Moscow, veering back and forth in an agony of indecision. Looking back now, it is not easy to recall why what I saw and heard had such an appeal. My revulsion at the ugliness and hardness of life in Russia under Communism was natural enough, but why did I feel so drawn to it, like a moth to a flame?

I had a room in the Grand Hotel, one of the three or four hotels that catered to foreigners. The tourist trade was at this time being actively promoted by the authorities as a source of foreign exchange, much needed for the purchase of foreign machinery and materials. Intourist already had a sizable bureaucracy of guides and interpreters to help the foreign tourist. Traveling alone in Soviet Central Asia, I had not been in the care of Intourist guides, and I took pride in using their services sparingly after reaching European Russia.

I was grateful for the shop that catered to foreign visitors, selling fancy goods not available to Russians for dollars and other foreign currencies. Here I spent an unconscionable amount in American Express checks to buy rich chocolate bars for which I especially hungered, and these I consumed guiltily in my hotel room, as a kind of solace for the deprivations the Revolution seemed to have in store for me.

A small foreign colony of Americans and Britons had settled in Moscow at that time, people like me, fascinated and repelled at the same time; we spent hours in hotel restaurants discussing the pros and cons of the Revolution, and what we saw of its results. I bought pamphlets in English—from a series called the Little Lenin Library—summarizing the works of Marx and Lenin.

I read the English-language *Moscow Daily News*, with its recurring stories of economic disaster and social upheaval in the rest of the world. The English pound went "off" gold during the month of my stay; there was a "hunger march" on Washington; the Japanese imperialists invaded Manchuria. My world was crumbling, while the triumphs of Soviet industrial production under the Five-Year Plan were everywhere proclaimed.

I had seen enough of the sleazy construction in the new towns and industrial complexes I had visited to be skeptical of the triumphs claimed, but still I could not doubt that in this country there was progress while the rest of the world was in decline.

I was encouraged in this view by a Mrs. Hanna, an enthusiastic if sentimental believer, who was running a small American travel agency in Moscow called the Open Road. She put me in touch with American and British contemporaries. But she told me that if I really wanted to understand what was going on, I should take part myself in the great work of building socialism. She told me some visitors like me had found jobs teaching English in one or another of the foreign language institutes then popular in Moscow. I told her I planned to be in Moscow only a month, but she said that even in that short time I could contribute something and learn a lot. She referred me to a Mrs. Borodin, who would be directing a fall program in foreign languages about to begin at an adult education center for Communist party members.

She told me Mrs. Borodin was the wife of Michael Borodin, who, as emissary of the Kremlin, had played a large part in the Chinese Communist movement in the 1920s. I had heard about Michael Borodin from my father, who had met him in 1927 while visiting China as a United States Senator. I recalled my father telling how he had probably saved the life of Mrs. Borodin. He had had an audience with the Manchurian warlord, Chang Tso-lin, then in control of Peking. Chang had boasted that his troops had raided the Soviet embassy and seized prominent Communist leaders including Mrs. Borodin, and she was to be executed the next day. My father commented that such an execution without trial would adversely affect Chang's standing abroad. The warlord angrily agreed to give her a trial before her execution. It was later learned that Peking Communists bribed the judge assigned to try her, and she escaped to Mongolia and then proceeded to Russia. She was now in charge of the foreign language institute, and her husband was editing the *Moscow Daily News*.

I sought her out. She seemed not to know of my father's role in saving her from execution, though she acknowledged that Americans in Peking at the time had been of great help. Actually it was the American journalist Vincent Sheean, as he later revealed in his autobiography *Personal History*, who was most closely involved in her flight. In any case she gave me a job.

And so for two or three weeks, I was in the pay of the Soviet Union as a part-time teacher of English. My duties were simply to provide an advanced class, then being organized, with practice in conversation.

Before beginning to teach, I attended an organizing session of about twenty Communist party members. I was struck by the democratic procedures to which they seemed accustomed: the group elected its own chairman who then battled with Mrs. Borodin in trying to control an often heated discussion on how to schedule class meetings. It was finally decided to meet two evenings a week from six to eight o'clock, a conclusion that could well have been announced in advance by the director but was actually a group consensus.

Toward the end of my class's second session, I learned what such a consensus meant. Noting that two or three of the students were dozing, I suggested we stop ten minutes early. I was promptly charged with attempting to shirk my duties, and we continued till closing time.

315

I was then invited by a friendly student in an army officer's uniform to go to the movies with him. We were joined by a young woman who I learned worked in the Moscow post office. She was not unattractive, and I soon found myself holding hands with her in the darkened theater. I felt I was getting on in my penetration of Soviet society.

I made a further inroad when Mrs. Borodin invited some of the young English and American teachers in her institute to her home to meet her husband, as described in my journal:

> The Borodins have a large one-room apartment, rather bare except for a scarlet Chinese cloth thrown over the beds. The bookshelves were full of American and English books on the Far East, on economics, on general political subjects. We were served coffee with sandwiches, caviar, cake, a very nice bourgeois collation. Mrs. Borodin did not talk much, but her husband, after a preliminary period of some suspicion, while he tramped about the room like a caged animal, opened up genially and talkatively. He was a thick-set man, reminding me of pictures of Stalin, except that his stiff bushy moustache was narrowed to a ridiculous pair of wisps. His face was seamed, strong and dark, rarely smiling: it somehow failed to appear aristocratic or intellectual but one wondered why.

He and his wife had once lived in Chicago and spoke English with not much accent. He warmed into a discussion of his beliefs. Communism was a distant ideal, but someday it would mean freedom, equality, and a high standard of living for all humankind. As I left, he assured me that my class status was not an obstacle to my becoming a Communist. His confidence in the possibility of my conversion I found profoundly disturbing.

From the outset of my brief teaching career, I brashly took advantage of the opportunity to encourage discussions of Communist theory and practice and the differences between the American and Soviet systems. In halting English rather than halting Russian, I was continuing the conversations I had had on my long train journeys. But in the third week, I became suspicious of the role of a large and florid woman member of the class, who had apparently once lived in the United States: she already spoke a fluent if crude English, and seemed not particularly interested in my correcting her pronunciation. She left the room at one point and returned with another woman whom I took to be an official of the institute. They sat in the back of the room and listened. I began to have an uncomfortable feeling that I was being spied on for ideological deviations. I became more careful in the opinions I expressed. The next week I resigned before I might be further investigated.

I was ready to go on my way. Yet none of the painful conflicts in my mind had been resolved. The professed goal of the Revolution, whether called socialism or communism, I was ready to accept: a society in which all people sought the common good was, it seemed to me, simply the Christian ideal of the Kingdom of God under another label. I had seen so many instances of kindly concern for me and for one another on the part of Soviet citizens that

I was inclined to believe that only in the Soviet Union and under Communist rule could a person be wholly a Christian. Yet the doctrine of a class struggle in which the "proletariat" would establish a dictatorship and "liquidate" the capitalist class was grim and hardly Christian.

I spent three days in Leningrad marveling at the beauty of its palaces and canals. Despite Communist ideology, the regime seemed bent on preserving the beauties of the past. And along with beauty, the memory of luxury seemed worth preserving. In one of the palaces in the outskirts now known as Dyetskoi Syelo, the living quarters of the last Czar and his family, remodeled for comfort and even coziness, had been preserved to the smallest detail, with family photographs still on the library table, and a children's slide with other nursery equipment forlornly inappropriate in a gilded salon.

Nostalgia for graciousness emerged in a performance I saw of Chekhov's *Three Sisters*: the lavish setting, the stylish clothes, the leisured elegance of society in the old regime were lovingly portrayed and, reminding me of the tasteful opulence of my grandmother's household, heightened my aversion to the harsh deprivations of the Revolution.

At the same time, my Puritan ancestors had cautioned me that luxury was wrong, and sacrifice of creature comforts was more likely to lead to heaven. My social conscience, now fully aroused after a year of observing the misery in which most people on the planet seemed to live, told me that the friendly egalitarianism I saw as the Communist goal should prevail over the selfish materialism of the capitalist world.

Most compelling was my growing conviction that socialism was efficient and capitalism was not. As another visitor to Russia about that time, Lincoln Steffens, succinctly put it: "I have been over into the future and it works."

Looking back now, more than sixty years later, it is easy to say I was wrong. What was then called the capitalist system has triumphed in competition with the centrally planned economies of the socialist world. We can now see why: human nature being what it is, the desire to serve the common good, noble as it is, fails as an incentive in comparison to the individual's need to advance his or her own welfare. No central planning can be as efficient a regulator of production and distribution of goods and services as the market. The centralization of economic power requires a centralization of political power, and the combination leads to the stagnation and corruption of a self-perpetuating bureaucratic totalitarianism.

Yet even if I could have followed that logic at the time, I would still have been moved by the ideal of a classless society. I knew nothing of the ways in which a market economy of private enterprise could be not only regulated to avoid its predicted doom but combined with a growing socialist sector organized not for profit but for the general welfare.

In any case, when I packed my books and papers and headed south, I was still torn between the attraction of much of what I had seen in the Soviet Union and my dismay at its ugliness. I visited Kiev, went on to Odessa, and

317

there took ship for Istanbul. It was now November, and cold weather was approaching in Russia. But across the Black Sea, summer seemed to be returning. My journal took on a new vitality:

> Dawn in the Bosporus: the sun rising over Asia and reddening the hilltops of Europe, white villas set among cypresses, bronzing oaks, a clustering harbor with fishermen's sailboats slowly tacking. Early morning sounds came from the land, cocks crowing, dogs barking, a wagon rumbling, like music. Here was grace and beauty and quietness. Here was the world breathing more easily.
>
> Finally Constantinople, recently renamed Istanbul, ancient battleground, home of Caesars and Sultans, with its minarets and domes, palaces and gardens, came resplendent into view. The new tall apartment houses looked like homes of comfort and prosperity after Russian jerry-building.
>
> Then to anchor in the Golden Horn, and to be rowed ashore in a tiny boat through the world's shipping, was a sort of liberation. More and more the things I had missed in Russia came to mind. Even the shouting and the stink of automobiles was pleasant. I noted well-dressed people in the streets, shops crowded with fruit and vegetables, colorful goods in the stores. And finally a hotel with courtesy and cleanliness and most decided comfort. Russia suddenly seems preposterously primitive. Or am I just too soft?

CHAPTER 45

The Appeal of Fascism

In Turkey, as in other countries I had visited, I used my father's status as a U.S. Senator to approach American diplomatic officials and my own status as a roving correspondent to talk with Turkish newspapermen and political figures. Though I "did" the usual tourist sites—I exulted in Hagia Sophia as one of the three most beautiful buildings in the world, the others being Chartres and the Taj Mahal—I was still giving priority to study of the contemporary world. In interviews with journalists in Istanbul and members of the Turkish parliament in Ankara, I learned of a revolutionary model quite different from that of Marx and Lenin.

Mustafa Kemal Atatürk and his Young Turks had changed the face of the country in less than ten years. The moribund Ottoman Empire that had made Turkey the "sick man of Europe" was replaced by Mustafa Kemal's dynamic new regime. Men's fezzes and women's veils were outlawed. The Arabic script was replaced by the Roman alphabet. Traditional Islamic ways of social control gave way to the disciplines of a modern state. Land reform and industrialization were raising living standards.

In Ankara I engaged in a long conversation with a newspaper editor who was also a high-ranking figure in the ruling party. Like the Communist party in Russia, he said, the new People's party provided a disciplined leadership to a population that was still predominantly a backward peasantry. Until a new, educated generation took over, democracy was out of the question. He denied a class basis to the regime, however. Turkey had no significant industrial proletariat, so the Marxist formulas did not apply. Private enterprise on the Western model was encouraged, but it was strictly controlled and guided by the political leadership.

Etatism was a word I heard more than once to describe this nationalistic and authoritarian system in which the state dominated economic and social development. The analogy to Italian fascism was sometimes cited, despite insistence on the purely Turkish road to a better society that Mustafa Kemal and his followers had charted. I began to feel I should not attempt a final judgment on communism till I had learned more about fascism.

Before going to Italy, however, I made a planned visit to Greece, where I had arranged to meet my brother Mitchell. Almost six years my junior, he had opted for a career as an artist, and, instead of following his brothers to Yale after graduating from Groton, he had headed for Paris, with classmate Fuller Potter, to study painting on the home ground of the French impressionists. He had planned to spend the winter in Greece, and there I joined him in mid-November of 1931.

For much of the six weeks we spent together, I engaged him in discussions of the agonizing uncertainties planted in my mind by my visit to Russia. The world we had been brought up in seemed to be falling apart. Which side of the barricades would I be on when the revolution came? Mitch agreed with me about the precarious state of the world, and his sympathies were with the oppressed rather than with oppressors. But having chosen to be an artist, he was not subject to the compelling demand of an aroused social conscience to choose sides and become engaged—as I was.

We lived in a pension, and while he was out painting, I read history and anthropology and wrote poetry. I also followed my established routine of interviewing political leaders, including the then premier Eleutherios Venizelos and the foreign minister. I engaged them in a discussion of the world economic crisis and the prospects for a Communist revolution; no doubt thinking that my newspaper connections were important, they expressed their concern over America's aloofness from Europe's problems.

Meanwhile "the inner struggle over Communism goes on," as I wrote in my journal on December 11:

> Were Marx's predictions of the inevitable collapse of capitalism and the
> historical necessity of proletarian revolution valid? And must I take sides?
> It seems hopeless to try to decide, for nothing short of a lifetime study of

history and economics and a thoroughly established philosophy of life would be sufficient to make a sound judgment possible. I feel at the least I must wait till I have studied Fascism and Socialism in Europe, and such economics as I can muster, and then have spent a few years in hard work on the ground at home. Yet, having settled down to that extent, could I ever take flight again? The day of doom is close, close. And I am not ready.

Two days later I did come to what I thought was a decision. I recorded the event in my journal in what I felt were fateful words for my entire future:

At 11:30 p.m. on December 13th, 1931, in the cafe lobby of a theater, in the intermission of a sentimental movie, I became a Communist.

What did it mean to say I had become a Communist? I had not become a Marxist. That would require further study, and my skepticism about doctrines of any kind would ultimately leave me unconvinced. Moreover my enthusiasm for what I had seen of Communist Russia was riddled with doubts and misgivings. Yet I felt at the time as if I had had a religious conversion. And a few days later I continued:

I don't know just what it means yet, beyond my assurance that it does mean something: perhaps only that I am now devoted to the cause of the underdog. Something will yet come from that declaration.

The same note of concern for the poor appears in my journal a couple of weeks later in Naples. I was ensconced in a luxury hotel room with a fine view of the Bay and Vesuvius. But it was January in the depths of the Great Depression.

The Grand Hotel is a melancholy place. I have seen only two other guests and doubt if there are more. To sit in the dining room alone and have three full-dressed waiters standing around me is so absurd I could laugh aloud. It is the patent absurdity of the whole present system, which makes the superior things of life the monopoly of a wealthy (even foreign) class; and when that class stays home all the paraphernalia of their enjoyments is unused. As for allowing the people to benefit who most need and would most appreciate a little luxury, that would never enter the head of anyone. We are all mad.

I went on to consider another madness, the madness of nationalism. It was now 1932 and Hitler was reaching for power. Fear of war was in the air.

These Europeans are much alike in habit and looks and thoughts. The idea of their engaging in mutual slaughter is as ridiculous as it was in the case of the Greek city states. The only sphere for autonomy of a national or linguistic or racial group is in its culture: political autonomy is a false shibboleth, and the cause of most of Europe's woes. I have been reading Harold Laski's *Grammar of Politics*. His plea for international government I find completely convincing.

320

My mind was stretching. I had become a social reformer. I wanted to reform not only my own society but the whole world. Clearly the world was a single interdependent community and should be governed as such. But how? *The Communist Manifesto*, with which I was by this time familiar, conceived of the "workers of the world" as the instrument to establish not only a new social order but a unified world. And Lenin had focused Marx's vision, as I had gathered from my "Little Lenin Library," by giving the leading role to a disciplined party to effectuate the "dictatorship of the proletariat." But my mind had rebelled against the emphasis on the role of the industrial working class.

My childhood rearing had made me fearful of the "muckers" from the industrial districts of New Haven. And the recent summer jobs I had taken, especially the spell of factory labor, to find out "how the other half lives," while somewhat relieving my fears, had given me a sense of the pitiful weakness and degradation of the industrial working class rather than of any latent powers of leadership. Still I had accepted the goal of socialism—as a world-wide society planned and operated for human welfare—and the need for a disciplined leadership to achieve it.

In Rome I presented myself, as I had in other national capitals, to the American ambassador. Again, as the son of a U.S. Senator and as a newspaperman, I was treated with deference and given official introductions to significant figures in the hierarchy of Mussolini's government. I was impressed by the high quality of these professional men, largely intellectuals, some with ties to the landed aristocracy. They spoke of the high aims of Fascismo, and I duly reported my impressions in my journal:

> The ideal of Fascism is not equality or democracy, but it does believe in giving every individual as nearly equal a start and as nearly equal an opportunity as possible.

I was told of the greatly expanded services for mothers and children, and the *Dopo Lavoro* or "after work" organization that provided leisure-time opportunities for all parts of the population. I was reminded of the "palaces of culture" I had been shown in the Soviet Union, but when I saw a large group of young people carrying skis on their way to a mountain holiday organized by Dopo Lavoro, I felt the Fascists were aiming at an even higher level of "culture" for the masses.

Mussolini was then at the peak of his power, and with Hitler still a semi-comic figure in the wings, the Italian leader loomed larger than any other Western European. On a second visit to the American embassy, the ambassador offered to request an interview for me with Il Duce. He suggested that I mention my recent visit to Russia as a means of arousing Mussolini's interest and getting him to talk. I was also told that he was learning English and liked to practice conversing in English.

The interview was arranged. At the appointed time, I presented myself at the door of the Palazzo Venezia. I was ushered through strangely empty hallways and up a vast marble staircase, and left alone in a high-ceilinged ante-room. In a few minutes a door opened, and a flunky in a tailcoat ushered me into a great ballroom where at the far end, as if seen through the wrong end of a telescope, I made out a little balding man seated at a desk. My heart was pounding as I walked across what seemed half a mile of marble floor. Putting down a paperback book with the pages open as if impatient to resume his reading, the man rose and came around the desk to greet me cordially in English, then seated me in a chair facing him.

I quickly launched into the suggested topic, saying I had just spent three months making a study of Soviet Communism, and was now in Italy making a comparable study of Fascism. I hastened to add that I realized Communism and Fascism were at opposite poles and hardly to be compared.

This opening sparked an unexpected response.

"Fascism and Communism are not opposites," he expostulated. "Fascism is Socialism. Fascism is Communism. We have the same aims."

I knew that he had once been a socialist and had left the party primarily because of its internationalist stance at the outbreak of World War I, joining a militant nationalist movement before organizing the Fascist party. But this was an amazing statement. He insisted that Fascism was not concerned with preserving capitalism but with controlling capitalism in the interest of the whole nation.

He asked what I had seen in Russia, and I told him of my impressions of rapid economic progress under the first Five-Year Plan.

His interest was clearly aroused. A telephone on his desk rang. He lifted it briefly off its hook without answering it, while putting a question to me, as if to signal that he wanted the interview to continue. The question, in his halting English, was about the impact of collective farming on the peasants—pronouncing the word "peesents" till at his request I corrected him. I boldly suggested that I was fluent in French, and he might find that language easier than English. He seemed a little taken aback, and I quailed at my presumption, but the interview went on in French.

As for the collectivization program, in which, as it is now known, millions of peasants died, I knew little and could only deplore the fanaticism with which the Communists were pursuing their goals. The man whom I considered the second most powerful man in Europe broke in to defend Stalin.

"Fanaticism is needed to accomplish any great work," he declaimed. "It is faith that moves mountains. After a task is finished, then you can afford to be liberal, to look at both sides." I was reminded of the fervor of some of the young Communists I had met in the Soviet Union.

Italy, he continued, his voice rising, needed discipline and pride in her national heritage if she was to be restored to greatness. His eyes bulged as he went on to declaim as if he were on a balcony making a speech to thousands.

322

I got up to leave. He became fatherly, encouraging me to continue my studies.

As I walked back to my pension, I was treading on air, overwhelmed by the attention he had paid me. I was almost ready to believe Fascism provided a means of achieving a planned society and of assuring the welfare of the whole population without liquidating the ruling class. That seemed to be Mussolini's message.

I read about the Fascist program for disciplining private enterprise and compelling it to serve the national interest, the so-called corporative state. In each industry, owners, workers, and the public were to be represented in a governing body that would rationalize the industry and make it conform to the overall needs of the nation. It was an idea that owed something to the anarcho-syndicalists on the one hand and Roman Catholic theorists on the other, and was soon to become a feature of Roosevelt's National Recovery Administration under the symbol of the Blue Eagle.

I particularly emphasized this feature of Italian Fascism in an article I wrote at the time for one of the Connecticut newspapers on my string:

> The "corporative" idea is bringing Italy closer and closer to Socialism. Freedom of economic life without governmental interference is considered an outworn shibboleth. Instead governmental regulation is held natural and necessary under modern conditions. This regulation may involve subsidizing weak enterprises, preventing undue competition, forming mergers, indirect control of prices and wages, government ownership or control where necessary, and so on. Private ownership and private initiative are still the general rule, and it is the declared policy of the government to uphold them. But more and more, especially in the exigencies of the economic crisis, the government takes an active part in the economic life of the country. This action is clearly consistent with the theory of the supremacy of the State over all the life of the country.
>
> These indications are sufficient to show the far-reaching nature of the Fascist Revolution and to suggest that it is not yet nearly completed. When one adds to this development of a new theory of the relations between government and economics, the great effort that the government is making to raise the standard of living of its people at all points, the housing and recreational and cultural facilities of the laboring class, the care of women and children, the educating and propagandizing of the whole people to a new conception of national community, it will be seen how vast is the transformation that the Fascists are trying to bring about.

The economic and social program being pushed by Mussolini and the Fascist party clearly implied continuing repression—though a less cruel and destructive dictatorship, it seemed to me, than that of the Soviets. And there were democratic features in the representative assemblies of the corporative state.

So I was favorably impressed by much of what I saw in Italy in early 1932. At the same time, I was repelled by the nationalist bombast that led Mussolini— even in a private interview—to roll his eyes and pound his desk in a declamation on Italy's imperial destiny.

While in Rome, I lived in a pension near the gardens of the Villa Borghese. I took Italian lessons with one of my fellow boarders and practiced my still rudimentary Italian at the boarding-house table. I spent my days reading, writing, sightseeing. My principal objective was to learn what I could about Italian Fascism, and with the help of people at the American embassy, I made many contacts in the American colony and the diplomatic world as well as with government officials. But in line with the original purposes of my travels, I was also trying to learn what I could about life, and this quest was forwarded by my again falling in love.

Jane Ewell was a first cousin of a school friend of mine, Sherrill Bigelow, and it was probably through a letter from him that I heard she was traveling in Italy with her mother. I sought her out at their hotel. Her mother, a proper Bostonian, found me eligible and invited me to join them on a motor tour of the hill towns, including Perugia, Siena, and Assisi. Jane, barely out of her teens, was charming and high-spirited, but more interested in horses and dogs and a gay life than in fascism and communism. Still we found each other mutually attractive. Ever self-analytical, I wrote in my journal:

> While I am talking bad Italian to Fascist officials and visiting medieval cities, the world is drawing ever nearer the abyss—and I am in love. It is love, really, that matters. This month will either see the world go berserk, or start recovering from wars and horrors, but that is an old story that will be told in newspapers of the year 1932, and I am only concerned with a sweet face that smiles and offers gentle but passionate lips.

I never allowed myself to go beyond her lips. I was ready not just for an affair but for marriage. She seemed too young and vulnerable, and I felt, probably with good reason, that she would never be able to keep up with my grandiose dreams for myself and the world. But the glow that accompanied being with her on excursions or over an evening glass of wine colored all my days in Italy.

Ever since my encounter with Cynthia Davis in Manila, I had continued to think I was still in love with her. At this point I felt I had to choose between them. When I now heard Cynthia was in Paris, I made a sudden decision to go see her and check out my feelings for her before going further with Jane. On meeting Cynthia at a cafe on the Champs-Elysées, I found her no longer the simple flower girl I had preserved as my image but a sophisticated ornament of Paris society, to me no longer attractive.

My amorous thoughts could now be focused on Jane. I was moved not simply by sexual desire. The future that lay ahead of me on my return from my world tour included marriage and a family as increasingly insistent goals, and Jane now seemed the way to reach them. But when I began to think of her as the mother of my children, I was reminded of an opinion, voiced by a doctor in the Yale infirmary during my sophomore year in college, that I would probably never be able to have children: I had had a bad case of mumps, complicated by inflammation of my pancreas and my testicles. I had not taken the opinion too seriously at the time, but now that I was definitely considering making an offer of marriage, I wanted a current evaluation of my condition. I could not propose to so honest a person as Jane without my knowing and telling her how much of a husband I could be.

In Geneva I sought out a specialist. After microscopic examination of a sample of semen, he confirmed the Yale doctor's judgment: I was almost certainly incapable of fathering a child.

When I went on from Geneva to a rendezvous with Jane at an Austrian ski resort, I was prepared to tell her that if I were indeed sterile I would not object to her being impregnated by another man's sperm. However, I never got around to telling her. When I first saw her on the ski slopes as an awkward and timid novice instead of the glamorous princess I had been dreaming about, the flame suddenly flickered and went out, and I found I was no longer in love with her. Actually the doctors' opinions were proved wrong a few years later under fateful circumstances to be related in due course.

Although I had seen a doctor for affairs of the heart, my visit to Geneva in that winter of 1932 had been prompted by events on the world stage. Six months before, just after I had crossed Manchuria on my way into the Soviet Union, Japanese military forces in Mukden had taken control of the province and, in coordination with a seizure of power by militant nationalists in Tokyo, had started a process of aggression against northern China that was in effect the opening round of World War II. China had appealed to the League of Nations for sanctions against Japan, and now in March a formal meeting of the League was about to be held in Geneva to consider the case. It was superimposed on continuing sessions of the Disarmament Conference that had opened in February with participation not only of League members but of the United States and the Soviet Union.

I had a sense of the world's fate being decided in Geneva and went there to watch. What I saw was disappointing. "It seemed that the city should be humming with the reverberations of this memorable period," I wrote in my journal,

> but instead the Geneva newspapers only mentioned the League's and the Disarmament Conference's work in a small back paragraph, beyond the Municipal Council news. The ramshackle old hotel that houses the League Secretariat made it seem like a temporary convention of some organization that could not afford very fine quarters. Finally the people in evidence were disquietingly uninspiring.
>
> I went to get a press gallery ticket and found the office behind a little propaganda bureau where earnest American women were trying to sell

325

literature about the League; a harassed and ineffective Italian distributed tickets, but only after various formalities and wirepulling. I had two talks with another harassed gentleman, an American in charge of the Information Section, a Mr. Sweetser, whose inspirational posters about the League's work were tacked up in the hall. He was a thorough YMCA type, and what with the bespectacled women interested in uplift who hurried around the corridors, the whole League began to take on the look of a YMCA convention.

In the main hall where the Assembly was to convene in two days, strange people were milling about from all countries, with Orientals, young earnest ones, particularly in evidence. It seemed an odd collection of freaky people.

It is, of course, unfair to draw conclusions so soon. But I felt the whole show at once tragic beyond comprehension, and ludicrous to the point of hilarity. Here is the hope of the world—peace, millions of lives, perhaps civilization itself may depend on what these people can do. Yet the shadow of Woodrow Wilson, the academic, the impractical professor, the American idealist, hangs over it as does his picture here and there.

No one I talked to expects much from the Assembly, yet there seems to be a feeling that if it fails the League is permanently done for. It appears to me that a new League will be necessary before long.

I attended the opening session a couple of days later on March 3. With little formality, after some remarks by the presiding officer Paul Boncour, the Chinese and Japanese spokesmen began to present their cases. I felt it a "historic day," as "one of the great powers of the world is brought to the bar of justice at which most of the world's nations are represented." It might have been the opening of a new era. Yet even before the proceedings began, they were clearly only a charade. Power lay in those days not with leaderless black-coated diplomats but with Frankenstein monsters in jackboots.

CHAPTER 46

Blueprint for an American Utopia

At the end of March 1932, I was nearing the end of my freewheeling travels. I had three months more of the two years I had set aside to round out my education. By summer I knew I must get back into some kind of harness. I had planned to start practicing law as a base for a career in politics, but what I had seen of a world in the throes of revolutionary change had irremediably altered my conception of a career in politics.

I had become convinced that the ordered upper-class society in which I had been brought up—a society of private wealth and public empire—was crumbling. I saw it being replaced by collectivist regimes. I was persuaded that the Communist system was working in the Soviet Union, but its Marxist-Leninist ideology I found unconvincing and pedantic, and I was appalled at how much I would have to renounce in a Communist revolution.

Italian Fascism seemed to provide a more attractive means of achieving a collectivist order. With its mass base in the middle classes, it seemed more applicable to American conditions than a program that would make the proletariat the ruling class, but its fanatic nationalism offended me. So feeling an urge to learn more about democratic roads to socialism, I decided to spend my remaining time in Germany and England. The Weimar Republic was, to be sure, a battleground for the clashing forces of Communism and Hitler's brand of Fascism, but it was also the home of Social Democracy. Britain's Labor party, under the ideological spur of the Fabians, had been developing its own program for achieving democratic socialism.

I spent two months in Berlin, mostly as a boarder in the home of a middle-class family of Social Democrats. On May Day, I went with two younger members of the family to a big party gathering:

> It was a gay dance for young people and the boy and girl from this family were there. The hall was hung with red banners. It was a delightfully homely gathering, simple, democratic. Before the war the children of the upper and lower classes would not have mixed as here. Here was the spirit of the village green brought into the city, as an augury of what the future may be.
>
> The world can be such a lovely place. I am becoming more and more of a utopian. I went last Saturday with Bill Hinkle [a Groton and Yale classmate then living in Berlin] to spend a day in the sun, wind, and water on one of the lakes near Berlin. It was indescribably lovely, a little village, woods, villas, breezy weather, and we sunned ourselves with almost nothing on. Cheap, almost available to all.
>
> I have never seen such a vision of what the world could be like. It could be so great and glorious for all. I could hardly wish for more for anyone than I have had, and my own opportunities almost represent the ideal for me. But I can see the day when no one will be less fortunate than I have been—though it may be centuries before the glad day comes.

After reading George Bernard Shaw's *Intelligent Woman's Guide to Socialism and Capitalism*, I had been persuaded that if we organized the production and distribution of wealth intelligently, if we put the idle men and idle resources to work, we could all be rich. But how could the potential be made real?

I went to mass meetings of Communists, Nazis, and Social Democrats; I talked to journalists, diplomats, and members of the Reichstag. I visited an office in the slum district of Wedding where thousands of gaunt men and women came to get their dole.

327

I came to some conclusions about the possibility of achieving socialism by democratic parliamentary methods. The Weimar Republic had given Germany a welfare state of public housing and social security, but the Social Democratic party had failed to develop either a program or a leadership able to transform the collapsing market system into an effective planned economy. Its base in organized labor left the unorganized and unemployed subject to the rival demagogies of the Nazis and the Communists, and it denigrated the increasingly important but increasingly disaffected lower middle classes as the "petite bourgeoisie." Moreover, the parliamentary process itself began to seem incapable of achieving the necessary changes.

My reaction to a day spent watching the Reichstag in session was summed up in a letter I wrote home:

> A Communist denounced all the other parties as slaves of big business and brutal scoundrels, and when he finished speaking, the eighty Communist members cheered lustily, and all marched out of the chamber so as to have nothing to do with the rest of the members or listen to their speeches. Then a Hitler member got up and made a fiery speech calling the Social Democrats and the Centrists all the names in the calendar, while they tried to drown him out by laughing and shouting till the chamber was in an uproar. And the Social Democrats hate the Centrists, with whom they have been cooperating, as the paid representatives of the Pope. And there are numerous smaller parties, all sure they are right and everyone else is wrong.

This was "pandemonium" and I was more than ever dubious of the possibility of peaceful change.

I was hardly able to predict what happened less than a year later when a fire destroyed part of the Reichstag building and provided a pretext for Hitler to take power. But some of the rationale for the Nazi movement was brought home to me by a contact I made at this time with a member of the landed aristocracy, Count Grote, heir to a vast estate in Mecklenburg. A sister-in-law of mine had given me an introduction to his American wife, Rachel, who was an old school friend of hers. I met the count and countess in Berlin and was duly invited to visit them on their estate.

Fritz and Rachel lived in an enormous but crumbling mansion, a hundred-year-old manor house surrounded by vast stretches of rich farmland. They told me that Communist propaganda had been reaching their workforce, landless peasants who cultivated the eight-thousand-acre estate and lived in a squalid village outside the manor house gates. The Grotes, despite an instinctive dislike for Hitler and his lower-class following, had come to see the Nazi movement as the only effective defense against a Communist revolution. They had joined the party and promoted the organization of a party unit in the village, with one of their peasants as leader and Fritz participating democratically as a follower. They had put their Cadillac in dead storage and drove only a battered old car of German make when in residence. The class struggle was under control.

A few years later, after Hitler's conquest of the low countries, Fritz was put in charge of civil affairs in the Netherlands, but was so horrified by the realities of Nazi rule that he sought transfer to active military duty on the eastern front, and there was killed. In the last months of the war, Rachel fled with her children from the advancing Red Army, and eventually made her way back to America.

At the end of my Berlin stay, I was finally coming to a resolution of the conflict between the demands of my social conscience and my plans for a political career. I considered myself now a socialist rather than a Communist. Yet I was sure the socialist label, while popular in Europe, was to be avoided in America as politically unsalable. Moreover, I was unable to accept the Marxist theory that the industrial working class would lead the transition to socialism. I saw the Fascist movements in Italy and Germany as revolutionary movements that drew their strength from unemployed white-collar workers and other middle-class elements. I tried to imagine how the restlessness of the threatened middle classes might become the instrument for a democratic transition to socialism.

On April 27, 1932, I wrote in my journal:

> My mind has been running on grandiose ideas the last few days. I fear my own unhealthy ambition, yet I know it is not merely my ambition that makes me think I could help awaken America. What the country needs is a great breath of fresh air, common-sense idealism which would give it a new perspective.
>
> I have conceived the idea of an organized movement calling itself the Community, which would appeal alike from the selfish individualism of capitalism to the selfish sectionalism of nationalism. Revolting against hunger in the midst of plenty, it would emphasize the Christian ideal of neighborliness. It would promote a new form of socialism suited to the American temperament. It would appeal to the active community spirit of America. It would be frankly utopian in its ultimate ideal, but insisting on the practicability of the utopia it preaches, and in its immediate program limited by common sense.
>
> It is a dream. But it is capable of fulfillment.
>
> I am thinking of preparing the road for it with a booklet called "Common Sense."

Actually the manuscript I began to put together then and finished some weeks later had a longer title, "Common Sense and the Community," while the magazine I helped organize before the year was out was called *Common Sense.* But in May, I was only at the beginning of formulating a prospectus.

After Berlin, I went on to Paris and then returned to London, the first stopping place on my world tour, and in both places found a mood of deep pessimism. In London I obtained an interview with a Labor party leader who had been given a title so the party could have a voice in the House of Lords. Lord Morley in formal attire greeted me in an elaborately decorated reception room in the Lords' wing of the Houses of Parliament, and in the well-modulated voice of an Eton and Cambridge education, told me blandly that a revolution was imminent and that it would be a good thing if it toppled the rotten class-ridden British social order.

Yet I could see little evidence to support his expectations. I watched a Communist party rally of the unemployed in Trafalgar Square and found it dispirited and unimpressive. I interviewed Harold Laski and other left-wing intellectuals, and gathered that the Labor party, despite its vague socialist goals, was too much dominated by conservative trade-union leaders, anxious to preserve past gains, to provide a revolutionary leadership.

How had I been persuaded in Russia that a worldwide Communist revolution was historically predestined? I decided to retest what I had taken to be almost self-evident six months before, and undertook a quick return visit to the Soviet Union. Back in Moscow, I looked up a young Briton with whom I had had long soul searchings on my previous visit. He had since joined the Communist party, but being an insider had only given him a closer insight into the defects of the system. My journal was dotted with references to squalor, hunger, all-night queues. Yet if Moscow was a slum, I was still able to see it as a "glorious" slum, and its "miserable" people as still "heroic"—"working, working, working, forever on the go, often in circles, yet generally forward, exulting over the doom of the rest of the world."

I renewed acquaintance with a young woman, a few years older than I, whom I had first met in the English class I had taught the preceding autumn. Her father, a Czarist army officer, had died in the Revolution, as had her mother. She had protected and raised a younger brother. Married early, she had borne two children, both of whom had died young; now divorced, she was living in a one-room apartment with her younger brother, still a student. She worked in the post office. We were attracted to each other, and carried on a passionate love affair on a couple of long evenings in her apartment, while her brother discreetly stayed away. A vivid memory remains of my crossing Red Square at three o'clock in the morning after one such evening, with a red sunrise lighting up the clock on a Kremlin tower, and not another human being in sight. Anya's placid cynicism about what was happening in the Soviet Union helped dispel the remnants of my former enthusiasm for a Communist-style revolution. Yet as I returned to London on a reassuringly comfortable Soviet steamer, I still believed the Communists would succeed with their Five-Year Plan while the rest of the world would have to find other answers to the collapse of the old order.

The end of my travels was now only a month off. I felt I had the answers to the dilemmas that had long troubled me. It remained only to put my manifesto into final form.

In the meantime I was making the most of a new wave of self-confidence. I had renewed the contact with Lady Astor made on my earlier visit to London, and perhaps finding my sudden conversion to a belief in socialism of some interest, she invited me to visit her at Cliveden, the great estate overlooking the upper Thames that was to become notorious as the hotbed of "appeasement" a few years later. A taxi at the local station took me through the gates and up a tree-lined avenue to the portico of the great house, where I was relieved of my bag by a uniformed footman. He ushered me up the grand staircase to my room and embarrassed me by unpacking my bag and laying out my things, including not only my dinner jacket but also a few odd rubles left from my Moscow trip. At dinner I expounded my views on the success of the Soviets' first Five-Year Plan, and was surprised at the support I received from the Astors' student son David. He railed at his parents for the lavishness of their surroundings in comparison to the hunger and misery of the masses. Lady Astor contented herself with good-naturedly chiding us youngsters for claiming to have answers to all the world's problems.

Later I received formal invitations from Lady Astor to receptions at her London house in Berkeley Square. On one occasion the Prince of Wales, who a few years later was to become briefly King Edward VIII, was a guest, and on another I met the Duke and Duchess of York, who would in time become George VI and Queen Elizabeth. On still another occasion, George Bernard Shaw and Helen Keller were the celebrities.

I was now moving in the highest circles. I was glad that I had brought along my full-dress accoutrements of white tie and tails—my wardrobe trunk had followed me to India and the Far East, and across Siberia—and now at last all my finery was to be displayed. I even had a top hat, sent from home for the London season at my request. At the same time I was fashioning my own version of revolution.

I retired to an ancient inn in Winchester where as a boy traveling with my parents I had first made contact with British aristocracy, and there in the week remaining before my sailing date, I put the final touches on the manifesto I had been working on for months.

The vision I had of a perfect world was so overwhelmingly bright and obvious that I imagined my manifesto as having an impact as immediate as Thomas Paine's *Common Sense* at the time of the American Revolution, and as powerful as Karl Marx's *Communist Manifesto* in the nineteenth century. I saw my program doing for America what Lenin's Communist program seemed to be doing in the Soviet Union or Mussolini's Fascism in Italy, transforming a bankrupt capitalism into socialism.

Capitalism meant idle workers and idle productive capacity. A rational system would replace production for profit with production for use. This would require effective governmental control of the entire economy by an enlightened elite of technical experts. The inception of the new system would require a measure of dictatorship, willing and able to counter the violence to be expected from the wealthy minority that would suffer loss. But the ultimate goal was a democratic society in which all people would cooperate willingly in the service of the common good. I cited Communist Russia and Fascist Italy as having successfully initiated such a transition, but emphasized that America could and should find its distinctive way to the new social and economic order.

I was now ready to dedicate myself to the task of persuading the American public to accept this vision. My medium would be a magazine.

CHAPTER 47

Common Sense

When I told my father on my return from my travels that I was not going on with my law career but intended to be a journalist, he was obviously disturbed, but he simply asked me if I now planned to go to the Columbia School of Journalism. I had no such intention. I had a sense of mission, a message to proclaim so powerful and appealing that no professional training seemed called for. As for the skills necessary to publish a magazine, I felt my experience as editor-in-chief of my school publication, *The Grotonian,* and as a member of the *Yale Law Journal* editorial board had given me enough training for the task. Where then to begin?

I discussed my project with Sylvia. Her image had come to dominate my thoughts of marriage. The romantic attachments that had possessed me on my travels had all faded out with time and distance, and I was back where I had been at the start of my travels: I saw Sylvia as an ideal partner, with whom unfortunately I was not in love.

During the two years of our separation, we had corresponded occasionally. I knew that while pursuing graduate studies in psychology at the University of Berlin, she had become engaged to a college classmate of mine but that the engagement had been broken off by him. (I did not learn till later how deeply traumatic this rejection had been for her.) She could not afford further graduate studies and was now looking for work. She had had secretarial training after graduating from Bryn Mawr and had recently been employed as private secretary to a visiting German lecturer. But she was now at loose ends. She liked my ideas for a magazine, and I thought if she worked with me on my project our closeness might ripen into love. It was understood between us that if the project got off the ground she would have a part in it. But I needed a more professional staff.

332

John Chamberlain was the only person I knew whose interests and experience might be appropriate for a left-wing magazine. Though he was two years ahead of me at Yale, I had known him as a genial fellow member of Zeta Psi fraternity. He had started a career in journalism at the *New York Times* and had written *Farewell to Reform*, a book about the American progressive movement, which suggested that more than liberal reform was needed to meet the present crisis. He showed an interest in my magazine project and promised to write for it if it got under way, but could not see his way clear to leaving the *Times* and joining me in a risky new venture. He suggested I contact William Harlan Hale, a brilliant younger man just a year out of Yale, now launched on a writing career at *Vanity Fair*. I went to see Hale, who also was interested in my project, but he could not be persuaded to give up his promising connections to the magazine world.

A few weeks later I learned that Hale's connection with *Vanity Fair* went beyond a paying job. Clare Boothe Brokaw was the editor, and she and Hale had apparently found each other mutually attractive. He told her about me. She wanted to meet a real revolutionist, so he invited me to have dinner with them at a fancy restaurant where we had much to talk about. Dancing with Clare, I fell under the siren spell that was later to make her the wife of Henry Luce, the head of the *Time-Life-Fortune* empire. I thought she was equally attracted to me. But when after dinner Hale announced they were going on to a nightclub, and I expected to be included, I suddenly found myself standing alone on the sidewalk as they drove off in a taxi.

Hale told me about Selden Rodman. He and Rodman had edited and published an iconoclastic student magazine at Yale known as the *Harkness Hoot*, the name derived from its critique of the flamboyant Gothic that Edward Harkness's millions had imposed on the expanding Yale campus. According to Hale, Rodman hoped to carry on his revolt against the establishment on a larger stage and had talked about starting a new left-wing magazine of national circulation.

I sought out Rodman during the summer of 1932, and almost immediately we found each other's journalistic ideas congenial. He read my "Common Sense and the Community," with its advocacy of a political and social revolution, and I learned about the cultural revolution he and Hale had launched at Yale. His interests were more in the arts than in politics or economics. I had considered—and still consider—the Harkness tower beautiful, but I did not quarrel with his iconoclasm, and he was ready to accept without question my belief that the capitalist system was doomed and a social revolution inevitable.

We discussed the financial aspects of starting a new magazine. We had heard that the *New Yorker* had succeeded a few years earlier with an initial capital of $100,000. Our own personal resources were limited: Selden said he had no capital to invest. He had a small private income, which had enabled him to travel abroad for a year after his Yale graduation in 1931, but far from being able to contribute to our venture, he would need a salary.

My own financial situation was more favorable. At this point, my brothers and I were each assured of annual incomes of two thousand dollars from Annie Tiffany Mitchell's trust for her grandchildren. At the depth of the Depression in 1932, two thousand dollars a year was more than ample for a bachelor to live in comfort. I told Selden I could get along without a salary until the new magazine became profitable.

Moreover, I could provide a substantial part of the $50,000 in capital we estimated as our minimum need. For in this same year, 1932, my grandmother, then in her late eighties, distributed her holdings in Tiffany & Co. to her children and grandchildren. The Tiffany shares, then worth over a million dollars, were divided into equal parts, and before the year was out, she distributed one-third to my mother, one-third to my aunt Charly Mitchell Jeans, and the remaining one-third to her eight grandchildren, to be divided equally among the seven Bingham brothers and Olivia Jeans.

I had just received my portion of the distribution, forty-one shares. I was willing to pledge my shares as an underwriting fund, and ultimately I put into the magazine something over $30,000 derived from their sale.

Rodman and I set out to raise outside funds. I heard of some wealthy young Harvard men who were known to give to radical causes. Like me, Corliss Lamont, son of a Morgan partner, had visited Russia and had been favorably impressed with the Soviet experiment. I met him for lunch at the Harvard Club. He was sympathetic with my planned venture but was obviously not prepared to be an angel. He put me in touch with two other Harvard men, Frederick and Osgood Field, heirs of the Vanderbilt fortune, and they too expressed interest but were unpersuaded to become more than token contributors. (Fifty years later Frederick Field, in his autobiography *From Right to Left*, disclosed that in the 1930s he had joined the Communist party and was subsidizing the party-line *New Masses*.)

Another wealthy young radical willing to contribute, with indications of more to come if the magazine lived up to its prospectus, was John Henry Hammond, Jr., a breezy enthusiast whose principal interest was the history of American jazz. A sister of his had recently shocked the world of the *Social Register* by marrying the great jazz clarinetist Benny Goodman; their mother, not to be outdone by her unconventional offspring, was soon to turn over the family's great estate in Westchester County to Dr. Frank Buchman and his Moral Re-Armament movement.

John Hammond's support seemed to be in part dependent on our offering a job to his protégé C. C. Nicolet, an unemployed and disillusioned newspaperman ready to work for any publication, whatever its politics, that would pay him a salary.

Another unemployed writer who helped shape the magazine's first few issues was Walter W. Liggett, a big florid Midwesterner with an established reputation as a crusading muckraker in the style of Lincoln Steffens. He had recently launched a magazine himself, but had been unable to raise capital for more than one issue. It was clear that he looked on Rodman and me as inexperienced amateurs, with no likelihood of success where he had failed, but with unlimited wealth behind us. He was not interested in becoming an editor but undertook to write a series of exposures of municipal corruption that, he assured us, would be sensational enough to put the magazine quickly on its feet. He urged us to go ahead with our project without delay and encouraged us to call it *Common Sense*, a name he had thought of using for his own magazine.

By the end of the summer of 1932, within three months of my return from my travels, Selden and I had rented a two-room suite on the twenty-fourth floor of an office building at 155 East Forty-fourth Street, hardly a block from Grand Central Station.

Neither of us had an established residence in the city. Selden was living with his mother in an Upper East Side apartment building, and I was staying at a residential hotel on East Thirty-eighth Street during the week and returning to my parents' summer home in Salem, Connecticut, over weekends. Now with an office, a staff, and a growing sense of commitment to the enterprise, I had to become a New Yorker. With old college friend and law school classmate Charles Grimes, who was in the first stages of a distinguished legal career, I rented an apartment at 25 Prospect Place, in Tudor City just off of East Forty-second Street.

We moved in on the first of October. The arrangement was happy enough for me; I could walk to my office. But Grimes, though a loyal friend, was not interested in revolution. He was on his way up the corporate and social ladder. Before our year's lease was up, he married a charming young woman from a wealthy and socially impeccable family. As an usher at the stylish wedding, I wore my cutaway and top hat for the last time. The bride and groom left on a honeymoon and later moved into an apartment with an address more distinguished than Tudor City.

My own marriage was still two years away. I had come back from my travels ready to marry Sylvia Knox. But in the meantime, she became a part of the new magazine venture *Common Sense*, and we saw each other in the office each working day. But it was not an arrangement conducive to romance. Sylvia acted as the office manager, bookkeeper, and general secretary but had no hand in editorial content.

CHAPTER 48

Editor and Left-Wing Activist

The first issue of *Common Sense* was being put together on Election Day in November 1932. I drove up to Salem to vote, uncertain till the last minute how I would mark the paper ballot. Finally, as a gesture of filial goodwill, I put my "X" before my father's name as the Republican candidate for another six-year Senate term. But I had as much scorn for the Democratic presidential candidate Franklin Roosevelt as the Republican Herbert Hoover. Nor in my revolutionary fervor could I support the "reformist" candidacy of Norman Thomas and the Socialist party. I did not believe in the Communists, but I felt the urge to make the strongest possible protest against the status quo, so I marked my ballot for Foster and Ford—the Communist candidates for president and vice-president.

I had not calculated correctly the effect of my protest vote on the ballot counters in a farming community with less than two hundred voters. A ballot marked for Republican Bingham and Communist Foster was an aberration. I was undoubtedly under suspicion. My local reputation as a "parlor pink," if not a Communist, had some continuing effect in the community when I entered conventional politics eight years later.

The outcome, Roosevelt's defeat of Hoover, seemed to me of little consequence, as I wrote in my first editorial. Neither of the "old parties" recognized that the capitalist system was in its death throes and that revolutionary changes were ahead.

I expected a mass audience for the magazine, and a hundred thousand copies were printed of the first issue. It featured a lurid cartoon of Andrew Mellon on the cover, and the cover story was a long exposure by Walter Liggett of the Mellon family's corrupt rule in Pittsburgh.

When my father saw that issue, with its blatant caricature of his admired friend Mellon, he flung the magazine across the room, according to my mother, and so far as I know, never looked at *Common Sense* again.

Walter Liggett had persuaded Selden Rodman and me to hire a friend of his named Martin as circulation manager. Martin went out to Pittsburgh to assure that the magazine was prominently displayed on local newsstands. He sent one wire back before moving on to other cities, saying that *Common Sense* was selling like hot cakes. For a few days we had dreams of success and even wealth. But even before the second issue was distributed two weeks later, we were smothered by bundles of returned copies of the first, and had to face the fact that the magazine would never have significant newsstand sales.

Obviously it was not a "mass" magazine, despite our efforts to enliven it with cartoons and sensational "exposures." Within a couple of months, with our funds almost gone, we lowered our sights. The magazine would be issued once a month instead of biweekly, and would depend on subscriptions rather than newsstand sales.

We were saved from an early demise by an affiliation with a leftist political organization, the League for Independent Political Action. Since 1928, the LIPA had been calling for a new party to challenge the Republican and Democratic parties, which were seen as hopelessly conservative. Its program was vaguely socialistic, with an emphasis on public ownership of utilities and key industries. The leadership of Professor John Dewey of Columbia University and Professor Paul Douglas of the University of Chicago was academic, but it had connections with the La Follette Progressives in Wisconsin and the Minnesota Farmer-Labor party, and other Midwestern populist movements. Its chief asset in 1933 was a mailing list of about twenty-five hundred "members," with whom it kept in touch with an occasional bulletin.

We agreed to include the bulletin in our pages and to send the magazine to all members. They became the core of our subscription list. Gradually over the years, the twenty-five hundred grew to nearly ten thousand.

In spite of its small circulation, *Common Sense* had a considerable impact. We were able to attract well-known writers. Selden was able to persuade many literary figures, including Theodore Dreiser and John Dos Passos, to write articles. My participation was more ideological and political.

The intellectual and literary left in New York at the time, confronted by the horrors of the economic breakdown, had been much influenced by Marxism, and a substantial number were persuaded to follow the leadership of the Communist party, either as members or fellow travelers. Yet the Communists, frustrated by their failure to win a mass following, were torn by internal divisions. And as time went on, particularly when the great purge trials began in Moscow in the mid-thirties, many lost faith in Communism and the Soviet Union. Some of the disillusioned were attracted to *Common Sense*.

One of the popular ideas at the time the magazine was launched was "technocracy." It held that if the productive capacity of the country were taken in hand by engineers and technicians, and organized in a rational way, enough would be produced to meet all the needs of society. "Production for use" would lead to "abundance for all," as we proclaimed in *Common Sense*. It was the old dream of the Utopian Socialists in the trappings of modern technology.

What conservative critics in the 1930s pointed out was made manifest by the total collapse of the Soviet system many years later: central direction of the economy requires absolute dictatorship and a monstrous bureaucracy; and dictators, whether engineers or a party elite, no less than petty bureaucrats, inevitably abuse power and make mistakes, while the workers under their control inevitably become malingerers. However, in the vision of the

337

new society as presented in the pages of *Common Sense*, none of those dire consequences would occur under leaders dedicated to democracy.

During the first months of *Common Sense*, two groups approached us, both in the hopes of manipulating our editorial policy. One approach came from a Nazi agent about the time that Hitler was consolidating his power in Germany. The populist tone of our magazine, evoking American national traditions of revolt against the moneyed interests, was similar to the appeal of Hitler's National Socialist German Workers party.

We had recently published a laudatory article entitled "The Lindbergh Who Was Almost Lynched," about Charles Lindbergh's father, the Farmer-Labor congressman from Minnesota who had opposed this country's entry into World War I against Germany, calling it "J. P. Morgan's war." The Nazi agent cited the elder Lindbergh as the American equivalent of a National Socialist. I did not like the comparison and gave no encouragement to Hitler's agent, but I had to admit that there were some parallels between Midwestern populism and National Socialism.

If some people labeled *Common Sense* as having Fascist tendencies, others thought we were Communists, and at least one Communist thought we were close enough to be converted. His name was Albert Weisbord. One of the founders of the American Communist party, he had followed Trotsky at the time of his split with Stalin, and then disillusioned with Trotskyism, he had founded his own tiny Communist sect. He offered to give me and others associated with me a concentrated course in Marxism in return for two weeks in the country that summer.

Sylvia was interested in joining the seminar, and the first week was spent in Peru, Vermont, on the slopes of Bromley Mountain, where Sylvia's parents owned a cottage. The only other person whom I was able to persuade to join the group was my old college roommate John Pierson. A second week was spent in Salem in the Mumford House where we were guests of my grandmother, and on one occasion, she was driven out from her home in New London in her great battleship-gray Locomobile limousine, big enough for her to stand up in—to listen in on one of our sessions on revolution.

Weisbord, a Harvard graduate with a brilliant mind, was an inspired teacher. In our daily morning and afternoon sessions, he outlined the essentials of Marx's philosophy, economics, and revolutionary politics. I found it heavy going and was particularly put off by Weisbord's almost religious faith that every word of Marx must be taken as true. I felt afterwards as if I had been permanently inoculated against the disease of Marxism—certainly not the result Weisbord had intended.

I did find Marx's method of understanding history in terms of class struggle useful. But I felt it had not been applied to an analysis of present-day society in America and other advanced countries, where the industrial working class, seen by Marx as destined to become the new ruling class, was challenged by rising middle-class elements.

It seemed to me significant that the only revolt against the existing political establishment in this country in recent years had come not from the industrial East but from the farm states of the Midwest. Robert La Follette, running as a Progressive, had garnered five million votes in 1924 and actually carried the state of Wisconsin. And the Farmer-Labor party in Minnesota had elected a governor and two senators.

The tie-in between *Common Sense* and the League for Independent Political Action enabled me to make contact with the leaders of that Midwestern insurgency. The intermediary was Howard Y. Williams, an ordained minister who had left a pastorate in St. Paul to become executive secretary of the LIPA. He was active in the Farmer-Labor politics of his home state and had cultivated sympathetic individuals in neighboring states.

With names and addresses provided by him, I set out in the spring of 1933 to tour that area. The most important man I met was Thomas R. Amlie, a former congressman from Wisconsin. Of Norwegian extraction, somewhat ponderous and slow-moving, he and I were mutually drawn to each other. A student of Thorstein Veblen, with a brother who had become a Communist, he had a natural affinity for the technocratic-socialist program Rodman and I had been developing at *Common Sense*. Though nominally a Republican and elected to Congress as such, he had worked with the La Follette Progressives. He had joined LIPA in the hope of seeing a national third party come into existence. He was critical of the elder La Follette's two sons, Robert Jr., who had won his father's seat in the U.S. Senate after his father's death, and Philip, who had become governor of the state, for returning to the Republican fold after the 1924 campaign.

In Tom Amlie and Floyd Olson, the Farmer-Labor governor of Minnesota, I felt I had found the experienced political leadership that could make a reality of a new national party. In September of 1933, the LIPA called a conference in Chicago to consider the feasibility of running a third-party candidate in 1936.

The main features of Roosevelt's New Deal were by that time in place, but there had been no real recovery from the Depression, and from the point of view of believers in socialism—whether Communists, Socialists, or independent radicals like those at the LIPA conference—the New Deal measures seemed wholly inadequate.

The conference set up a new framework called the Farmer-Labor Political Federation, with Amlie as chairman. I was named Executive Secretary. Howard Williams had held that position in LIPA, but was now given the new title of National Organizer. In effect I supplanted him as the chief executive, a move for which I now feel some discomfort, if not shame.

I had had very little experience as an executive or administrator. Williams, at least, had been in the field as an organizer for some years and had long-standing personal ties, particularly in the Midwest. He continued to cultivate these as National Organizer, while I attempted to win a popular base for those academics who had rallied to John Dewey's leadership in the industrial East.

Despite the failure of *Common Sense* to win a wide readership, I remained under the illusion that, as the Depression dragged on, only a spark was needed to kindle a mass revolt against the "system" that had reduced millions to penury. Now that I had a political vehicle in the Farmer-Labor Political Federation (FLPF), I thought it possible to build a mass movement on its bold program of Americanized socialism.

Back in New York, the first step would be to call a "mass" meeting. The Cooper Union hall, with its historical associations as the site of a famous speech by Abraham Lincoln, seemed an appropriate place. It was a few blocks south of Union Square, near the headquarters of both the Communist and Socialist parties, as well as of the more politically advanced labor unions. A big poster announcing the meeting and the names of the speakers was set up in front of the old building on Cooper Square a week in advance.

The most prominent of the speakers was Milo Reno, the fiery leader of the Iowa Farmers Union and of the National Farmers Holiday Association: his direct action program, forcibly halting milk supplies to the cities in an effort to raise prices, had made headlines in the national press. A. F. Whitney, the head of the Railway Trainmen's Union, represented labor. Tom Amlie and Howard Williams were to present the revolutionary program of the FLPF.

When it came time for me to open the meeting as self-appointed chairman, I faced a vast wasteland of empty seats. The hall held hardly more faces than were assembled on the platform. The speeches were too many and too long. Milo Reno, who as the principal speaker was being held to the end of the program, left the platform in disgust at not being called on, and was only with difficulty persuaded to return and give his speech.

Clearly our revolution was a long way off. The only New York adherents to our new "political federation" were a group calling themselves the Knickerbocker Democrats. Its support initially sounded encouraging, but we soon found out that it was a Communist "front" organization, apparently more interested in sabotaging than promoting our movement.

We contented ourselves with the thought that the makers of the Russian Revolution were at one time only a handful.

In the Midwest, meanwhile, the outlook for a new national party was more promising. In Wisconsin, Amlie was elected to Congress in 1934 as a Progressive, and the Minnesota Farmer-Labor party, with Williams as chairman of its platform committee, adopted the full anti-capitalism program of the FLPF, and elected a full slate of candidates headed by Governor Floyd Olson. To be sure, Olson and the party leaders explained away the party platform as merely a statement of long-range goals.

By 1935, with another national election only a year away, and enthusiasm for the New Deal seemingly ebbing, Williams, Amlie, and I decided to call another conference to promote the new party. We had become persuaded that the Farmer-Labor banner, though appealing in the Midwest, was not inclusive enough to attract a following on the East and West coasts, or in fact throughout middle America. In the prairie provinces of western Canada, a new radical party had made headway as the Canadian Commonwealth Federation. In the state of Washington, a group of liberals and progressives had followed suit by successfully organizing the Washington Commonwealth Federation. Perhaps if we abandoned the "Farmer-Labor" label and became the American Commonwealth Political Federation, we would attract a wider following.

Again we met at the University of Chicago, courtesy of Professor Paul Douglas, with the same stalwart Eastern liberals and Western populists in attendance as two years before, and again we adopted a radical platform and called for a new party to enter the 1936 election campaign. But the American Commonwealth Political Federation, or the ACF as we called it, had no more political muscle than the FLPF, and the change of name had little if any practical effect.

The truth, as I gradually came to see it, was that Roosevelt's New Deal, while it had not ended the Depression, had won the support of the discontented and had transformed the Democratic party into the party of social change. Our slogan, "production for use," found no readier response among pragmatic Americans than had "socialism."

A year later, in the election campaign of 1936, all the office holders and political realists in the Wisconsin Progressive movement and the Minnesota Farmer-Labor party, as well as the nascent third-party leaders in other states, were supporting Roosevelt, and in the editorial pages of *Common Sense*, I recommended that our readers vote Democratic.

CHRONICLE XI

Husbands and Wives

CHAPTER 49
War and Politics

$\overline{}$

While I was starting my career as an editor and activist, my parents' marriage was crumbling. The rift that was now widening in their marriage could be traced back many years—to the beginning of my father's political career.

After his discovery of Machu Picchu in 1911, my father had had several unsettled years. He had been virtually expelled from Peru when, on his third Peruvian expedition, the authorities claimed he was illegally exporting archeological treasures. By this point, he was no longer interested in exploration, nor in going back to college teaching. The humiliation he felt as an American in a Latin American country was accentuated by the coincidental sinking of the *Lusitania* in the spring of 1915, when South American public opinion saw the American reaction as faint-hearted. My father had turned to the British embassy in Lima when the American embassy offered no help in meeting the Peruvian charges.

My father had no use for Woodrow Wilson after his sad experience at Princeton, and now Wilson's Secretary of State William "Grape Juice" Bryan (as one of my father's friends in Peru had dubbed him) had met the German atrocity with "mild notes."

As a new career, my father thought of politics. He had a sacred cause to pursue in reaffirming American authority over and superiority to the peoples and nations of Latin America.

He contacted the Republican party machine in Connecticut and secured appointment to the 1916 Republican National Convention as a delegate. But it was not until 1922 that his aspiration for public office was fulfilled. In the meantime, he had written books about his expeditions and spent the years of America's entry into the war in Europe as an aviator. Regardless of his being the father of seven children, he dreamed of glory as a combat pilot. Instead, the War Department recognized his academic credentials, and he became the commander of the largest establishment for training American aviators in France. He was in command of thousands of personnel while still only a lieutenant colonel. On his return from the war, he sought to capitalize on his glamorous careers, and wrote a book entitled *An Explorer in the Air Service.*

He was more than ever an eligible candidate for political office. However, he had to wait for his opportunity. After two or three years of psychosomatic illness, his chance finally came when the Republican boss of Connecticut, J. Henry Roraback, brought him forward as a candidate for lieutenant governor of the state in 1922. In 1924 he became a candidate for the governorship.

But in the middle of the campaign that fall, Senator Frank Brandegee, one of the senators from Connecticut, committed suicide and a vacancy for his senate seat opened. Within weeks of his election as governor, my father was nominated in a special election for the senate vacancy. As a professor going into politics, he had carried the Yale community with him up to this point, but many of his academic colleagues, feeling he was guilty of overweening ambition, turned against him. One of the local newspapers, despite its Republican sympathies, declared him guilty of "political Binghamy." Nevertheless, he was elected at the special election in December, with the public understanding that he would take office as governor and immediately resign to take his senate seat, in order to avoid another special election.

As governor for a day, he delivered an inaugural address to the General Assembly and attended the gala Inaugural Ball with his shy and somewhat bewildered wife. He was sworn in on the U.S. Senate floor two days later.

CHAPTER 50
The Widening Rift

When in early 1925 Alfreda joined her husband in Washington as a senator's wife, it was to mark a break in her life. For twenty-five years she had been an adoring wife, and devoted herself to her seven children as they came along one after the other. During her husband's many long absences as an explorer or as an aviator, she naturally had many days and hours of loneliness. The brief diary she kept gave evidence of her occasional feelings of abandonment and loneliness, but she was persuaded that her life with Hiram was or ought to be a happy one.

The only life of her own that she was able to maintain revolved around music. Otherwise she was mistress of a household that at its peak had a good many children to care for, even with the help of nurses and governesses. But now her children were either in boarding school or college, and she found the life of a senator's wife opening before her with no appeal. She had found state politics and politicians uncongenial, but now she felt she had moved into a higher level of her husband's public life where she would not need to be so concerned about knowing politicians by their first names. Never able to associate herself closely with her husband's career, and making her own career out of being a mother, she now found herself without a purpose and only superficially associated with him and his new activities. She almost felt her life was over and probably, in depressed periods, wished for death. Despite the emptiness of her life, she had disciplined herself to maintain a cheerful exterior and also a certain measure of inner contentment.

In the suite at the Hotel Powhatan on Pennsylvania Avenue, a few blocks from the White House, that they had decided to make their temporary home, she devoted one morning to an appraisal of her present life, which she called "A Complete Life." Written just as she was turning fifty, it was a very private document, and no one saw it until after her death many years later. It was written on hotel stationery.

A Complete Life

Winter of 1924–25

If I should have to die soon, let none of my dear ones sorrow. Let none of them mourn my going! I wish them to realize, as I do ever so strongly, that my life has had more happiness crowded into it than any life I know. I have lived in a lovely home as a girl, had out-of-door pleasures nearly all my childhood, winters turned into summer with the joys of swimming and riding and keeping the beauties of Nature all the year round. To be sure I lost most of the pleasures of school friendships in that way, but on the other hand I had for compensation the exquisite joys of companionship with Natural objects, ocean waves on the seashore, mountain heights and views, communion with trees, plants and flowers. What purer joys than those!

When a girl and romance filled my mind, I had an outlet for romantic feelings and sentimentality in my violin. It filled my craving for sympathy in youth, it nursed my ambitions, it comforted any sorrows. And what an example of quiet contentment and peaceful enjoyment I had in the sight of my father always reading in the atmosphere of his books! Also what example of companionship with trees I had in the sight of my father's pruning and budding in his orchard or cutting away to make room for the best trees and beautifying his woods.

I had faults which caused some distress and worry, and jealousy was always the enemy I dreaded most, but on the whole what a happy childhood, what a glorious young womanhood, and then, what a crown of life to have become the wife of the man I did! I used to say when the first child was born, "what a miracle that I should be the mother of a boy!" One boy! And then there were two to make me happy and then the third to complete a mother's pride and joy. I used to think in those days: "if only these sons of mine when they grow up could be as happily married as I am!" It is a good deal to hope for and that is my greatest wish now. And with it goes another: That they turn out as good and fine men as their father. I cannot ask that they become as distinguished altho' it is a sweet dream I dare hope. I know moreover that they will be good men, brave men, loyal and true, patriotic and loving their country because all these traits have shown themselves already in them, some more in one or two, some in others. They can take comfort in Nature because they were brought up close to it as little boys, they ought to respect the sacredness of marriage life because they have seen nothing else, they ought to respect womanhood because this was unconsciously before them in the home.

347

The Mother's place as a helpful companion but also as an inspiration and an ideal is what my old-fashioned attitude has been. I have liked to place woman on a pedestal and worship her when at her best, and so perhaps have they imbibed a little of that spirit! Oh daughters of mine to be: do not disillusion my sons! Women can be angels on this earth and bring sunshine, starlight and moonlight into every home if they will. If women have wisdom and recognize their soothing influence, their help in time of need, their beneficent radiance, their men will be better men and the "Kingdom" of Heaven will be here. Our America would be the happiest place on earth.

But be happy young lives in the generations to come! Build for a better country, a world growing wiser and better. The sweetness of innocent children bless you and the pure goodness of wives and mothers. I trust my sons to choose wisely and they must look only for the purest and best. So may the next generations build upon the past, higher and nobler and greater...

But to return, if I pass away today I could be content and satisfied. I am happy, "Ich habe geliebt und gelebt." I have had a world of blessings in my life. I have had the joys of motherhood sevenfold! The pangs and sorrow of worrying motherhood are as nothing to its blessings! How I used to watch each baby mouth and hug each little body and admire each baby's fingers. What endless interest in the unfolding of their different characters. How engrossing was their company when their father was away, how proud of father when he returned. And what years of pride and happiness I have had lately in the wonderful development of his career, in the recognition of my husband's ability. I could die today, content, more than happy in the success of my husband, seeing him honored and respected of men! I am blessed, blessed in the love of my seven sons and beloved husband.

My father, meanwhile, entered the hurly-burly world of Washington politics with renewed vigor and zeal. In contrast to his wife, who felt her own life closing in, my father now saw new and exciting vistas opening before him. For him, this new glamorous and fast-paced world represented the attainment of a long-sought dream. With natural aplomb, he ascended into the heady atmosphere of smoke-filled rooms, power politics, and masculine camaraderie. The rift with the cloistered and refined world of his wife widened. Within weeks of his arrival in Washington, at a Saint Valentine's Day dinner party, my father met and began to fall in love with the wife of a congressman. The attraction was mutual and developed in time into a deep and lasting romantic attachment.

Throughout his years in Washington, he was able to hide his extramarital connection from his wife, because politically and financially he could not afford to break up his marriage. He was no doubt still fond of his wife and had a strong sense of loyalty, despite his acute sense of her limitations.

Over a turbulent period of eight years as a senator, my father expounded the philosophy of "rugged individualism" that was the cornerstone of conservative Republicanism. He conscientiously devoted himself to his duties as a legislator, making as his specialty legislation concerned with aviation. One of his more important legislative contributions was the Air Commerce Act of 1926, which became the foundation for all subsequent legislation dealing with commercial aviation.

Although he never gained the place he hoped for on the Foreign Affairs Committee, his chairmanship of the Committee on Territories and Insular Possessions gave him an opportunity to address some of the problems of a world of declining colonial empires. In 1927 he made a three-month fact-finding tour of the Pacific, which included forays to Japan, China, and the Philippines. Although he was passed over for the number two spot on the 1928 presidential ticket, my father loyally supported the new president, Herbert Hoover, in the last halcyon days before the Great Depression.

The year 1929 was one of disaster for my father's career. The great stock market crash, though it failed to seriously affect my father's finances, triggered a political shift towards greater government intervention and social welfarism that signaled the end of the conservative policies my father supported. The same week of the crash, he was publicly censured by the U.S. Senate for having hired a lobbyist, who was still on the payroll of the Connecticut Manufacturers Association, to advise him during Finance Committee hearings on a tariff bill. It was one of only half a dozen such incidents of public censure in the U.S. Senate's history. My father's political career was seriously damaged. By 1932, when he was up for reelection for his third term, the dominant role of conservative Republicanism was at an end, and with it his political career.

Chapter 51
Financing Second Marriages

The year 1937 was a crucial year in this family history. It was the year of the death of the Tiffany heir Annie Tiffany Mitchell and of the breakup of my parents' marriage.

Sylvia and I had married in November of 1934. Our first Christmas together—and the only Christmas we ever had together without children—was divided between New York where we were living, and Washington where we visited my parents. Sylvia's parents had come down to New York from Stonington, Connecticut, and the Knox family gathered for Christmas dinner at the John Knoxes'. John, Sylvia's oldest brother, and his wife Lucy, not long married, lived in Tarrytown, New York, from where he commuted daily—as he did for the rest of his life—to a job on Wall Street with Brown Brothers Harriman. Sylvia's youngest brother, Sam, with whom she had been sharing an apartment in New York before our marriage, drove out to Tarrytown with us for the occasion.

The next day we took the train for Washington. That year my parents were living in an apartment in the Shoreham Hotel. They had given up the impressive rented apartment in "Embassy Row" on upper Sixteenth Street, while completing plans to build a house on a lot they owned on the edge of Rock Creek Park. My mother was delighted with Sylvia and arranged for a photographer to take some formal portrait pictures of Sylvia and me. We were included in a formal dinner party in my parents' suite for Supreme Court Justice Hugo Black and his wife.

My relations with my father were restrained but polite. He and I had reached a friendly understanding a few months earlier during a drive in my car to Salem from my brother Brewster's wedding in the Boston area, and we had agreed that we would avoid controversial political issues in order to maintain a fond personal contact. The radical views I was expressing in the pages of *Common Sense* at that time were obviously irreconcilable with his staunch anti-New Deal Republicanism, and we agreed to respect our differences.

The only time tempers flared that Christmas was at a small family dinner when my father could not avoid expressing a controversial opinion. Sylvia brightly tried to enter the conversation, prefacing what she was about to say with the words, "I don't agree with you, Father." He interrupted her with an angry, "I am not accustomed to being disagreed with at my own table." Much of the time during that visit my father was absent, "at his club," as my mother said.

And I had other concerns too, attending a "Continental Congress" of socialist and labor groups where I tried to promote my dream of a third-party candidate in the next year's presidential election. My mother was sympathetic when I told her about my doings, but I was embarrassed by her uncritical acceptance of everything I said as if it were gospel. I had gathered that her support of my utopian ideas was widening the rift between her and my father.

A year later Sylvia and I again visited my parents in Washington over Christmas, this time with a nursing baby. They were then living in a small but comfortable rented house overlooking Rock Creek Park near their building lot. Plans for building their own house were still in abeyance. After a relatively modest Christmas dinner, my father departed for "his club." My mother said she was planning to have some music with Mr. Gregor, the pianist who had been at the Camp in Salem the previous summer with another musician, a cellist. Since my father's election to the Senate and the move to Washington, her music had been more than ever a comforting preoccupation; but a violinist needs a pianist or other instrumentalist for the playing of chamber music, and when amateur friends were not available she was quite willing and able to pay an accompanist.

So Henry Gregor appeared that Christmas day, and it was quite clear from their talk and their glances that their intimacy, at least in making music together, was of long standing. Accordingly it was no great surprise to me a few months later when my mother came to visit Sylvia and me at our Tenth Street apartment in New York, and I noticed that she was not wearing a wedding ring. She told us she was in love with Henry Gregor. Was she going to get a divorce and marry him? That was not decided. He had been married before, and though he and his wife had been long separated, they were not divorced. A composer as well as an instrumentalist, he was teaching music at a girls' school in Washington, and was the organist and choir master in a Washington church. Born in Moscow of a German father and a Russian mother, Gregor had been brought up in Germany. He was forty-nine years old. My mother was sixty-one.

What about Father? She did not like to leave him. But he was now in good health (I had sometimes noticed in recent years that the only times she had been close to him was when he was ill and bedridden and she could take care of him), and she felt pretty sure he would find somebody else to take care of him. She thought he might be interested in a certain Mrs. Hull whom she had met and been favorably impressed by. Sylvia and I did not discourage her. I had been aware of the estrangement between her and my father for several years. I remembered the time the previous summer when she had broken down for almost the only time in my memory, and told me how unhappy she was, and how she felt it was my father's fondness for whiskey that had ruined their marriage. Yet I had seen her be cruel to him in putting him down in ways that were most hurtful to his self-esteem.

By the summer of 1936, my mother had reached a decision. She established a legal residence in Florida, where she had been taking care of her dying mother, and initiated divorce proceedings alleging mental cruelty. She was still not aware of my father's long unfaithfulness. Also during this time, she asked my father to return the Tiffany shares given to her by her mother in a distribution of the company stock in 1932. At that time he had advised my mother to put them in his name for tax purposes. Now he insisted the Tiffany shares had been a gift to him and refused to return them. My mother did not press the matter.

After a painful court trial in early 1937, a divorce was granted in March. At the end of April, a Washington court granted Suzanne Carroll Hill a divorce from her husband, and in June she became Mrs. Hiram Bingham. A month later my mother and Henry Gregor were married.

Both my mother and my father found more happiness in their second marriages than they had in their first. My father and Suzanne shared twenty years of married life, spent mostly in Washington where they lived in a town house belonging to Suzanne. My father's political career was over.

My mother's marriage to Henry Gregor lasted twenty-six years. They shared a common love of music, and were temperamentally well suited to each other. Henry Gregor, who had struggled for many years as an immigrant in America before his marriage to my mother, was now able to enjoy a more comfortable existence. Over the course of their marriage, Henry built up a sizable personal fortune, much of it accrued through shrewd investments in Florida real estate, the investment capital for which had been provided by my mother's Tiffany inheritance. Henry was also able to bring over two sisters and their families from Germany, thus saving them from the vicissitudes of life in war-torn Europe. His wife's money, siphoned through Henry's beneficent hands and with Alfreda's full and informed consent, bought his relatives houses and cars, employment, and continuing support for their children. Although precise records are not available, approximately $1.5 million of Tiffany money was passed on in this way over the span of my mother's and Henry's marriage.

CHRONICLE XII
In the Establishment

CHAPTER 52

I Acquire a Family

Sylvia was a loyal follower during the first year of *Common Sense* and my involvement in third-party politics. I had hoped in the beginning, when she joined me in the establishment of the new magazine, that our intimate cooperation on that project would lead to love and marriage.

But in the grimy day-to-day business of a publishing office, romance did not blossom. Selden heightened the difficulty by his latent anti-feminism, which contributed to our decision that Sylvia's role would be confined to the business part of the operation, with no participation in editorial content.

Obviously we needed a competent business manager to keep track of financing the enterprise and to build a subscription list. Sylvia was willing to take responsibility in these areas. But, like us, she thought of them as secondary to the main purpose of our venture. After somewhat more than a year, both Sylvia and I realized that our relationship had become more distant and more formal rather than closer.

I was nearly thirty years old. I wanted to get married and have a family. In almost every respect, I had felt for years that Sylvia was a nearly perfect mate for me. But I had never felt any strong sexual attraction to her. Mere propinquity did not help. I came to the conclusion that sexual involvement was needed as well as intellectual compatibility. I felt we should make love if we were to fall in love.

In the spring of 1934, we began spending weekends together. With a good deal of self-doubt and trepidation on both sides, we set out in my car for our first tryst on the New Jersey shore, south of Sandy Hook. We found a small hotel right on the oceanfront in a place called Normandie Beach. After dinner at a restaurant and somewhat fortified with alcohol, we repaired to our little room. The roar of the surf was in our ears as we undressed.

Sylvia was a virgin, and I was more moved by scientific curiosity than desire as I examined her. She left all initiatives to me, as if my experience were not limited.

In retrospect many years later, she told me the encounter was a nightmare. She particularly resented the fact that I had taken her to a cheap hotel without even a private bath. I had thought it an almost ideally romantic spot. We were both tenderly solicitous. But it was far from a perfect beginning.

The next weekend we went to a resort hotel in the Catskills. In both places I registered as man and wife, and I provided Sylvia with a dime-store make-believe wedding ring. But the pretense was another irritant. I decided that we should continue our experiment more directly in a place that belonged to me: the log cabin in the Salem woods that I had built as a refuge and a place to write before going on my world safari.

There for a number of weekends in July and August we camped out. We would drive up from New York after office hours on Friday evenings, a grueling three-hour trip, ending on a rough logger's trail into the wilderness. We parked the car and carried our baggage and supplies over a tiny brook for a final quarter-mile hike by flashlight. The cabin had an iron cot and the rudiments of housekeeping equipment. And there we attempted, with more or less success, to make love. I varied between thinking it was all idyllic and wondering if it was all a mistake. Sylvia doggedly followed my lead. Having boasted of her prowess as a mountain climber, she did not complain of the ruggedness of my love nest.

The next day we often moved to the Camp, where my mother was in residence, acting as if we were just up from New York, and luxuriated, if separately, in the amenities of civilized life, with meals cooked and served by a household staff.

By the end of the summer, it was evident to me that my experiment had failed. I was not falling in love with Sylvia. And she was obviously not happy and was showing increasing signs of nervous strain. On a chilly afternoon at the Waterford, Connecticut, beach, where we huddled against the side of the bathhouse to avoid a cold breeze, I opened up the subject and blurted out that I thought we should end our "affair." Sylvia sadly agreed, and we talked about the future. She would give up her job at *Common Sense* and perhaps take a trip abroad. It was bitterly painful for me to give up my long-held romantic dream of love and marriage with Sylvia, but, as I found out later, it was even more excruciating for her. She had missed her period and believed herself pregnant. But she would not and did not tell me.

At the offices of *Common Sense,* now located in a loft building at 315 Fourth Avenue, she told us she was leaving in mid-October and going to Europe. On her last day of work, I had arranged to drive her to her parents' house in Stonington. She had been working overtime to see that the magazine's business affairs were in order and to train others of our semi-volunteer staff to handle the circulation and bookkeeping tasks she had mastered. She was clearly at the end of her rope; she fainted dead away on two occasions that last morning. I put it down to fatigue and nervous strain. I helped her into my car, picked up her baggage at the uptown apartment she shared with her brother Sam, and headed up the Boston Post Road. I realized she was in pain, and when she fainted again sitting in the front seat beside me, I became seriously alarmed and decided to stop in New Haven and try to have her see Dr. Arnold, the Bingham family doctor, whom I had kept in touch with all through college and law school. Sylvia desperately protested, saying she was just having a painful menstrual period, and that was what she told the doctor when I found him in at his office. She would not let him examine her, and he could do no more than accept her explanation and pass it on to me.

Ten days later I had what was to be a farewell visit with her at her parents' mountain hideaway in Vermont. She was booked to sail for Europe two weeks later. We went for a walk along the highway the first morning. She told me she had something to say that she could not have told me before—that she had become pregnant, and that the painful episode on the day she had left *Common Sense* was a miscarriage. Now that it was all over she could tell me, but she had not wanted to force my hand by telling me before, and had planned to have the baby in Europe.

I felt weak in the knees and had to sit down on a boulder beside the road to absorb the shock of this revelation. I thought back to our encounters at the cabin in the woods and realized I had been reckless in using a condom only on two occasions, believing what I had been told by two doctors—that I was probably incapable of fathering a child. I was overwhelmed by Sylvia's heroism in carrying her secret. I was astonished and relieved to find out I was not sterile after all.

Sylvia was reassuring. She was now recovered and felt we could put the past behind us. But I found I could not. In the next few days I wrestled with my feelings.

I was filled with admiration for Sylvia's courage and forbearance. I now saw her as a splendid and beautiful person. I felt acute sympathy—and guilt—for what she had suffered on my account. To help sort out my feelings, I tried putting them down on paper. As I wrote, I began to realize that I loved her. In a flood of tenderness, I knew I loved her. I knew she loved me. I knew I wanted to marry her.

Two days later, at my urging, she came to New York, and in my tiny two-room apartment, at the back of an old brownstone that faced on Stuyvesant Square, I proposed to her. I was confident of her acceptance, and she did indeed accept me. Yet I felt she had some mental reservation, and years later I found out what it was. She wondered whether my decision was not simply a reaction to finding I could have a child by her. That certainly was a factor, but what was most important, and what she later masochistically refused to believe, was that I had fallen in love with her.

We were married nine days later, November 9, 1934, at her parents' home in Stonington, and that same night we sailed for Europe together on the *Bremen*. The anxieties that had blocked the fullness of making love before were gone, and even in the narrowness of a cabin bunk, we reveled in sex. Four days short of nine months later, our first child was born.

The next few years were the happiest of my life. I was happily married. I was producing children. I had work to do that I believed in, editing and publishing a magazine of increasing distinction and significance. And I was writing books.

Selden was largely responsible for my career as a writer. Even before my marriage, he had promoted the first book that bore my name and his as editors: a selection of articles from *Common Sense* that appeared in 1934 as *Challenge to the New Deal.*

John Dewey, the distinguished philosopher who had been chairman of the League for Independent Political Action, agreed to write an introduction to the book but, to my dismay, was unable to get to it before taking off for South Africa on a speaking tour. I saw him before he sailed, and he promised to write it and send it to me, but he did not reject my suggestion that if he grew too busy he might be willing to have me ghostwrite it for him. Some days later came a cable from South Africa with the single word "Ghost" and his name. And when the book came out, it contained an "Introduction by John Dewey" written by me, not too immodestly praising the work of the two young editors of *Common Sense.*

Compiling a collection of magazine articles is not the same as writing a book, and Selden urged me to put the ideas that had inspired the magazine and its political program into book form. A year of research and writing (for part of which I hired a research assistant) produced *Insurgent America: Revolt of the Middle Classes* published by Harper & Brothers in 1935.

Looking back on it now over fifty years later, I am astonished at my productivity, editing a magazine, promoting a third-party movement, founding a family, and still engaging in serious research and writing. Part of the research was combined with my marriage; I took a typewriter along on my honeymoon to Germany to record my impressions of Hitler's brand of fascism.

My research there carried more than a spice of danger. I had a friend in New York, who had left a position as a Foreign Service Officer at the American embassy in Berlin to become an agent of the revolutionary "New Beginning" group, an offshoot of the German Social Democratic party not yet wiped out by the Nazis. Furnished with false names and secret instructions, Sylvia and I made contact with the underground group when we got to Berlin.

A phone call to a memorized number, a visit to a Herr Doktor (whom we never saw) to bring greetings from a Miss Violet Banks (whom we had never met), led to a botched introduction when I was supposed to give my name as Jonathan Brown and instead blurted out "Jonathan Bingham," only to be reassured that my real name was already known. Some meetings were arranged with members of the New Beginning group, the first at a restaurant next to an orchestra where we could not be overheard, a later one with a larger group at our Christliche Hospice hotel room after inspection had determined that it was not bugged or next to a room from which we could be overheard.

It was all conspiratorial in a way I found amusing as well as terrifying, for we had gathered that if any of the group were found they would most likely be tortured and killed (as we heard a year later they had been), and we too might have been imprisoned. Sylvia called up some friends from the early

1930s. The Psychological Institute where she had done a year's graduate work had only a skeleton staff of non-Jews left. We had tea with the family of a wealthy businessman Sylvia had known and found them expressing satisfaction that noisy political demonstrations, often erupting in violence, were now no more: "Alles ist ganz ruhig" ("Everything is completely peaceful") was their theme song. Their only complaint against the new Nazi regime was that mail boxes, which had always been painted green, were now red. But it also seemed clear that they were afraid to talk, and references to Hitler were guarded and few. He had been in power for only a year and a half, and neither his military buildup nor his war on the Jews was yet in full swing. Nothing occurred during our visit to undermine my generally tolerant and objective view of the Hitler regime. I was looking for positive elements in the Nazi movement, and I was impressed with the creative energies that seemed to have been unloosed.

We spent two weeks in Germany, visiting Dresden and Munich as well as Berlin, and returned home via Paris and London. We spent Christmas with my parents in Washington. Sylvia was pregnant.

Insurgent America, when it appeared some months later, was my most original and successful book. Most contemporary literature was heavily weighted with the Marxist dogma that the industrial working class was the predestined instrument of social change. Left-wing interpretations of fascism all located it on the capitalist side of the barricades. By contrast, I wrote that fascism was a revolutionary challenge to the old order fueled by middle-class discontent.

I analyzed population data and noted that the percentage of the American work force engaged in manufacturing, mining, and transportation (the blue-collar occupations) had by the 1930 census become smaller than that in white-collar and middle-class occupations. The class struggle was not what Marx had described. I argued, as I had argued earlier in *Common Sense*, that America was a middle-class country, and that the class forces making for social change in America were more middle class than working class. For evidence of a coming new American revolution, I cited the rise of the Progressive and Farmer-Labor movements of the Midwest.

The book was favorably reviewed, and one publisher, W. W. Norton, who had turned down my manuscript at first, now said he wanted to be my publisher. He brought out an edition with his own imprint and offered to publish my next book. Harper meanwhile had issued a paperback edition, which we hoped would become the Bible of the third-party movement.

With three editions on the market, sales were significant if hardly overwhelming, probably reaching no more than five thousand. Still I felt I was now an established author, even perhaps an authority.

I went on at once with the new book for Norton. Whereas *Insurgent America* had focused on the politics of social change, my next would deal with economics. I had two readerships in mind. First were the liberal reformers who believed capitalism could be reformed and made to work for the general good. Second were the radicals, both Socialist and Communist, who accepted Marx's prediction that capitalism was doomed by its self-destructive tendency to deprive industrial workers of the surplus value they created and drive them to revolution.

I was much influenced at the time by the newly emerging interest in semantics. To escape what Stuart Chase had called the "tyranny of words" in his book by that name (1938), I decided to base my presentation on my own experience and the evolution of my own thinking. "Adventures in Economic Discovery" became the subtitle of a book I called *Man's Estate*, both to suggest the maturing process and the abundance of the world's goods made possible by modern technology.

The result was a semi-autobiographical work in which I traced my own intellectual progress from conservatism to liberalism to radicalism. My travels in Asia, Russia, and Western Europe a few years before provided a rich background for my observations about the nature of socialism, communism, and fascism. I devoted fifty pages to an analysis of Marxist economics, which—after plodding through all three volumes of *Das Kapital* and finding much of them unrelievedly turgid—I entitled "Through Marxism Darkly." I then went on to an analysis of capitalism as it had evolved and as it had been subject to increasing government intervention.

The result of my "adventures in economic discovery" was what I called a "new New Deal." I saw the New Deal, particularly in its early phase, as tending toward a managed free enterprise system. The terms *socialism* and *capitalism*, I argued, were of little value. Whether enterprises were privately owned or publicly owned made little difference. I had begun to think by then that strategic planning might achieve full employment and an ironing out of the fluctuations of the business cycle. I was no longer calling for revolution.

Abandonment of my more radical stance was no doubt assisted by my becoming a family man. Sylvia and I welcomed our first child in the summer of 1935. We named her Alfreda after my mother. Sylvia did not like the shortened form of the name that my mother used, "Freda," and to call her "Alfy" seemed to impinge on my territory, so we called her Elfy. The nickname was more appropriate for a small child than a grown woman even if she was petite, but within the family she is still known as Elfy.

We brought her back from the hospital to a newly rented basement apartment at 117 East Tenth Street. The building was one of a group of ancient houses adjoining the churchyard of St. Mark's-in-the-Bouwerie. The church had acquired the block of half a dozen houses, modernized them, and thrown their backyards together, to make a charming enclave of upgraded but still reasonably priced apartments. For a monthly rental of sixty-five dollars, we had a three-room apartment with a fireplace and a patio, as well as access to the common landscaped area.

We thought it charming, even luxurious, though when my father gave us a visit, he was horrified by our living in what he considered a slum dwelling.

Elfy slept in a crib in our bedroom, but after Christopher was born in 1937 and we had two babies in our bedroom, we began to feel crowded. Elfy was particularly restless at night. Looking back at that period when it seemed we could never get a good night's rest, I can recall my rage when Elfy's crying woke me up. Sylvia was nursing Kit, as we called him, so she would get up at night for him, and we arranged that I would take care of Elfy when she cried. Sometimes I was angry enough to strangle her. I am not surprised today when I read stories of child abuse.

That fall we moved into a larger apartment in the same block of buildings where we had two bedrooms with a corridor and bathroom between. We were on the fourth floor of a walk-up, but the apartment had big windows overlooking the churchyard on one side and the backyard garden on another. At eighty-five dollars a month, it seemed ideal for our purposes. The building, bigger and more pretentious than the others in the block, even had a western exposure, giving light as well as air to our small bedroom and the kitchen next to it. Sylvia salvaged some gold damask curtains from her Doughty grandfather's Brooklyn home, now being sold by his estate, and with new red-flowered curtains for our bedroom, our apartment began to look sumptuous.

We had a maid who came down from Harlem six days a week to clean and cook and help Sylvia with the care of the two children. Bright, attractive, and soft-spoken, Marion Tedo was in her teens when she first began to work for us. Sylvia treated her as a colleague in the housework, and they became lifelong friends. The laundry was done in a tub in the kitchen, and Sylvia would lug the heavy laundry basket up two more flights of stairs to the roof where clotheslines were strung.

In summers we would take the children to Central Park or Bronx Park or, best of all, to Jones Beach on the south shore of Long Island. Our car, garaged on Twelfth Street, enabled us to spend occasional weekends in Connecticut, either at my mother's Camp in Salem or in Stonington, at the big Doughty mansion on Darling Hill, the home of Sylvia's parents since her father's retirement, and where we had been married.

Sylvia had been one of four children; I was one of seven. We now had two of our own, but both of us felt we wanted more. However, the next pregnancy ran into trouble. Early in 1939, at five months of gestation, the amniotic sac ruptured, and Sylvia, in the effort to hold the fetus, was hospitalized for two months in the New York Hospital with total rest prescribed. Her mother came to live with me and take care of Elfy and Kit. Finally at seven months, a baby girl was born but lived only a few hours. Apparently the attachment of the fetus to the wall of the uterus had been deficient, and we comforted ourselves with the thought that the child would probably have been defective.

I had a talk with our pediatrician, Dr. Benjamin Spock, an old New Haven neighbor and friend, who was to become an international celebrity. His wife also had lost a baby, and to minimize the psychological trauma, they had surrendered the body to a hospital for research. On his precedent and advice, we did the same with ours—but not before I had a glimpse of the tiny shriveled body in the hospital morgue.

Sylvia felt the pain of her loss would be mitigated by a prompt replacement, and within a few months she was pregnant again—and I was once more reminded of the fallibility of the medical opinions I had received some years before as to my infertility. We were to have two more children: Douglas, born June 14, 1940, and Stephen, born April 23, 1942.

CHAPTER 53

Politician

From the time I had decided to study law, I thought of politics as my real vocation. I projected a political career growing out of the practice of law in New London. This scenario was laid aside when my world travels gave me a new perspective: I began to envision my political activity in terms of social reform if not revolution, and became a magazine publisher and editor instead of a lawyer. That led in turn to association with the progressive Farmer-Labor and other third-party movements. But by 1940 I had to accept the fact that the Democratic party under Franklin Roosevelt's leadership had become the party of social change.

Meanwhile the rise of Hitler and the imminence of war in Europe had transformed the world situation. Instead of the problems brought by the Great Depression, the focus of public attention was the looming conflict in Europe.

It began with the civil war in Spain in 1936. While support for the democratically elected government was general in the United States, most of the liberal and progressive movement and its press uncritically backed the loyalists, even when it began to be evident that the Communists had gradually taken control of the legitimate government. *Common Sense*, under my editorial direction, supported a policy of neutrality. It seemed to me that the struggle in Spain had become a struggle between two similar forces, the Fascists and the Communists. I wrote a series of editorial articles aimed at the liberal press, later issued as a pamphlet denouncing what I called "War Mongering on the Left."

My argument followed naturally from the views I had worked out on my travels as to the nature of fascism: a revolutionary movement against the established economic and social order differing from communism only in its class base—middle class rather than working class—and its lack of an intellectual rationale. The Communists enjoyed an intellectual base in the pseudoscientific certainties of Marxism, for lack of which certainties the Fascists depended on the emotional appeals of nationalism and racism. But both movements were trying to impose a collectivist (that is, socialist) economic and social order, and the method of both was brute force. Enlightened Americans, I argued, should put their energies into finding an evolutionary and democratic path to the same end, rather than taking sides in the struggle between communism and fascism.

I took a somewhat similar stand in the face of the looming war in Europe. British and French opposition to the demands of Hitler for more *Lebensraum* ("living space") was motivated, I thought, by concern for the British and French colonial empires rather than for democracy, and this country should not be drawn into the impending war to save those empires.

In *Common Sense* we called the policy we advocated from 1936 to 1941 "non-intervention." We distinguished it sharply from the isolationism that had characterized much of the Midwestern populist movements from which we had hoped to see a new party emerge.

The Farmer-Labor Political Federation and its new persona, the American Commonwealth Federation, vanished without trace during those years, and my dream of a utopian "production for use" society was laid aside as the economy began to revive under the stimulus of Europe's race toward war. My desire to contribute to the coming of a better world found a new objective overseas: I visualized a new united Europe as a possible and desirable outcome of the great struggle building up on the continent, and I began work on a new book.

My recently published book, *Man's Estate*, had received some favorable comment, the *New York Times* reviewer going so far as to call it "a courageous piece of work" and "an excellently knit statement of an optimistic and highly civilized point of view." But it made no splash. Sales were minimal. From a publisher's perspective, it was a failure, and I heard no more from Norton of his desire to be my publisher. However, in Charlie Duell, a good friend and college classmate who had organized a new publishing firm, I found an enthusiastic supporter, and my next book appeared under the imprint of Duell, Sloane and Pearce. It was entitled *The United States of Europe*.

The idea of a united Europe embracing the continent's many ethnic groups was as old as the Roman Empire, and I traced its history through Charlemagne and the Holy Roman Empire to the recurrent wars for hegemony as the national state became the dominant mode. In the inter-war period of the 1920s, the ideal had been revived by the French political leader Aristide Briand, and a "Pan-Europe" movement was launched by an Austrian publicist, Count Coudenhove-Kalergi. I saw the war now unleashed in Europe as a civil war between different parts of a close-knit continent, and suggested that the war offered the possibility of realizing the old dream. I even projected the possibility of a European federation that included the fascist dictatorships as well as the democracies if, as seemed likely at the time I wrote, neither side could win a decisive victory.

Up until Pearl Harbor, I clung to the liberal "non-interventionist" line, urging in the pages of *Common Sense* that this country should stay out of the conflict and use its power to influence a constructive postwar settlement. I joined a group known as the Post-War World Council, organized by socialists and pacifists to promote liberal terms of peace.

The National Council of Churches about this time set up a commission under the chairmanship of John Foster Dulles to consider the terms of a possible peace settlement, and on one occasion I shared a platform with him at a panel discussion on American foreign policy at the Cosmopolitan Club in New York. Twelve years later, as Eisenhower's Secretary of State, Dulles became a major figure in the Cold War against the Soviet Union, but at that time he was associated with the peace movement.

It was a time of painful soul-searching for churchmen. My brother Brewster had recently been a student at the Union Theological Seminary on upper Broadway and had taken a course with Reinhold Niebuhr. I had two memorable contacts with Niebuhr. A socialist, he had become persuaded that the Marxist emphasis on the industrial working class was not wholly applicable in America, and was interested in the third-party prospects we had been promoting in *Common Sense*. At his request I joined a small gathering in his office to consider the future of left-wing politics. Lewis Corey, an ex-Communist who had recently written *Crisis of the Middle Class*, was present. Out of that meeting and others emerged the Union for Democratic Action, which later became Americans for Democratic Action, a liberal lobby that strove to work within the Democratic party and give direction to its liberal and progressive elements. As I had by this time given up hope of a new party, I would have liked to participate in the new undertaking. But Niebuhr was strongly committed to support of the Allies against Germany, and I played no further part in the new enterprise until after the war, when the ADA became for a while the left wing of the Democratic party.

From the perspective of half a century later, I have often asked myself whether I was wrong to oppose America's entry into the war. It must be remembered that even in the 1940 presidential election campaign neither Roosevelt nor Willkie, the Republican candidate, openly espoused intervention, even though France had surrendered and Britain was fighting for its life in the Blitz. Public opinion especially in the Midwest was still, if not isolationist, at least against entry into the war. Place names like Auschwitz and Buchenwald were then without significance.

While struggling with the ethical and moral problems of what America should do about the war in Europe, as seen from the Olympian heights of an editorial writer, I was in 1940 going through a highly personal inner struggle involving both my own vocation and my family. *Common Sense* had peaked as an independent left-wing journal of opinion and seemed to be going no further, and I no longer felt it had a special mission either for me or its readership. I no longer had expectations of a new political movement in which I might play a leading role. My political activities had involved considerable contact with Senators and members of Congress as well as state governors, and I began to feel I belonged in Washington rather than New York, participating in the making of policy rather than just commenting on it.

On the day Hitler entered Paris, June 14, 1940, my son Douglas was born, and this addition to my family raised the question of a more permanent home than our rented apartment on Tenth Street. Elfy and Kit would soon be ready for school, and despite our theoretical opposition to private schools for the privileged, Sylvia and I did not want to subject our children to the New York City school system. We even thought of moving to Fairfield County in Connecticut, from which I could still commute to New York while our children attended what presumably would be a higher quality public school. We actually looked at some houses for sale in the Riverside section of Greenwich.

I was ready to declare myself a Democrat, and with my Connecticut background I fantasized about running for Congress that year and so getting back on a mainstream political career.

I had been made a voter in Salem when I turned twenty-one. Eastern Connecticut clearly offered more opportunity for a New Deal Democrat than Fairfield County, but there was in fact, as I found out, a New Deal Democrat already representing the Second Congressional District. Congressman William Fitzgerald was a rough diamond from the labor movement. I called on him at his home in Norwich to suggest, in my exaggerated sense of my own qualifications, that he step down in my favor.

It was hardly the way to ingratiate myself with the Democratic party leadership in the area, but I was in a hurry to get into Congress. I had in fact, some months before, made myself known to the local party leaders as a potential office seeker, thanks to Yale classmate Guy B. Holt, who had preceded me as a would-be politician, relying on his father's political standing, by serving as state treasurer: Holt suggested I volunteer to become a member of a statewide committee of sponsors for the Jefferson-Jackson Day dinner in February of 1940. This gave me publicity as the son of a former Republican Senator converting to the Democratic party.

My hope of running for Congress in 1940 was clearly a fantasy, but I found that the Democratic leadership in New London County was looking for a candidate to run for the state senate in the staunchly Republican Twentieth or "Shoestring" District (so-called because its string of sixteen small towns encircled the cities of Norwich and New London). I was nominated as a sacrificial lamb, and then to the surprise of many—including me—I was elected by a margin of less than a hundred votes. Franklin Roosevelt, running for his third term as president, swept many Democrats like me into office.

I had moved my family for the summer into the Mumford House, a vacant old family mansion in Salem, inherited by my brother Hiram, who was then in the U.S. Foreign Service. With my election, this house now had to be considered my permanent residence. As it had been used only occasionally as a summer home since its acquisition by my Mitchell grandfather and had never been winterized, I now set about installing a central heating system.

For the first five months of 1941, I commuted daily from Salem to the state capitol in Hartford and occupied seat Number 20 in the senate circle. There were thirty-six senators, their desks arranged in two semi-circles before the presiding officer's dais. The senator from the Nineteenth District, Joseph Downes, sat on my left next to the aisle. I already knew him, and he became a close friend. He had by then served two terms and instructed me in the intricacies of legislative procedure.

The Democrats had won a majority of the senate seats in the last election, but with Connecticut's antiquated system of representation, the Republicans were in firm control of the lower house. Under the 1819 state constitution, each town no matter how small was entitled to at least one representative, while the cities of Hartford, New Haven, and Bridgeport could have no more than two.

Two issues dominated my brief tenure as an elected politician, milk and birth control.

My constituency of sixteen rural towns explained my assignment as the chairman of the Agriculture Committee. The chief grievance of the state's dwindling farm population, most of whom were dairy farmers, was the whipsawing to which they were subject in the open market; they felt the dealers who bought their milk at ridiculously low wholesale prices had them at their mercy. I knew nothing about the problem or how to solve it, but I was taken in hand by the Farm Bureau lobbyist and a professor at the state's agricultural college. They persuaded me, and through me the committee, to hire an expert in milk marketing legislation, and he in turn drafted a workmanlike bill regulating the dealers.

Hearings were held under my chairmanship over a series of weeks until the provisions were acceptable to all parties, and the bill passed successfully through the legislative process.

I was impressed by the valuable function of lobbyists representing special interests, particularly where the parties were reasonably well balanced in power and influence.

I was also impressed by the effectiveness of the down-to-earth, non-theoretical process by which the framework of laws in a civilized society is kept up-to-date and functioning. Dreams of a new social order were relegated to "pie in the sky." The politician is less a leader than a broker mediating conflicting interests. I found my fellow senators to be on the whole reasonable and well-intentioned.

Most of them, however, spoke a different language from me. Though on the floor of the senate in formal session all speech was dignified and restrained, the language of the streets was the rule in the caucus room where we met to determine the party line each morning, and I never became wholly accustomed to the flow of four-letter expletives that this all-male group indulged in off the floor. They were only slightly more decorous when the senate's presiding officer, Lieutenant Governor Odell Shepard, in whose office we met, was present. Shepard was of an older generation, white-haired, the soul of dignity and old-fashioned courtesy, a retired professor of English literature at Trinity College and an author of historical novels; his brief venture into politics paralleled mine, and we became good friends.

The senate agriculture committee, which had a Democratic majority, held hearings jointly with the house agriculture committee, then under Republican control. Partisanship was not extreme, and I found that the two-party system, with parties never too far apart on policy matters, gave stability and continuity to the legislative process. In the drafting of the Milk Marketing Act, the conflicting demands of the farmers and the big dairy companies who bought their milk were successfully mediated.

By contrast, the other issue with which I was involved was beyond mediation. For years liberal forces had sought the repeal of Connecticut's absurd ban on contraception, always to be thwarted by the Catholic opposition. The Democratic party in Connecticut, as in other industrial states, was largely Catholic in composition, and the Democratic majority in the state senate was far from ready to abandon its traditional championship of the Catholic position.

I was approached early in the session by the Birth Control League of Connecticut (later Planned Parenthood), asking me to sponsor the repeal bill. I agreed without hesitation, believing that my party standing would not be adversely affected. In the Democratic caucus, of course, I stood alone. The only other non-Catholic among the Democratic senators, a Jew, faithfully went along with the New Haven city machine of which he was a part.

The day of the floor debate, as it happened, was the day Sylvia had promised to take our two older children to Hartford to see "Daddy" in his role as senator. When I rose to argue for the repeal of the ban against birth control, I was disconcerted to see my four-year-old son Christopher squirming in the front row of the balcony directly above Senator Joe Cooney, attorney for the Hartford Diocese and the Catholic spokesman on this issue. My peroration of course changed no votes. The chamber divided along religious lines, and the law that made contraception a crime remained on the books.

I was later lauded by liberal admirers for having risked my political future on a matter of principle. But I made a study of the impact of the issue on my subsequent political career. During the debate, I had received a letter signed by a hundred parishioners of a Catholic church in Lisbon, a small town in my district, threatening to vote against me in the next election if I did not alter my stand. I found no significant difference between the vote in Lisbon and neighboring towns in the election of 1942. I concluded that my stand on the issue was not the reason for my failure to win reelection two years later. Rather, the normally Republican Twentieth District had reverted to type without the magic of Roosevelt's name on the ticket. And repeal of Connecticut's birth control law had to wait until the U.S. Supreme Court held it unconstitutional some years later.

At the end of the legislative session in June 1941, I was voted by the capitol press corps one of the members of the Assembly most likely to make a mark on future Connecticut politics. At the time I did not pay too much attention to such plaudits. I was not primarily interested in Connecticut politics. World War II was raging in Europe, and with Hitler's invasion of the Soviet Union in June of 1941, the relation of Communism to the liberal democracies called for some hard rethinking.

I was not ready to abandon my role as a left-wing publicist and molder of public opinion. I still had a tenuous position as an editor of *Common Sense*, ostensibly on leave, but I had left New York and did not want to resume the burden of putting out a monthly issue. I decided to use my new free time to write a book on a subject that I had for some time been wrestling with, the relation of socialism and democracy.

In Stalin's Russia, the monstrous purges of the mid-1930s had taken all the bloom off the great experiment that had for a while enthralled me and so many other left-leaning intellectuals. Why had the idealistic expectations of the believers in socialism turned into the realities of Stalin's terror? Like many liberals, I was inclined to blame the theories of Lenin and the Communists, which espoused dictatorship as a necessary if temporary aspect of the revolution—but absolute power tended toward absolute corruption. Still, a growing school of thought held that democratic socialism was a mirage: without a free economy, without free enterprise, political freedom was impossible.

Among the advocates of this view, I was most impressed by John Chamberlain, a friend and fraternity brother in the class ahead of me at Yale. His earlier *Farewell to Reform* had seemed to parallel my own shift from liberalism to socialism. Now he was shifting back to what seemed to me a conservative position, for if socialism led only to tyranny, then even the "socialistic" measures of the New Deal were suspect. I wanted to establish that a socialist or planned economy could be democratic; my brief experience with practical politics had given me new insights into the democratic process. I was now ready for another venture into authorship.

But at this point my domestic life was in some turmoil.

CHAPTER 54

Home in Salem

In settling into the Mumford House after deciding to move to Salem, I felt I was finally in a home of my own. We had put a central heating system into the old house, and Sylvia had begun repapering the more shabby rooms. I tended to overlook the fact that the house did not belong to me.

I was, of course, a tenant of my brother Harry. The old Mumford farm had been put in his name by my grandfather Mitchell, but Harry had never occupied the house during his years as a Foreign Service Officer. He had served in Japan, Poland, and England, and at the outbreak of war in 1939 he was stationed in the American consulate in Marseilles. He shipped his family out when France was invaded in 1940. Rose and her five children (a sixth was on the way) found temporary shelter with her parents in Georgia, until he was reassigned to the American embassy in Buenos Aires. In the summer of 1941, he took accumulated leave and asked us to vacate his Salem house so that he could spend a couple of months in his own home with his family.

Another old family house, the Woodbridge House, only a mile across the valley from the Mumford House, was untenanted that summer, and we had no great difficulty in making that our temporary home. A handsome eighteenth-century mansion, it had been built for my great-great-grandfather Nathaniel Shaw Woodbridge, but it went out of the family for lack of male heirs about 1850, then was bought back, with its adjacent family burial ground, by my Mitchell grandfather at the beginning of the twentieth century. In return for being allowed to name my parents' first-born son—and he chose his grandfather's family name Woodbridge—he put the title of the Woodbridge farm in the name of his new grandson, though reserving a life use to himself. Like the Mumford House, it had been occupied by family members only during summers.

Woodbridge, who was now at the University of California at Berkeley, teaching Chinese history, readily agreed to my offer to pay him rent for the summer. And so I moved my family into this second ancestral property only a hundred yards from my great-great-grandparents' graves. But Sylvia found the move wrenching. She remembered her own secure childhood in what seemed a permanent home in New Canaan, and longed for the certainties of a home not dependent on the whims of my brothers. At the end of the summer, after moving back to the Mumford House, we began looking for a house to buy.

I too had been left a farm by my grandfather, the Beebe farm across the highway from the Mumford farm, also a part of the original Woodbridge estate. The acreage included Mitchell Pond, the fine bottomland around it, capacious dairy barns, and an old house. But the house, located next to the barns and barnyard and of poor design, had no appeal to us as a permanent residence, and was already occupied by a tenant farmer.

We heard that the Henry Darling farm south of the Mumford House might be for sale. The farmhouse there, dun-colored and remodeled in mid-Victorian style, did not attract us. However, on a fine day in September, with the leaves just beginning to turn, I was driving to Hartford for a meeting of the Highway Safety Commission to which I had been appointed, when just beyond the Salem-Colchester line I happened to notice Henry Darling at the wheel of an old car, waiting at an intersection for the highway traffic to pass. I drove on for a quarter of a mile till I suddenly decided that my Hartford appointment could be deferred. I swung around, chased after him, caught up with him a couple of miles down the road, and when he pulled over, I asked him whether his house was indeed for sale.

"It was," he said, "but it's been sold. I'm on my way to Old Lyme to sign the deed at the lawyer's office. I'm sorry I didn't know you were interested. I'd rather have sold it to you than the New York man. Of course, at the last minute, if he isn't ready to close, it might come available again."

I asked if he could wait long enough for me to have a look at the house and consult Sylvia about making an offer. He guessed he could be half an hour late.

I chased back, found Sylvia at the Mumford House, told her what was afoot, and drove the half mile to the Darling house, where we found Henry waiting on the lawn. The charming setting, with big sugar maples touched with orange along the road, and the magnificent old white oak tree shading the lawn, gave the dingy old house a romantic glow.

We asked Henry how much he was selling it for. He said five thousand dollars. The fact that so much acreage went with the house—about two hundred and fifty acres, he thought—had made the place hard to sell.

Sylvia and I conferred. The house was certainly shabby and unattractive; it lacked running water (except for a hand pump in the kitchen), central heating, and electricity; but it could be made temporarily livable. We told Henry we would pay six thousand for the place if today's deal with the New Yorker didn't go through.

And in this chancy manner, we acquired a beautiful home that is still mine. Henry Darling's New York purchaser was not satisfied with the title; the purchaser's lawyer wanted an easement cleared before a warranty deed could be accepted. The easement, allowing an entry onto the land to cut laurel, did not bother us, and the sale to me and Sylvia went through in due course.

We hired a New York architect, Julian Whittlesey, an old friend of ours, then achieving an international reputation. He found only the frame of the house and some of the floors in sound condition, and the central chimney with four fireplaces could be rebuilt. Only slight improvements were needed to transform the adjoining sheds into a two-car garage, and the old hay barn with room for a dozen cows in the basement was in fine shape. But the house itself had to be largely rebuilt, and a new two-story wing, containing three new bedrooms and baths, replaced the old kitchen and woodshed.

So we ended up not with a makeshift temporary shelter, as I had at first foreseen, but with a large permanent home. The ultimate cost was many times the original price, but I had recently inherited my share of my grandmother's three-million-dollar estate and had no difficulty paying the bills without a mortgage.

A few years later, when Sylvia was chafing at being surrounded and submerged by Bingham relatives, I transferred the title of the property to her, to give her the feeling that it was her home, and I have now in my old age only a life use of it. But for over fifty years, it has been a family home to which my four children and their children have often returned.

While our children were still at home, we had servants. As a boy, I had taken a big house staffed by a full complement of servants for granted. On my world travels I had gone so far—in complying with what I conceived my status entitled me to—as to have a personal servant when I was in India, though my growing social conscience rebelled. When my travels in the Soviet Union made me think of myself as a revolutionary socialist if not a communist, my moral objections to domestic service became an article of faith. But when I married Sylvia, who sympathized with my classless ideals but would not let theory control our life together, one black maid-of-all-work after another came in by the day. The last in the series, Marian Tedo, a teen-ager when she first came to work for us, became Sylvia's treasured friend even after her marriage ended her employment with us.

In our last year on Tenth Street, 1939–40, with war breaking out in Europe and the plight of the Jews under Hitler becoming evident, Sylvia obtained the services of an Austrian Jewish refugee, wife of a prominent Viennese cardiologist. Her husband hoped to resume his medical practice in this country but found that only two states, New York and Connecticut, allowed a noncitizen to obtain a medical license, and then only after passing a rigid examination. Dr. Ehrenstein felt he would need at least half a year to prepare for such an examination. Sylvia found a small apartment for the couple only a block from where we lived, and there the Ehrensteins moved in with their dachshund and such meager possessions as they had been able to take with them when they fled the Third Reich.

Ilse Ehrenstein, a little elderly lady, came down the block every day to help Sylvia with the housework. After a couple of months, during which Ilse improved her English and her knowledge of an American kitchen, her husband learned he could work as a doctor even without a license in a Louisiana hospital, and they left us with mutual expressions of good will to go to New Orleans. Two weeks later they were back. They had found the color line in the Louisiana hospital so like the racist policies of Hitler from which they had sought escape that they could not tolerate living in the South—even with a salary.

The Ehrensteins were unable to go along with us when we moved to Salem in the summer of 1940. They scraped by for a year or so more on her meager earnings. Then we heard he had passed his medical exams and had secured a hospital appointment in upstate New York, and eventually he joined the teaching faculty at the University of Rochester.

With three children and the big Mumford House to care for, Sylvia and I now thought we should get a couple to live with us. An employment agency in New York found a Polish couple who were agreeable to living in an isolated country house. But I could not find enough for the husband to do, and when he was asked to wait on the table as butler, he appeared in his undershirt on a hot day—and we decided we did not want a married couple after all. For a while we had two girls from Stonington, cousins whose fathers were part of the Portuguese colony of commercial fishermen there. But they had to return to high school in the fall.

Calling on an employment agency again, we obtained a French peasant woman who wanted to live in the country. Her name was Julianne. She was big and easygoing, and the high point of her employment was the evening she went out to fish for eels and came back with a basketful.

She was with us in the spring of 1942 when Sylvia went to New York to have our fourth child. During the last two weeks of her pregnancy, Sylvia was a house guest of Ben and Jane Spock. Ben was our pediatrician, and I had known both him and his wife from my boyhood. Sylvia made herself useful during that stay by helping to read page proof of Ben's soon-to-be-famous *Baby and Child Care* and was rewarded with an acknowledgment in the first edition. During her absence I was further supported in Salem by the presence of Frances Bingham, my brother Brewster's wife, so the household was not entirely in the care of Julianne.

Sylvia came back with our new baby, Stephen, at the beginning of May. The lilac hedges beside the drive into the Mumford House, as well as the lilacs around our new house, were in full bloom.

In the architectural plans, we had provided a spacious bedroom and bath beyond the kitchen with extra radiators to ensure Julianne's comfort. But during the process of moving, Sylvia began to notice that minor articles of houseware and clothes were disappearing. She took advantage of Julianne's day off to check her bedroom and found a drawer full of pilfered items, including some from a collection of miniature animals and bric-a-brac. On being confronted with the evidence the next day, Julianne shrugged and was meekly driven to the railroad station in New London.

Another married couple worked for us briefly as we settled into our new house at the end of the summer. Having a man-of-all-work available was helpful as we collected our furniture from various places of storage and arranged it in what was at last a home of our own. Sylvia had been the beneficiary of a generous distribution of furniture when her Doughty grandparents' home in Brooklyn was sold; I had received my share of furnishings both from my grandmother Mitchell's estate in 1937 and from the sale of my parents' home in New Haven, much of which I had put in storage. Between Sylvia and me, we had inherited enough to furnish our new seven-bedroom house in a fairly lavish style with four-poster beds, colonial reproductions of chairs and tables, Oriental rugs, and antique chests of drawers. I had only a few twinges of social conscience when I thought of my recent revolutionary biases.

They were being modified all through this period of home and family building, as I worked on new books. The war in Europe had come to overshadow my interest in social reform. Although I had once been a near convert to Soviet Communism, the purge trials of the late 1930s, when Stalin exterminated many of the old Bolshevik leaders, appalled me. When Stalin made common cause with Hitler in carving up Poland and then went on to subdue Finland and absorb Estonia, Latvia, and Lithuania, while Hitler overran Denmark and Norway, there seemed little to choose between Nazism and Communism during the winter and spring of 1939–40. Britain, France, and the Low Countries awaited attack. It seemed clear to me that the era of small sovereign states was over in Europe. The only alternative to the precarious balance of power between the great powers lay in European federation. Perhaps that might be the outcome of the war.

I was researching my book called *The United States of Europe*. I found there were numerous supra-national agencies in Europe already functioning to regulate river and rail transport, communications, and trade. The book came to fruition in the months of the so-called Phony War, before the Nazi invasion of the West. As part of a flood of speculation about the consequences of the war, it had a modest success. Fifty years later, the ideal of European unity is now more than ever finding expression in supra-national institutions like the European Community, while ethnic and nationalist rivalries spring to life in the collapse of empires.

Another book soon followed, entitled *Techniques of Democracy*, also published by Duell. In it, I analyzed the various possible meanings of the word *democracy*. As a form of government, democracy might be no more than, first, the right to vote and, second, the making of political decisions by majority vote. But a democratic society depended on much more. I saw it as requiring that every individual have the right to participate in all decisions affecting him or her. Since becoming part of a small-town community and experiencing an intensive course in the nature of government as a member of the state senate, I had found there were many ways in which individuals could assert themselves other than by simply voting on election day. These ways I called "techniques." I divided them into "traditional" techniques, such as the ballot box, parliamentary procedure, and civil liberties, and new techniques, such as labor unions, cooperatives, and devices of scientific management that enlist the positive participation of workers in the administration of large enterprises, whether public or private.

It was hard to concentrate on my writing after Pearl Harbor, but I persuaded myself that I could make no better contribution to the war effort than to continue with the development of a thesis that might well have a bearing on the postwar world.

Selden Rodman was shortly to be drafted, and the editorial direction of *Common Sense* tended to be more and more dependent on Sidney Hertzberg. He was an able young intellectual. As a former member of the Socialist party, he was so opposed to American entry into the war that he became an active promoter of the America First Committee.

That Committee had brought together a strange combination of socialists, pacifists, and liberals on the one hand, and populist isolationists on the other. Among its early adherents was Chester Bowles, who was leaving a successful career in advertising to become increasingly active in public affairs and politics. His first political statement was an article he wrote for *Common Sense* distinguishing between isolationism and "non-intervention," which he defined as avoiding military involvement in the war while playing an active role in international affairs—the policy we were advocating in *Common Sense.*

Chester Bowles, having achieved the financial success he and his Yale colleague and partner William Benton had set as a prerequisite to careers in public service, was now living in a handsome mansion he and his second wife "Steb" (née Dorothy Stebbins) had built overlooking the Connecticut River near its mouth in the town of Essex. It was on this estate, half an hour's drive from Salem, that I first met the Bowleses at a Democratic party picnic and rally during the 1940 campaign. We were both entering Connecticut state politics and had much in common; it was Chet who persuaded me, after my election to the state senate, that it was possible to make my permanent home in Salem while still maintaining my New York contacts.

After Pearl Harbor, Japan's swift conquest of Malaysia and Indonesia had cut off this country's chief source of rubber, and the rationing of tires was an immediate necessity. Bowles was appointed by Connecticut's Governor Robert Hurley as the state administrator for tire rationing. Within a few months, gasoline, sugar, and other scarce items were also subject to rationing. Bowles set up a system of local rationing boards, one to each municipality in the state. The delicate task of deciding who in each community might have new tires or extra gasoline was entrusted to unpaid local citizens rather than to a network of bureaucrats. Here to my mind was another new "technique" of democratic administration replacing what would otherwise have been sheer bureaucracy.

With the manuscript of my book now in the hands of my publisher, and still uncertain as to my role in a country at war, I accepted a job offer from Bowles to become the "State Organization Officer" in what was now called the Office of Price Administration (OPA). My job was to see that the 169 local rationing boards and 8 appeals boards in the 8 counties were provided with guidelines and supplies. Bowles, interested in my future career, explained to me that through the contacts I developed with local administrators and town officials throughout the state, I could build myself up for future political campaigning.

For five months of 1942, I commuted from Salem to Hartford. The OPA was a federal agency, and I became a part of the national civil service. As such, I was required to resign my seat for the remainder of my first term in the state senate. Since the General Assembly met only every other year, this resignation seemed of no consequence.

I was provided with a secretarial staff as the paperwork piled up and with five "field officers" when it became apparent that I could hardly keep in personal touch with almost two hundred local and county rationing boards.

However, by midsummer I was finding the routines and pettinesses of government bureaucracy increasingly tedious and unrewarding. I felt I was not contributing anything that another could not do as well or better, and I was still attracted to the challenges of elective politics. I resigned my job and accepted renomination to the state senate, only to lose—in the absence of Roosevelt's name on the ballot.

CHAPTER 55

I Go to War

A number of my friends and members of my family were in uniform by the end of 1942, a year after Pearl Harbor. Three of my brothers were commissioned officers: Woodbridge in Navy Intelligence, Charles in the Navy Medical Service, and Jack in Army Intelligence. Two Knox brothers-in-law were abroad with commissions in the army and navy. My father had offered his services to the navy as a lecturer on the Pacific islands at naval officers' training stations, and I felt he would like to see me also in uniform. After my thirty-eighth birthday in February of 1943, I was no longer subject to the draft, and with four children I would probably have been exempted anyway. I began work on another book, this time a summary of what in my previous books seemed relevant to the war and the postwar world. I called it "The Practice of Idealism." But I was eager to take some more active part in the vast changes the war was bringing about. What did my background and experience have to offer?

I read somewhere about the constructive role that professional men and civilian specialists were playing in restoring civil administration in territory

375

liberated from the Nazis. North Africa was now under Allied control, and the Allied invasion of Sicily followed. An extensive program of recruitment and training of "military government officers" was under way as the prospect of liberating Europe opened up, and I heard that the New York Yale Club was a recruiting center.

There, in the summer of 1943, I filed my application for a commission. Weeks went by. In September I received a notice that I was commissioned a captain in the Army of the United States, Civil Affairs Division, and should await orders as to when and where to report. More weeks went by. I bought a uniform at Brooks Brothers and read an *Officer's Manual.* Finally in December came orders to report to a training camp in Michigan the day after Christmas.

Now I had a place in the war effort. Now I was in the mainstream. Now for the first time since I had become a rebel, I belonged. Yet with some trepidation I considered the dangers that might lie ahead: even if I were not to be a combat soldier, I would be entering some combat zone immediately behind advancing combat troops. The function of military government was to provide an administrative structure for occupied territory, and occupied territory was sure, at first, to be a place of wreckage and turbulence.

On Christmas day, 1943, after the morning ceremonies of opening presents around a Christmas tree, I left home. Sylvia and the children saw me off in my new uniform at the New London train station. As the train pulled away, my feelings were mostly relief at shedding the burden of family responsibilities.

After a night on a Pullman sleeping car, I arrived at Fort Custer outside Battle Creek, Michigan, and became a willing cog in the vast bureaucracy of the military. I filled out forms, was assigned a serial number and "dog tags," and rounded out my equipment. We studied training manuals and heard lectures on "standard operating procedures" (SOP). The several thousand trainees were all officers, and our instructors, mostly enlisted men, treated us with deference.

It was like being back in boarding school, and I reverted to a comfortable feeling that grownups would make all decisions for me. I liked the scheduling, the close-order drill, and instruction in the use and maintenance of a carbine and a 9mm handgun. When I was summoned by the colonel in command of my unit, I was as pleased as a little boy, and came running to salute smartly and receive fatherly recognition. Colonel Babcock had been police chief of New London and, seeing my name on a roster and knowing I had been a state senator, was only keeping his political fences in order.

Then suddenly we heard we were being sent overseas without further training.

With Italy in Allied hands, the liberation of France from both south and north appeared imminent, and the collapse of all German resistance seemed a possibility. Ready or not, military government might be needed sooner than expected, and military government officers for the European theater, now several thousand in number, should be on the European side of the Atlantic.

We were first transported to a staging area near Youngstown, Ohio. Sylvia, desperate not to lose touch with me, had already begun the practice, to which I had dutifully responded, of almost daily letter writing. Now, thinking she might never see me again, she traveled to Youngstown for a frantic farewell in a hotel bedroom. But we moved to another and final staging area near Taunton, Massachusetts, from where I drove in a rented car to Salem for another few hours together in the middle of the night. The children were all asleep, and I did not rouse them. But it was clear that I had not been able to put my family wholly behind me.

Then in the middle of the next night, on a blacked-out Boston dock, I accepted a Red Cross cup of coffee and a doughnut and marched up a gangplank to a troopship. I was finally off to war.

By February 1944 the North Atlantic was relatively safe, but we traveled in a convoy. I was assigned a meaningless job watching over the galley, which ran by itself anyway. But I came down with a bronchial cold—the last hectic days ashore with inadequate sleep had been too much for me—and I gratefully spent a couple of days in the ship's hospital.

We landed at Liverpool at night and were taken on a long uncomfortable ride in army vehicles through the blacked-out countryside—to find ourselves in the morning at a magnificent barracks complex in the south of England. It was still February, and we had left snow and ice at home, but here the grass was green and spring was in the air, and the big estate on which the military training center had been built just before the war provided a surprisingly luxurious setting for the assembling and organizing of the European Civil Affairs Division (ECAD).

I spent three months in this bucolic setting, learning that the chief occupation of soldiering is waiting. Between various training exercises, assemblies, "parades," orientation sessions, I had time to explore the neighborhood with one or another congenial fellow officer.

The village of Shrivenham with its ancient church and a pub or two was near by. Across a wide valley three or four miles away loomed the South Downs, and if it had not been camouflaged, I was told, one could see a great white horse carved in the turf of a chalk hill. I remembered having been given a prize book at Groton entitled the *Scouring of the White Horse* about an ancient folk festival in the village of Uffington, and now I found myself serendipitously within sight of Uffington Castle, a prehistoric earthwork above the famous white horse. By writing Sylvia to send me that book, I was able to let her know where I was stationed.

It was a strangely happy period in an enchanted English spring, with the horrors of war only seen on psychological training films. Airborne troops would soon be dying across the Channel, but now we chair-borne soldiers only glanced up at the gliders being towed by planes that sailed overhead.

General Eisenhower visited our encampment, and our West Point commanding officer staged a formal parade, but the General dismissed the parade and asked us to fall out of our formations and gather round him, all two thousand of us, and gave us a moving talk on the importance of our coming role.

We were sorted out into teams targeted for particular areas. At first we understood there would be a joint Allied occupation of Germany, but the plan was changed to separate occupation zones—the American zone to be the Ruhr and northwest Germany, the British in the southwest, and the Soviet Union in the east. Then for reasons no doubt connected with the general strategic plan for the invasion, the British and American zones were switched.

D-Day, the unknown date for the invasion of the continent, was near, but how long it would take to achieve a Nazi surrender was anyone's guess. Months of further waiting and "training" were ahead. On June 6, my unit set out in a convoy of trucks for Manchester; on the way the rumor spread that this was D-Day and that landings on the beaches of Normandy were now in progress.

In Manchester I found myself billeted in a private home with the unexpected privacy of a tiny bedroom under the same roof as an only slightly resentful working-class couple. I only slept there and saw little of them. The headquarters of my detachment and of the rest of the military government personnel preparing to take over civil affairs in Germany was now in a branch of the University of Manchester in a suburban area a mile or two from the city center.

Marches and military formations were behind us. The university provided instruction in the German language and in the organization of local and regional government in Germany. One of my instructors, an Austrian Jewish émigré named Heinz Arndt, became a congenial friend, with whom I maintained contact for some years after the war, even when he became a professor of political economy at the National University of Australia.

The officers in regional detachments like mine now were given specialized functions. There was a legal division, a public safety division, and an agricultural division, among others. I asked to be and was assigned to the labor division, which also had jurisdiction over social insurance and welfare.

The same functional divisions had taken place in the civil affairs branch at Supreme Headquarters in London, and a staff officer of the labor division named David A. Morse contacted me. He had been part of the liberal-left-labor milieu I had been close to as editor of *Common Sense*. After the war he became the head of the International Labor Office (ILO). Now he was friendly and helpful.

He told me of the scrapping of the plans he and others had been working on, aimed at promoting a democratic renewal in postwar Germany, with special reliance on the Social Democratic party and the Social Democratic trade union organization. At the Quebec Conference in September, Roosevelt and Churchill had opted for the wholly punitive "Morgenthau Plan," which called for the total destruction of Germany as an industrial power. Moreover, there was to be no fraternization between the military government apparatus and the civil government of Germany, even after all officials tainted with Nazism had been replaced.

For the present, Morse told me, with the Allied forces still trying to break out of their Normandy bridgehead, military government personnel would face more waiting in idleness, and he suggested I might like a tour of temporary duty in London. He arranged for me to be ordered to London headquarters to prepare a staff study on the problem of unemployment in Germany after its surrender.

It was clearly a "make work" project, but I was delighted to be nearer the center of things. The air blitz was by now ancient history, but London was at this point under siege by robot planes, or "buzz bombs," and for the first time I felt I was under fire. Several times a day the air raid sirens would sound, and I would hear the strange buzz of an approaching bomb. So long as the sound could be heard, the robot was still flying, but when the buzzing stopped, it meant the flying bomb was on its way to earth. Those nearby held their breath until a muffled thud, usually distant, was heard, and people would then resume an interrupted sentence. Only once was a bomb so close that I could hear the tinkle of glass from shattered windows following the explosion.

The subway platforms at night were generally covered by recumbent bodies, mostly those of families with children, trying to get a quiet night's sleep. I realized the tension under which everybody lived when one day, as I was walking down a street, I noticed that I was twisting and untwisting my fingers.

Back in Manchester after this brief London interlude, I found our departure for the continent was imminent. Paris had been liberated, and it seemed that military government personnel might soon be needed in Germany; we were to be brought closer to the front. Each detachment had by this time its own trucks and jeeps, and they were being fitted with high exhausts and air intakes to enable them to function in the surf in a beach landing.

Then early in September came our own D-Day, and we were moved to the next staging area. It was a long exhausting push, down from the Midlands at night to Southampton, embarkation on a crowded transport, daybreak on Omaha Beach where a makeshift dock had been constructed so our vehicles did not have to splash through the surf, and another long push through shattered towns and cities (St. Malo seemed to be nothing but rubble, though military police had cleared and marked a route through the city), and arrival after dark in a pine grove where we were told to pitch our pup tents.

The next day revealed the most romantic as well as the most primitive setting of my wartime experiences. Above a steep incline behind our encampment was a marble palace next to a ruined castle, and formal gardens with lawns and flower beds, overlooking a vast green landscape of woods, fields, and villages. The village at the foot of the cliff on which stood the castle was called Rochefort-sur-Yvelines. The great marble mansion, built perhaps at the turn of the century by a rich Paris tycoon, was a center for fashion shows before the war. There our top brass was housed, and some pretext of further training and language instruction carried on, but for the most part we spent the next month making ourselves as comfortable as possible in our wooded encampment, and using freely granted leaves to hitch rides into Paris thirty miles away.

Paris on my first visit—only three weeks after its liberation—was still in a holiday mood, and American soldiers were greeted everywhere with smiles. One of my first objectives was to look up my old French governess. For years I had sporadically corresponded with her and knew that her last address, even up to the beginning of the war, was in a Catholic "retraite." After a long ride on the Metro, feeling ungainly and conspicuous with my helmet and side arm—all American army personnel in Paris were still required to wear full battle dress and carry a weapon—I appeared among the startled but welcoming nuns, and was told that dear Mademoiselle Leonie Bernard had died the year before.

There were other visits to Paris, usually in the company of congenial friends, sometimes in an ECAD "personnel carrier," sometimes hitching a ride on an army vehicle or in a farmer's truck powered by woodchips and carrying farm produce into the city. We would catch the Metro at the end of the line and make our way into the heart of the city, perhaps the Place de l'Opéra to have an aperitif at a sidewalk table in front of the Café de la Paix or at the Ritz bar, basking as liberators or pretending to be just tourists—and marveling that Paris had magically escaped war damage.

We spent a month at Rochefort camped in the pine grove, sleeping in pup tents and fed from field kitchens. But as autumn was passing, the Allied forces were stalled somewhere to the northeast and had not reached the Rhine. One morning I found ice in the helmet that I used as a wash basin in front of my tent. It was clear that our military government detachments would not be moving into Germany before winter.

Instead we were moved into winter quarters in a former French army ordinance depot near Troyes, eighty miles east of Paris. There I spent four months, interminably waiting. Training exercises were devised to keep up some semblance of activity. Back in Manchester I had been assigned to a regional detachment pinpointed to Stuttgart and the Württemberg region. We were about thirty officers and as many enlisted men, the officers representing civilian specialties—law, public safety, and the like.

The class structure of the army was more in evidence here than before. The barracks we lived in were segregated by rank, though there was probably little difference between the officers' quarters and the enlisted men's. The enlisted men were mostly assigned to driving our jeeps, trucks, and personnel carriers, and to taking care of field kitchens from which we were fed.

One day I was accosted by a grimy-looking private.

"Captain Bingham," he began, "You may not remember me, but we've met in New York. My name is Murray Gross and I was an organizer for the International Ladies' Garment Workers' Union. I've read *Common Sense* and know about your efforts to promote a Farmer-Labor party; I am a member of the Socialist party myself. After basic training I got myself assigned to the Civil Affairs Division, since I speak German and know something of the German labor movement. But I've been put in the motor pool. I was promoted to PFC [private first class] and then I was demoted for talking back to the lieutenant running the motor pool. I wonder if you could get me assigned to your detachment."

I was fortunately able to have Murray Gross assigned not only to my regional detachment but also to my Labor Section. He turned out to be more fluent in German—and more conversant with social conditions in Germany and the German labor movement—than any of the officers. After I entered Germany, and for the year I served as regional chief of what became the Manpower Section, I relied on his understanding and good judgment more than on any of the guidelines or field manuals provided. But for the moment, in the post we were in, there was little that could be done to change his lowly status.

It was a hard winter, but we had shelter and after a couple of weeks even a crude hot shower. I was able to get my laundry done in the nearby village where the cake of GI soap I provided was a treasure. At Christmas I was invited to a holiday celebration in the home of a formerly prosperous businessman in Troyes. His wife and six children took me in and gave me some of the feeling of being part of an affectionate family.

Another family that welcomed me lived in the little town of Romilly-sur-Seine, a few miles west of our base. The middle-aged head of the household, owner of a small furniture store, had been active in the "Résistance"—or so he said. I was skeptical, for it seemed clear that the vast majority of the population in a conquered area were docile and accepted the presence of a conquering army as a fact of life without risking their lives to harass it.

The housewife and their giggling and plump eighteen-year-old daughter were welcoming and full of little jokes and laughter, piling my plate with meat and potatoes until I was stuffed and protesting. Yet I knew that the civilian population everywhere in France was on desperately short rations.

At one time that winter, the reality of the war suddenly seemed close. In the so-called Battle of the Bulge in Belgium, the German army had succeeded in breaking through the Allied lines in a desperate counterattack, and was now threatening the Allied rear where our headquarters were located. We were civilians in uniform but still under military command. Armed with rifles and pistols, we were told we would have to try to defend the base if the enemy approached.

Few of my fellow officers considered resistance to an armored column feasible—it seemed a totally quixotic idea. Fortunately the Battle of the Bulge ended in the defeat of the Nazis; surrenders of German units began to become common; and we were thrown back to waiting for our turn to enter the fray.

In March I received orders to move to Paris, along with a colleague named Spencer Meredith, who like me was catalogued as being reasonably fluent in French. We were to establish liaison with an educational project aimed at training French military government officers for service in Germany.

We were luxuriously housed in a Paris hotel and attended lectures at the Sorbonne on some of the subjects in which we were supposedly already trained—the rules of war, military justice, and selection and supervision of local civilian officials to carry on local administration.

Our duties were minimal and Paris in early spring was still in a holiday mood. Well fed in a sumptuous officers' club, I began to feel guilty over my high living in the middle of a devastating war, and visited an army hospital to try to get some sense of the suffering and death that the great war machine was grinding out. As in any hospital, the suffering and death were behind sanitized curtains, and my conscience was not eased.

After a month of sybaritic living came word that our detachments were moving out of winter quarters. The Allied armies had crossed the Rhine, and the Nazi forces were being pushed steadily back; the occupation of Germany was beginning. Meredith and I caught up with our units and rode in our jeeps through the devastated and empty ruins of Saarbrücken into Germany.

The destination of my regional detachment was Stuttgart—still in enemy hands. In the meantime, I was given my first assignment directly connected with the occupation. Thanks again to my linguistic knowledge—more fluent in German than most of my fellow officers—I was put in command of a four-man "Documents Team"—to search for incriminating Nazi documents.

CHAPTER 56

In Occupied Germany

The preservation of documentary evidence of Nazi crimes was a new concern of the high command. Apparently, a few months before, when Strasbourg fell to American troops, the former headquarters of the SS (the Schutzstaffel, or Security Police responsible for crushing resistance to the German occupation of France) was used as a barracks, and all its files were burned. At this point, with the growing interest in bringing Nazi war criminals to trial, military government was charged with safeguarding such documentary material for later war crimes trials.

For two or three weeks, I took my little "Documents Team" to town halls and other likely repositories. We even searched an old ruined castle that we were told had been an SS headquarters. Bothered by smoke from the still burning wing of the castle, we found cabinets in the main tower containing old family records, but nothing of current significance. We drove to the next town through the verdant spring countryside, the air sweet with the scent of apple blossoms. We passed women carrying sprays of lilac back to their ruined homes, oblivious of the occasional thud of a distant explosion.

For a few days we were "attached," for housekeeping purposes, to a mysterious "task force" that I later learned was searching for evidence of German progress in the production of nuclear weapons.

The only fruit of my little unit's search was in Stuttgart. The city had been abandoned by the German military three days before. Bypassed by the American Seventh, it was occupied by French colonial troops, units of the First French Army, recently assembled by General De Gaulle—mostly from North Africa. From American military police directing traffic, we heard reports of rampaging French colonials raping German women. We located the SS headquarters and found it stripped of current files. But in the former recruitment office we found, under piles of stationery and promotional literature, some cartons of old personnel records, mostly applications for officers' commissions, containing each applicant's résumé.

We sent these records back to our headquarters, and wondered later whether any SS officer was ever identified from these documents in the war crimes trials held in Nuremberg and elsewhere.

Stuttgart had not been the target of the thousand-plane bombing raids that had flattened Frankfurt, Hamburg, and other large German cities, and while much of the center of the city was in ruins, destruction was spotty, leaving many fine buildings virtually unscathed. The palatial government office building, ultimately the headquarters of the regional military government to which I was attached, had suffered not much more than broken windows. The State Opera House dominating the central square was likewise found mostly intact. Yet my first impression was of a dead city. Aside from military vehicles, the only sign of life on the streets was a few furtive civilians carrying jugs of wine from looted municipal cellars.

I was to live in Stuttgart for most of the year of my active service in military government. For my first billet, I was assigned to a private house on a tree-shaded residential street, the only visible occupant of which was an elderly lady who spoke reasonably good English. She had once lived in Philadelphia, she said, married to an American, and claimed to be still an American citizen. She had draped an American flag over her ornate front door. She welcomed me in effusive agitation.

It was standard operating procedure at this time to fraternize with no one and to remain at all times in battle gear. When I lay in bed that night, in clean sheets for the first time in weeks, I kept my own armament, a 9mm automatic pistol, within reach on my bedside table. The night passed quietly. Weeks later I heard reports that my landlady had been a prominent Nazi, but I never saw her again after my two nights as her house guest.

The regional military government detachment to which I was assigned back in Manchester was supposed to locate in Stuttgart, and assume supervision of all the local detachments in Württemberg. But I soon found that Stuttgart had become a pawn of geopolitics. General De Gaulle had assumed leadership of the Free French and was determined to salvage what he could from the defeat of France.

Roosevelt, Churchill, and Stalin had reached agreement at Yalta on unconditional surrender for Germany followed by a tripartite occupation of German territory. De Gaulle now demanded a share in the military government of its traditional enemy and a zone of occupation for France. His makeshift army had fortunately been able to take possession of Stuttgart after German forces withdrew. The French general in command refused to give up the city as ordered by General Eisenhower, the supreme commander of the Allied Expeditionary Forces. After a few days of confrontation, the news filtered down to us that the conflict had been resolved at the highest level, that is, by Roosevelt, Churchill, and De Gaulle: France would be assigned a portion of the American Zone of occupation, consisting of the southern half of Württemberg and Baden, but De Gaulle would give up the occupation of Stuttgart, though only after the First French Army had marched through the city in a victory parade.

As it happened, I had a small part in this arrangement. When I contacted my regional detachment, at this point marking time in the town of Schwaebisch-Gmuend, some twenty miles east of Stuttgart, my duties as a member of the Documents Team were terminated, and I was ordered to remain in Stuttgart as a liaison between the French and American military government personnel. My only duty, as it turned out, was to stand on the reviewing stand with General De Gaulle at the victory parade. When I presented myself there in my best captain's uniform, the General had not yet arrived. Awed by my prominence, I waited to be saluted by what I took to be a French lieutenant bearing one star on his shoulder (my service at the French military government school in Paris had accustomed me to French military insignia), only to discover after I had taken my place at the back of the reviewing stand that he was a Brigadier General, presumably the highest American officer in the area at the time.

De Gaulle arrived—an incredibly tall, incredibly thin, distant figure—and loftily shook hands with all those on the reviewing stand. Then, erect and unsmiling, he took his place at the front of the stand to receive the salutes of the First French Army as the soldiers began to march by. It was a ragged army, mostly colonial troops from Senegal and Algeria. Many of them wore desert robes, but they were led by French officers, some in borrowed American uniforms. For hours they straggled by, while the ramrod at the front of the reviewing stand never faltered.

I returned to Schwaebisch-Gmuend. Within the regional detachment, I had expected to be at the head of the so-called Labor Section, but a Major Rafferty, outranking me, had also been assigned to that section. Until he was reassigned, I had to remain under his orders. Happily I found he had already organized the section by hiring a secretary, and I soon fell heir to her. A personable lady of good education, fluent in English, Frau S. had left her former husband in East Germany and moved with her twelve-year-old daughter, Annalies, to Schwaebisch-Gmuend. There she had become acquainted with one of the town's leading citizens, Reinhold Maier. When I began my duties and was looking for untainted but competent Germans to head up the administration of the services under my jurisdiction—employment offices, labor relations, health insurance, public housing—she suggested I see Dr. Maier.

Dr. Maier, she told me, had been a prominent lawyer and a member of the last Reichstag, where he had headed a small independent political party, the Democratic party. After the Nazi takeover, he had retired to practice law in this small town and had kept out of trouble with the Nazis. I later learned that anti-Nazis viewed him with suspicion for having cast his vote in the Reichstag for the crucial Ermaechtigung Gesetz, the law under which Hitler took power in 1933. But since there seemed no way to stop Hitler's rise to power at that point, it was possible to believe that his power would be more responsible and restrained if he came to it legitimately.

At our first meeting, I discussed a whole range of topics with Dr. Maier, not only my labor and manpower field but the political and economic situation generally, and in spite of language difficulties—his English was as limited as my German—I was much impressed by his openness and enlightened views.

I reported back to my commanding officer Colonel Dawson (a former Northwestern University Law School dean and now Military Governor of the Württemberg area) and suggested that when it came time to appoint a responsible head of a new Württemberg government, Dr. Maier might be a good choice. I arranged for them to meet and was present at their first meeting; Colonel Dawson subsequently appointed Dr. Maier "Minister-President" of Württemberg-Baden. As it turned out, he was a logical choice; I don't know how important my initiating the contact may have been, but my relation to him remained cordial, and he spoke generously about me in his later published memoirs.

A year later, when the process of rebuilding a democratic political order in West Germany had reached the point where the Germans elected their own local and regional officials, he was elected to the same post of Minister-President that he had held by appointment. And later still, when the West German government received full sovereign rights and the military occupation was terminated, Dr. Maier served as president of the Bundesrat, West Germany's upper house.

As Hitler was coming to power, Dr. Maier had sent his Jewish wife and their two children to England where they had spent the war years. He divorced her to save her property—and, no doubt, his own standing. But after his appointment by Colonel Dawson, special arrangements were made for her return to Germany, and, as he movingly told in his memoirs, they were remarried. He brought her to meet me a few days after her return.

The detachment to which I belonged was finally able to set up its head-quarters in Stuttgart where it had been targeted. A largely undamaged office building near the heart of the gutted old city was made usable, and there, as chief of the Manpower Section, I was provided with a spacious office.

I also was assigned a room in a house where two or three other officers were billeted, in a residential part of town half a mile from the city center. A lavish officers' mess was established in a large mansion nearby, and there I enjoyed the privileges of a conqueror, furnished not only with basic army rations but with the best of requisitioned farm produce, meats, eggs, and vegetables from the area, as well as choice wines.

That first year of the occupation, particularly the bitter winter months of 1945–46, was a time of great suffering in Germany, as it was for the millions of other Europeans, victims of Nazi aggression. But it was hard to fasten the blame on the German children we saw scavenging the garbage dumps.

My social conscience had been largely anesthetized. I accepted the situation as it was. My uniform helped: I was a soldier in a hierarchy in which higher authorities made the decisions.

Only in one area was I able to develop my own ideas and perhaps affect the policies applied by the occupying powers. Labor relations came under the overall jurisdiction of the Labor or Manpower Division. Since my conversion to a radical point of view in 1931, I had tended to accept the Marxist concept of the positive role of labor unions in social change. From what I knew of German history, it seemed to me that the most promising center for the revival of democracy lay in the German labor movement, especially in those unions that had been the backbone of the Social Democratic party. This opinion was much reinforced by the fact that the former official of the International Ladies' Garment Workers' Union, Murray Gross, had been assigned to my section. Ostensibly only a jeep driver, he was my chief counselor and advisor.

The pre-Hitler head of the Social Democratic labor movement in Württemberg and Baden came to my office one day and asked permission to try to pull together and reorganize the old labor movement. I satisfied myself about his credentials—he had served part of the war years in a concentration camp, as his scrawny pallor seemed to confirm. I consulted with Murray Gross, cleared it with Colonel Dawson, and told Herr S. to go ahead. Shortly thereafter came a request that he be allowed to hold a meeting of old union leaders. About the same time, I was visited by a representative of the American Federation of Labor (A.F. of L.), then traveling alone in the American Zone sounding out the prospects for a revival of democratic unionism. Permission was given for the meeting; I went with the A.F. of L. man and Murray Gross, and sat in the back of the dusty basement hall where the meeting was held.

With my still limited knowledge of German, I could not follow the discussion closely, but it seemed evident that these were old union leaders who had suffered under the Nazis but had survived, and were now ready to try to reestablish the old Social Democratic unions. The A.F. of L. man was invited to address the gathering and gave a rousing speech offering help from American labor. He obviously looked on those present as friends and allies.

A month later, a very different kind of meeting was held in which some of the same German unionists were treated as enemies. Sidney Hillman, head of the Congress of Industrial Organizations (CIO) and confidant of Roosevelt, was touring the American Zone under the guidance and auspices of two unlikely partners, the Army brass and the Communist party.

The Communist line was of course the Soviet line, and in an important respect it jibed with the official American line: no revival of the old unions was to be permitted at this time. The Communists did not want the old Social Democratic unions, with their inveterate hostility to communism, to get the jump on them in organizing workers as industry revived. They favored a strategy, based on experience at the end of World War I, of organizing workers in factory councils, which they felt would be easier to control than industrial unions. The U.S. military took the same line and opposed the revival of the old labor movement—but for different reasons. The military mind is almost instinctively anti-union. To defer organization of German workers until they were back at work fitted the notion that it might take a generation to eradicate Nazi ideology. Military government policy at this time held that the only safe way to allow the Germans to organize democratic institutions was from the ground up, and that meant only in local government and in individual enterprises. At the meeting I arranged at our headquarters, Hillman and his advisor John Abt, known in New York left-wing circles as a dedicated Communist, together with high-ranking officers from SHAEF (Supreme Headquarters Allied Expeditionary Forces), sat on one side of a conference table, and the Germans on the other. Hillman gave them a lecture as if they were all suspected Nazis, warning them against any attempt to organize.

The Manpower Division at SHAEF had been the target of rival infiltrators from the American Communist, Socialist, and Labor movements, many of whom had obtained status as civilian advisors to OMGUS (Office of Military Government United States). During the first few months of the occupation, the Communist influence was dominant. A New Yorker named Wolfe, believed by the other advisors to be a Communist sympathizer, was the American representative who sat with the British, French, and Soviet representatives on the quadripartite committee that was determining labor policies for occupied Germany. It was this committee that had banned the revival of the Social Democratic union movement.

Not long after Sidney Hillman's visit to Stuttgart, I was ordered to report to General McSherry, the chief of the Manpower Division at OMGUS in Berlin. About the same time, a young captain appeared in Stuttgart with orders to investigate the operations of the regional Manpower Division, which I had been heading. I turned over my files to him and left for Berlin. Later I heard that on the basis of my notes and memoranda, he reported back to Berlin that not only had I violated the policy of non-recognition of unions by giving the green light to Herr S. to revive the old unions, but I was thereby encouraging a revival of the Nazi labor movement. The implication was that I should be replaced and possibly court-martialed.

But on my arrival in Berlin, I found that a much-respected advisor to General McSherry was David Saposs, a Socialist writer and labor historian with whom I had had some contact when editor of *Common Sense*. Moreover, the deputy chief of the Manpower Division, Leo Wirts, a civilian with the "simulated" rank of colonel, was trying to eradicate the Communist influence in the Manpower Division. As it turned out, I was at the center of a struggle for power between Communist and Socialist advisors in the making of labor policy in occupied Germany.

I had two meetings with General McSherry. The first was a dinner meeting at the luxurious villa in a Berlin suburb where the general was quartered, with only Wirts and another aide present. There I got a taste of how a conquering army can behave. That afternoon, on a tour of the shattered city, not far from the Brandenburg Gate, I had seen a woman trying to saw out a plank from a park bench in the Tiergarten—almost the last bit of firewood among the stumps of trees to be found in the devastated park. But General McSherry had a blazing fire in the fireplace of his already overheated villa, while we relaxed with Scotch highballs after dinner. That first meeting was more of a friendly social gathering. But at the general's office the next day, I was gently chided for not following the official guidelines.

Not long thereafter, I learned that the struggle for influence in the Manpower Division had ended with the rout of the Communist "fellow travelers," and the policy was changed from banning to encouraging the revival of the Social Democratic union movement. The officer who had reported that I was fostering a revival of the Nazi labor movement was transferred out of the Manpower Division. (I later learned that he found a new slot in the Office of Strategic Services, which ultimately was absorbed into the CIA.)

I felt vindicated and took some pride in having participated in what later appeared as a significant step in the revival of German democracy.

Another step for which I was given some credit had to do with the revival of local self-government.

Colonel Dawson called me into his office one day and asked my opinion of a request from some local officials for permission to hold a meeting of their counterparts from all the towns and rural districts in the Württemberg region—to consider their common problems. By this time the local detachments, supervising the "de-Nazification" of these towns and districts, had installed officials who appeared to have clean records. I told Colonel Dawson that the proposed gathering seemed a significant development in the revival of democratic self-government. He agreed and asked me to attend the meeting as an observer and to report back to him.

The meeting was held at an inn in a small town about twenty miles east of Stuttgart. The driver of my jeep was Murray Gross, and I took him in as my interpreter. The gathering reminded me of meetings of small-town politicians I had attended in southeastern Connecticut. There was a good deal of backslapping and bantering familiarity among the participants, some of whom might not have been in touch with one another since the demise of the Weimar Republic. Yet it was a serious and decorous gathering, with the participants describing what they had done in their localities to bring order out of the chaos of military defeat and the collapse of the Third Reich. There was a general agreement on the need for vigorous initiative in reconstruction (with participants keeping in close touch with one another), and for a revived administrative structure in the region—all in full cooperation with the American military government.

I sat as a silent observer most of the time, but at the conclusion of the meeting, I offered a few words of encouragement in my halting German. Afterward I reported my favorable impression to Colonel Dawson, and with his approval, I attended subsequent meetings of the same group in different small towns of the region. Over the next few months, I saw the development of what in time became the legislature of the state ("Land") of Württemberg-Baden within the Federal Republic of Germany.

Reinhold Maier, who presided at the first meeting, later wrote in his published memoirs that this meeting in Murrhardt was the "first sprouting" of a new German democracy and gave me credit for its favorable reception by the American military government.

CHAPTER 57

Nuremberg

One of the perquisites of my position in the regional military government was the possession of a civilian motor vehicle. My initial rank as captain was not high enough to rate me a large luxury model such as the colonel and the lieutenant colonels drove, but I was happy with my small Mercedes-Benz coupe, requisitioned from a local doctor. How the doctor managed without it was a question that did not occur to me at the time.

It enabled me to make a memorable trip to Nuremberg to attend a session of the first war crimes trial. I had read of the convening of the International Tribunal and had noted that an assistant U.S. prosecutor was Thomas Dodd of Connecticut, whose home was in the district I had represented in the Connecticut state senate. Sylvia had mentioned in a recent letter that she had met Dodd's wife at a Democratic political rally and had told her where I was stationed, which seemed to explain the letter from him inviting me to come to see the trial as his guest.

I asked George Friede, a member of my detachment who had become a close friend, to come with me on a private junket and, after getting a few days leave, we set off in mid-January of 1946. George and I took turns at the wheel. A requisitioned old car, even a Mercedes-Benz, provided uncertain transportation for the hundred-mile drive over snowy roads to Nuremberg. Two flat tires on the way almost terminated the expedition. But we made it by nightfall, found a comfortable hotel room, and dined with Mr. Dodd.

His natural friendliness was no doubt enhanced by his political ambitions: as he put it, "men of integrity" were needed in politics back home. He had his eye on the next Democratic nomination for governor of Connecticut, and I had been a Democratic state senator with presumed influence in his home district. (Tom Dodd was defeated a year later by Chester Bowles who won the gubernatorial nomination, but he went on to become a congressman and then a two-term U.S. Senator. His son Christopher later won the same Senate seat once occupied by my father.)

The next morning Dodd sent his car to take us to the courthouse. I described the spectacle in a letter to Sylvia.

Nuremberg
January 14, 1946

My Dearest:

I spent the morning at what may be the most important trial of our time. There were the great ones of Nazidom, who had made the whole world shake with fear, murdered millions upon millions of people, brought most of the cities of Europe to ruin—now in the prisoners' dock, looking small and pathetic.

We got good seats in the front row of the visitors' gallery, where we could study their faces by the hour.

First, of course, was Goering, looking expansive, even in a fawn-colored uniform that is now many sizes too big for him. Next to him was Hess, a fanatical-looking ghost of a man with years of prison pallor and eyes so deep set you can't see them. Then Ribbentrop, worried and kindly looking, with Rosenberg just beyond him, also quite decent-looking, so that one wondered how they got into such a den of thieves. Then came Frick, sharp-faced, with a gray bristle on his head, and the loathsome Streicher, looking like a half-witted janitor, small, chewing something most of the time. Beyond him was Funk, the financial wizard, now shrunken and slouched and revolting, and at the end of the first row Schacht, still trying to look suave, but still only a small-town banker.

In the back row were the two admirals, Doenitz and Raeder, pretty tough specimens, then Baldur von Schirach, the pretty boy of the gang, a little like a YMCA secretary. Next to him was Jodl, behind Keitel whom I forgot, both still in uniform though without insignia. The mightiest of militarists, now under the watchful eye of some simple GI's in the white helmets of MP's. Then came Sauckel, the manpower and slave labor czar, looking like an obsequious delicatessen salesman, Frank, the grim tyrant of Polish extermination camps, and Seyss-Inquart, bully of Austria and Holland, both expressionless and surprisingly young. There was von Papen too, horse-faced and reserved, and von Neurath, still a smooth diplomat, and Speer with an attractive sensitive face, who had been czar of war production.

Facing them across the courtroom were the judges, two Russians, youngish and in uniform, two Englishmen, two Americans and two Frenchmen, all robed. The defense lawyers sat in front of their clients, with the prosecution and the press at the end of the room beneath the gallery.

The morning's proceedings were not too exciting, witnesses being a Czech doctor out of Dachau, and a young German naval officer, plus a long recital by one of the British prosecutors of Nazi violations of international law in submarine warfare.

Everyone wears earphones most of the time and hears questions or answers or pronouncements instantly translated in his own language, English, French, Russian, or German.

It was a fascinating show. In spite of criticism it seems as if a real honest trial were being given these astonishing men. It is hard for me to believe in the evil men do. Even the worst like Streicher were just vulgarly brutal, or like Frank pursuing a policy without pity. I could not help but feel they were as much the victims of the horrible machine they helped create as its masters. The human animal simply hasn't learned how to control his social mechanisms.

The enormity of the Holocaust was such as to lead one to expect that its perpetrators would be criminals of extraordinary proportions. Instead, looking down on them from a balcony a few feet away, they seemed quite ordinary human beings. In the little courtesies they showed one another, I could see that they were not fiends, and I began to feel sorry for them.

Some months later, when I described these compassionate feelings to a liberal American friend, he became indignant with me. I was carrying tolerance and Christian forgiveness too far. His own righteous anger against the Nazi monsters was spilling over onto me. Yet I believed then and still believe that self-righteous moral indignation is dangerous, if not "sinful."

The Hiroshima and Nagasaki bombs had been dropped on Japan a few months before. Mixed with relief at the end of the war, which followed shortly thereafter, was a feeling of alarm at the misuse of science and technology.

And the boundless suffering caused by these atomic explosions seemed to me comparable to the suffering caused by Nazi genocide.

To focus judgment on specific human targets like those in the dock at Nuremberg is no doubt helpful in dealing with that enormous tragedy, but it is hardly the last word. If one were to look for a focus for responsibility in the case of the Hiroshima bomb, one should perhaps look at Harry Truman, who said, "The buck stops here." He also was reported to have said he never lost sleep over the decision to drop the bomb. And by any account he was a kindly man and not a fiend.

How to assess blame for the horrors perpetrated by the Nazis was a perpetual subject of discussion among military government personnel. The Germans with whom they came in contact, particularly the young German wives and widows who became their interpreters, secretaries, and mistresses, felt innocent of Dachau and Auschwitz. Again I could find a contemporary parallel in the lack of concern on the part of Americans today for the fact that a million of their fellow citizens are behind bars, and millions more in our inner cities are living subhuman lives.

Back in Stuttgart I found the excitement and glamor of being a part of the liberating forces giving way to bureaucratic boredom. The war was over, and the principal function of the military government, the restoration of responsible German government administration, had been largely achieved. Years of a continued American military presence in Germany might be required to finish the job of "de-Nazification," but it was already clear that the hold of Hitler's ideology on the German people had died with Hitler and the destruction of his power.

Allied policy makers had assumed it would require a generation or more to eradicate the poison that had led to the Holocaust and the war. As a part of their training, military government personnel were warned that guerilla warfare might continue for years in Germany, and that fanatics of the Hitler Youth would become "Werewolves," engaging in sabotage and keeping alive the doctrine of German racial superiority.

Nothing of that kind occurred. From the moment of the collapse of Nazi power, the hold of Nazi ideology evaporated. To be sure, the contacts that I and other military government personnel had with German civilians were not likely to reveal Nazi attitudes. And doubtless Hitler would never have achieved power if there had not been in the German psyche elements that facilitated his conquest of their minds. But I believe that his indoctrination of the great majority of Germans was only skin-deep.

Our experience with Nazi totalitarianism ought to have prepared us better for the collapse of Communism in the Soviet Union in the late 1980s. Almost overnight, the seventy-year indoctrination of the Soviet mind gave way to a renewed search for a free society in the traditional styles of the West.

In 1946, however, Soviet armies dominated eastern Europe, and seemed to threaten the West. American power, especially after Hiroshima and the occupation of Japan, now seemed the only bulwark against further Soviet conquest. The Cold War was beginning. A fellow officer in my detachment, whom I thought of as relatively liberal, told me he thought the American army should, while at its peak of strength, invade Russia and put an end to the Communist menace.

I was horrified. I wanted no more crusades. I had briefly felt myself a target of Communist aggression when I was called to Berlin by General McSherry, but I still retained some of my earlier belief that the Soviet Union might point the way to a better world. And I was more than ever a pacifist: I had seen enough of cities destroyed. And I was ready to go home.

For a time in the early months of 1946, it was not clear when I would be able to go home, and it seemed possible that I might have to stay another year. Sylvia and I had discussed—by letter and lately even by telephone—the possibility of her bringing the children over to Switzerland and putting them into schools there (two of her brothers had attended a Swiss boarding school as teen-agers). We could then be more often together as a family.

My responsibilities as head of the Manpower Division for Württemberg-Baden were being diluted as the Office of Military Government for the United States (OMGUS) responded to the pressure within any bureaucracy to expand—in accordance with "Parkinson's Law" and the "Peter Principle." Two more junior officers and two more secretaries were assigned to my office in a new table of organization.

Meanwhile I had a glimpse of how the traditional hierarchy of the German social order was once more asserting itself. I was invited to Sunday dinner by the Princess zum Wied. She was a sister of the Count Grote I had visited in Mecklenburg in 1932. The count's American-born widow had been able, as the war was coming to an end, to take her children and their governess in the family limousine across Germany ahead of the advancing Red Army. She reached the American lines and so impressed American field commanders and military government officers that she was helped on her way to her sister-in-law's Stuttgart home. Somehow she got in touch with me and induced me to be a mail drop in a correspondence with an American whom she had fallen in love with after her husband's death. Eventually they were married. He had been a junior officer in the American embassy in Berlin before the embassy closed in 1941. The only postal service available was through American military channels. Now she was living with her sister-in-law, the Princess zum Wied, in an elegant establishment just outside the city.

The princess was connected with the old German aristocracy, though her mother had been an American. She could not understand how I, with an upper-class family background she knew something of, could be comfortable dealing with lower-class politicians. She, like the Countess Grote, had so impressed the American military government authorities as to come through her country's defeat with double ration cards for all the family. The Sunday dinner, served by her large domestic staff, was on a par with the fare I was by now used to at our officers' mess. Her children and her sister-in-law's children, sitting with their governess at an adjoining table, were clearly not going to suffer the pangs of hunger that most German children were feeling in that first bitter winter of the peace.

CHAPTER 58

A New World?

By the winter of 1946, I was on my way back to the United States. I had been abroad more than two years. As in 1932, after two years as a world traveler, I was faced with the question of what to do with my life. My social conscience had been reawakened by my encounter with the Princess zum Wied. But whereas on my return from my world tour I had a specific plan to work on— to start a magazine to preach a reshaping of the economic and social order according to what I was then convinced was common sense—now I was without a plan.

I did not want to resume editing and publishing what I now saw had been no more than a "little magazine." And as a matter of hard fact, *Common Sense*, for lack of financial support, had actually ceased publication with its April 1946 issue.

I made a list of possible careers open to me, and at the end of the list of options, as a last resort, was the practice of law, the profession for which I had been trained less as a means of livelihood than as a foundation for a political career.

By May I was demobilized. Getting home had been the dream expressed in many letters to Sylvia. But the reality of being master of a big household, with four bright and spirited children, was more than I was prepared for. In one battle with my six-year-old son Douglas, in a fury at his defiance of a father who had recently been a major in the Army of the United States, accustomed to being saluted by underlings, I broke down his locked bedroom door. Unable to beat him into submission, I induced him to help me repair the broken panel. But I found it impossible to erase a crayon caricature on his window screen with its caption, in the worst language Douglas could think of, "DADDY IS A DIRTY BRAT."

Despite the shock of a return to civilian life and uncivil children, I was able for a while to hold onto my dream of playing a significant role in changing the world. In Connecticut, as a former state senator and now a war veteran, I was asked on one occasion to substitute for U.S. Senator Brian McMahon as principal speaker at a Democratic party rally. In New York, my interest in the revival of democracy in Germany led to my association with an organization known as the American Friends of German Democracy, of which the distinguished left-wing theologian Reinhold Niebuhr was the chairman. When he retired from that post to take up more urgent challenges, I was made chairman in his stead. For a couple of years, under the executive direction of Maurice Goldbloom, a former editor of *Common Sense*, the organization, though existing largely only on paper, provided a platform for visiting spokesmen of the emerging new German Federal Republic.

In Stuttgart I had noted that those of my colleagues who showed the greatest sympathy for the emerging democratic leadership in Germany were Jews. Moses Moskowitz, our regional Political Officer, became the trusted friend and confidant of Dr. Maier and the new democratic leadership of Land Württemberg-Baden. Now back in New York, it was a Jewish intellectual, Maurice Goldbloom, who was promoting recognition of a new democratic Germany.

It was clear I needed a job; with my background I felt I was qualified for a high-level job. The State Department seemed a logical place to look. Before the war I had had some slight contact with Adolph A. Berle, whose coauthorship of *The Corporation and Private Property* had given me a benchmark for my own thinking. Berle was now an Assistant Secretary of State, and I sought him out.

He was at the time, as I later learned, much preoccupied with the recent revelation to him that Alger Hiss, then a high-ranking officer in the State Department, was suspected of being a Soviet spy. Berle apparently believed that, as editor of a left-wing magazine, I might be expected to have some knowledge of Communist subversion, and he asked me if I thought it possible for a real Communist to infiltrate the State Department. I told him I had no expertise in that area, and he suggested I see someone else in the State Department. I contacted an old school friend who held a prestigious position down the hall from Berle, and he in turn referred me to Hiss. He received me cordially, but neither of them, nor I myself, knew what kind of slot I was fitted for, and nothing came of my approach to the State Department.

I tried another old college friend, Sherman Kent, now a high official in the CIA, thinking that my background might make me useful in directing that new agency. He sent me to a personnel officer whose line of questioning about my "loyalty" ended at once any mutual rapport—and any expectation on my part that I could fit in there.

If my qualifications for statesmanship were not recognizable, perhaps such éclat as I had enjoyed as editor of a magazine of opinion would stand me in good stead. Chester Bowles had begun a career as a liberal spokesman with an article in *Common Sense*, and he and his wife had become friendly neighbors of ours. He told me of a project for a new magazine to be published by his former partner in the advertising business, William Benton, now owner of the *Encyclopaedia Britannica*. On Bowles's recommendation,

Benton hired me to explore the feasibility of the magazine, which would be published by the *Britannica* and devoted to the republishing of culturally significant articles from the world's more thoughtful journals.

I was installed in Benton's own presidential suite at the *Britannica's* Madison Avenue office. As my chief assistant, I enlisted Alfred Winslow Jones, a friend of many years, recently a writer for *Fortune* magazine. (Later he became a multimillionaire as the head of an innovative investment fund.) After a few months of intensive work, we presented Benton with a sample copy of a glossy magazine entitled "World," containing excerpts from dozens of foreign publications and dealing with science, the arts, and public affairs; we prepared an accompanying brochure estimating costs, circulation, and possible profitability. Our presentation did not sufficiently impress the owners of the *Britannica* to warrant the million-dollar investment we thought would be needed. The project was abandoned, leaving no trace except on my enhanced pocketbook—I had been well paid—and my depleted self-confidence.

I was depressed. I felt myself a failure, both as head of a family and as a breadwinner, to say nothing of my lack of accomplishment as a social reformer.

I began a long and expensive series of sessions with psychotherapists.

I was advised by a New Haven psychiatrist that I needed the in-deeper therapy of psychoanalysis. With no analysts available in Connecticut at that time, I undertook a two-year course on the couch with a New York analyst.

Meanwhile my family life was deteriorating. Spending more and more time in New York, I had become a weekend commuter to Salem. If I was to spend several days a week in New York with only my sessions with the analyst as a raison d'être, it was obvious that my spirits would not improve. For a few months, I worked in the American Civil Liberties Union office as publicity director and as editor of its monthly bulletin. This put me into daily contact with Roger Baldwin, the founder, executive head, and inspiration of the Union. Before the war I had been a member of the Union's national Board of Directors. As a friend and admirer of Roger Baldwin, I had supported him and the board chairman, John Haynes Holmes, in the 1938 "loyalty trial" of Elizabeth Gurley Flynn, an avowed Communist. It was decided that membership in the Communist party was incompatible with membership on the ACLU board—and she was ousted in a close vote. But my new status was as an employee rather than an employer of Roger Baldwin, and his many years of battling public opinion had made him impatient with any deviation from the procedures he had developed. I was unable to do the job he wanted done, and we parted.

For a while I became a candidate to fill a vacancy as New York State Commissioner of Labor, but I learned that my being in psychotherapy disqualified me.

I found a volunteer job for myself as an assistant editor of the *World Government News*, a pocket-size publication of the United World Federalists, with a circulation of a few thousand members. I had long been a believer in world government, and had seen much of its structure beginning to function—the World Court, the United Nations and its related agencies, multinational corporations, and financial and communications networks. In helping to report and comment on relevant public events in this little house organ, I felt I could still play a part in saving the world.

But I was neglecting my family, and without the Tiffany and Mitchell trusts then being liquidated, I would have been unable to pay my bills. To add to my anguish, I was becoming sexually impotent, and my marriage no longer seemed secure.

I finally made a decision. I was down to my last career option. I would return to the plan I had in mind twenty years before when I was finishing my law studies. I would join a law firm in New London and try to earn my living as a lawyer. At the same time I would continue to cultivate the local politicians in the hope of advancing up the ladder I had once begun to climb, with a seat in Congress as the next step.

The firm I probably could have joined twenty years earlier was then known by the euphonious name of Waller, Waller, Avery and Gallup. After deaths and retirements, it now was called Waller, Gallup and Anderson. Robert Anderson, a college classmate and friend, was now a partner and would soon be named a federal judge by a Republican president. I approached another firm, McGuire and McGuire; its senior member, Francis McGuire, had been a reform-minded Democratic party town chairman and, through this political connection, had become a close friend. He was skeptical of my ability to attract enough new clients to justify my becoming a member of the firm, and I had to satisfy myself with the offer of office space as an independent practitioner.

I sent out a professional card to everyone I knew in the county, including all members of the county bar, announcing the opening of my office for the general practice of law, and waited for clients. The little I remembered of my law school years gave me no assurance that I could provide professional legal services to anyone.

Francis McGuire's younger brother Morgan, who occupied an adjoining office, took pity on me and gave me advice on procedure when I asked.

My first and almost my only client was my brother Hiram. After eighteen years as a vice-consul and junior secretary in various diplomatic posts in Tokyo, London, Warsaw, and other foreign capitals—during the course of which he had married and fathered a large brood of children—he had resigned his appointment, and settled in the old Mumford House in Salem, which he had inherited almost at birth.

Harry, as I called him, was persuaded that he could make more money to support his still-growing family by going into business. He had two business projects in mind: one involved the promotion of a new steel-making process invented by a Yugoslav engineer whom he had met in Buenos Aires; the other was a game he had himself invented, a kind of miniature field hockey to be played in a small cage. Calling it "Florball," he hoped it might become as popular as basketball. All he needed was to raise the capital to promote it— and the steel project.

He made frequent trips to New York in his efforts to find investors. One day he got into conversation with a fellow passenger on the New York train, an elderly woman named Mrs. Robington, whom he described as "motherly." He told her of his projected business venture, and she professed great interest. She was herself a businesswoman, it seemed, buying and selling business properties in the then burgeoning field of shopping centers. She offered him a chance to make a quick profit in a pending purchase and sale of a new shopping center. She also promised she would help him finance his own projects at some later point. He took a chance and arranged to lend her a few thousand dollars; a week later at a prearranged meeting, she returned him his money, plus a thousand dollars or so—as his share of the profit she claimed to have made on the deal.

Mrs. Robington was almost ready to help him finance his projects, but first she offered him another chance at a quick profit on another deal she was engaged in. This time he signed over to her one hundred thousand dollars in U.S. treasury bonds recently received in the distribution of one of the Tiffany trusts. A month later, when unable to contact the lady, he consulted me in my new law office. He wanted at least to retrieve the bonds, and he would forget the promised profit.

The bonds were registered, and I was able to trace them. Mrs. Robington was in a bankruptcy proceeding and had given the bonds to a nephew, a chiropractor in Coney Island. I was able to reach him on the phone, and he told me that his aunt had swindled him and other members of her family, and he had already cashed in the bonds in settlement of her debt to him.

In my search for assets to attach, I visited her New York office at the address on Forty-second Street she had given Harry, and all I found in the otherwise empty cubicle was a chair and a desk. Tucked in a blotter on the desktop was a clipping from a magazine with these sententious words:

> Deep in the heart of every man lies the hope that sometime, somehow, somewhere, he will come upon a pile of money without sweat.

My trusting brother Harry had fallen into her trap. He never recovered any of his investment. It was small comfort to know that Mrs. Robington ultimately went to jail.

Not long after that episode, I was named by Chester Bowles, recently elected governor of Connecticut, to fill a vacancy as Workmen's Compensation Commissioner for New London County. This gave me a spacious office in Norwich with two secretaries, and somewhat restored my *amour propre*. There for two years I carried out relatively undemanding administrative and judicial service, deciding disputed claims over injuries sustained at work, and gained a recognizable status as a lawyer, after which I again set myself up in private practice, this time as an associate of Eli Cramer, a former school-teacher turned lawyer, with an office in Norwich.

I was now established as a small-town lawyer, and for a dozen years I shared the office with Cramer, and eventually with a younger associate, Morris Globerman.

Sylvia was only too well aware of my feelings of a blighted career. She had shared my dreams as a social reformer but had for some time come to realize that efforts to build a better world might as well begin with one's immediate neighborhood.

CHAPTER 59

The Neighborhood

A few years after my brother Harry had moved his growing family into the old Mumford House half a mile from ours, the Procters moved into the next house down the road (where Darling Road joined the state highway). I had been unable to salvage any of Harry's stolen property, but I did succeed in helping his troubled neighbors.

Like Harry, Sam Procter had a large and still-growing family. When his fifth child was born to his devoutly Catholic wife Marianne, Sam decided that the small town in Maine where they lived was too much of a backwater to enable him to support so many children. Like thousands of other "Down-Easters," he was attracted to the New London area by the high wages paid to men with no more than a high school education at the Electric Boat Company, the submarine shipyard in Groton. It was hard finding a rental for so large a family—five children going on six—anywhere near Groton, but he finally found what he needed fifteen miles from the Boat Company: he rented an old farmhouse in rural Salem owned by my brother Harry, who with eight children himself (going on nine at the time) was bound to be a sympathetic landlord.

I first knew the new neighbors were in trouble when I received a call at my Norwich law office from Mr. Procter, asking me to represent three of his boys at Juvenile Court. Luke, Bill, and Peter had been caught stealing an automobile radiator from a junkyard on Forsyth Road. They were spotted by the proprietor, Bob Maitlin, carrying away a radiator they had extracted from one of the junked vehicles in his pasture. It appeared that their father's car had been immobilized for some days after its radiator had burst following the first heavy cold spell of the season, and the boys had stolen the replacement their father could not afford to buy.

The juvenile court judge was sympathetic and put the boys on probation in the custody of their parents. I was most concerned about twelve-year-old Peter, the youngest of the three, who—as I had heard from my children—had recently appeared in school with a stamp collection given him, he said, by his grandmother, with which he was able to enter the active trade in postage stamps at the school. My brother Mitchell's house had been burglarized shortly before: his son Nat's second-floor bedroom had been entered by ladder when the family was away, and Nat's stamp collection was the only valuable item Mitchell could identify as missing and apparently stolen.

A few weeks later Mrs. Procter called me. Her husband had been arrested on many counts of burglary and larceny. Would I agree to see him and represent him if he wished?

He was more than willing to talk. He had already confessed to the state police responsibility for a long series of petty thieveries in rural areas around Salem.

Apparently work at the Electric Boat Company was slow. The company had discharged many workers and put many more on part time. Sam Procter had fallen more and more behind in his rent, and payday never gave him enough to cover his bills. Some months before, he had begun to take his three sons with him in his ramshackle car after hours to look for salvageable and possibly salable items on the garbage dumps in surrounding towns.

Sometimes they had found old tires behind garages that might or might not have been thrown away, and he had been able to sell them for a dollar apiece to fellow workers at the Boat Company. Sometimes he and his boys had found such old tires just inside a locked door or window, and the boldest of the boys, Peter, had begun breaking in to retrieve them. Tools and other usable items might also be picked up.

So it had become a routine. The boys would go off "junking" in the evenings with their father. From commercial garages they had turned to private garages and then to private homes in remote locations. Sam sat in the car while his boys went scavenging for loot. In one isolated Salem house, one of the boys reported that he had found some money in a bureau drawer.

"Hand it over," said the father.

"I didn't take it," said the boy. "I thought taking money would be stealing."

Up to that point they had been only "junking." After that, father and sons were a criminal gang, and they all knew it. But they told themselves it was to help feed the family.

Sam stopped going to mass on Sundays. He might drive Marianne and the girls to church, but he always made excuses why he could not go in himself.

When, as was inevitable, he was caught, he unburdened himself and confessed to more than twenty burglaries. Asked how much he had netted from his stolen goods, he estimated it at no more than five hundred dollars.

The judge who took his guilty plea stressed the enormity of involving his children in a course of crime, and he was sentenced to a five- to ten-year prison term.

While the case was still under investigation, I stopped by the Procters' house. I found one of the investigating state troopers, Sergeant Framboise, on his knees under the kitchen sink trying to help Marianne plug a leak that was sending waste water into the cellar. She had applied for welfare aid, but for a while the only money coming into the household was from Luke, the oldest boy, who had been mowing the lawn and doing odd jobs for my brother. But Harry suspected Luke of stealing some of the family silver and wanted no more thieving tenants: he would no longer employ Luke and gave notice to Mrs. Procter that she would have to find some other place to live.

I offered Luke, an appealing gangly fifteen-year-old, some work clearing brush at my place, and made it plain that my door would not be locked when he was there even if no one was home. And I undertook to find Marianne a home so she could move the family out of Harry's house.

I consulted a priest I had come to know in Norwich in connection with work I was doing as head of a County Bar Association committee on legal aid and lawyer referral. I had found that many applicants for legal aid in connection with family problems needed counseling as much as they needed a lawyer. Father Baldwin was the head of a Catholic social agency, the Diocesan Bureau, as well as a parish priest. With his help, I found a modest house for Marianne to rent near his church. She moved in with her brood and was soon getting more money and medical and dental care, thanks to the welfare system, than she had when dependent on Sam's earnings.

Sam was released from prison and placed on probation a few years later, having apparently been a model prisoner, and he sought my help in getting employment. I told his story to the manager of a manufacturing plant near Norwich, whom I had come to know as a fellow member of the board of trustees of New London Junior College, and he agreed to hire Sam on a trial basis. Eventually Sam became a permanent and trusted employee.

Once he called me in the middle of the night with a story about his younger son Peter, whose record as a juvenile offender had continued after his father's arrest and had landed him in the state's juvenile detention home in Meriden. Peter had phoned his father that night to tell him he had run away from the detention home and wanted his father's help in making his escape. Sam asked me what he should do. I told him he should go to the rendezvous his son had proposed and try to persuade him to return to the detention home—but neither help him escape nor turn him in. Sam agreed and asked me to go with him.

Half an hour later, he picked me up at my home, and we drove in his car to Meriden. About three o'clock in the morning, we spotted the shivering boy at a street corner. We offered him a choice of releasing him to his own devices or returning him to the detention center. After we drove around the empty streets for a while, Peter's resistance melted, and he agreed to be taken back into custody. His troubles with the law were now over. I sometimes felt that it was he who had led his father astray rather than the other way around. But the last time I saw him, he was successfully running a small appliance repair shop with skills he had learned in state prison.

The Procters were not the only family whose troubles I came to know intimately during my years of law practice. As a lone practitioner entering a competitive field after twenty years of trying to reform society, I was not able to attract a clientele of substantial citizens or business corporations. My clients were mostly poor. I even made a virtue of serving the poor by organizing a legal-aid and lawyer-referral system for the New London County Bar Association.

For a while I was the only lawyer living in Salem. I wrote wills for local people who had next to nothing to leave to their heirs. I searched land titles for neighbors and arranged closings for the sale or purchase of property. I was named Town Attorney for the Town of Salem and helped organize a Planning and Zoning Commission for the town when developers began to move into the area.

I was also named prosecutor of the Salem Justice Court. At that time and until its abolition in a statewide court reform some years later, an elected Justice of the Peace was named by the Board of Selectmen as Trial Justice at the first level of the state's judicial system. He in turn appointed one of the two elected Grand Jurors as the prosecutor.

When the Democratic party, of which I became the Salem chairman, won an election, the First Selectman, Joe Ploszaj or later Andy Zemko, would name Andy's brother Felix as Trial Justice, and he in turn would name me as Prosecuting Grand Juror. When the Republicans won the election, as they often did, Michael Urbanik became the First Selectman, and he would appoint Calvin McCall, owner of the garage at Salem Four Corners, Trial Justice. As there was no Republican lawyer living in Salem, Cal McCall kept me on as Prosecuting Grand Juror.

Whenever a lawbreaker was arrested in Salem by a state trooper (Salem at that time had only part-time constables), he would bring the case to me for presentation at the next session of the Justice Court. Most cases involved minor traffic violations or violations of the fish and game regulations, and the judge would impose a small fine usually accompanied by a moral lecture. But for more serious offenses, beyond the jurisdiction of a Justice Court, the judge would order that the offender be "bound over" (referred under a bail bond) to a higher court.

Thus I learned intimate details about some of my neighbors. There were cases of rape and assault and incest. In one case of incest between a father and his teen-aged daughter, I knew the father, a member of a large and trouble-prone family, for whom I had done occasional legal work, often unpaid; and after he had been bound over and served a few years in the state's prison, I was invited to the daughter's wedding and saw him escort his daughter up the aisle of the Congregational church and "give" her in marriage to a former schoolmate of hers.

If I was not acting as prosecutor, my legal advice might be sought by a victim of aggression. A former schoolteacher, married to a truck driver with a drinking problem, was herself an alcoholic. They had three children, and from my wife, who was a member of the local Board of Education, I learned of their superior intelligence. Occasionally when the parents engaged in a drunken brawl, the younger daughter, afraid her father would kill her mother, would run to a neighbor's house to call the police, and I would eventually find myself acting not only as a lawyer but as family counselor.

One midnight Sylvia and I were awakened by the angry voices of the couple on our front lawn. The husband had dragged his drunken wife down to demonstrate to me that he was not the only one at fault in their violent battles. We could not do much for the parents in that family, but we did help their bright younger daughter get into college with an anonymous scholarship arranged through her high school guidance counselor.

I found a new satisfaction in trying to solve social problems at their point of impact rather than from the heights of Olympus. I learned about the private and public welfare agencies that people with a social conscience had established in the area. Someone put up my name as a liberal-minded lawyer, and I was elected chairman of one of them—the Norwich chapter of the American Red Cross. I gave blood to its "Bloodmobile," and helped raise money for its programs of disaster relief and training in lifesaving.

I soon discovered that there was never enough money to meet the needs of all the private social welfare agencies. The Red Cross in its annual fund drive was competing with many other agencies. Most of them had for years merged their fund drives in a "Community Chest" in both New London and Norwich. I became involved in promoting a merger of the Red Cross drive with the annual campaigns of the two Community Chests, and became a board member of the new United Fund (later called the United Way) of Southeastern Connecticut.

When President Lyndon Johnson launched his boldly imaginative "war on poverty," I was prompted to initiate the organization of a New London County center to include Head Start, day-care centers, and various other new programs aimed at the problems of the poor. We called it the Thames Valley Council for Community Action, and as chairman of its board, I helped to channel millions of dollars of federal and state funds into the area. We did not end poverty, but we made a significant impact in helping the poor to help themselves.

Another civic enterprise in which I continued to take satisfaction was the New London Junior College, now known as Mitchell College. It probably would never have come into existence if I had not persuaded the other Tiffany heirs in 1938 to contribute the Mitchell family home and acreage as a site. And on at least one occasion of financial crisis, I was able to persuade the college's board of trustees not to close the institution. I served as chairman of the board for a number of years after the death of Waldo Clarke, the college's founder.

CHAPTER 60

Afterword

What, then, has this social reformer learned?

One lesson was in humility. My finite mind cannot expect to understand, much less remold, this infinitely complex spaceship Earth, with its billions of human passengers, each an infinitely complex thinking organism.

But then, as I join the multitude, my faith in humankind, my pride in being a member of the human race, overcomes my sense of impotence.

In the case of the troubled Procter family described in the last chapter, I might once have responded to their plight by writing an editorial in an obscure magazine, deploring the insensitivity of the corporate bosses who failed to pay an employee a living wage. I might have blamed the whole capitalist system for failing to reconvert a submarine shipyard to a peaceful purpose with the winding down of the arms race. But instead I recognized the worth of the members of a local family and helped them survive.

Not long after my involvement with the Procters, disaster struck my own family. My son Stephen, a lawyer, was charged in a criminal indictment with five counts of murder and conspiracy. Three prison guards and three convicts had died in an outbreak of violence in California's San Quentin prison. While visiting his client George Jackson, a militant revolutionary convict and member of the Black Panthers, Steve was alleged to have smuggled him a pistol. Even before Steve surrendered to face trial, I had spent half of my Tiffany inheritance on legal fees and investigations that I thought might contribute to his defense. Aside from other family contributions, Steve himself raised almost a quarter of a million dollars from friends and supporters. After fourteen years as a fugitive, Steve surrendered, stood trial on the charges of murder and conspiracy (smuggling a weapon into the prison was not included in the indictment as a separate offense), and was acquitted.

In the heated atmosphere of 1971 when the prison break occurred, such a happy outcome was not to have been expected. But by 1986 an uprising of the oppressed was neither hoped for by radicals nor feared by conservatives.

The revolutionary fervor that had inspired me in the 1930s—and a generation later had inspired young men like my son Steve and George Jackson to violent rebellion—had spent itself again.

In 1968, at the height of the second of those periods of revolutionary talk, I was offered the opportunity to collaborate on a book about the use of violence in social change. My brother Jonathan (whom I knew as Jack), then a seventh-term member of Congress from the Bronx, had been asked by a publisher to do the book for use as supplementary reading in schools and colleges. But as a congressman always facing reelection, he had neither the time nor the inclination to undertake the book, and he asked me if I would be interested. The result was my writing *Violence and Democracy* (World Publishing Company), which appeared under both our names in 1970.

I began writing the manuscript with an open mind, hoping to be able to justify at least some violence in the struggle for social reform. But the more I pondered the issue in the light of the history I had lived through, the more convinced I became that violence and democracy were antithetical and incompatible. Whatever the justification for the use of force in a struggle against autocracy or dictatorship, it could not be expected to lead to an open society. The collapse of the Soviet Union and the disintegration of the Communist movement in the 1980s and 1990s have demonstrated the folly of trying to achieve a better social order by means of a violent dictatorship.

These events also demonstrated the folly of trying to achieve a socialist utopia by destroying the free market system, sometimes called capitalism. Like any other animal, a human being needs the incentive to acquire what it needs for survival if it is to survive. Cradle-to-grave security can demoralize as well as liberate creative energy.

Thanks to the labors of my great-grandfather Charles Tiffany, I was able as a young man to see the world in long-range perspective and, in a burst of creative energy, to address the social problems of the day with the written word. From another great-grandfather, the first Hiram Bingham, I inherited the notion of saving humanity, promoting the Kingdom of God.

Now at the end of my life, it seems obvious that the human species must be concerned with both God and Mammon. Without the acquisitive drive—selfish pursuit of sustenance and happiness—or the "profit motive," inertia and stagnation take hold of an individual no less than a society. Without a vision of the unity of the human family, society becomes a jungle.

Capitalism and socialism once appeared to me as opposing systems of economic and social order. Now, even without articulating this idea, we live in a world in which the two systems are inextricably mixed. It is a far from perfect world. But it has been a good place to stretch my legs. I don't blame myself for trying to improve it.

405

INDEX

413

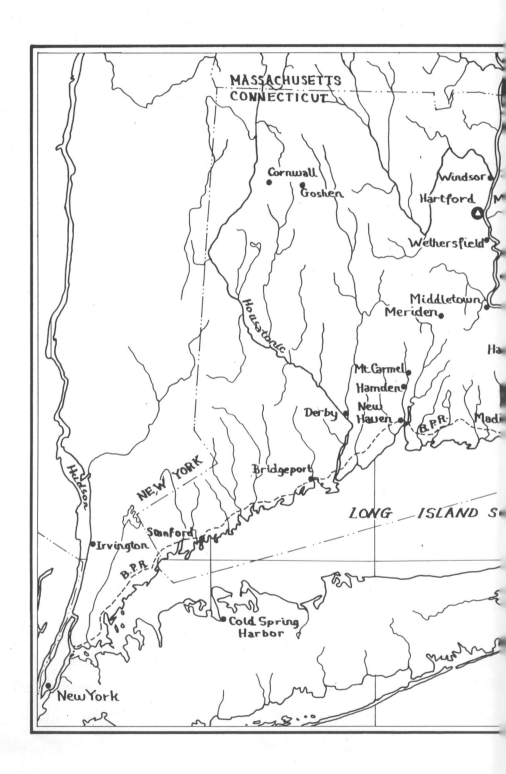